STELLA TENNANT

17 December 1970 – 22 December 2020

Stella was the perfect name for a quintessentially British, beautiful star.
She shone brightly and will be greatly missed.

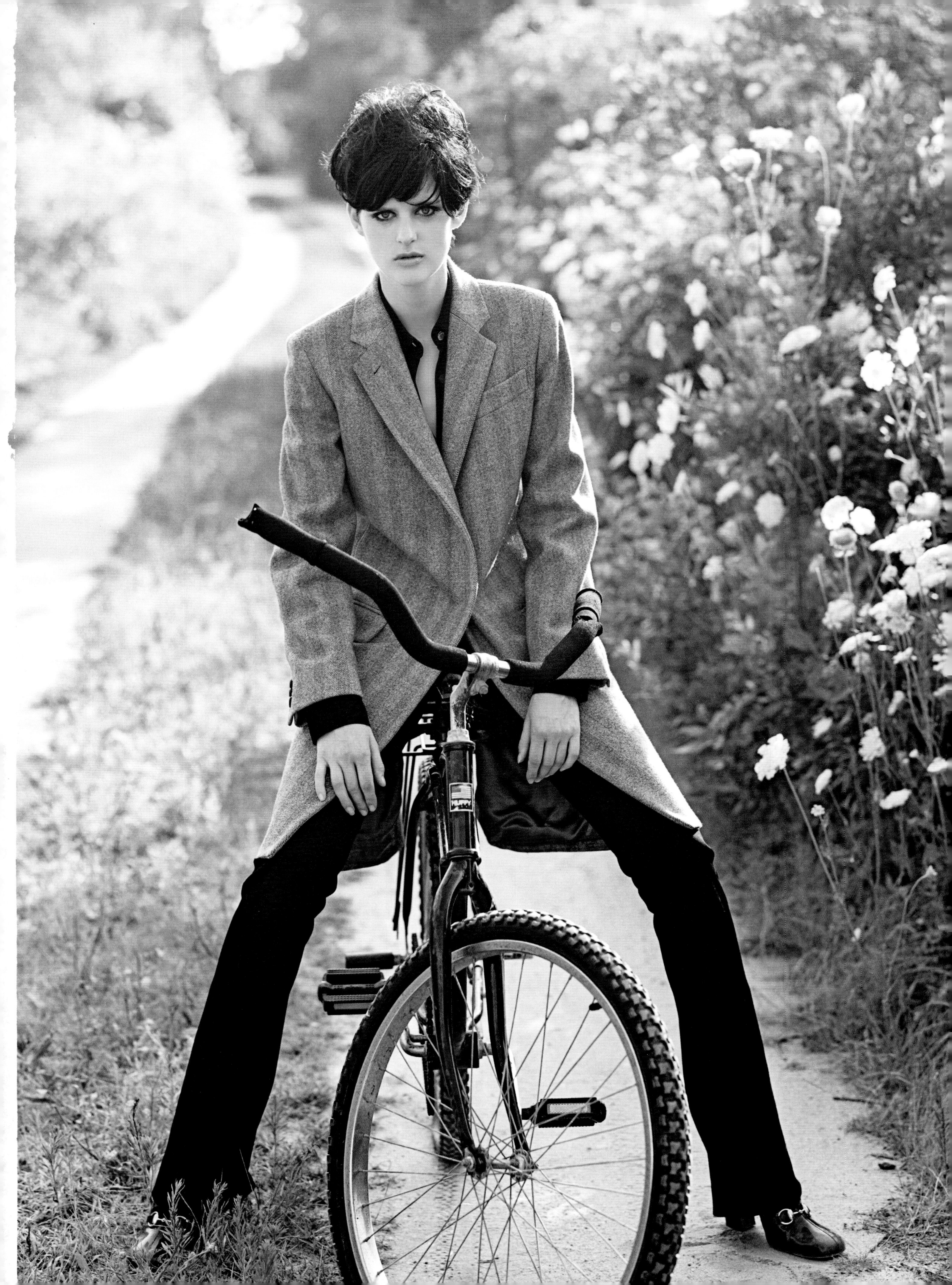

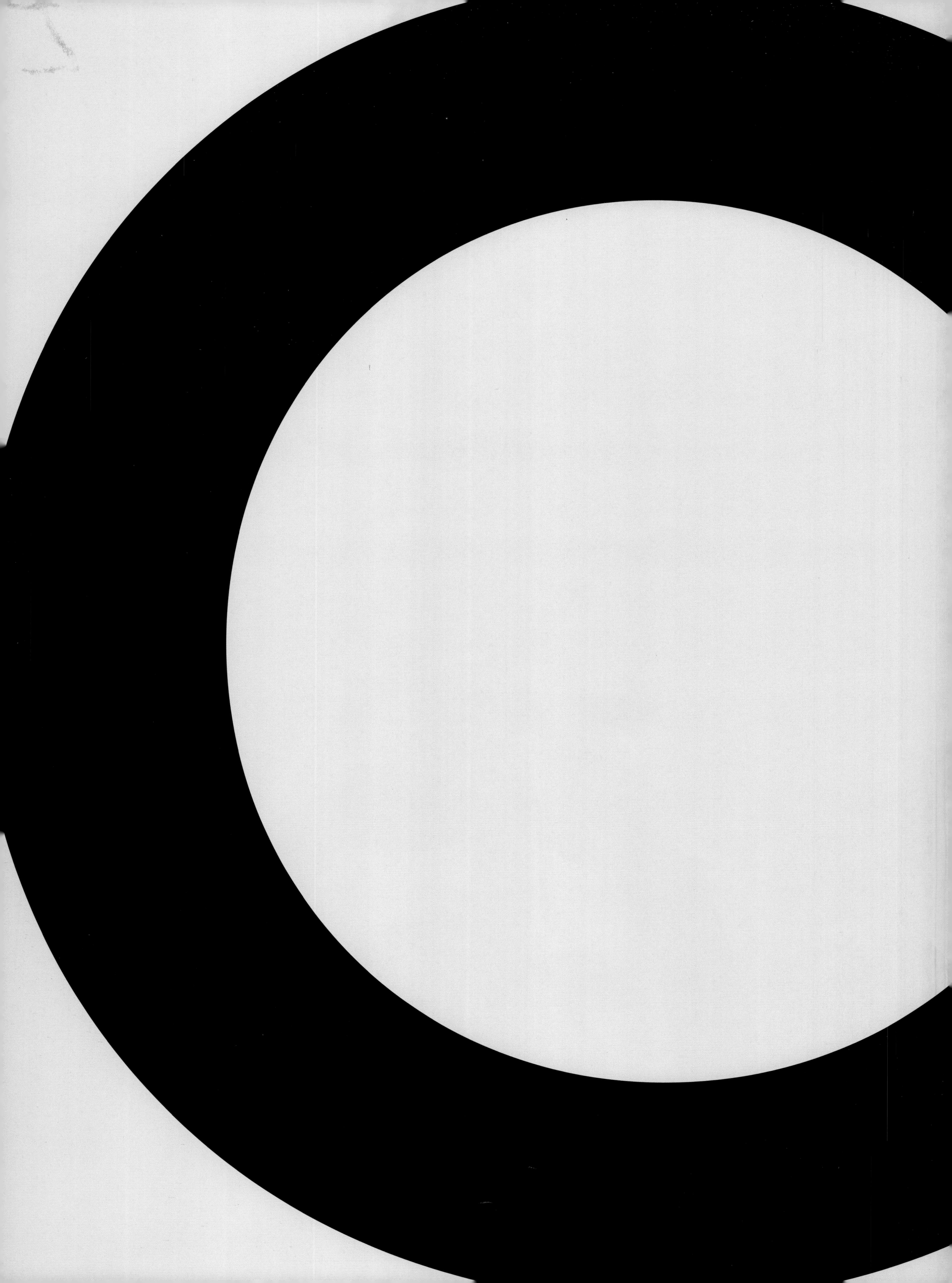

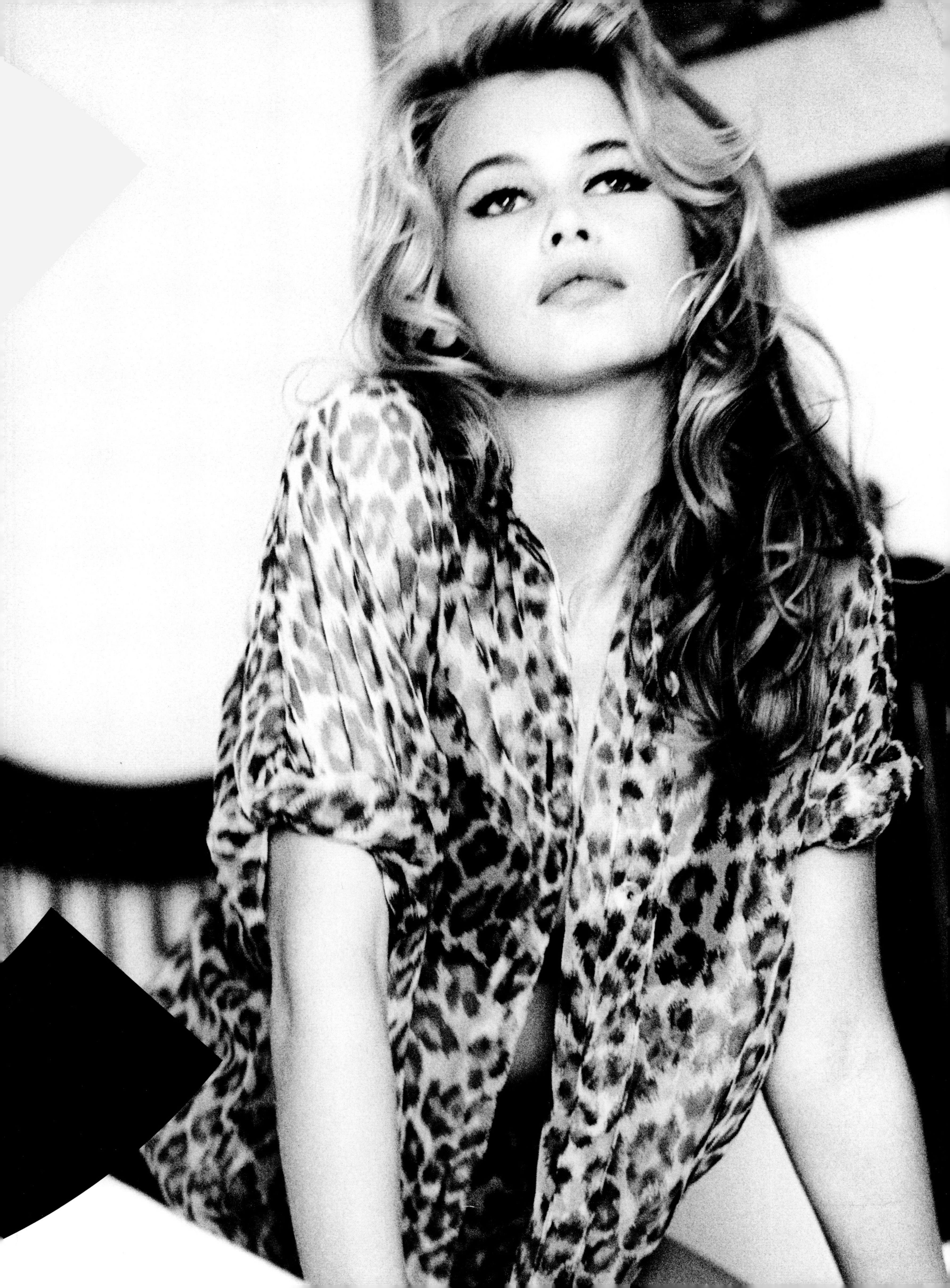

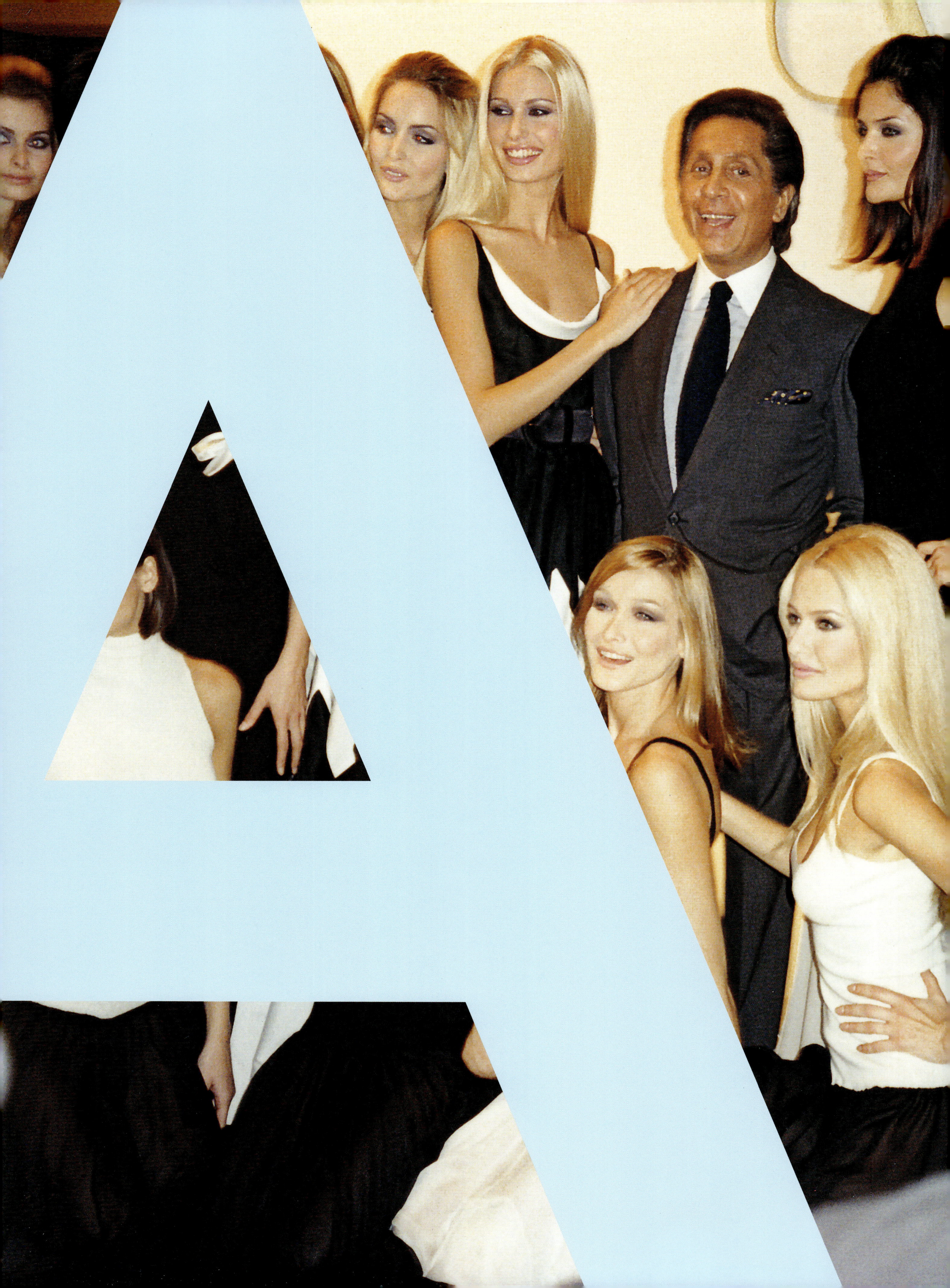

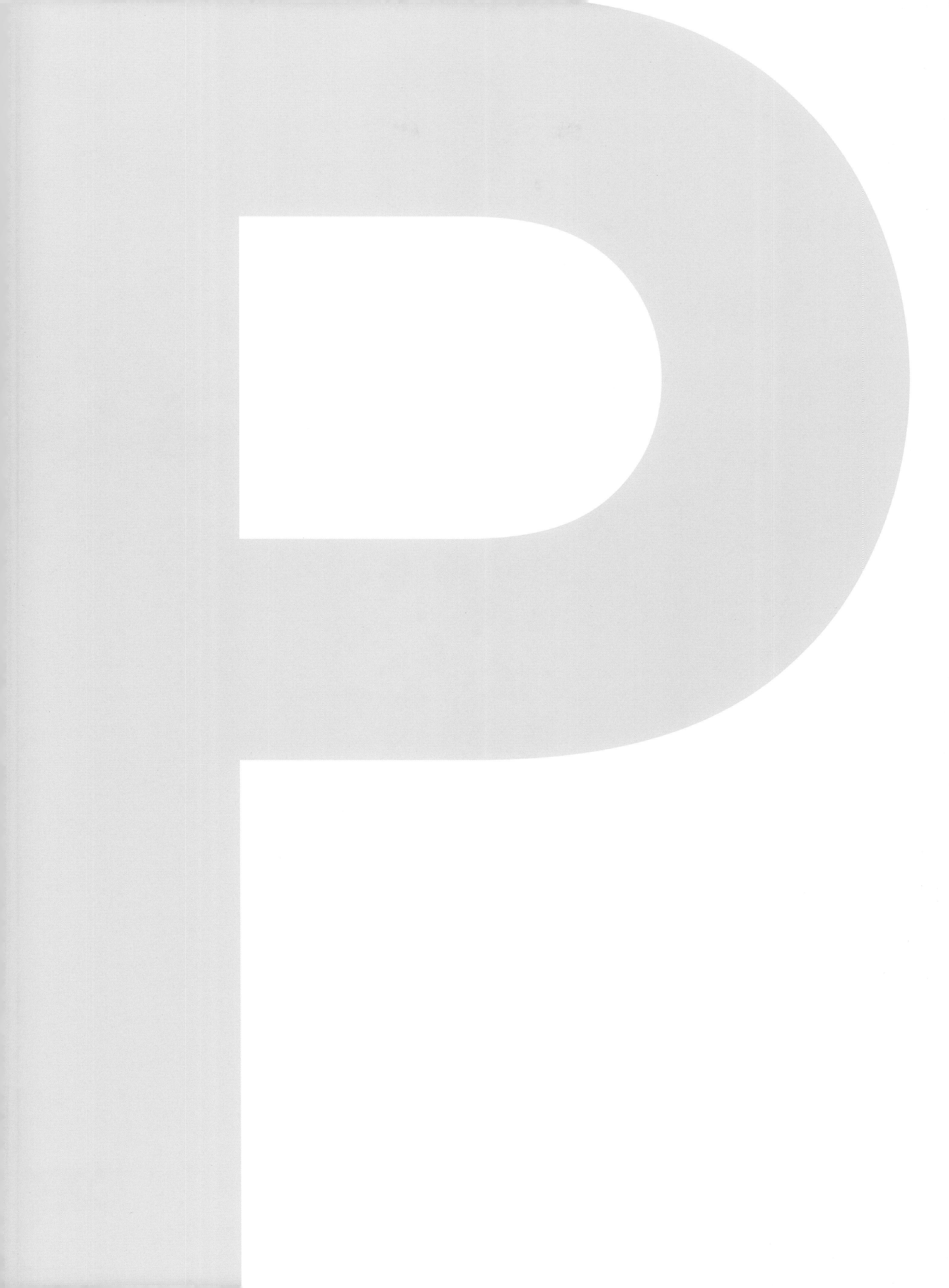

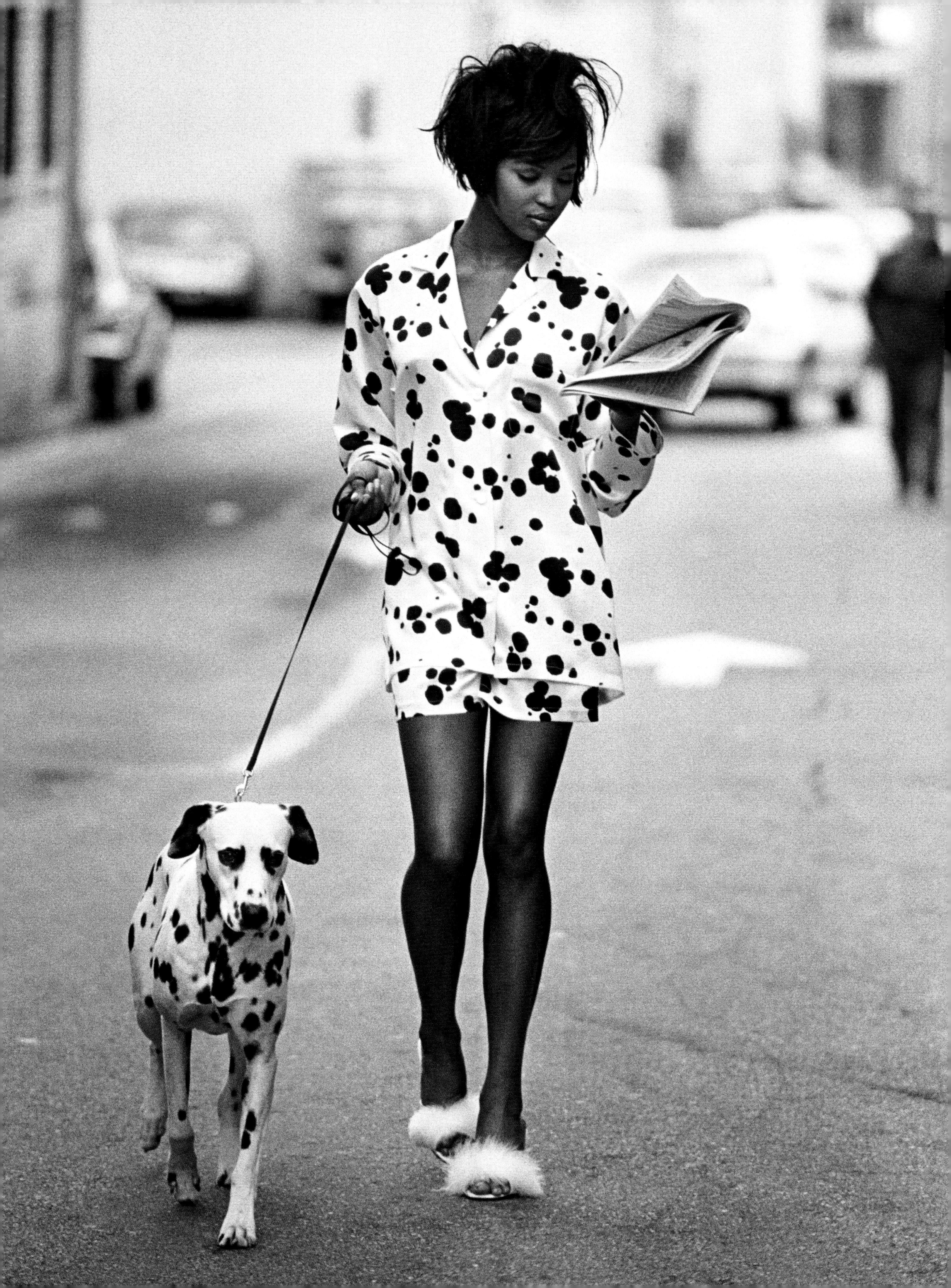

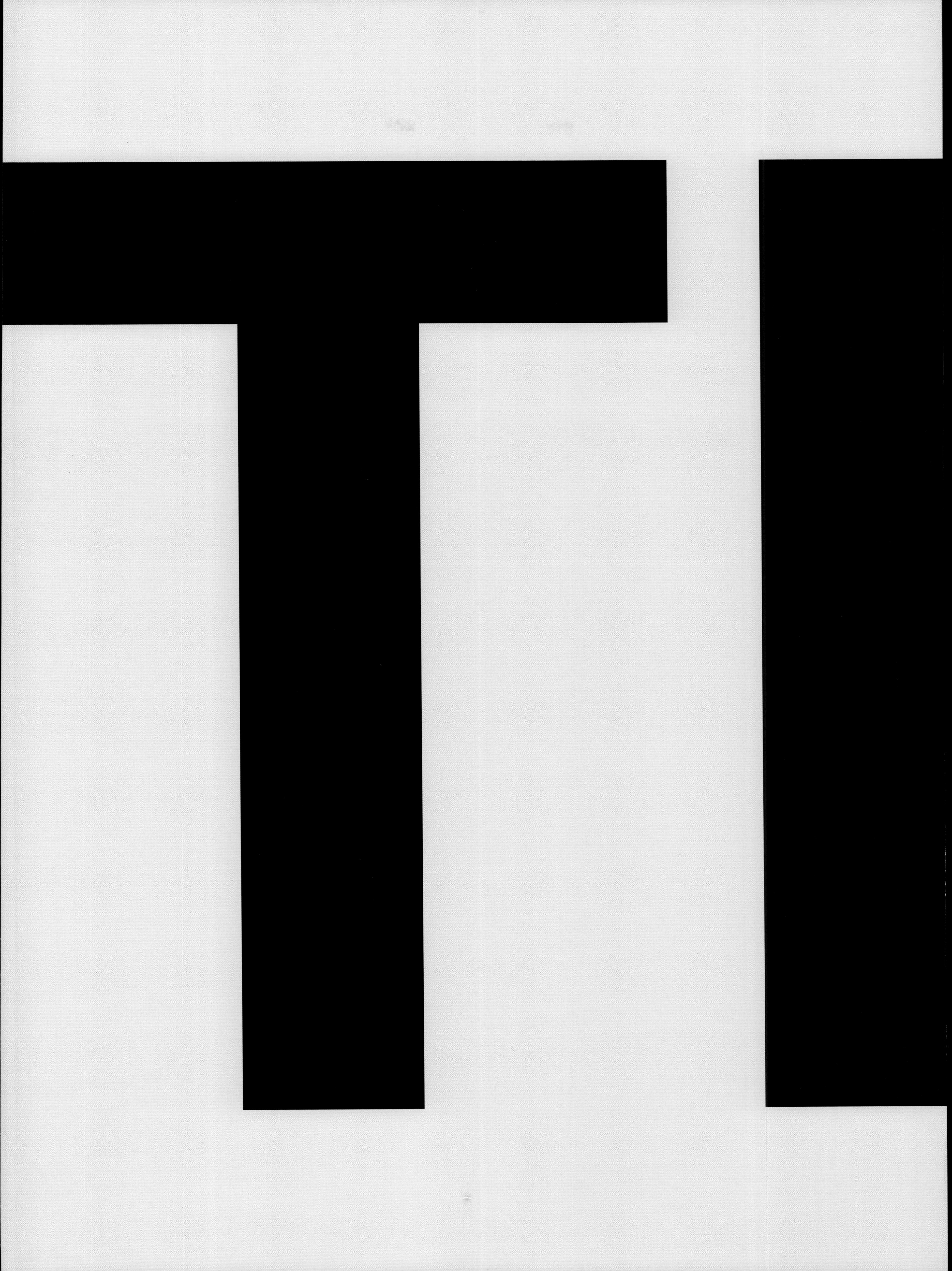

VATE!

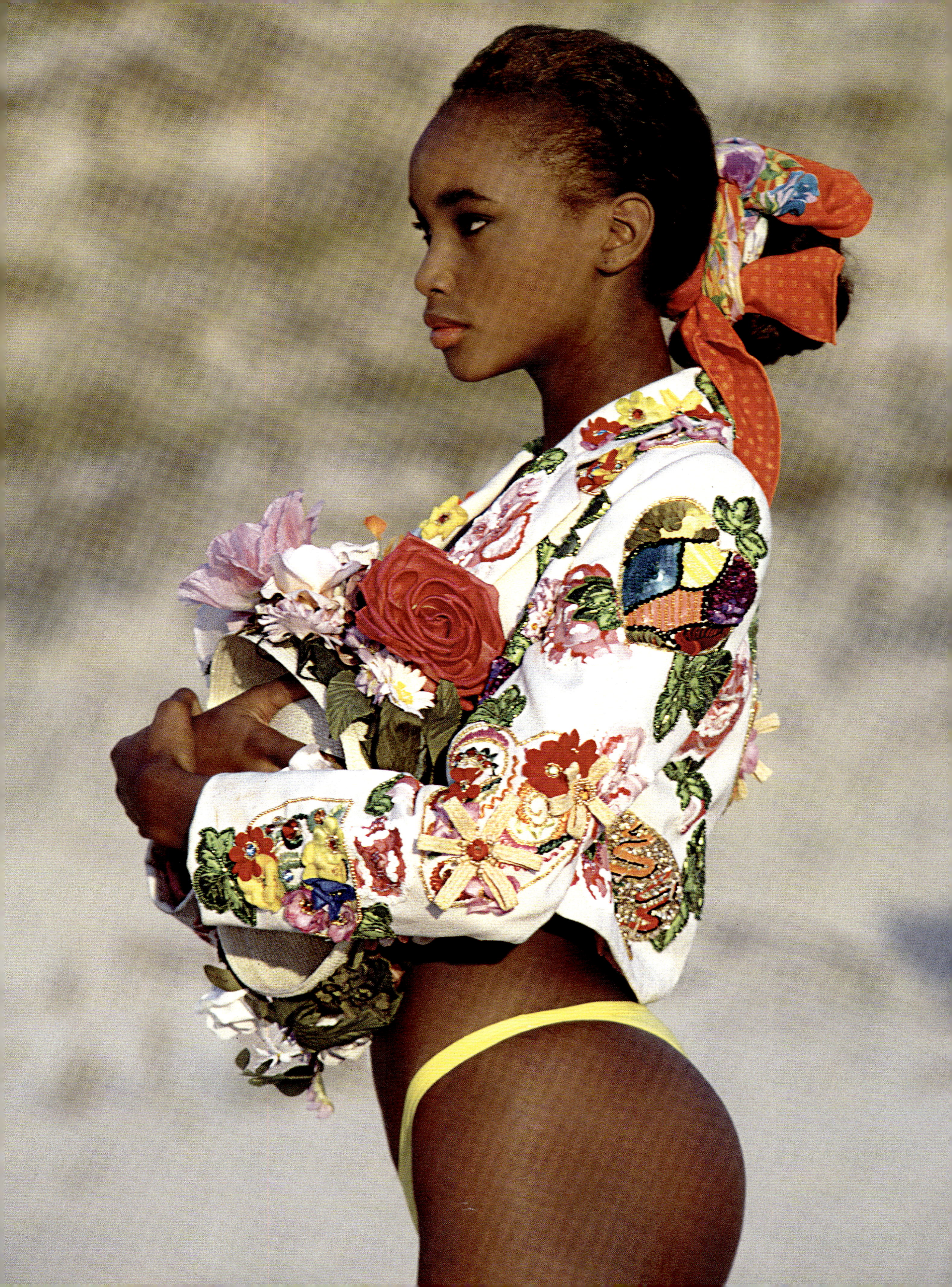

FASHION PHOTO-GRAPHY FROM THE '90S

FORE-WORD

When I became the director of the Kunstpalast in 2017, I already knew that I wanted to put together an extensive show on fashion photography – that powerfully influential genre of photography that has been encapsulating the zeitgeist for as long as anyone can remember. The theme would be the 1990s, a decade which has recently been experiencing a noticeable cultural revival, influencing contemporary art, design and pop culture.

From the start it was clear that pretty much no one would be better suited to curate the exhibition than Claudia Schiffer. Discovered in Dusseldorf in 1987, she then embarked upon a career as a supermodel – hence her close collaborations with the most influential fashion photographers in the world. She is a major figure on the fashion scene, as well as an informed observer, and this is precisely what makes her view of the subject so unique. To our delight, she accepted our invitation to put her very personal stamp on an exhibition as a first-time curator and to open up an individual and knowledgeable view of 1990s fashion photography.

The word *Captivate!*, which Schiffer chose as the title for her show, describes the ability of an image to mesmerise, and the way in which photographs can capture unique moments in time, and 'captivate' the viewer. And proof of this exact ability can be found in the photographs she has assembled for this exhibit. On the one hand, they seem playful, and on the other, determined: distinguished by spontaneity and a spark of brilliance, as well as elaborately detailed planning. They shift constantly back and forth between commercial purposes and a creative vision. Schiffer clarifies the various material forms fashion photography takes, from fine art print to Polaroid to the magazine page. Fashion photography reflects the status quo of what editors assess will be wanted by their readers. In the exhibition, the sets for fashion shoots become a hub for the varied interactions of different experts. It was their collaborations that allowed the shoots of the 1990s to become experiences. And in her show, Claudia Schiffer allows us to participate in this kind of experience.

Today, there is no longer any doubt that fashion photography belongs in an art museum, especially in a city like Dusseldorf, with its lively fashion scene. Many of the photographers presented here, from Herb Ritts to Juergen Teller, have already been honoured in international solo shows. Just before his untimely death, Peter Lindbergh invited the public on a journey through his unforgettable oeuvre here at the Kunstpalast. Again and again it is clear, that at the moment fashion photography is combined with an artistic vision, it begins expanding far beyond its original purpose, expressing the aspirations and yearnings of its time.

An exhibition project such as this one benefits from the support of passionate patrons of art and culture. Without their generosity, as well as their belief in the work of the curator and the Kunstpalast, such a complex show would not be possible. To begin with, I would like to thank the artists and lenders who were willing to part with their artworks for a while. This is the first time that many of these internationally celebrated stars of fashion photography have been represented together in a show, and this fact alone makes the project special.

An extraordinary team is needed to successfully navigate the process of staging an exhibition uniting the works of numerous international photographers from beginning to end, especially during the time of a global pandemic. *Captivate!* would not have been possible without the tireless, creative work of the Kunstpalast's staff. My special thanks go to the project manager, Svenja Schütte, and the head of the photography collection, Linda Conze, who, with the support of Vera Knippschild, acting as intermediaries between the curator and our museum, have helped bring the show to life. The fact that all of this had to be done via video conferencing was a special challenge, which they mastered with a great deal of elan, imagination and strong engagement. Working with Bastian Erhard and his team, they translated Claudia Schiffer's concepts into the real space of the Kunstpalast. Yasmin Limbach successfully oversaw the project's complex logistics, which involved many lenders. Claudia Schiffer's creative team, Erin Graham, Oscar Humphries and Lucie McCullin supported her curation and – thanks to digital technology – were regularly on site. I would particularly like to thank them for their commitment and enthusiasm.

Last but not least, my greatest thanks go to the curator. I am hugely indebted to Claudia Schiffer for agreeing to embark on this project with us to develop an exhibition that takes us straight into her version of the 1990s, when fashion and media history were being written. I am also grateful for her frankness, trust and, above all, enthusiasm for fashion photography, whose artistic potential is impressively revealed to us in *Captivate!*

Felix Krämer
General Director, Kunstpalast

'A PERFECT SHOT CAP-TIVATES THE IMAG-INATION'

A Conversation Between
Claudia Schiffer (CS) and Felix Krämer (FK)

FK What were your first thoughts when we invited you to curate an exhibition on 1990s fashion photography at the Kunstpalast? What attracted you to the project?

CS The Kunstpalast, Dusseldorf's art museum, has a rich history of showcasing contemporary photography and *Captivate!* honours that tradition. As a first-time curator, I wanted to encapsulate the vision of fashion that helped shape the perspective of a generation.

The 1990s was an extraordinary period which witnessed the birth of style culture, the rise of the supermodel and an explosion of creativity. Young designers, photographers, stylists and art directors, as well as hair and makeup artists, emerged and fundamentally changed the way we view fashion and design. It was an era of reinvention, rebellion and innovation, spearheaded by diverse talents and collaborators who merged the fields of fashion, music, entertainment and graphic art.

In photography, there was an exceptional range of visionaries, from the epic black-and-white romance of Peter Lindbergh, to the London-based David Sims and Corinne Day, who, together with Mario Sorrenti in New York, championed imperfection and the everyday, and coined what became known as 'dirty realism'. Defined neither by age nor social background, fashion was about visual experimentation and freedom of expression.

FK What is it that fascinates you about fashion photography? I know that you count works from Steven Meisel, Ellen von Unwerth, Mario Testino, Herb Ritts and so many others among the images in your private collection, some of which you've included in the exhibition. Which facets of fashion photography are you particularly interested in?

CS Fashion photography serves as a great cipher of trends, aspirations and dreams. While being born out of the moment, great fashion photography can, paradoxically, achieve a timeless status and capture a bigger story. The most memorable images are often provocative and challenge our perceptions of femininity and beauty. The 1990s made fashion photography and photographers a driving force in visual culture. Because fashion photography is a democratic art form, circulating on billboards, digital platforms, packaging and in magazines, it has an enormous sphere of influence.

The 1990s was an extraordinary time to be modelling. I worked with so many photographers who also became mentors. Figures like Ellen von Unwerth, Herb Ritts, Richard Avedon, Arthur Elgort and creative powerhouse Karl Lagerfeld gave me true insight into the artistry both behind the lens and off the set in the processes of art direction, editing and publishing. The model's role is to bring fashion alive but she or he is just one ingredient in the alchemy of image-making. Over time, and as my knowledge grew, I began to collect prints and original archive material. My own collection forms a part of the Kunstpalast's *Captivate!* exhibition. It's the first time that many of the photographers have been shown together in a group show.

FK What do you hope the impact of this show will be?

CS First and foremost, the impact of the pandemic has severely affected the economic health of the arts and culture sector across the globe. Galleries, institutions, studios and the people who work in both the public and private spheres are struggling for survival. My primary hope is that *Captivate!* attracts a wide audience to the Kunstpalast and boosts a love of fashion and photography. The experience of attending a show in real time is unbeatable. The curation of imagery and film resonates with the energy of the 1990s and is rich and varied. In essence, I hope that the exhibition will be inspiring, revelatory and rewarding.

FK Fashion photography plays a major role in our collective visual memory; we all have images in mind when we think about 1990s fashion. For me, those can be Von Unwerth, Lindbergh or Juergen Teller – this is quite a range. Which images did you immediately think of when you first heard about the project?

CS So many images – but also experiences – came to mind. Initially, I extensively edited my selection by choosing works that told the story of my own entry into fashion, which started with Von Unwerth's shoot in Paris, next to the Centre Pompidou. I was seventeen and wearing my own clothes, and Von Unwerth, a former model, was also just starting out as a photographer. Her work exudes freedom and intimacy. She showed the pictures to Paul Marciano, the co-founder of Guess, who decided he wanted both of us for the Guess Jeans campaign. It was our big break.

In the selection process, I was looking for iconic images that represented each individual photographer's eye. Von Unwerth's images stand in contrast to Lindbergh's cinematic vision or Teller's confrontational imagery that questions the nature of fashion and identity. Testino's glorious, glamorous shoots and Ritts's bold, graphic compositions exemplify further differing positions. While the 1980s were characterised by a perfectionist high glamour, the 1990s ushered in a new visual lexicon driven by energy, reality and personality.

FK Although it's your first time curating an exhibition, hearing you recite all those names and refer to those many stories in fashion confirms my initial motivation to invite you to lead the project: I was confident that you would bring a unique perspective, as much personal as versed, to the show. How did you proceed with your work on the exhibition? How did the chapter selection come about?

CS As I'd been faced with such an exceptional range of imagery, the difficult task was creating a blueprint for the show and the sections that could be navigated by the viewer within the Kunstpalast. From the outset, I didn't envision the show as proceeding chronologically but rather through synergetic groupings or chapters. The imagery also shifts between different formats: from Polaroids to magazine covers, from runway footage to candid backstage shots. Within these groupings, the larger arc of fashion is also reflected. The evolution from baroque glamour to minimalism is dramatic.

FK What criteria did you apply when choosing images for the exhibition? How did you differentiate between the strongest images and those less suitable for the show?

CS At every turn I asked myself the question: 'Is this 1990s?' What story is the image telling about the photographer, the creative teams and the model subjects? The starting point was the photographers and their respective archives. I wanted to mirror the impact of fashion photography experienced at the time, and to amplify it. To pinpoint around 150 images for the exhibition out of thousands of potential works was a huge task.

FK You've shared some memorable shoots; can you pinpoint any in particular that changed your career? Or any particularly important partnerships?

CS The Von Unwerth stories were pivotal. I also learnt so much from Lagerfeld, whom I started working with in 1990. What Warhol was to art, he was to fashion. He transformed me from a shy German girl into a supermodel and taught me about style and how to survive in the fashion business. The Lindbergh shoot for US *Vogue* in September 1991 was an epic production, featuring the 'supers' wearing ballgown skirts and leather jackets under New York's Brooklyn Bridge. It was an honour to work with Avedon for Versace. Every shoot that pushes you to excel in new directions is special.

FK One chapter of the exhibition deals with advertising campaigns from Chanel, Gucci, Calvin Klein, Versace and others. It demonstrates the power of images to affect taste. Could you elaborate a little more about this specific power? The images we see in the exhibition are somewhat historic, yet their impact still seems tangible today.

CS The 1990s was a watershed period. Campaigns became a valued part of visual culture, of our urban environment. Graphic artists, copywriters, art directors and photographers developed a bold language that upturned tradition and challenged notions of beauty and aspirational luxury. Fashion photography, 'the idealising vision', came to be seen as a democratic art form. In this way, houses and brands started a conversation with viewers. The competition to create definitive global campaigns was fierce. Consider Kate Moss by Sorrenti for Calvin Klein, with art director Fabien Baron, or Testino's legendary series for Gucci directed by Tom Ford and styled by Carine Roitfeld – these campaigns became part of the style conversation and, in turn, the imagery became collectible.

The dynamo was powered by the growing global appetite for fashion and the boom in media in the form of MTV, legacy magazines including *Vogue* and *Harper's Bazaar* and also a new guard of style titles such as *The Face*, *Self Service*, *i-D* and *V Magazine*. The era gave way to the birth of the superstar designer, stylist, model and photographer. Fashion creators became household names.

FK The exhibition starts in the late 1980s. In your opinion, what were the catalysts for the emergence of the new type of model in photography – for the supermodel phenomenon?

CS Supermodels were a product of the 1980s – a decade obsessed by image, power and glamour. Of course, previous eras had model stars – Lauren Hutton, Twiggy, Penelope Tree and Iman, amongst others – but the supermodels shared a fame that stretched beyond fashion, and we became symbols of a self-made success. The portrayal of sexual strength, freedom and optimism during the recession of the early 1990s helped keep fashion rolling. We were featured on the runway, in campaigns and on the covers of magazines, but we were also invited onto talk shows, to appear in films and on TV, and to become ambassadors for philanthropic organisations.

That level of exposure empowered us to take control of our careers in an entirely new way. When we all appeared together at runway shows, fashion shoots or ad campaigns, it was the ensemble that created the phenomena.

Behind the lens, Meisel, Lindbergh and Patrick Demarchelier championed us and directed our constant reinvention. It was an education and also a test of professionalism. I learnt about lighting, composition and the craft of fashion design, how to wear clothes and interpret the designer's vision. The supermodel's role was to project the image of a brand across the world at a time when brands were expanding globally. The catalysts were both commercial and creative but it was the democratisation of fashion and the boom in brand fortunes that allowed the supermodel to 'happen'.

FK When you told me for the first time of the 'triangle' that must come together for every great fashion shoot, consisting of the photographer, the designer and the model, I found that very convincing. What in particular would you say is the model's influence on the perfect shot?

CS Fundamentally, there needs to be rapport. As a model, you need to study a photographer's work and a designer's work, and learn how to translate those in front of the lens. Each photographer 'sees' in a different way. Helmut Newton was meticulous in every detail and that is what gives his imagery such graphic strength. By contrast, Elgort is a master at capturing exuberance outdoors.

Fashion design drives the story while the cuts, shapes, volumes and silhouettes make you feel and move in different ways – a model needs to be sensitive to the nuance. In Valentino you are transformed into a romantic heroine; in Versace into a siren; in Chanel into an effortlessly chic woman of the world. Modelling is a performance of sorts.

FK And what makes a perfect shot for you personally?

CS A perfect shot captivates the imagination. No fashion photograph can be called iconic at its conception. That status only comes with the test of time.

FK Could you tell me a little more about the different players and professions on the set of a large shoot in the 1990s – besides the photographers and the models? I learned from you that sets could be really crowded because so many different forms of expertise came together. What were the important steps for a perfect shoot? Where did it start, whose creativity had to merge, who set the tone?

CS The shoot is an intricate jigsaw of experts from all fields – photography, hair and makeup, location and set design, models, stylists, art directors and editors. Stories are conceptualised and rails of clothes edited prior to the shoot. Afterwards, the magic happens in the darkroom, in the printing, retouching and layout. A great shoot is the result of great teamwork. The photographer is like a conductor.

FK In your view, how has fashion photography changed since the 1990s? What is possible today that would have been inconceivable in the 1990s, and, conversely, what could fashion photography achieve in the 1990s that may have been lost today?

CS The 1990s was the last decade of the analogue era before the digital revolution. Everything was shot on film and tests were in the form of Polaroids to gauge light, composition and colour. Polaroids fade with time but to give the fullest possible impression of an analogue shoot, I wanted to include a section of these in the exhibition as well as of unseen and backstage images.

Today, the edit happens on the screen and imagery can be consumed instantly via social media. In the 1990s, the magazines were like the bibles of fashion, with every cover and page eagerly dissected. The budgets were bigger and that meant location shoots with ensemble casts which lasted for days, even weeks!

FK Today's top models also present themselves as entrepreneurs reigning over whole business empires based on their personal brands. What differences do you see between your own generation of supermodels and your successors?

CS There is so much talent today and models are true polymaths, entering fields such as activism, sustainability, philanthropy, fashion design, technology, interiors, wellbeing and acting. The rise of social media has helped accelerate multi-track careers. The supermodels provided the template.

FK Would you agree that there came a time, at the end of the 1990s, when the supermodel phenomenon 'outpaced' itself? You and your fellow supermodels were the first models to be seen as individuals. You were 'stars' and the public were as much interested in your personal lives as your work. You were confronted with cameras not only during fashion shoots but also on the streets, where paparazzi followed your every step. Do you think that, at some point, your generation became unwilling to blur the line between private and public any longer?

CS I think the industry is fundamentally the same, but it has grown exponentially. There are more collections, the pace is faster and social media has had a huge impact. It's been great for marketing fashion and beauty products, as well as providing a very effective way to manage your own exposure. What was special in the 1990s, though, was a sense of privacy.

FK Who, in your eyes, are the great fashion photographers of our time? And to what extent have the great icons of 1990s fashion photography influenced them?

CS There is a proliferation of talent. I've so enjoyed working with Inez & Vinoodh, and there are many more female photographers such as Tierney Gearon, who came to the fore at the millennium with her haunting double-exposure imagery. In this last decade, Cass Bird and Zoë Ghertner, who takes beautiful portraits of women of all ages, as well as Harley Weir, who is brilliant at capturing complex emotions. Fine art photographer Collier Schorr is also inspiring; we worked together on a cover story for Italian *Vogue* last year in an homage to Richard Avedon. Avedon's practice was to shoot alongside a mirror turned towards the subject, so that, as a model, you could see yourself as he did and gauge what was and wasn't working. Using the digital equivalent of a mirror, Schorr worked in the same way. It was a special collaboration and, just as with Avedon, her lighting was immaculate. I also admire the work of Tyler Mitchell. He has a fresh eye and I see some aspects of Guy Bourdin in his images. Every photographer must study the past first and then break away to create a vision of the present.

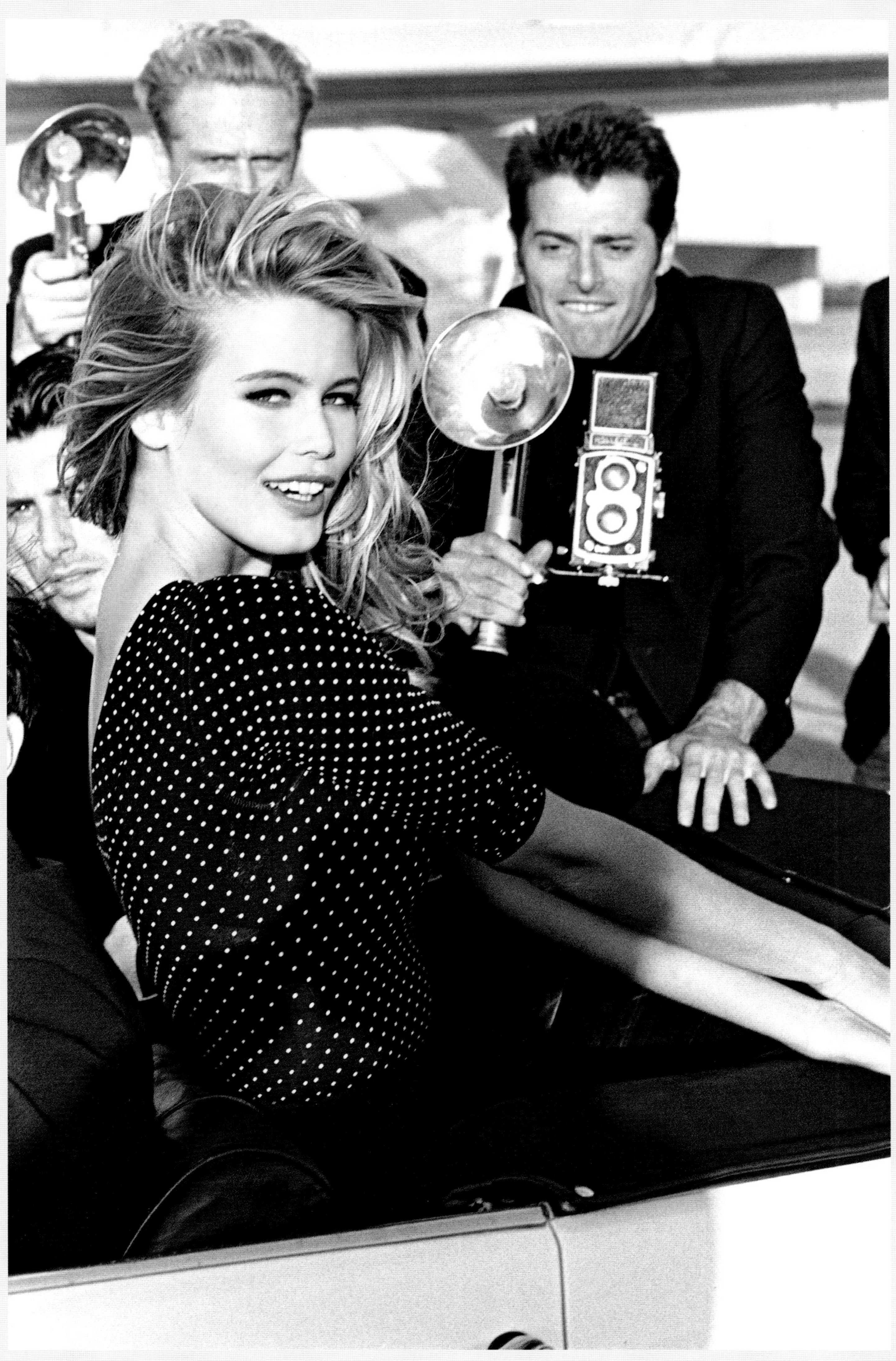

Ellen von Unwerth, model: Claudia Schiffer,
Morocco 1989 for Guess Jeans

INTO THE '90S

All texts by Claudia Schiffer

The divergent strands of the 1990s aesthetic didn't happen overnight but rather emerged through innovation, restlessness and experimentation. Fashion photography was pushing against the excesses and artifice of the 1980s towards a more individualistic, liberated vision, and that rebellion took many forms. Designers and stylists, influenced by postmodernism, pop music and street culture, were beginning to deconstruct fashion. They literally turned seams inside out and stripped fashion of its frills and gold buttons. Sartorial codes were mixed: haute couture with denim, biker leather with ballgown skirts. Style magazines emerged, exposing the cross currents of the counterculture and the street. It seemed that anything was possible.

For me, the move towards the impactful single-image campaigns associated with the 1990s had already begun in the late 1980s. Back then I was working with my friend, the German photographer Ellen von Unwerth, on the Guess Jeans campaign. She captured a slice of the 'Western cowgirl meets Brigitte Bardot' ideal with her playful yet seductive imagery. It chimed intuitively with the founders', the Marciano brothers, version of the American dream.

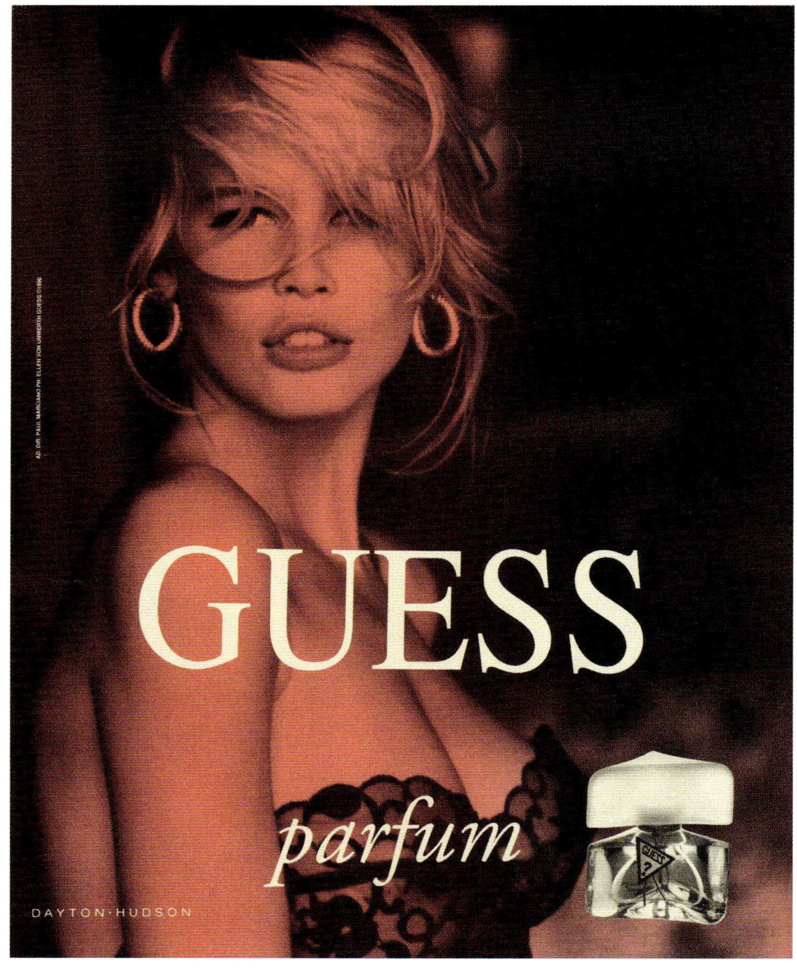

Guess perfume campaign 1990

Ellen von Unwerth, model: Claudia Schiffer, Viareggio, Italy 1989 for Guess Jeans

The chemistry between photographer and model is vital, as is a sense of trust. Ellen von Unwerth's specialty is to ask the model to move and express herself freely, rather than focus on a still pose. This campaign shoot was for Guess Jeans.

24/25
Ellen von Unwerth, model: Claudia Schiffer, Viareggio, Italy 1989 for Guess Jeans

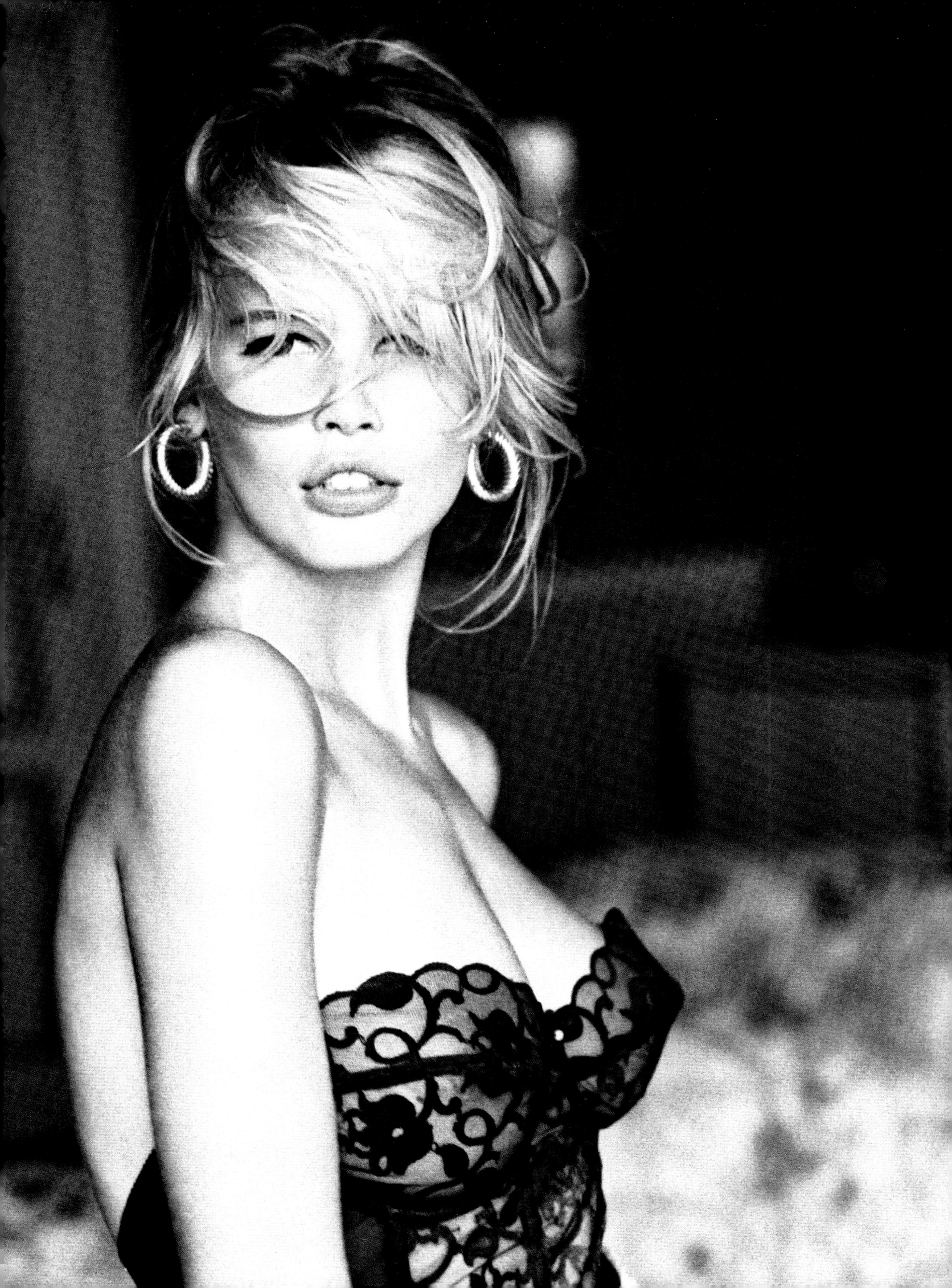

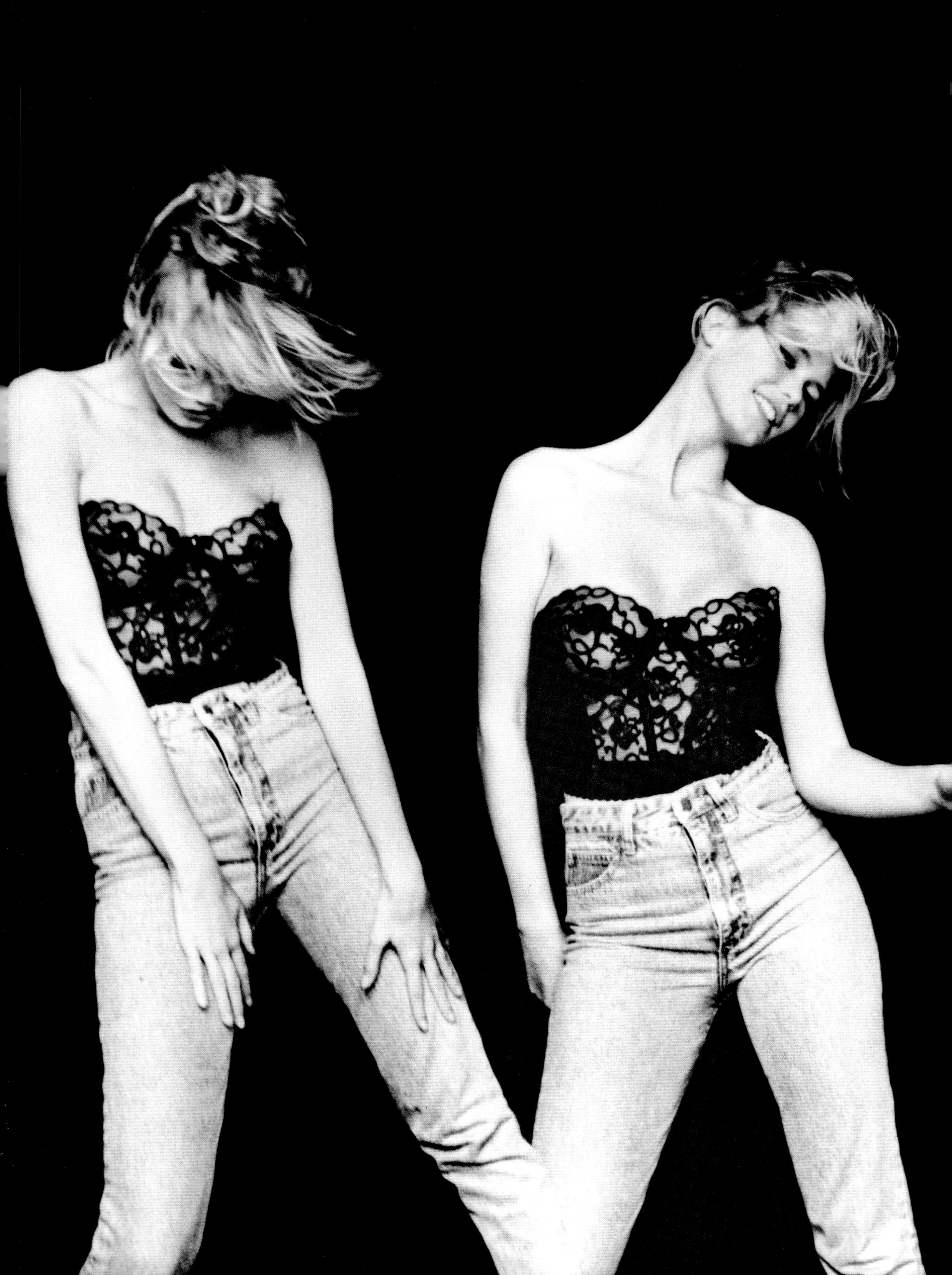

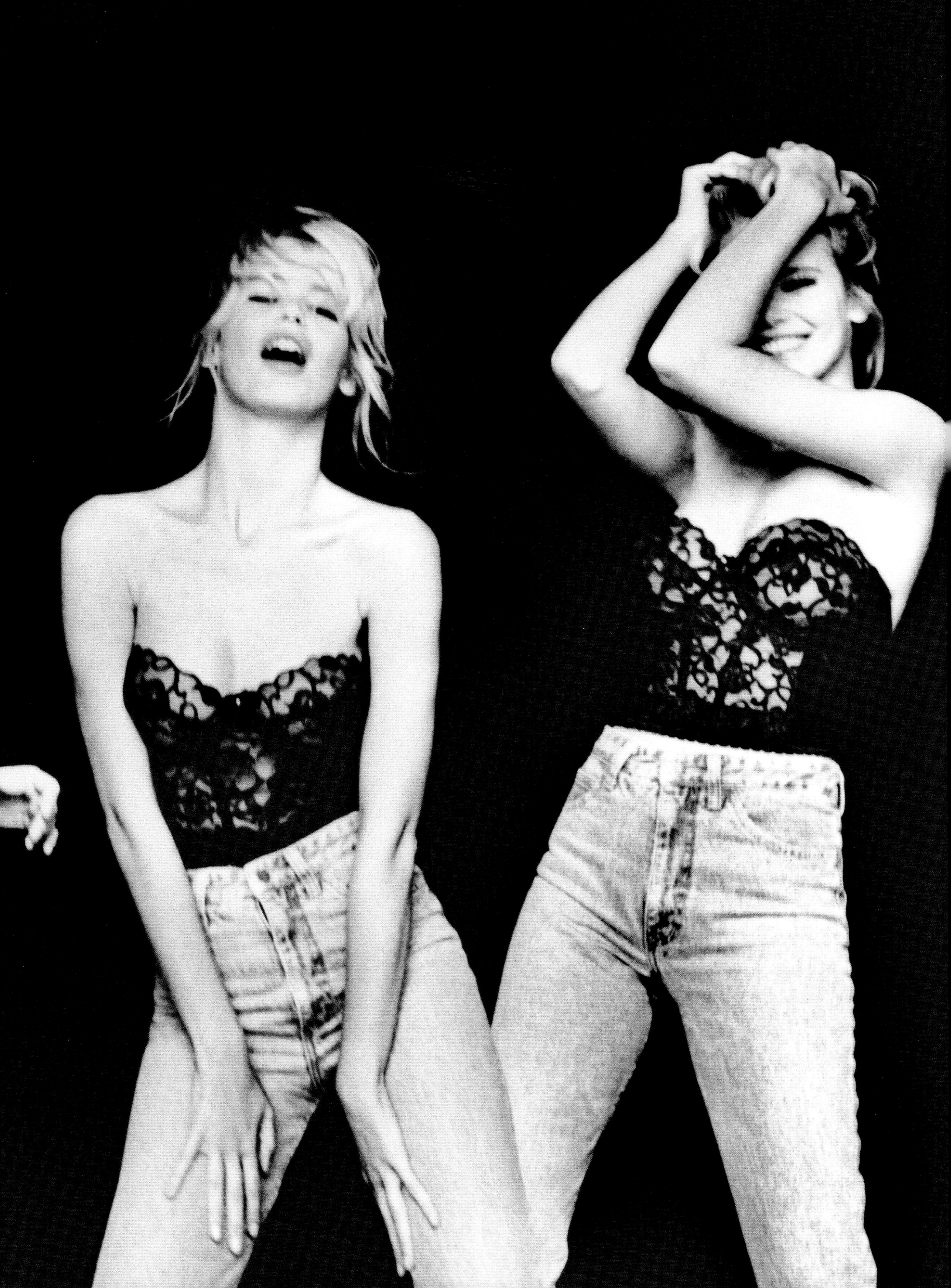

Ellen von Unwerth, model: Claudia Schiffer,
Nashville 1991 for Guess Jeans

28, 29
Ellen von Unwerth, model: Claudia Schiffer,
Pisa 1989 for Guess Jeans

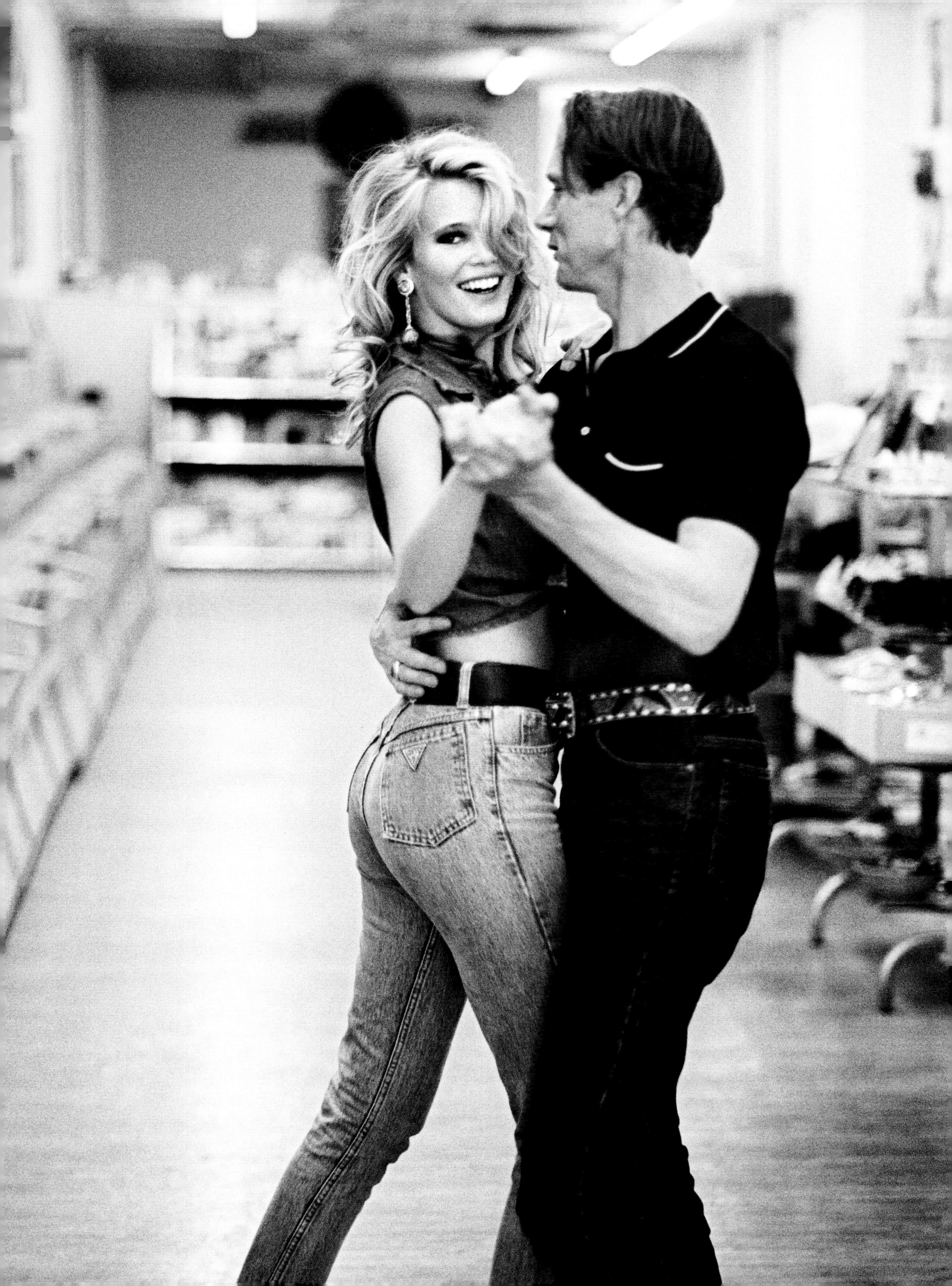

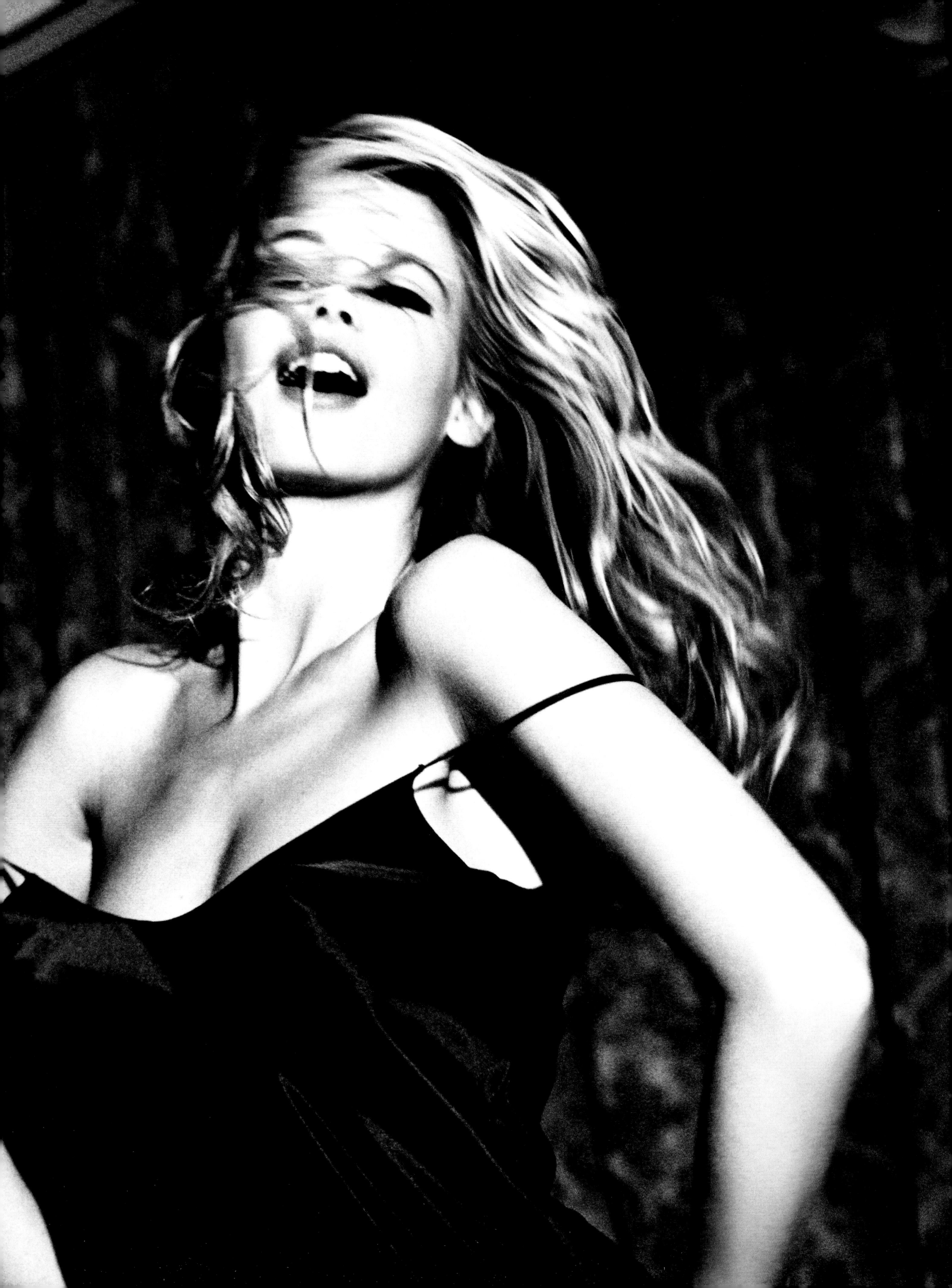

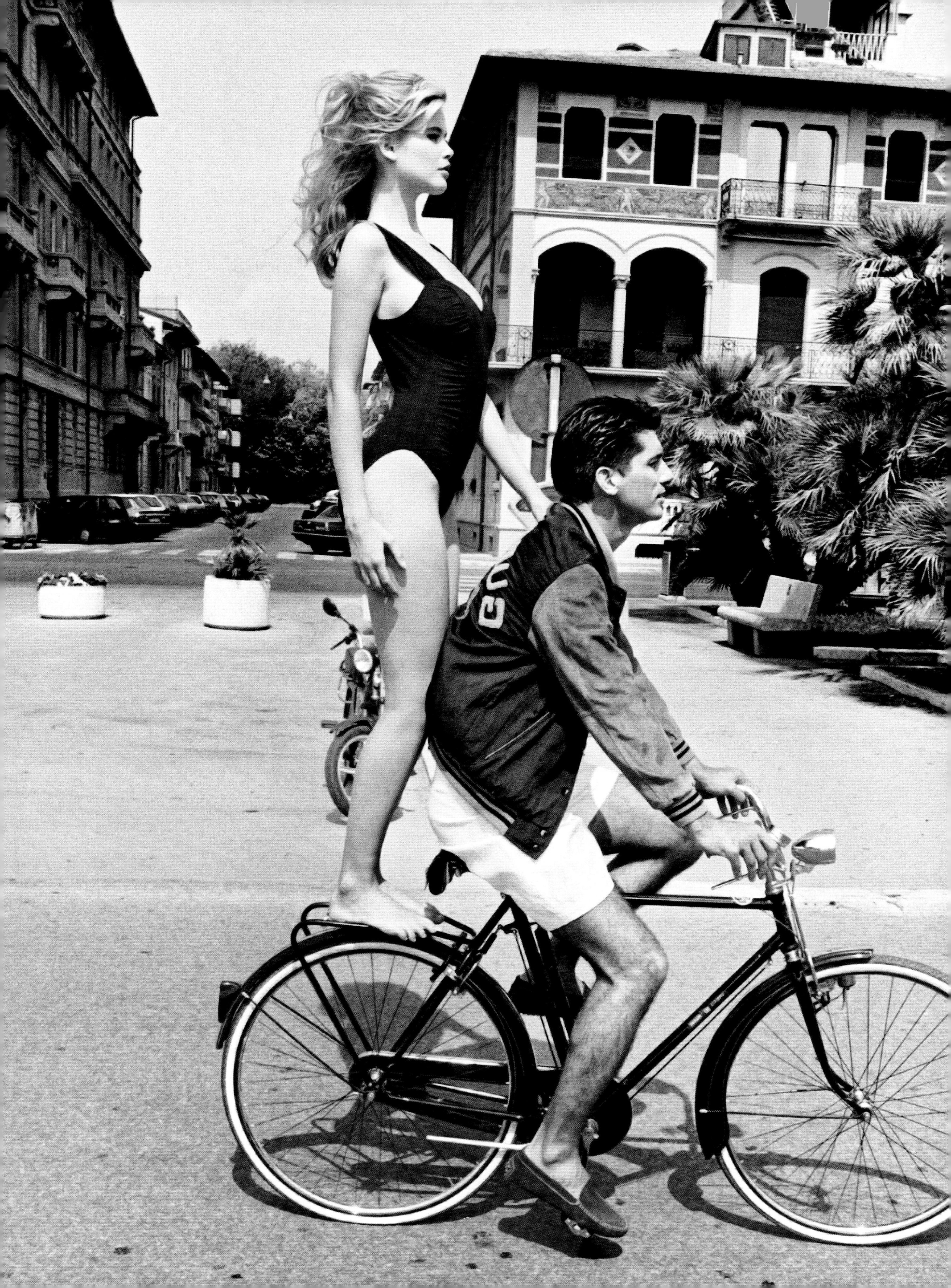

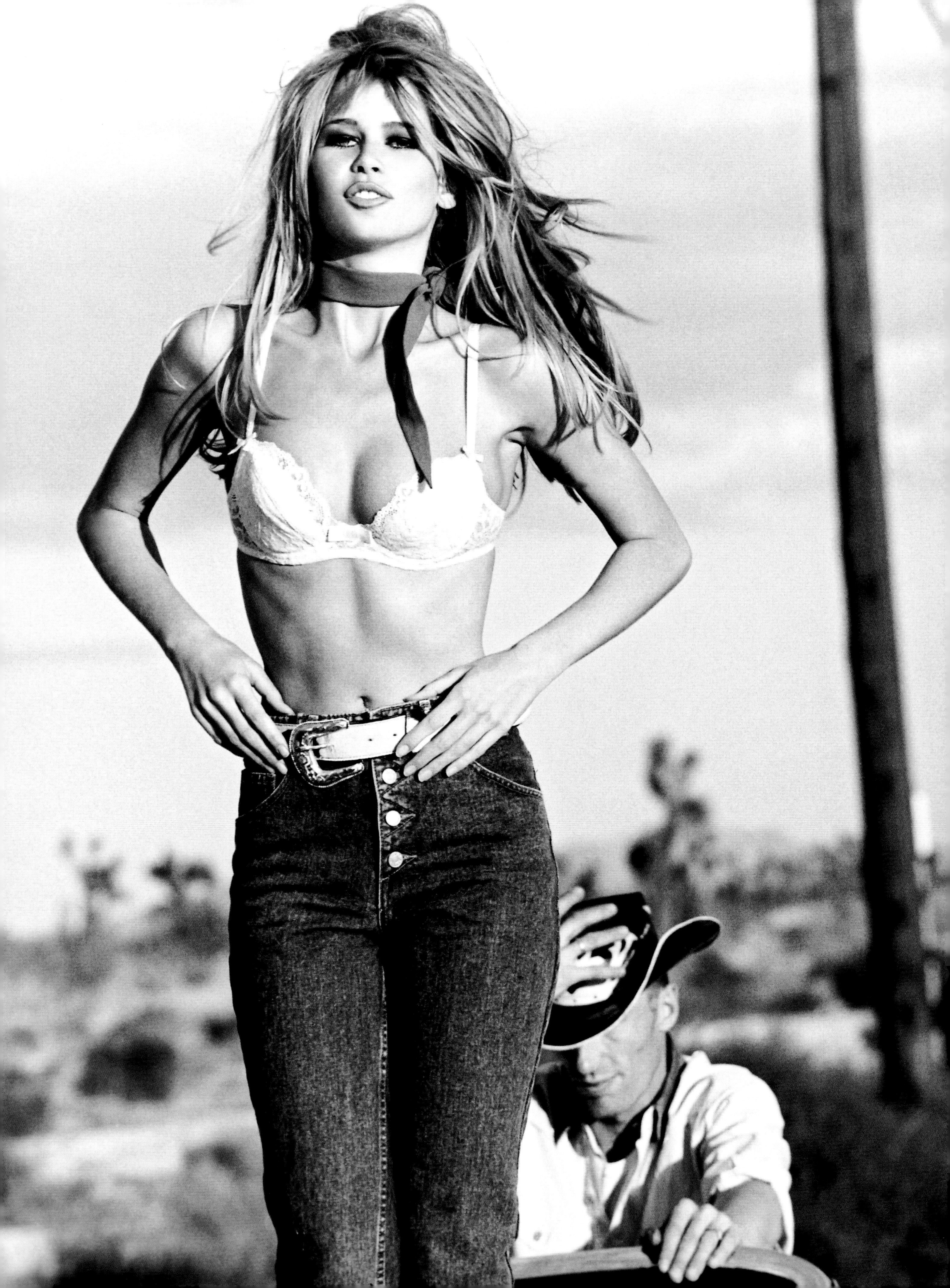

That's just the way I see women.
I see them as beautiful and sexy,
but also strong and in control of their
image – liberated and self-assured.

ELLEN VON UNWERTH

Ellen von Unwerth, model: Claudia Schiffer,
Nashville 1989 for Guess Jeans

SUPER-MODEL PHENOM-ENON

In the early 1990s, a group of models, including myself, began to be globally recognised and regularly called 'supermodels' in the mainstream press. We were transformed by designers, editors and fashion photographers, and came to represent freedom and self-made success in an era that championed female ambition. Whereas before models were largely nameless and categorised as 'runway', 'commercial' or 'editorial', the 'supers' were seen as individuals and traversed those boundaries. Supermodels were door-openers into the world of fashion that, until then, had been quite shielded. We worked in all areas and across the globe. Along with that influence came unprecedented fees and exclusive contracts. We took control of our careers. Today, the idea that a personality or individual can transcend the brands they work with is accepted, but back then it was very new. We helped to keep the glamour and optimism of fashion alive during the recession of the early 1990s.

In this section there is no 'top list' of supermodels. Rather, the supermodel phenomenon is presented as a collective of women. I selected iconic images to celebrate these outstanding women who reinvented the art and profession of modelling. Many have continued to work and remain globally recognised icons today.

You're trying to get to one moment with one frame that eventually may speak for your generation.

HERB RITTS

The spirit of this image is euphoric, it's upbeat. It gives you a wonderful sense of why we were all so obsessed by the supermodels of that moment, and what made each of them so uniquely alluring and appealing.

ANNA WINTOUR

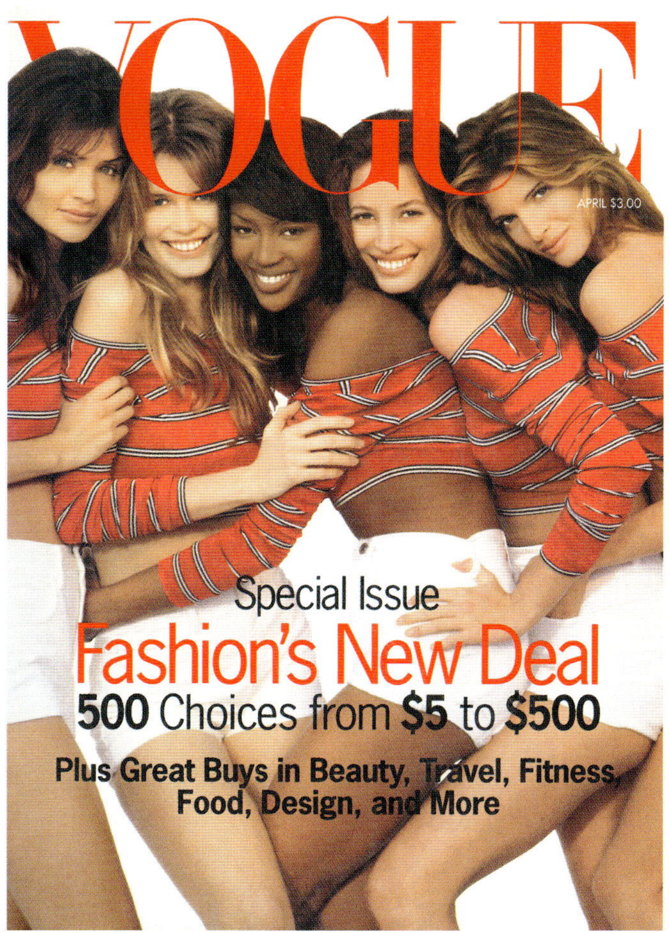

Vogue US, April 1993

Herb Ritts, models: Helena Christensen, Claudia Schiffer, Stephanie Seymour, Christy Turlington, Naomi Campbell, Hollywood 1993 for *Vogue* US

This image of Helena Christensen, Stephanie Seymour, Christy Turlington, Naomi Campbell and myself is quintessential 1990s. It was from a cover shoot by photographer Herb Ritts, who was a master at capturing natural moments.

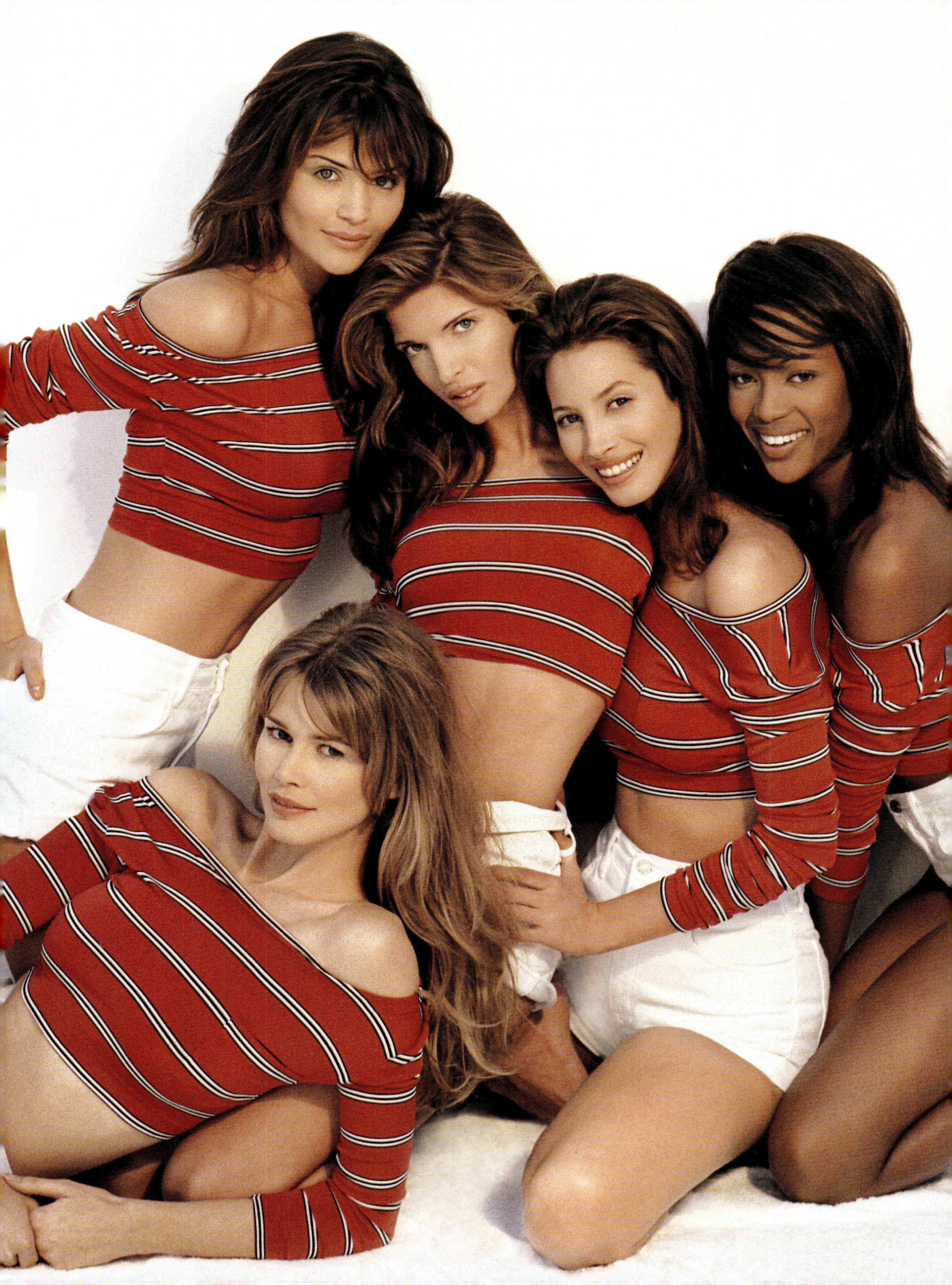

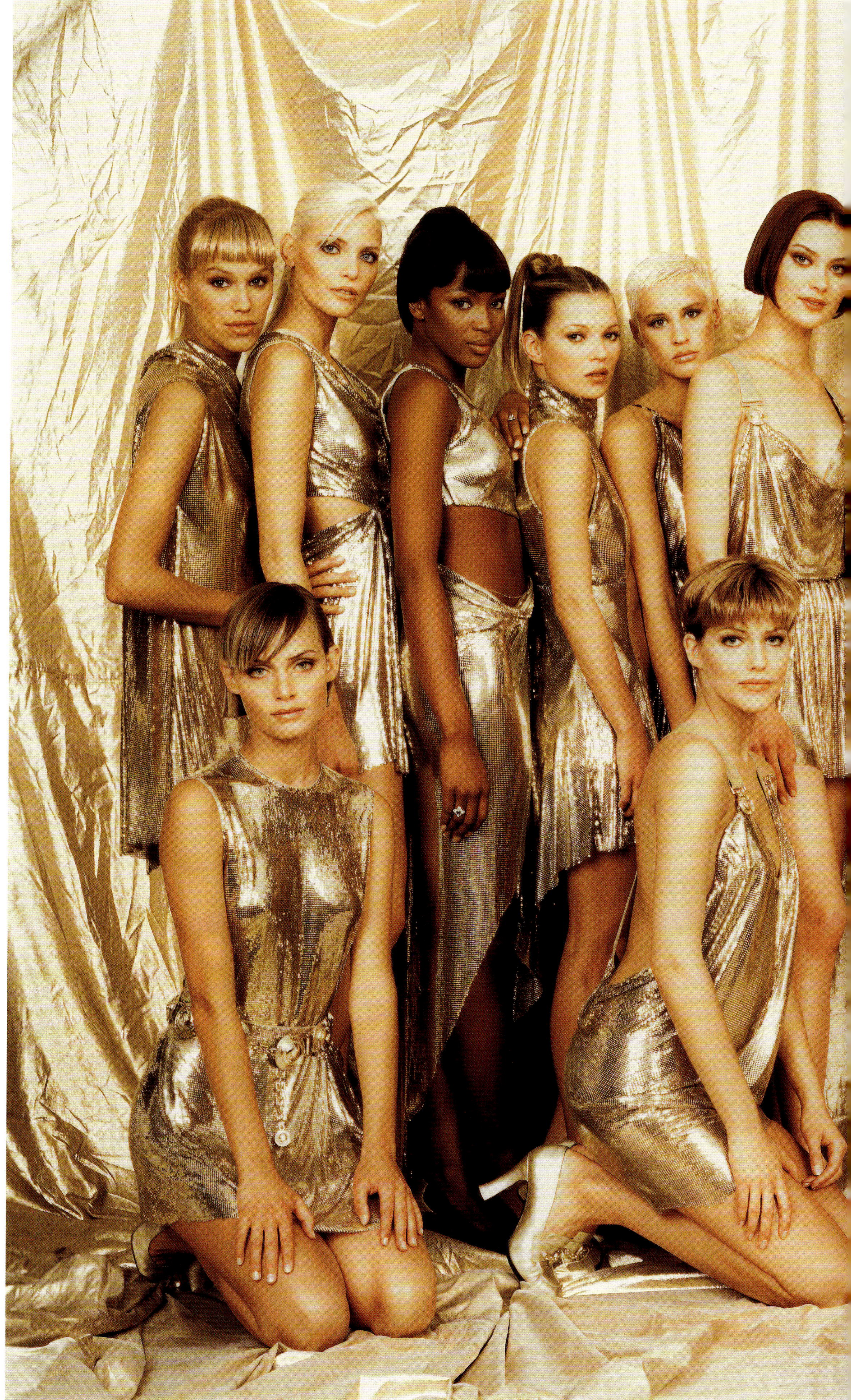

Doug Ordway, Golden Girls, models: Emma Sjöberg, Nadja Auermann, Naomi Campbell, Kate Moss, Ève Salvail, Shalom Harlow, Carla Bruni, Olga Pantushenkova, Christy Turlington, Linda Evangelista, Claudia Schiffer, Yasmeen Ghauri, Amber Valletta, Tricia Helfer, Helena Christensen, backstage at Versace RTW Fall 1994

This image by Doug Ordway unified and championed the supermodels as a group. Here we are backstage, dressed in Gianni Versace's famous gold chainmail dresses. Gianni electrified fashion, making it a driving force within pop culture.

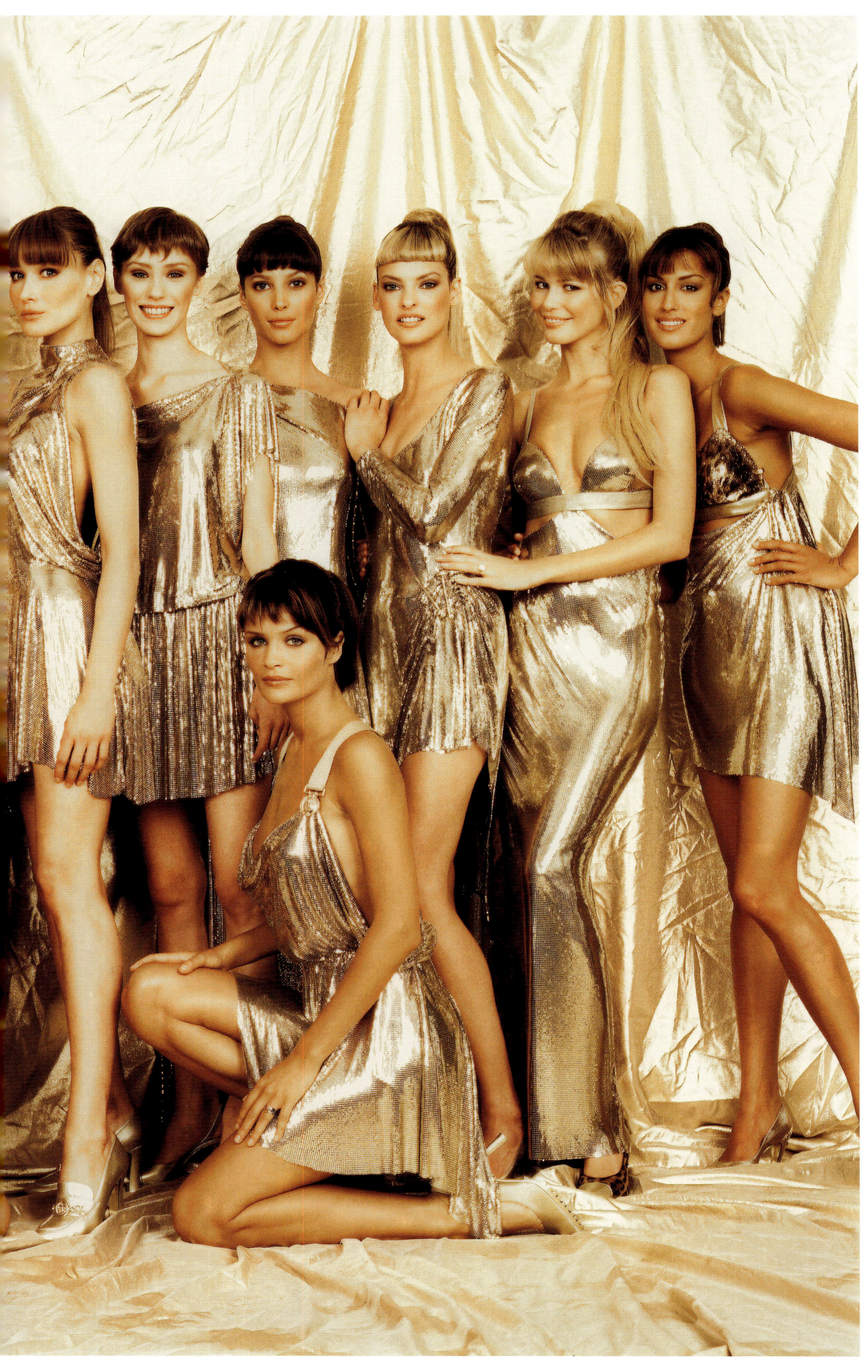

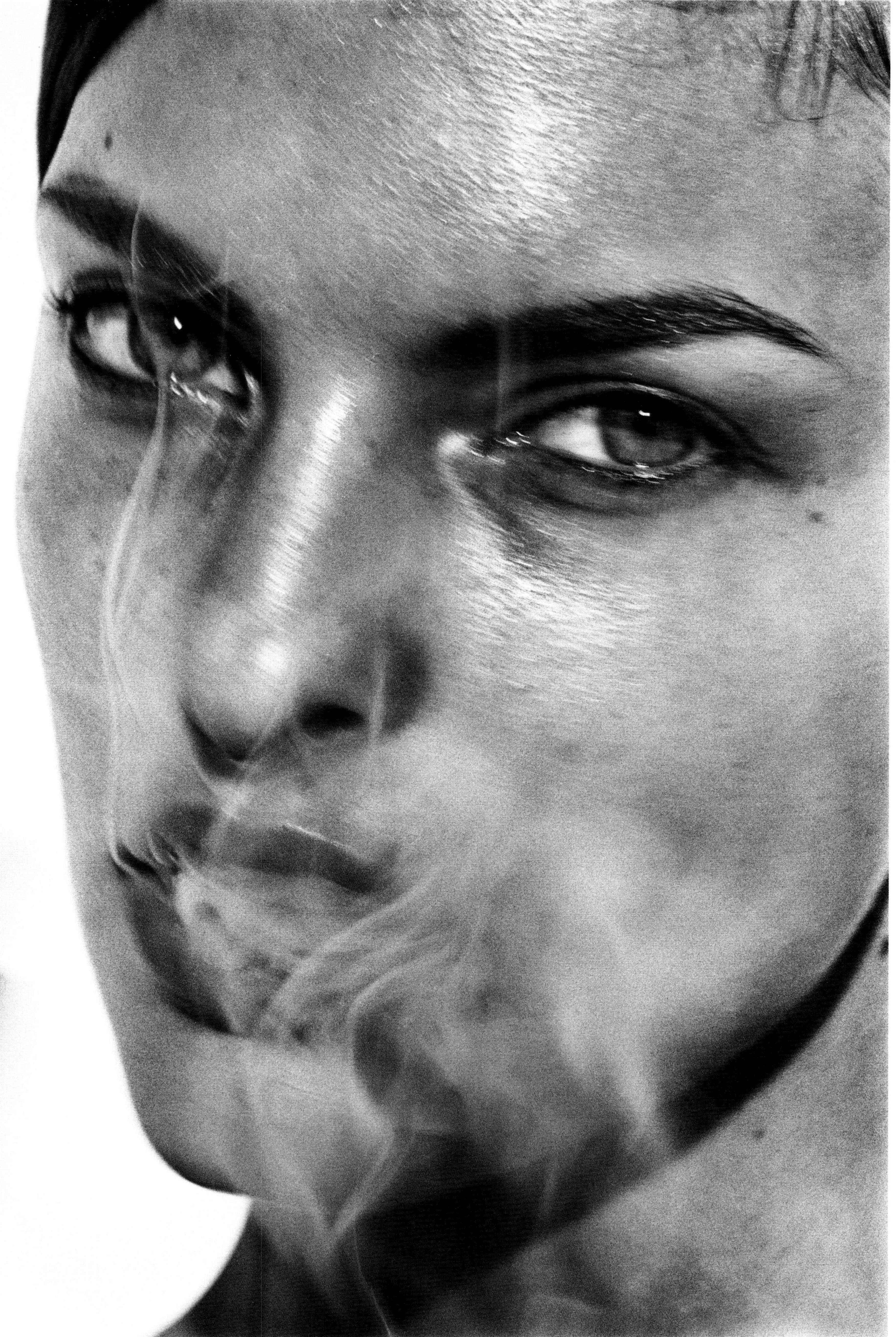

40/41
Peter Lindbergh, Seeing Spots, model: Naomi Campbell, Los Angeles 1990 for *Vogue* US

Peter Lindbergh brought black-and-white imagery back into the mainstream, at a time when pop culture was a rainbow of saturated brights. The image overleaf of Naomi Campbell in Geoffrey Beene seizes upon the sharp bite of black and white.

Peter Lindbergh, Linda Evangelista, 1990

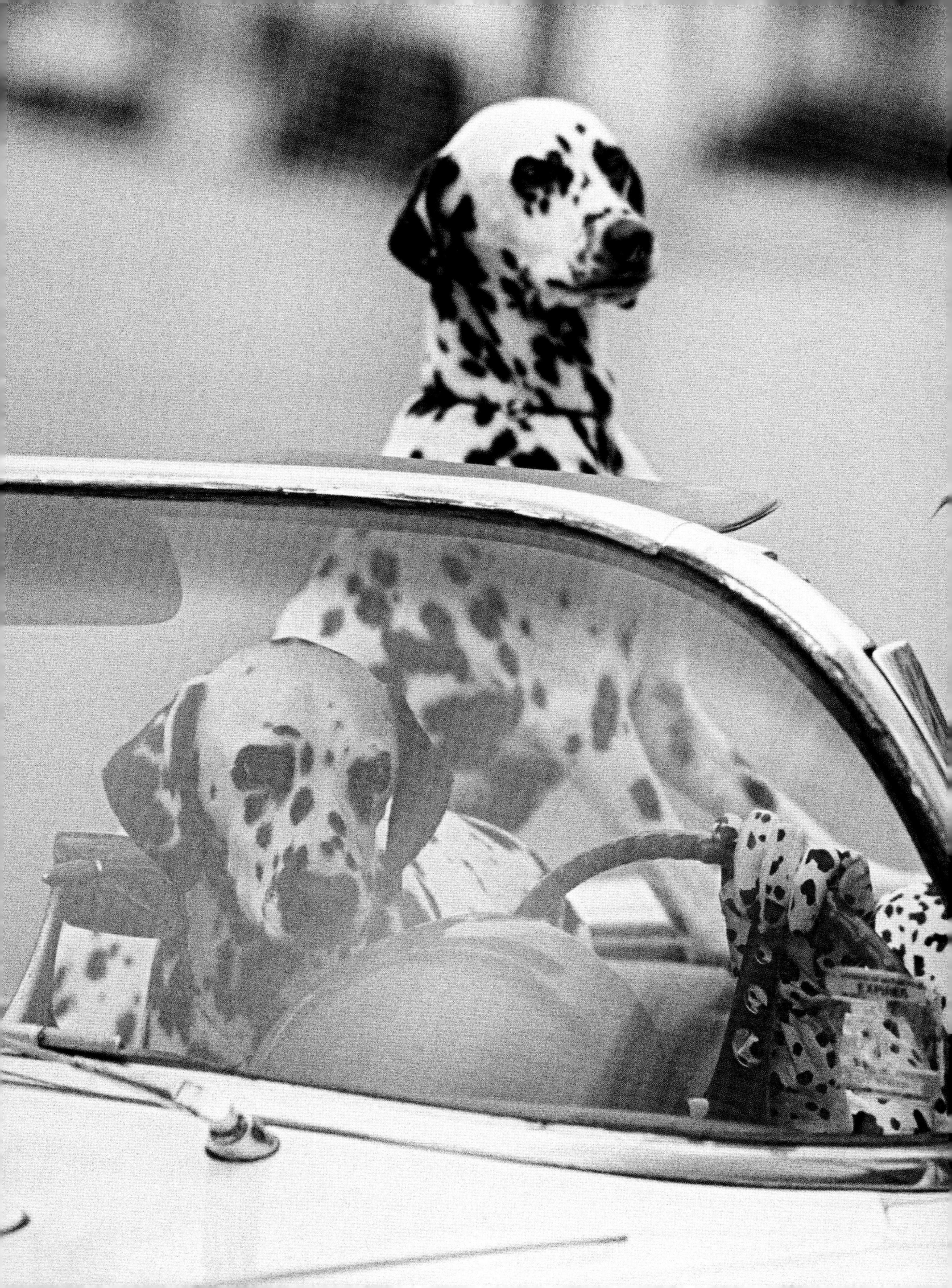

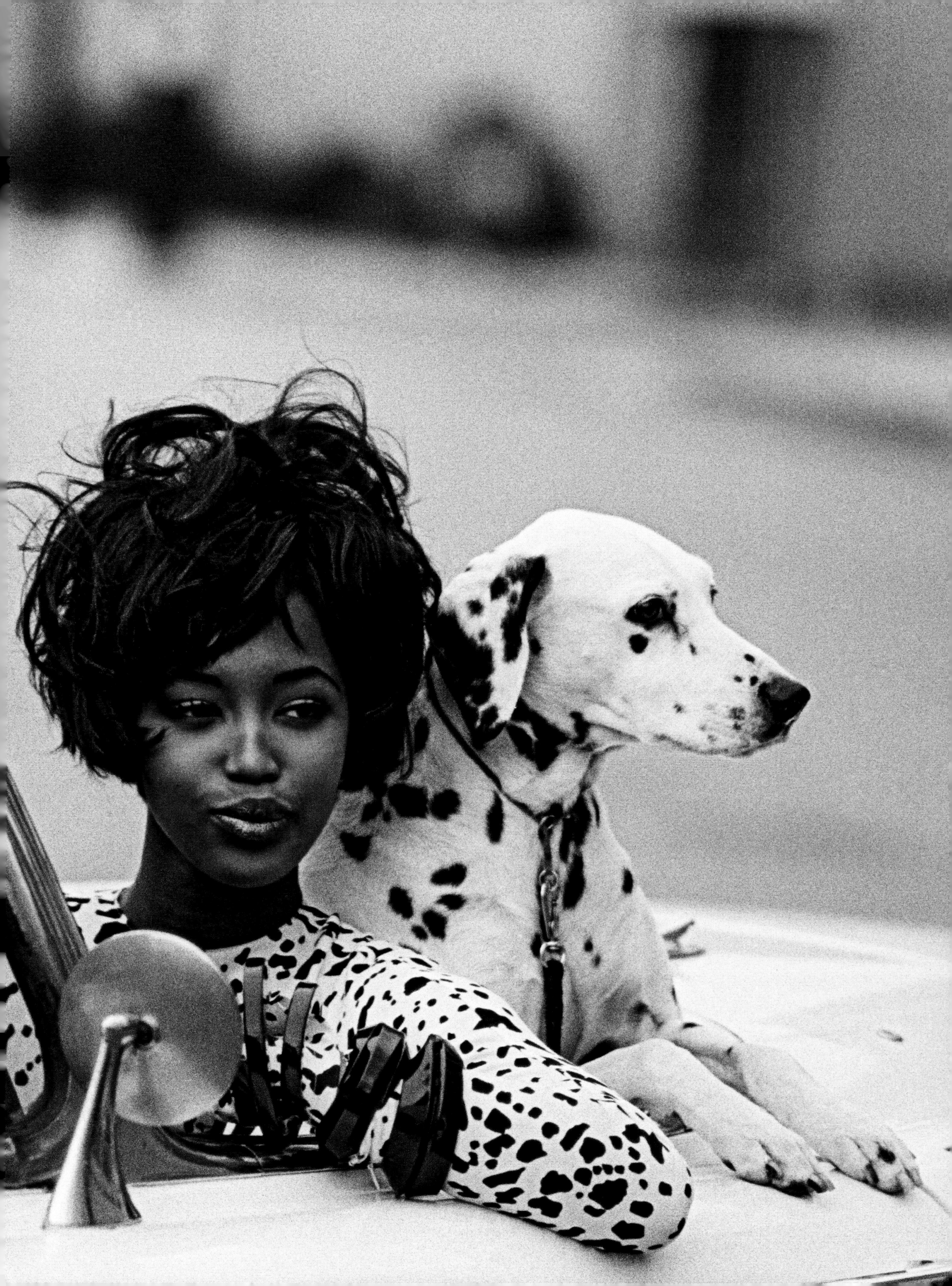

Herb Ritts, model: Claudia Schiffer, Palmdale, California 1992

Herb Ritts had an extraordinary eye for beauty, and this was amplified by natural light and graphic simplicity. He made his subjects feel absolutely at ease and his approach to fashion photography emphasised the personality of the model.

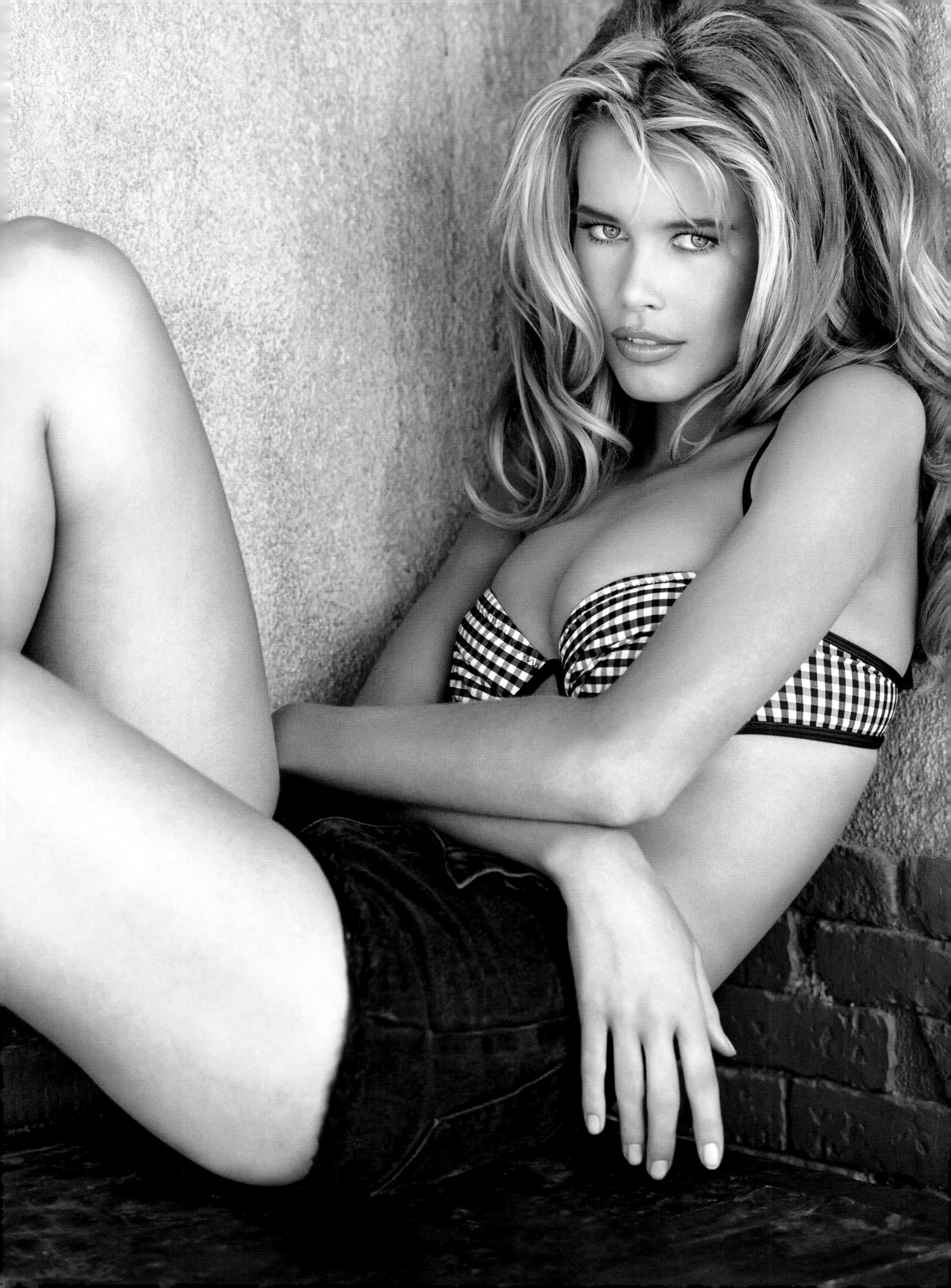

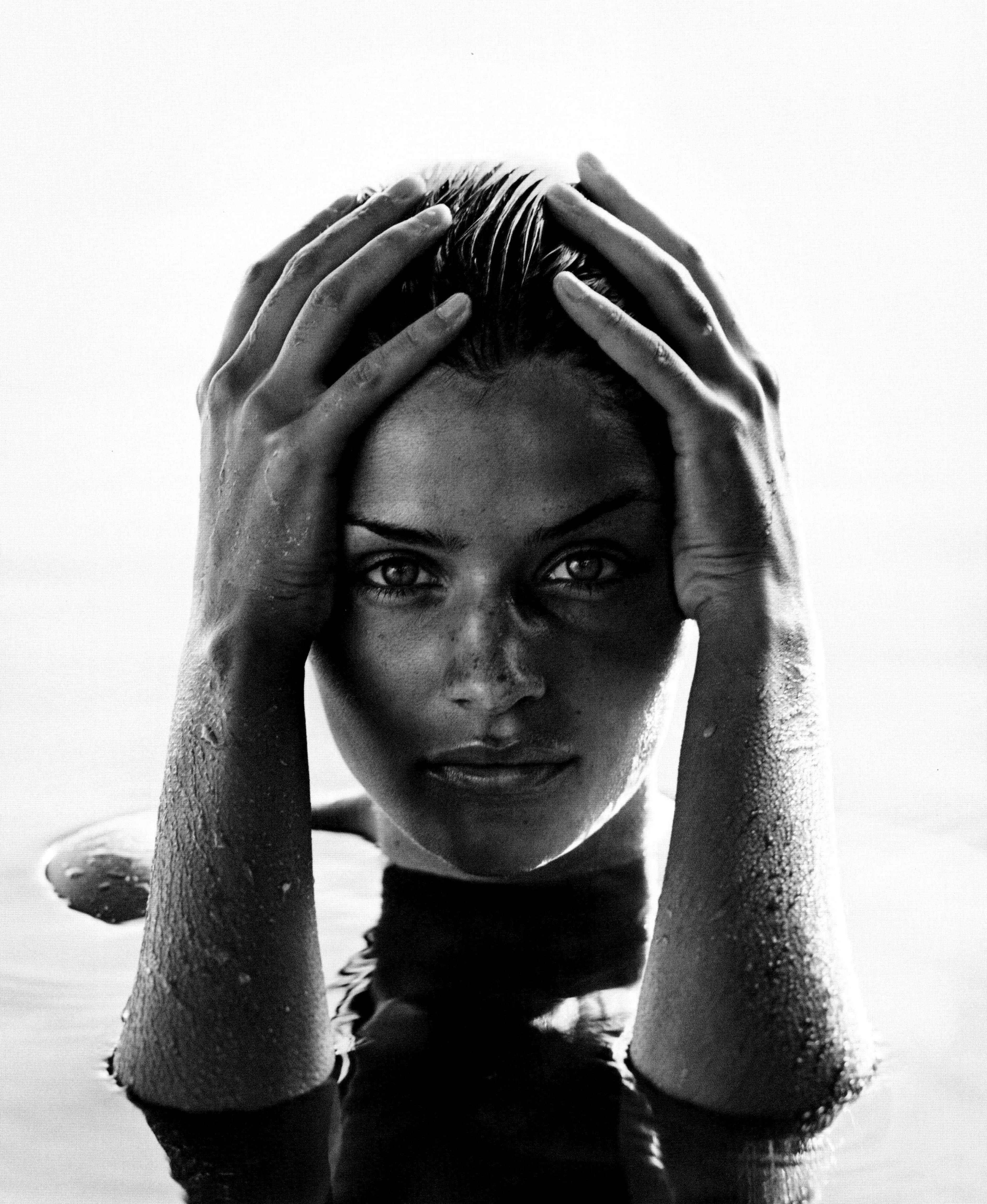

Herb Ritts, model: Helena Christensen, Malibu 1990

Bruce Weber, Seventh on Sale, models: Claudia Schiffer, Cindy Crawford, New York 1992 for Revlon

---

US-American photographer Bruce Weber seized on the idea of supermodel sisterhood, framing Cindy Crawford and myself in this campaign image for Revlon, one of the most successful cosmetic brands in the world at the time.

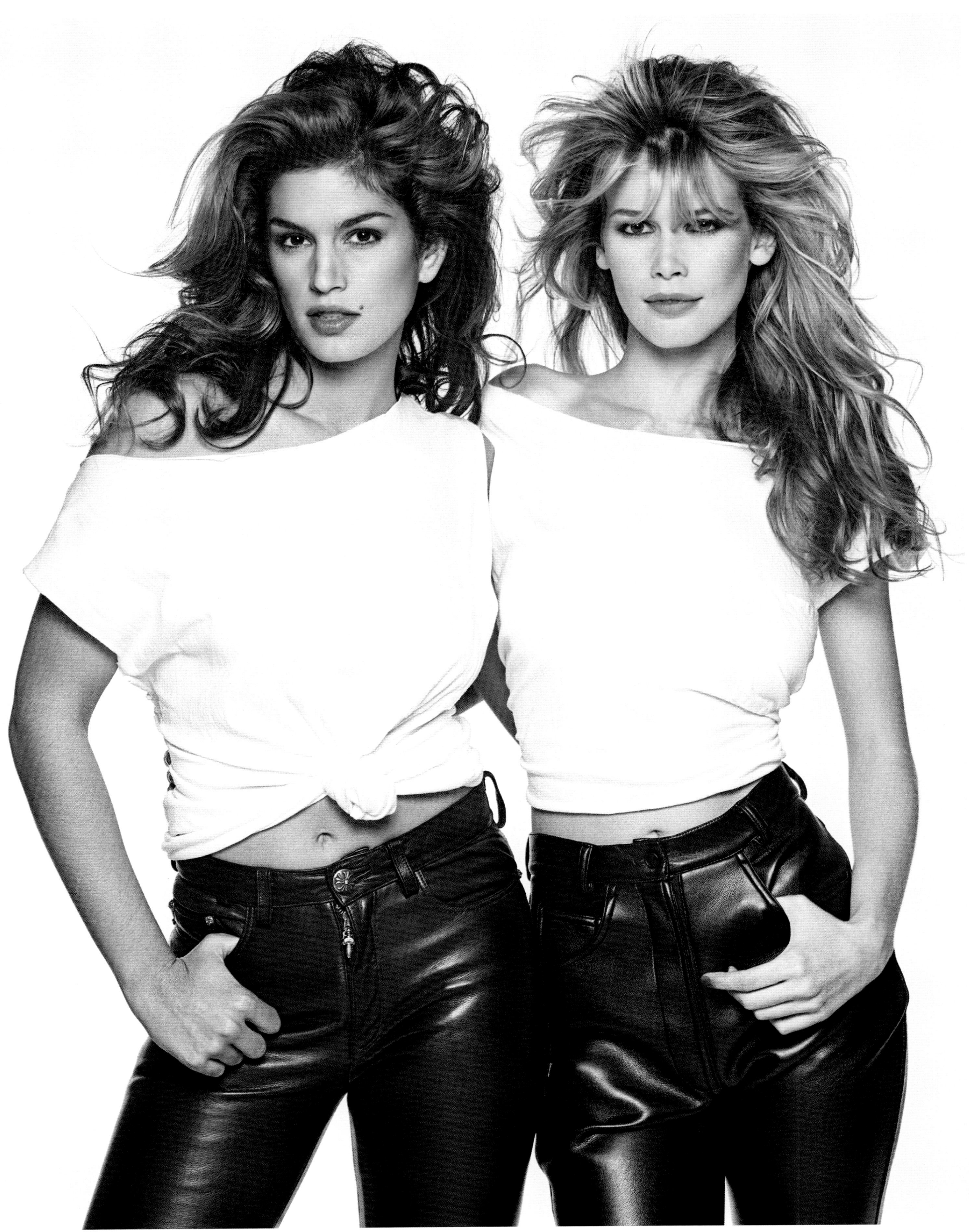

Working with Helmut Newton was like working with the Mozart of fashion photography, Iike being a part of fashion history.

CARLA BRUNI

Helmut Newton, model: Carla Bruni, Nice 1993 for Blumarine

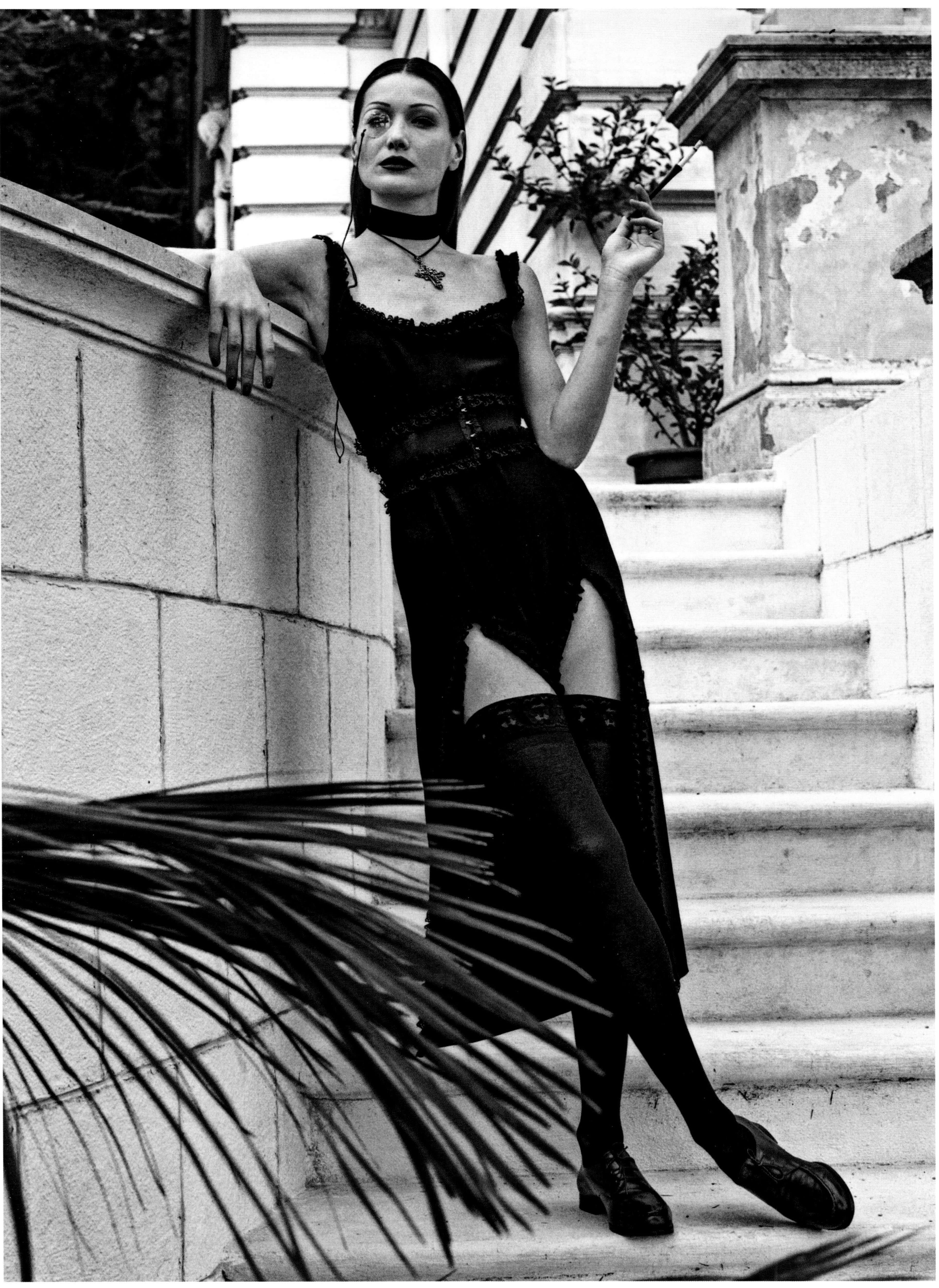

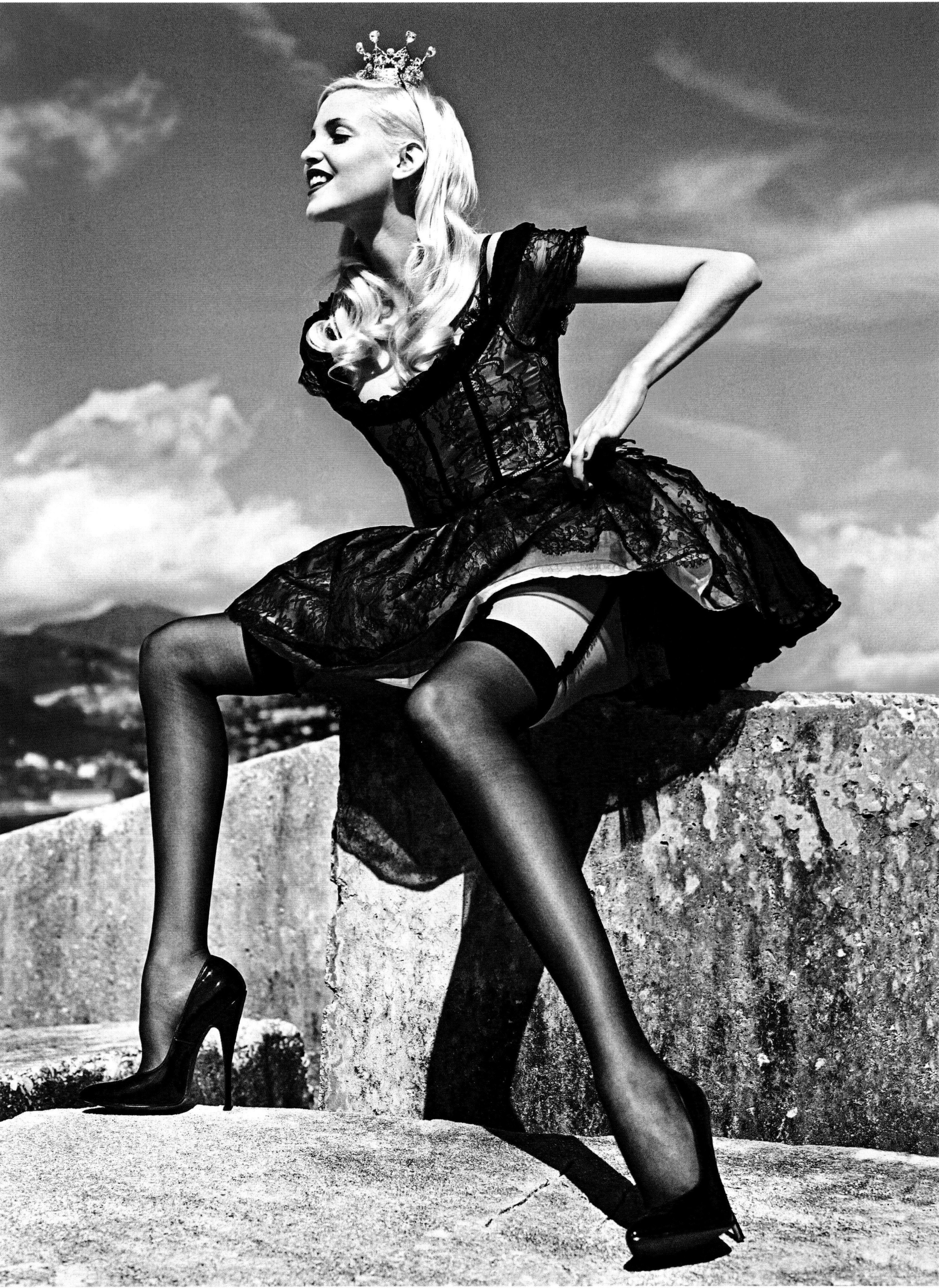

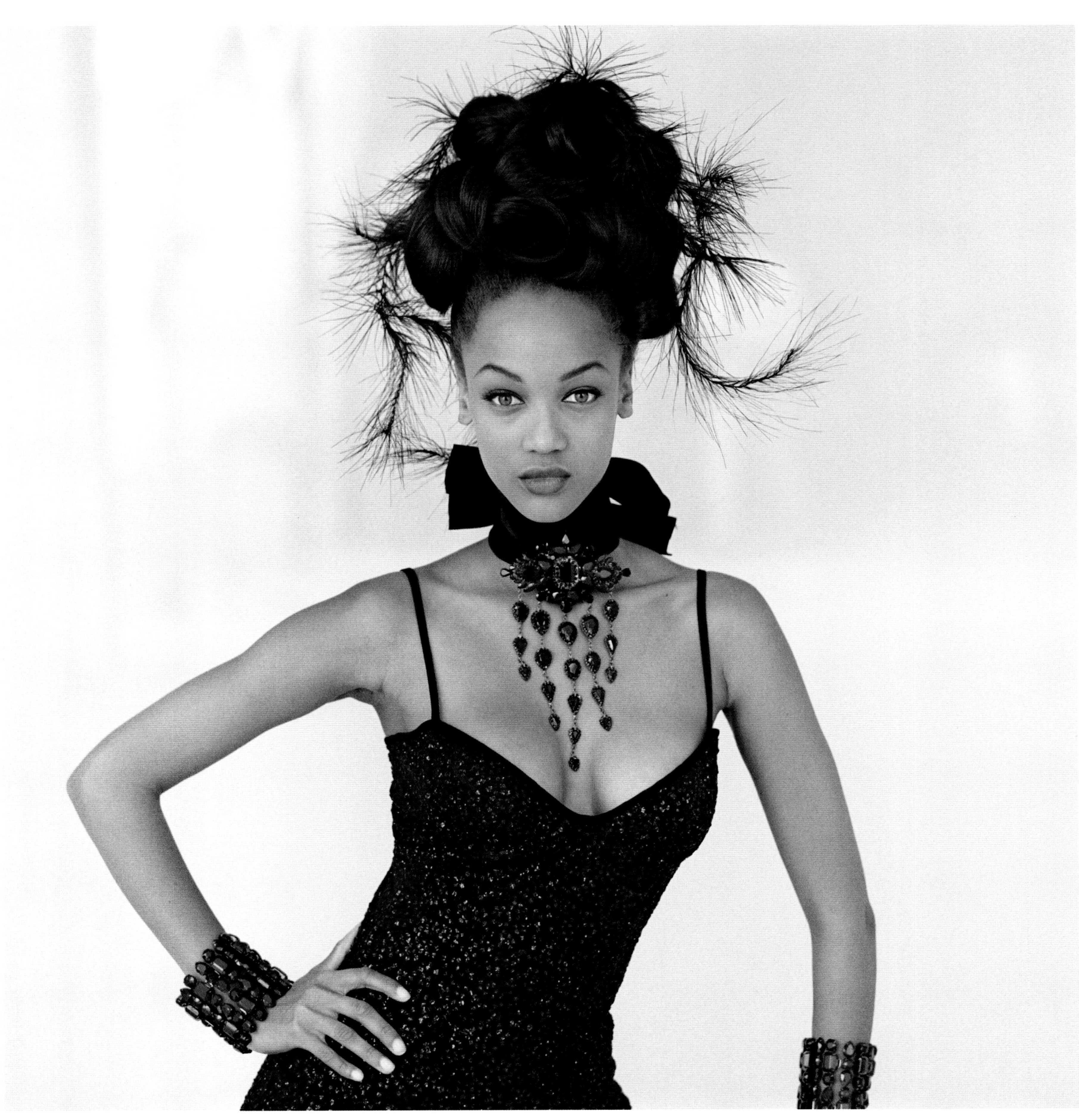

Helmut Newton, model: Nadja Auermann, Monte Carlo 1994 for Blumarine

Arthur Elgort, model: Tyra Banks, 1992 for *Vogue* UK

There was no Instagram yet.
You had to make people dream.
It was enough.

CARINE ROITFELD

Helmut Newton, model: Eva Herzigová,
Cannes 1996 for *Paris Match*

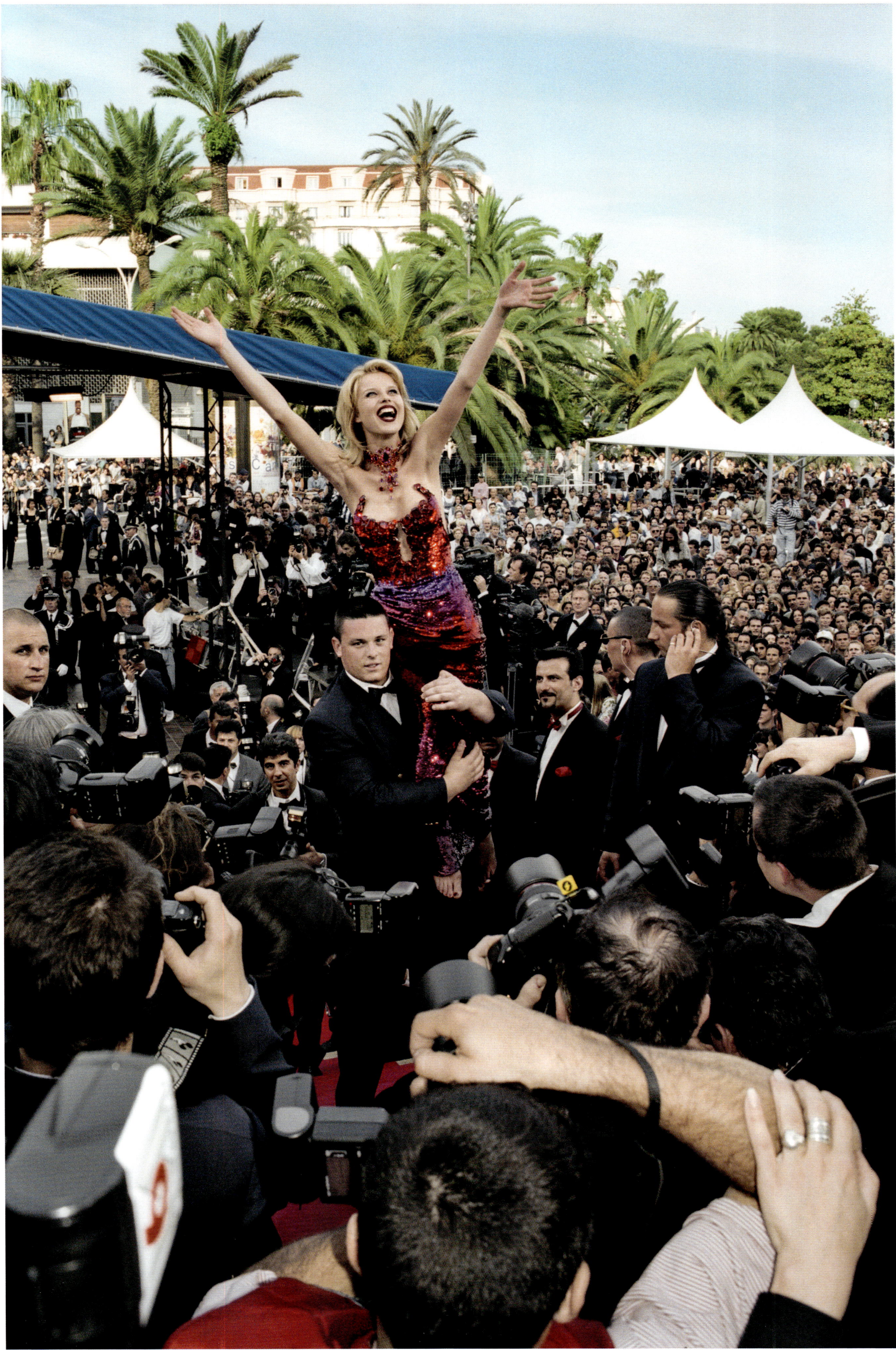

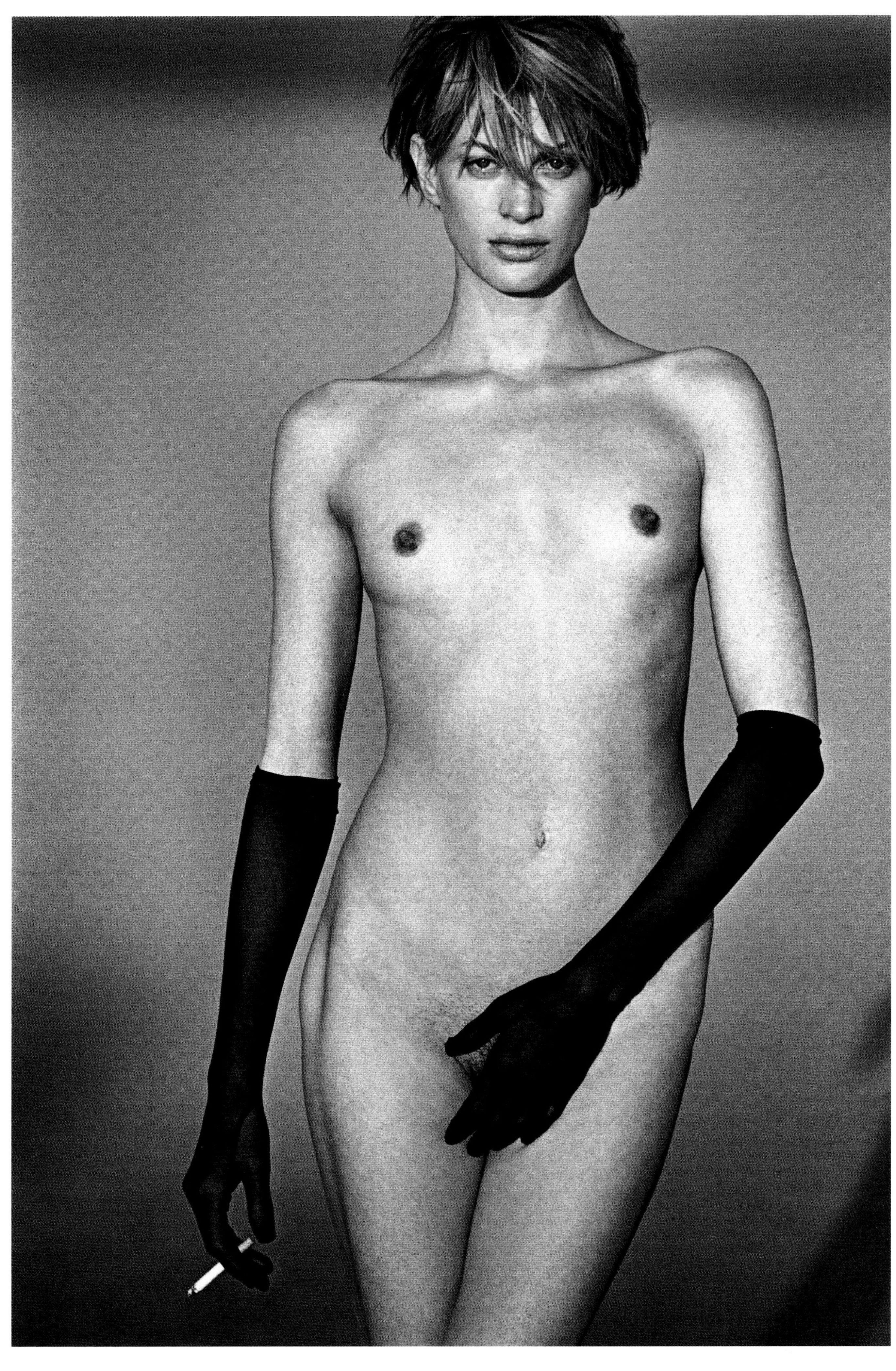

Peter Lindbergh, model: Kristen McMenamy,
El Mirage, California 1995 for Pirelli Calendar 1996

Herb Ritts, model: Stephanie Seymour,
1991 for *Vogue* US

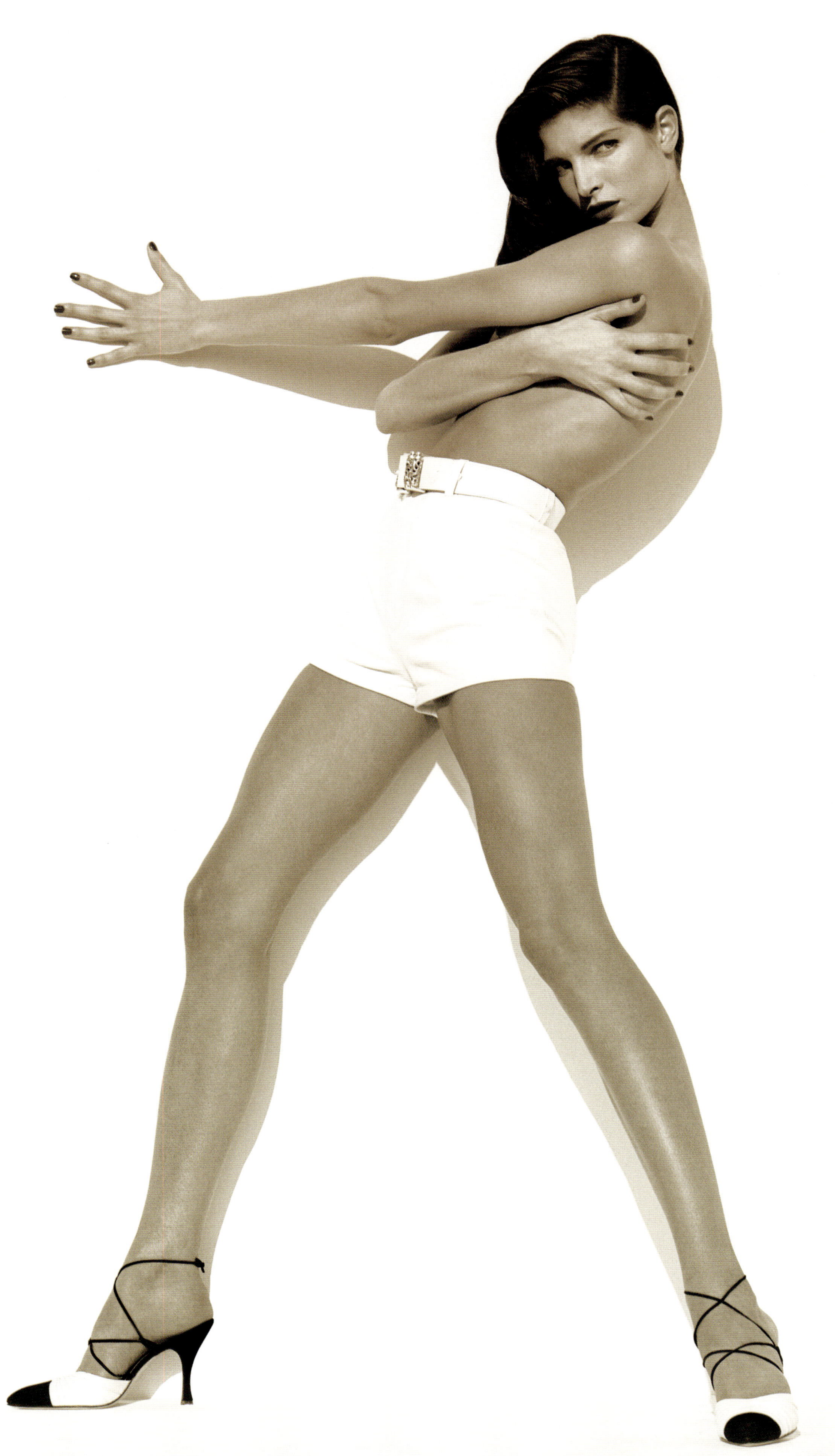

Peter Lindbergh, Ein starkes Stück am Strand, model: Tatjana Patitz, Deauville, France 1990 for *Stern*

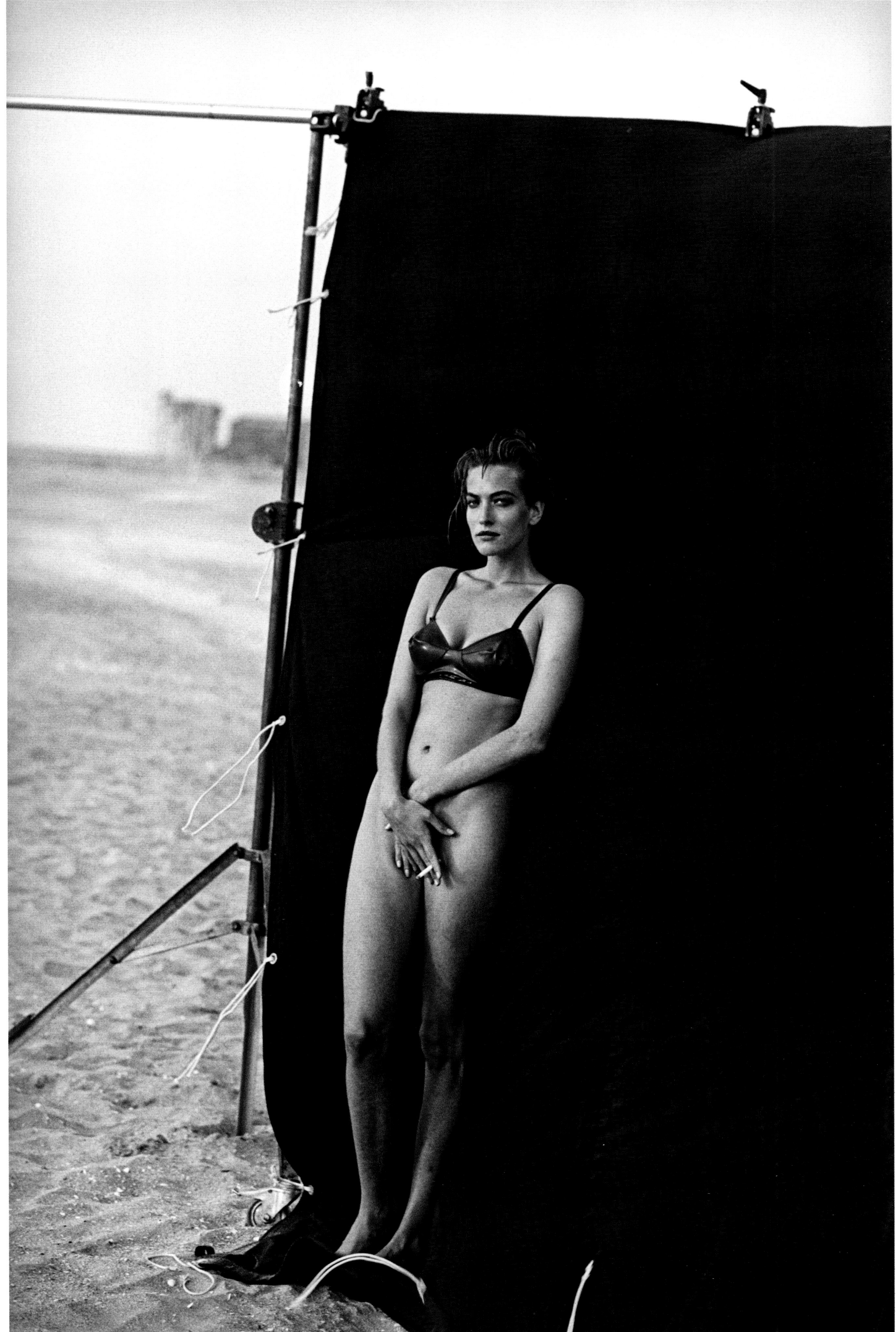

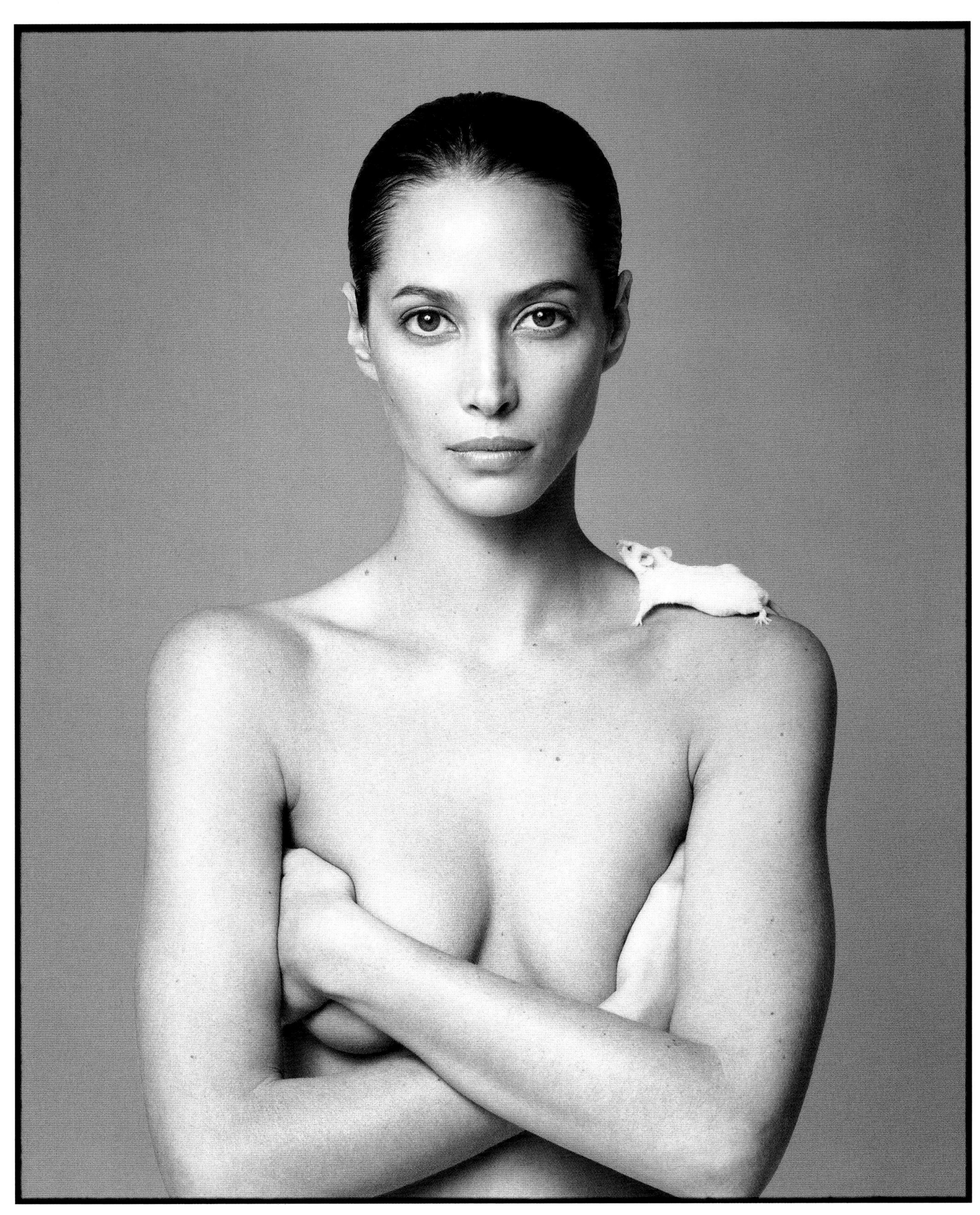

Patrick Demarchelier, model: Christy Turlington, 1999 for *Harper's Bazaar*

Patrick Demarchelier, model: Elle Macpherson, New York 1990 for *Madame Figaro*

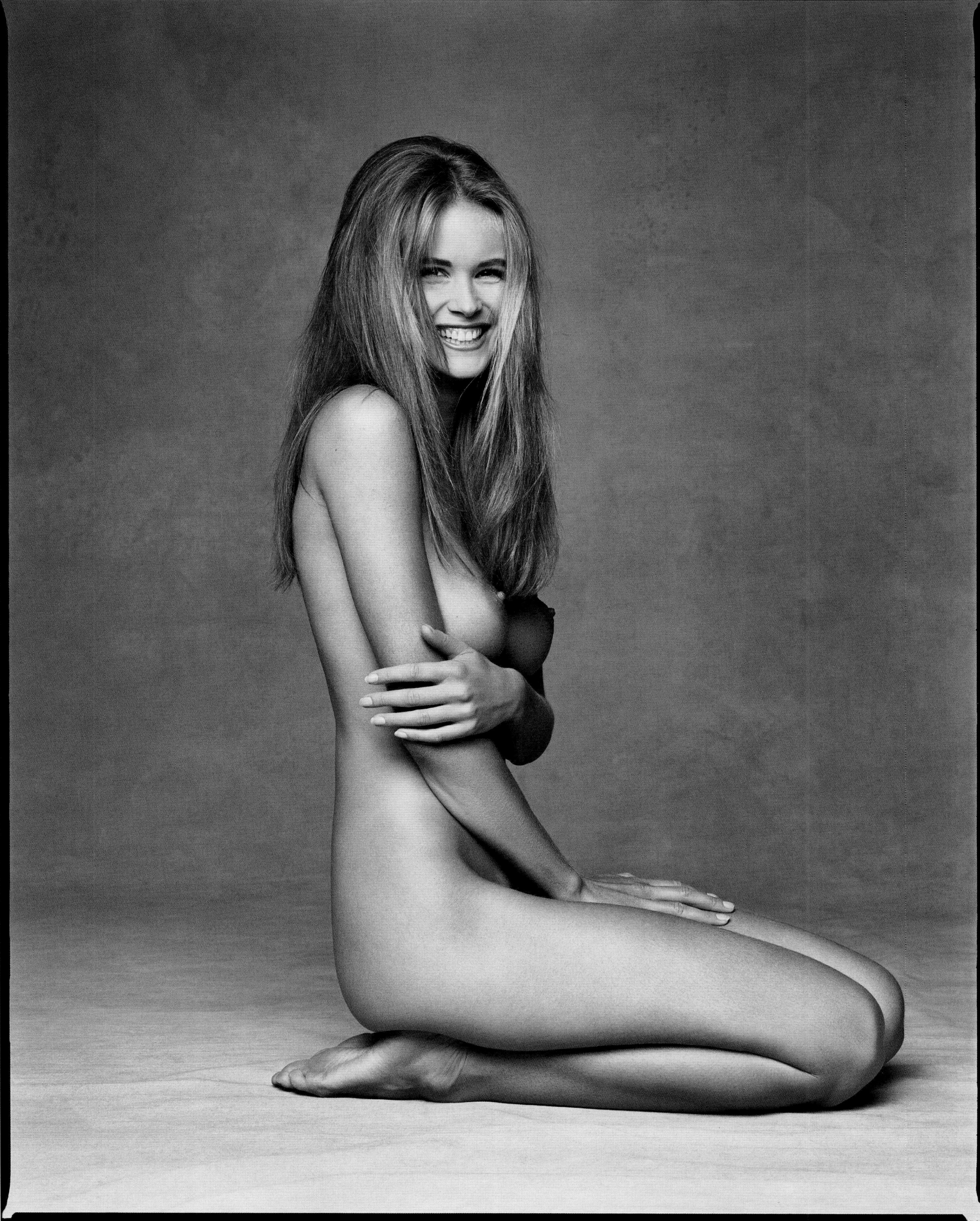

Michel Comte, models: Kristy Hume, Nadja Auermann, Nadège du Bospertus, Claudia Schiffer, Carla Bruni, Linda Evangelista, Naomi Campbell, Christy Turlington, Shalom Harlow, Brandi Quinones, 1994

A high-energy, classic 1990s Versace moment – we went straight from the runway to shoot for Italian *Vogue* in Versace's palazzo and on to the party together. Group compositions are complex and the skill is in directing everyone to work together. Michel Comte made it look spontaneous but there were numerous variations made over many hours before he arrived at the perfect shot.

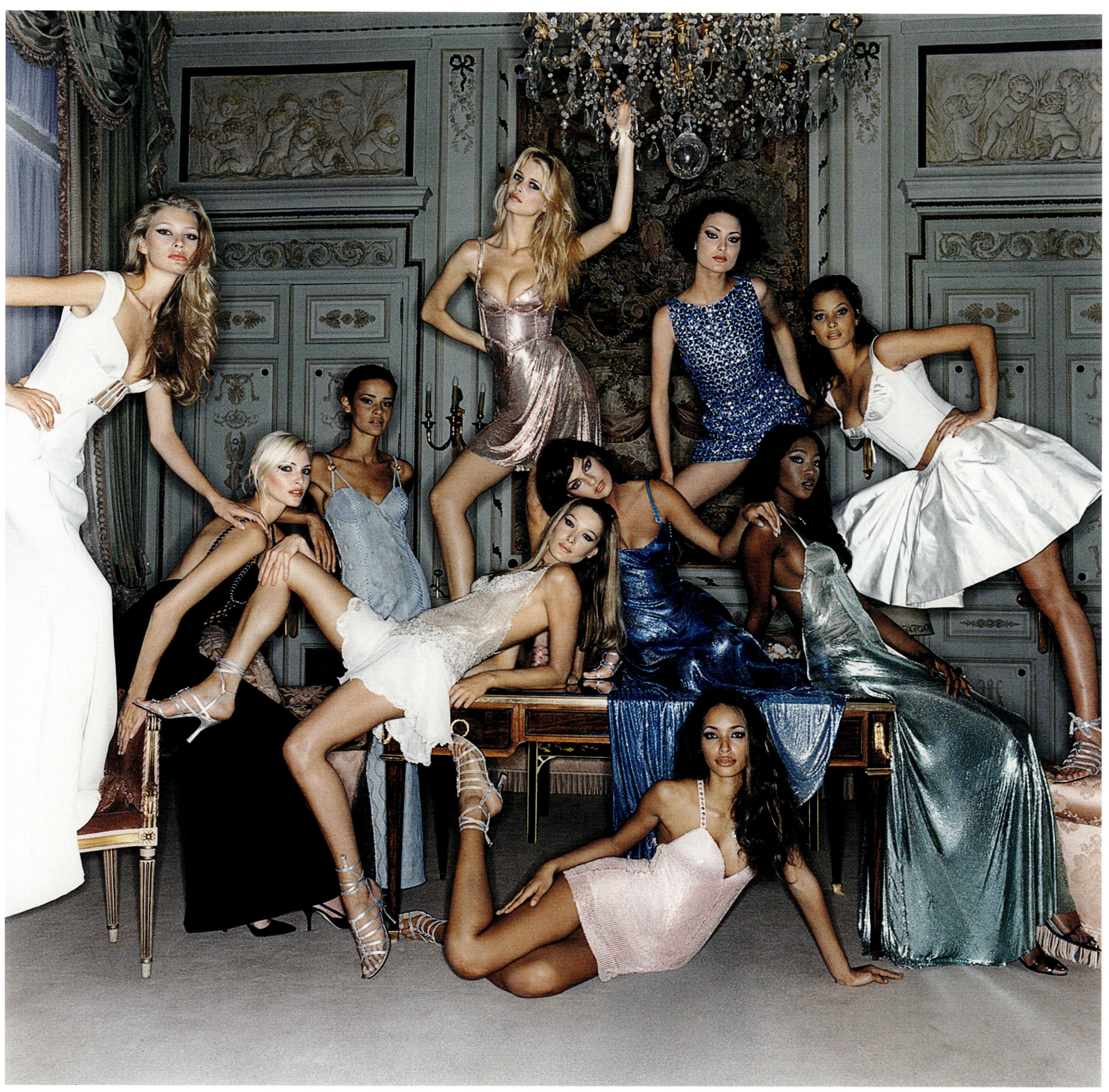

Herb Ritts, model: Cindy Crawford,
El Mirage, California 1995 for Versace

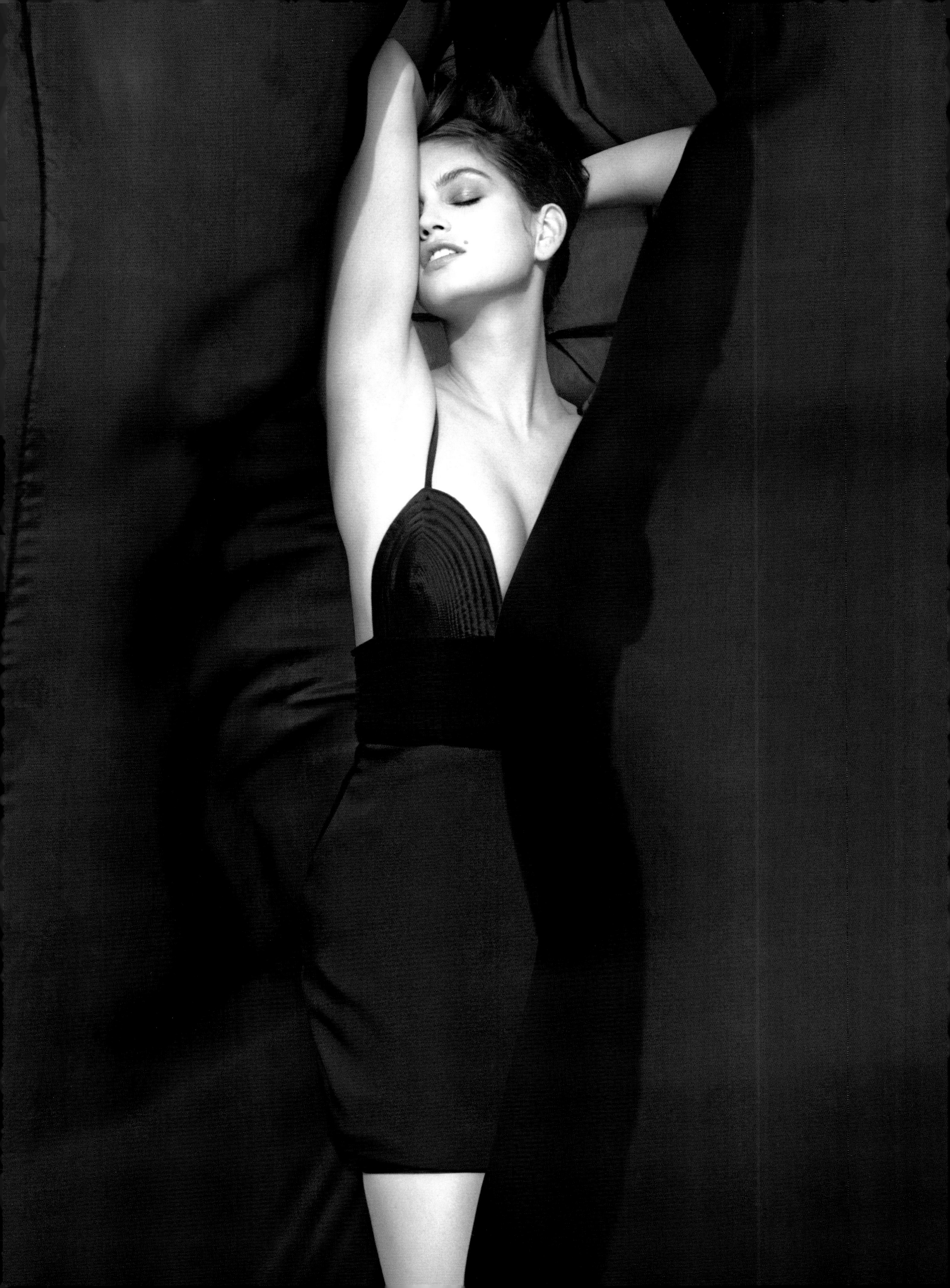

Herb Ritts, model: Naomi Campbell,
Los Angeles 1991 for *Interview*

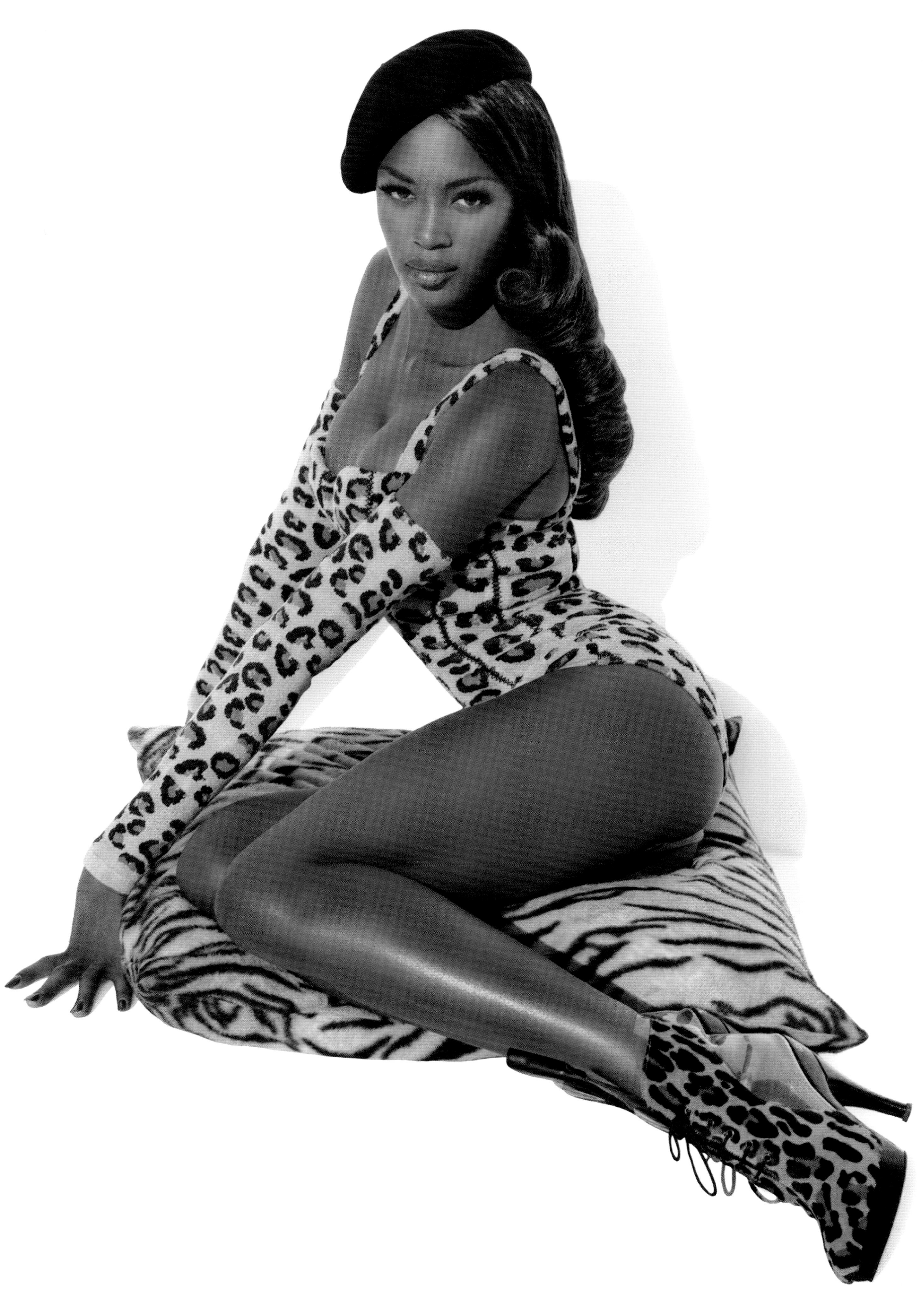

There were photographs before Instagram and smartphones, of course. They remain the true, authoritative and indelible record of the 'super decade': the 1990s, the age of the supermodels, the first time when it was not fashion that made the headlines, but the girls wearing it.

HILARY ALEXANDER

Ellen von Unwerth, model: Kate Moss,
Paris 1995 for *Vogue* US

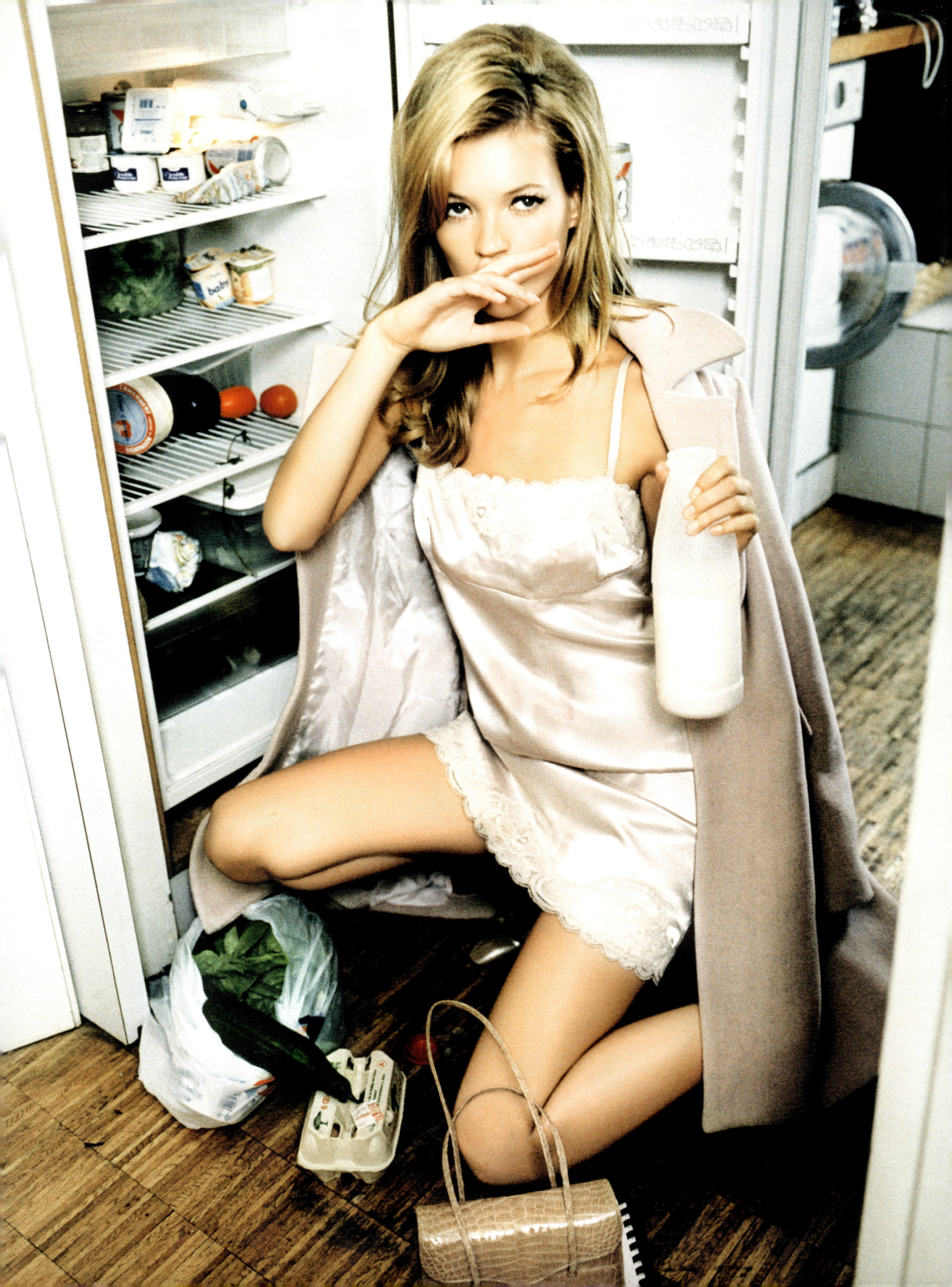
baby

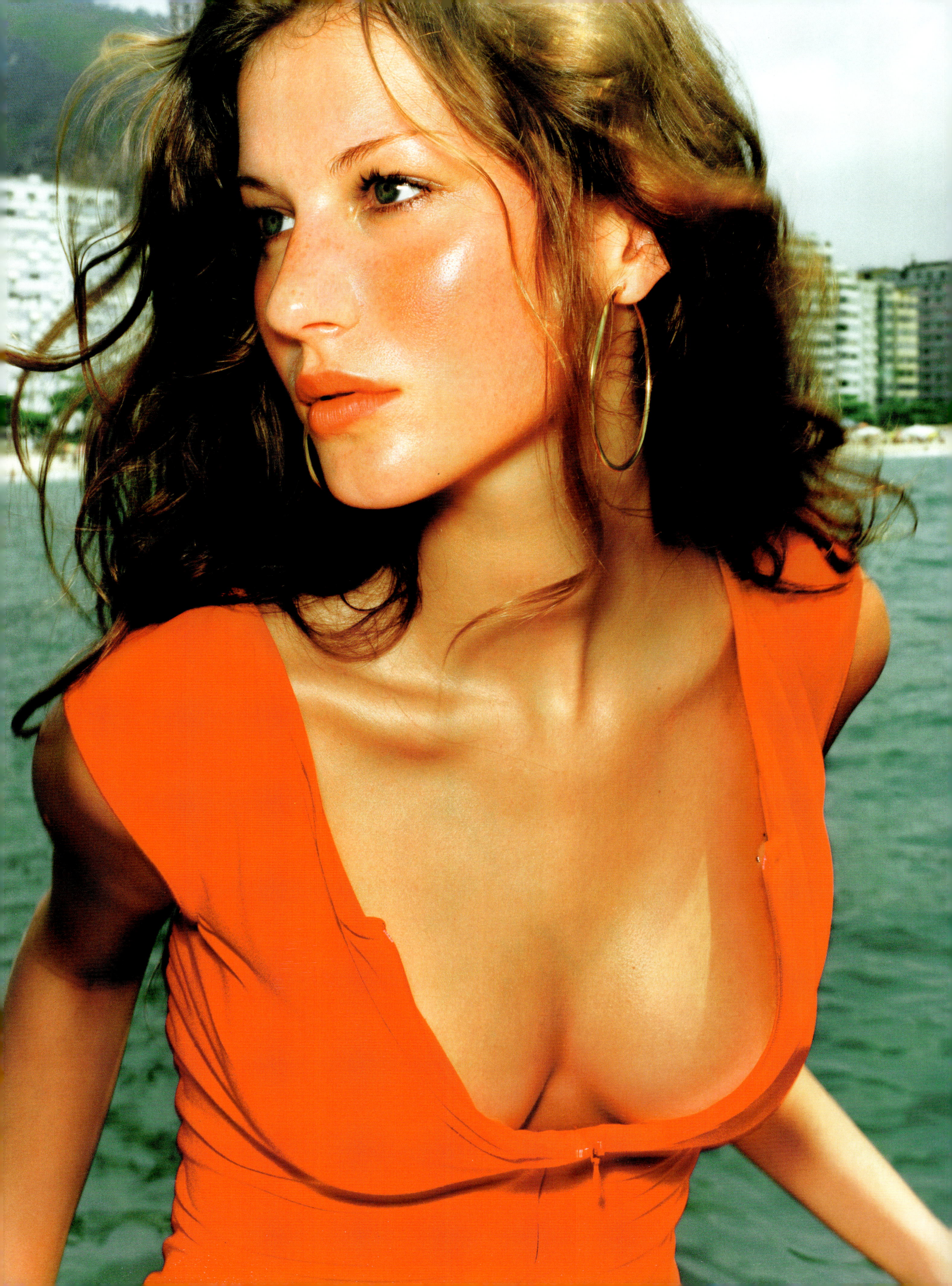

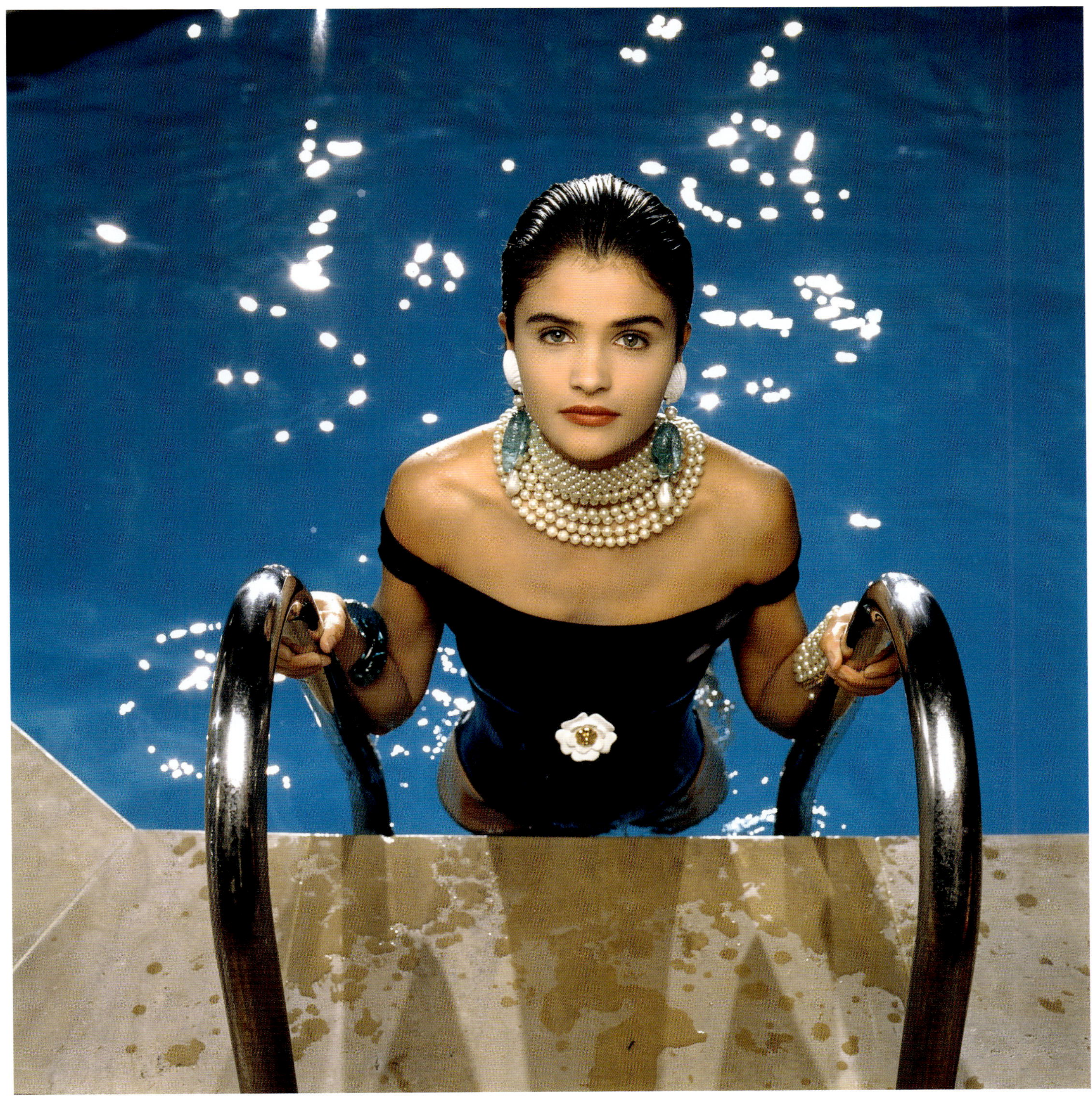

'Supermodel' – I thought it sounded cartoonish and just laughed at the word. I feel now that what it really means is longevity and staying power.

HELENA CHRISTENSEN

Mario Testino, model: Gisele Bündchen, Rio de Janeiro 1998 for *Allure*

Karl Lagerfeld, model: Helena Christensen, Deauville, France 1990 for Chanel

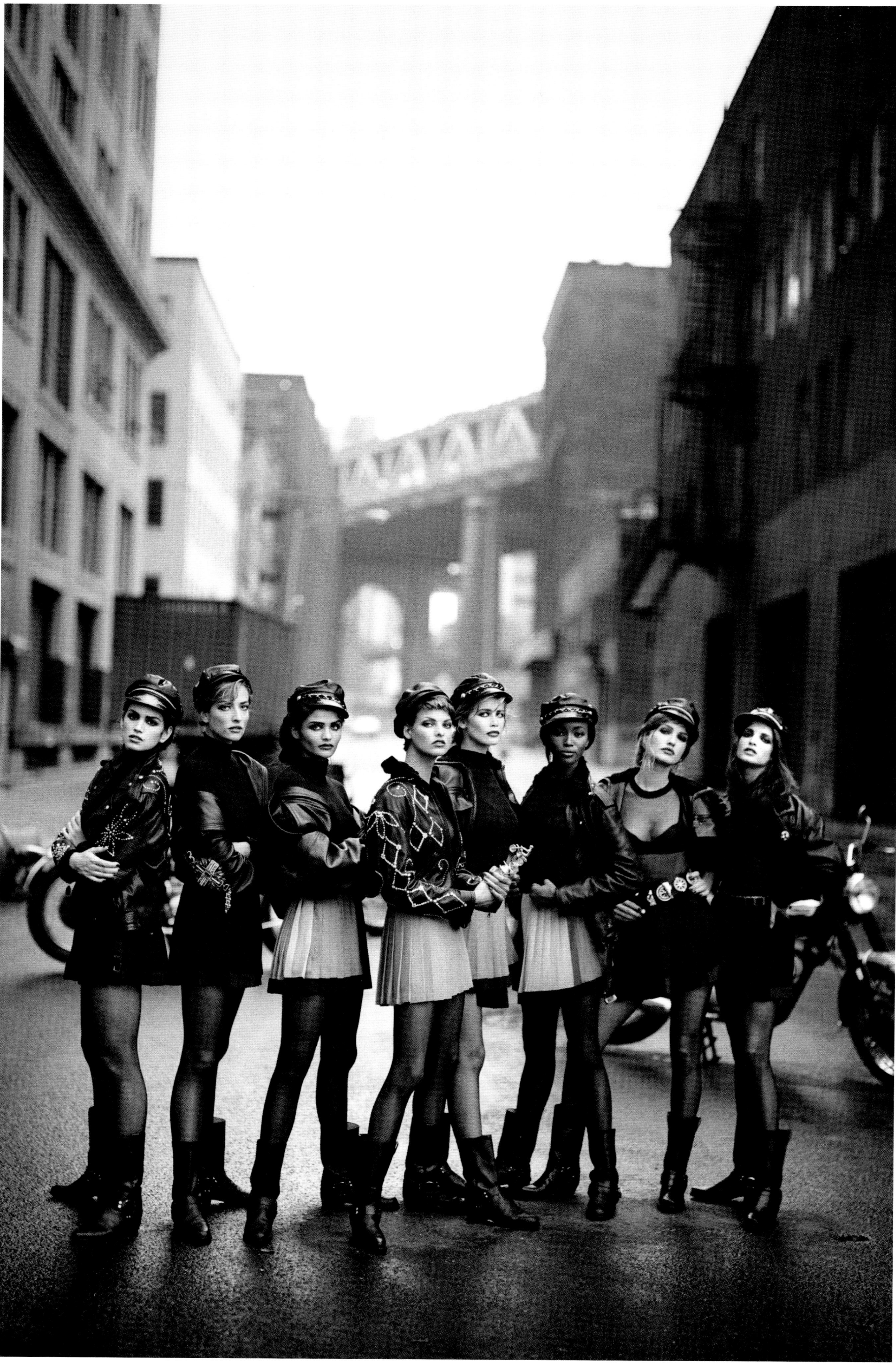

Peter Lindbergh, Wild at Heart, models: Cindy Crawford, Tatjana Patitz, Helena Christensen, Linda Evangelista, Claudia Schiffer, Naomi Campbell, Karen Mulder, Stephanie Seymour, New York 1991 for *Vogue* US

Wearing Chanel biker boots and leathers, we posed for Peter Lindbergh in downtown New York against the Brooklyn Bridge. The editorial shoot for the September 1991 issue of US *Vogue* was titled *Wild at Heart*, with a nod to actor Marlon Brando. Lindbergh had a cinematic vision informed by a deep knowledge of film. He was instrumental in defining the 1990s supermodel look. The art direction is defiantly glamorous, and projects female resilience and strength.

MY STORY

I was first discovered by a model agent at Checker's Club in Dusseldorf in 1987. Shortly after this, I took my first test shot and set card at the age of seventeen. A move to Paris soon after was where my journey into the modelling profession and the beguiling, maverick world of fashion began. This collection of images gives an insight into my story.

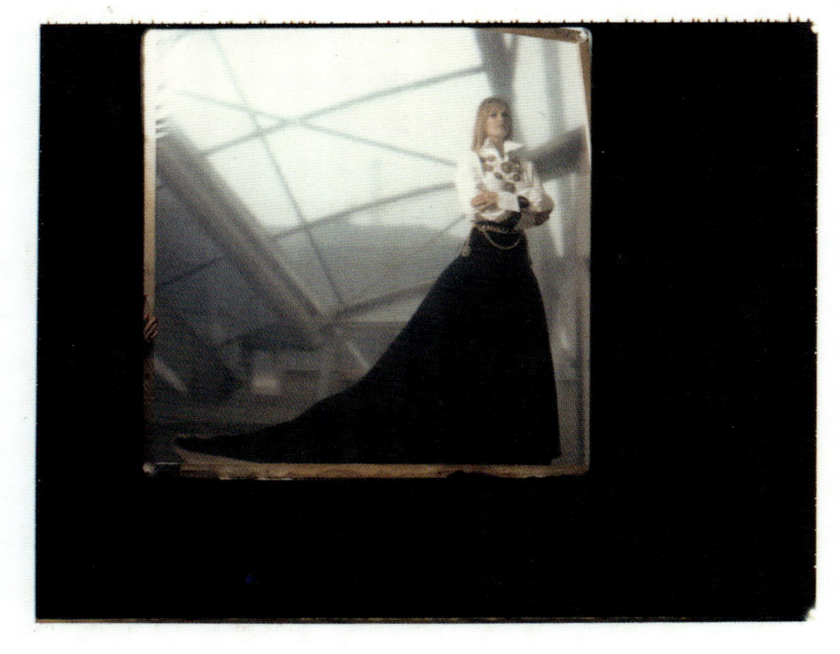

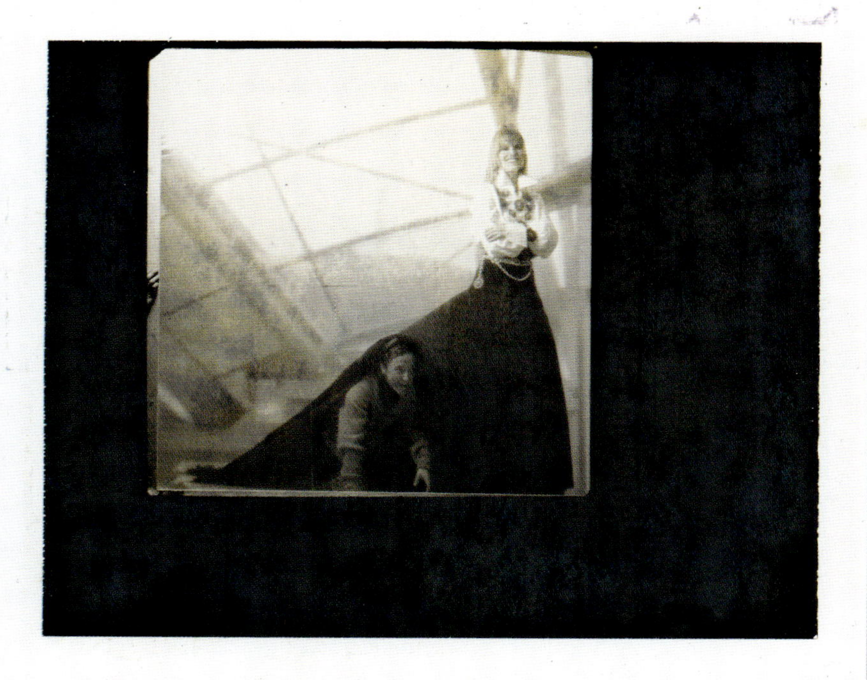

Here I am on set with Karl Lagerfeld for a Chanel campaign in the early 1990s. Franciane Bouscasse, then director of Haute Couture at Studio Chanel, was crouching under my dress to keep it voluminous while Karl Lagerfeld took the pictures. Polaroids by Karl.

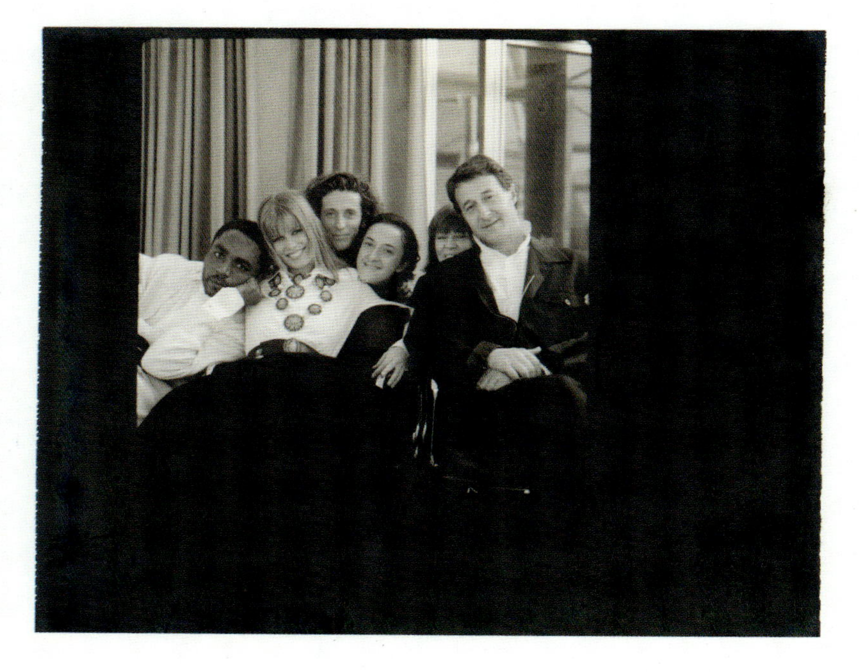

Behind the scenes with the Chanel team in 1993: here, Eric Wright, Julien d'Ys, Franciane Bouscasse, Heidi Morawetz and Eric Pfrunder. Polaroid by a crew member.

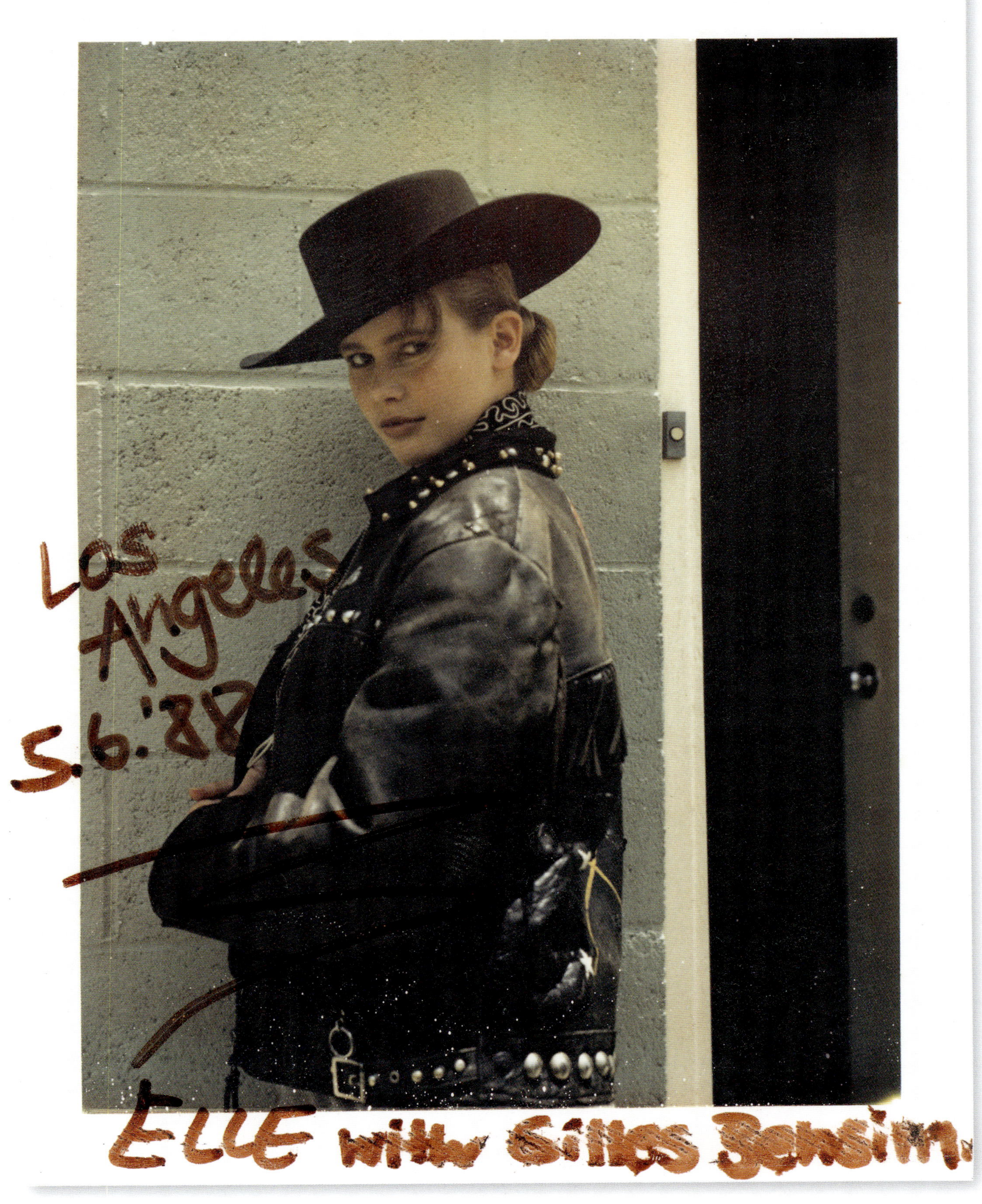

Here I am on set with Gilles Bensimon for an *ELLE* US editorial shoot in Los Angeles in 1988. Polaroid by Gilles.

Many supermodels become icons at the heights of their careers. But Claudia… when she hit the scene in her early years, she debuted as an icon.

TYRA BANKS

Hans Feurer, model: Claudia Schiffer, 1989 for *ELLE* FR

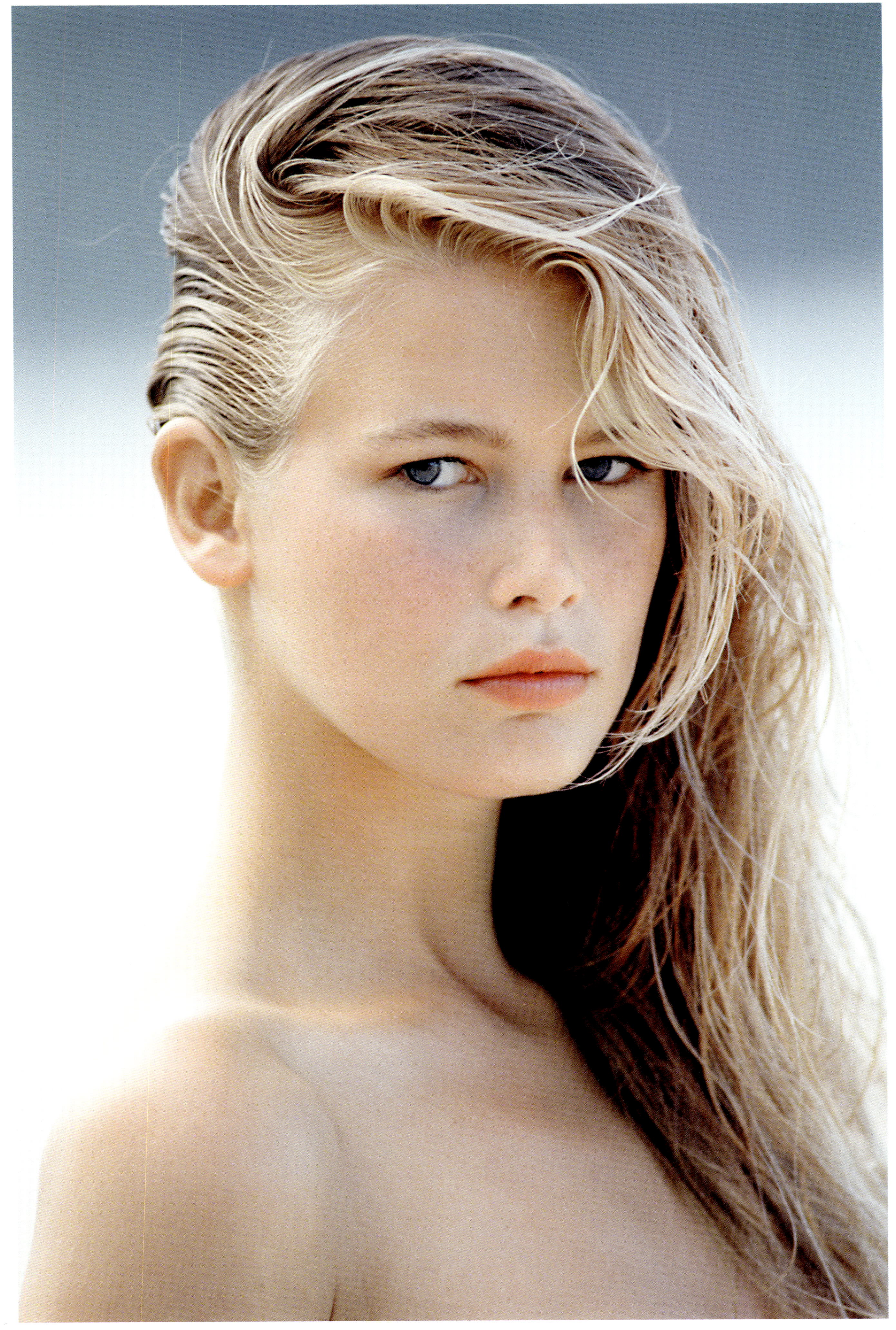

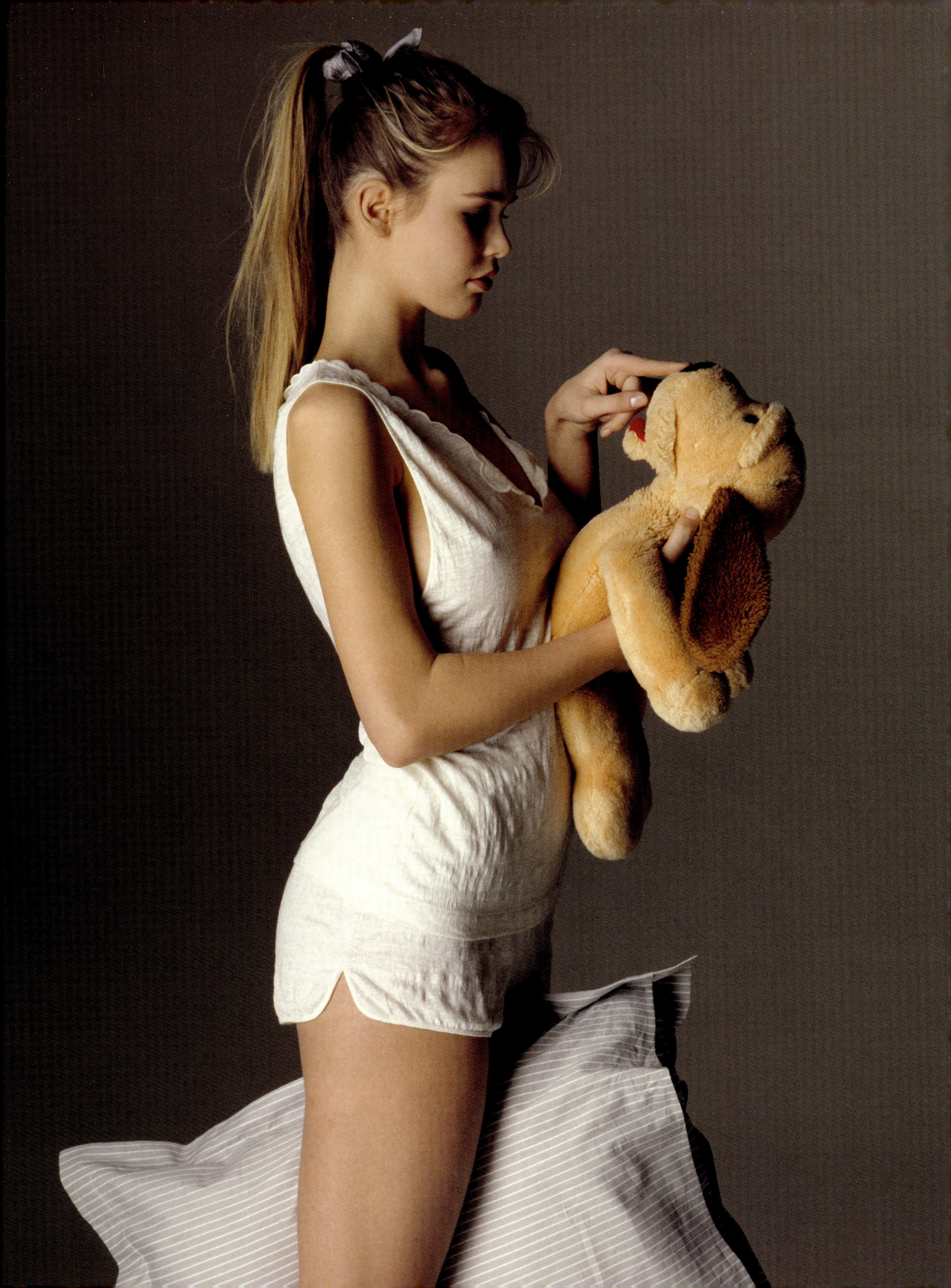

I relished the 1990s for its abundance of glamour, riches and dreams; it was the era when the supermodels came into our lives.

WALTER CHIN

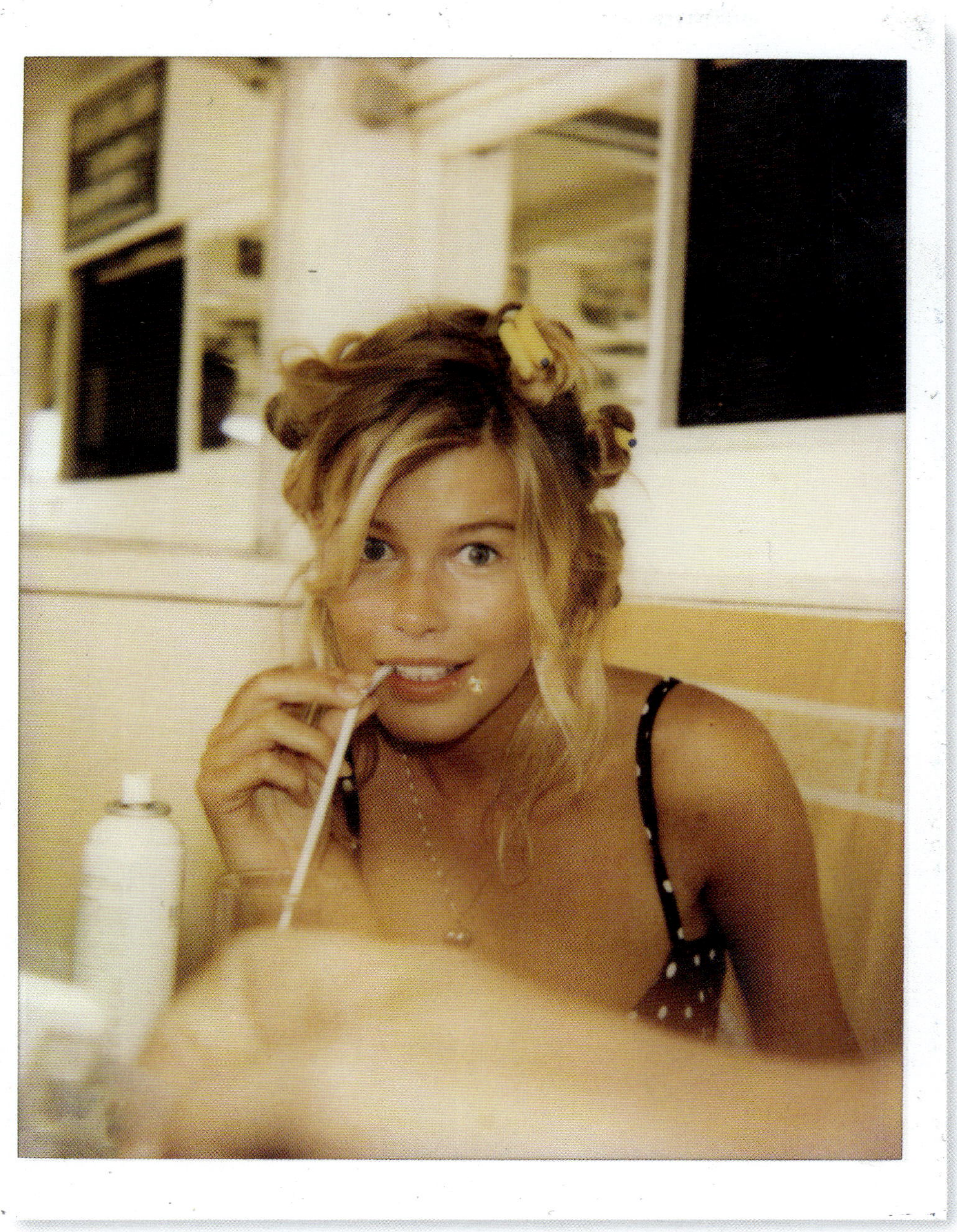

Here, I am on set in St. Tropez in the early 1990s for French *Glamour* magazine.

Walter Chin, model: Claudia Schiffer, 1988 for *ELLE JP*

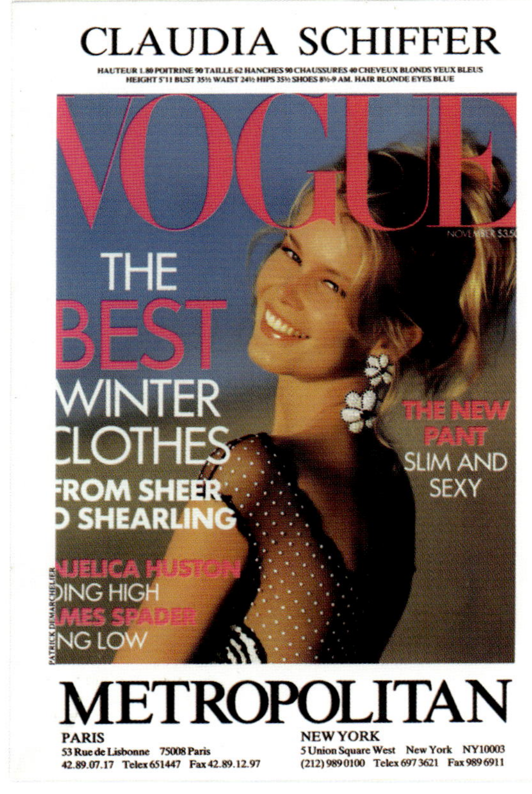

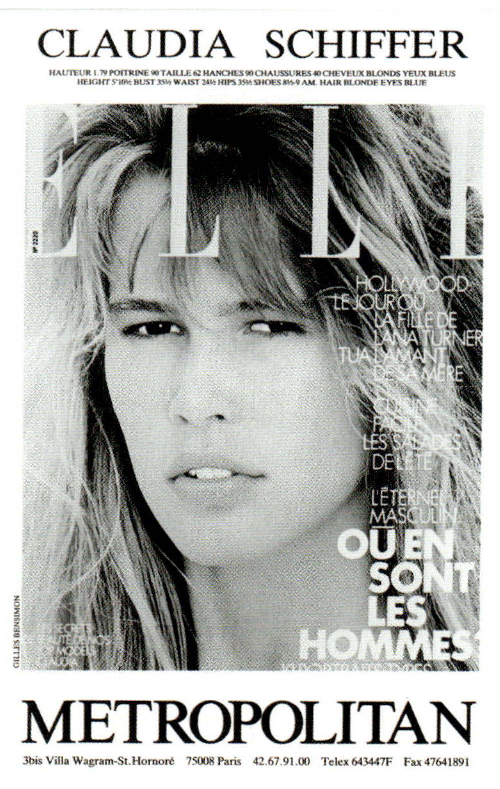

Comp cards, Metropolitan model agency (depicted covers: *Vogue* US, November 1990; *ELLE* FR, October 1989)

The model's 'comp card' was the equivalent of a business card. In the pre-digital age of the 1990s, a model would attend castings with fashion editors, photographers, casting agents and designers. You would present a portfolio and leave a model card printed with agency details and your measurements. I can still remember riding the Paris Métro for the first time, portfolio in hand, and walking kilometres to attend appointments. Within a month, I knew the Métro map and Paris by heart.

Ross Feltus, model: Claudia Schiffer, test shot, 1987

I was still at school here. Seventeen, hair crimped: this was my first ever test shoot, with Ross Feltus. In a test shoot, models starting out collect professional images for their portfolio to show to potential agencies or clients. Feltus was living and working in Dusseldorf at the time.

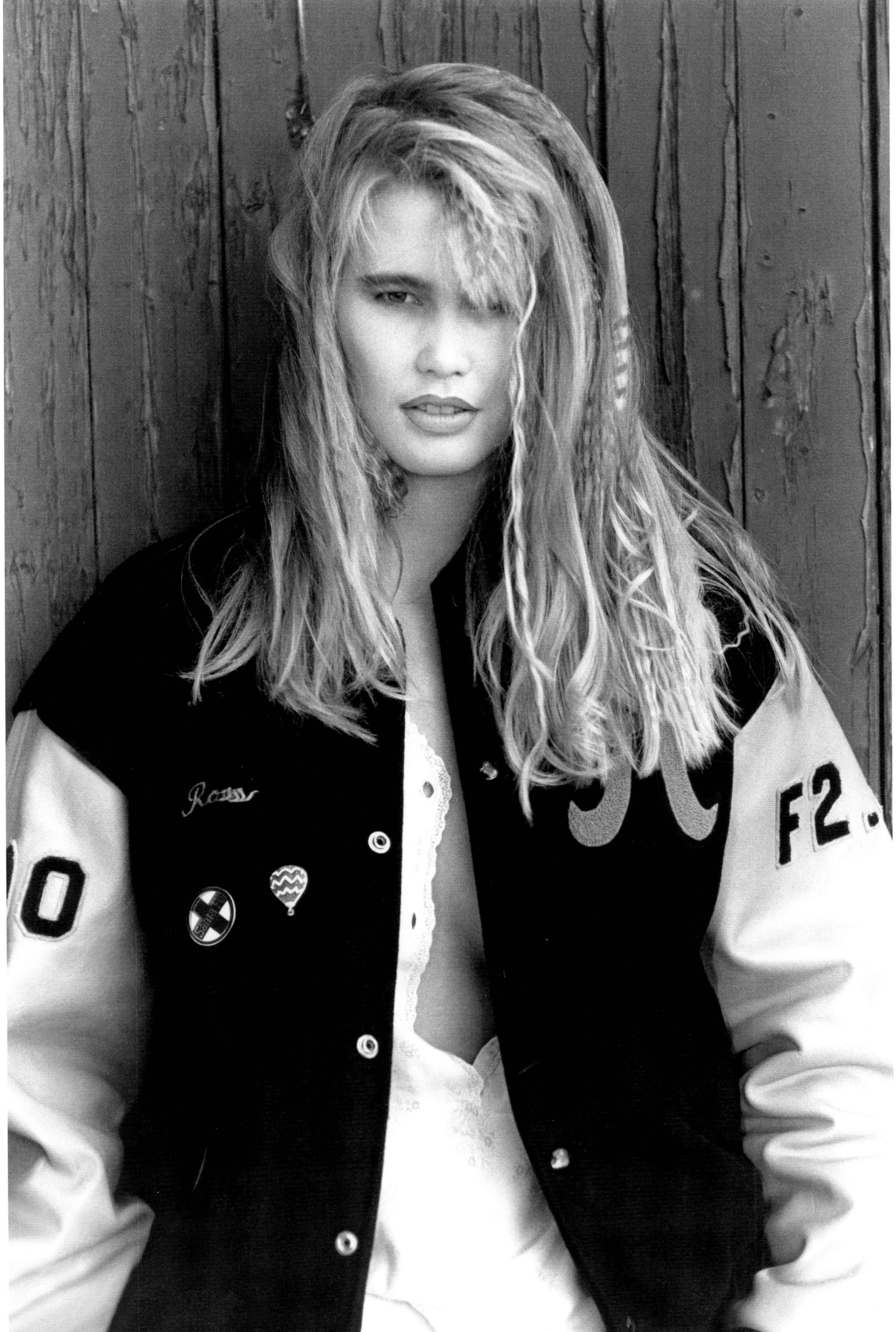
F2

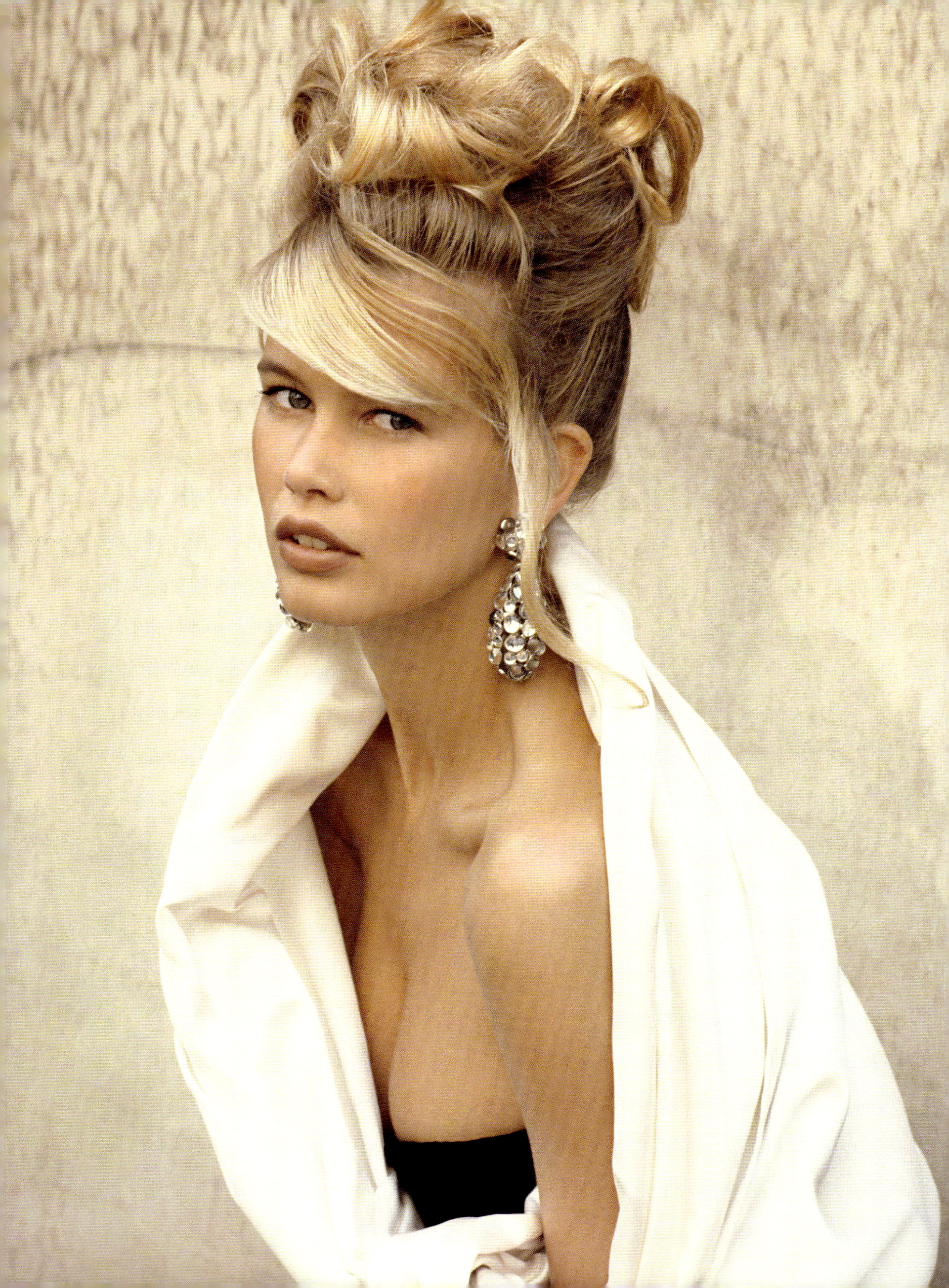

Claudia was like a young Brigitte Bardot, one of the best supermodels of the 1990s! J'adore la Claudia!

CARLYNE DU CERF

Herb Ritts, model: Claudia Schiffer, 1989 for *Vogue* UK

My first cover for British *Vogue* was modelling haute couture in Paris with Herb Ritts. The three-quarter pose as well as the draped shoulder and chignon hair are all reminiscent of nineteenth-century oil portraiture. I learned a lot from Ritts about how to work with the camera and the light to create the best shots.

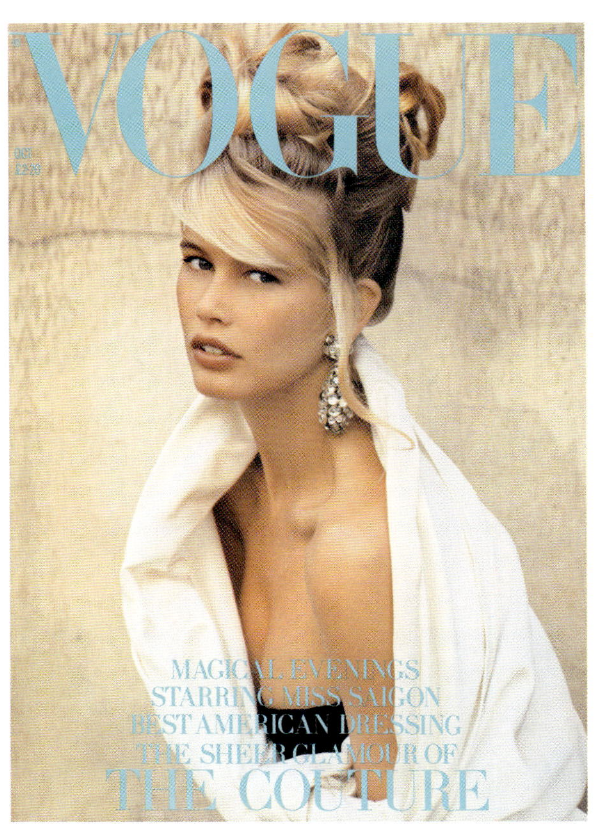

***Vogue* UK, October 1989**

Claudia Schiffer was the absolute image of youthfulness in the decade.

ANDRÉ LEON TALLEY

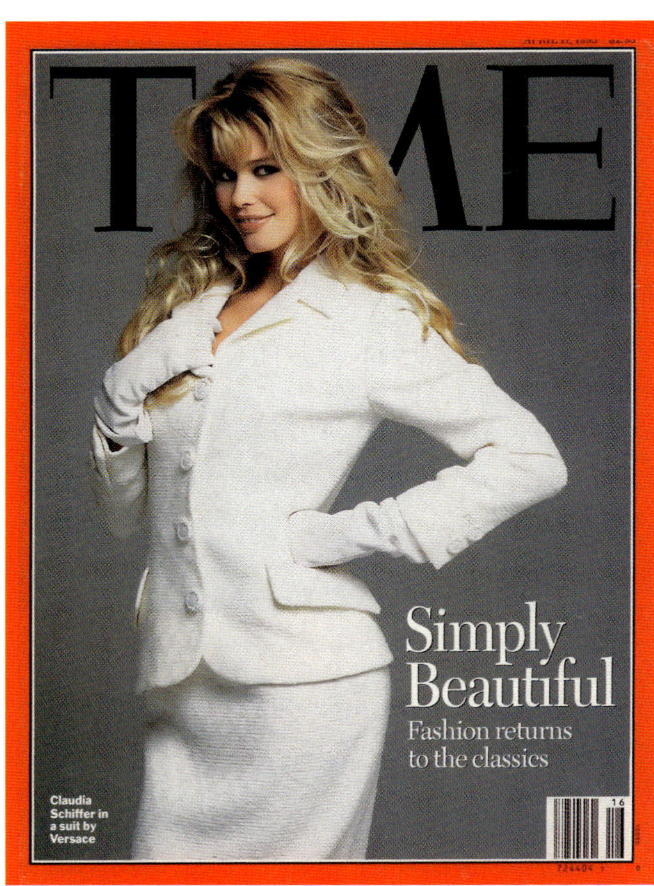

TIME UK, April 1995, photographed by Patrick Demarchelier, model: Claudia Schiffer

Ellen von Unwerth, model: Claudia Schiffer, 1989

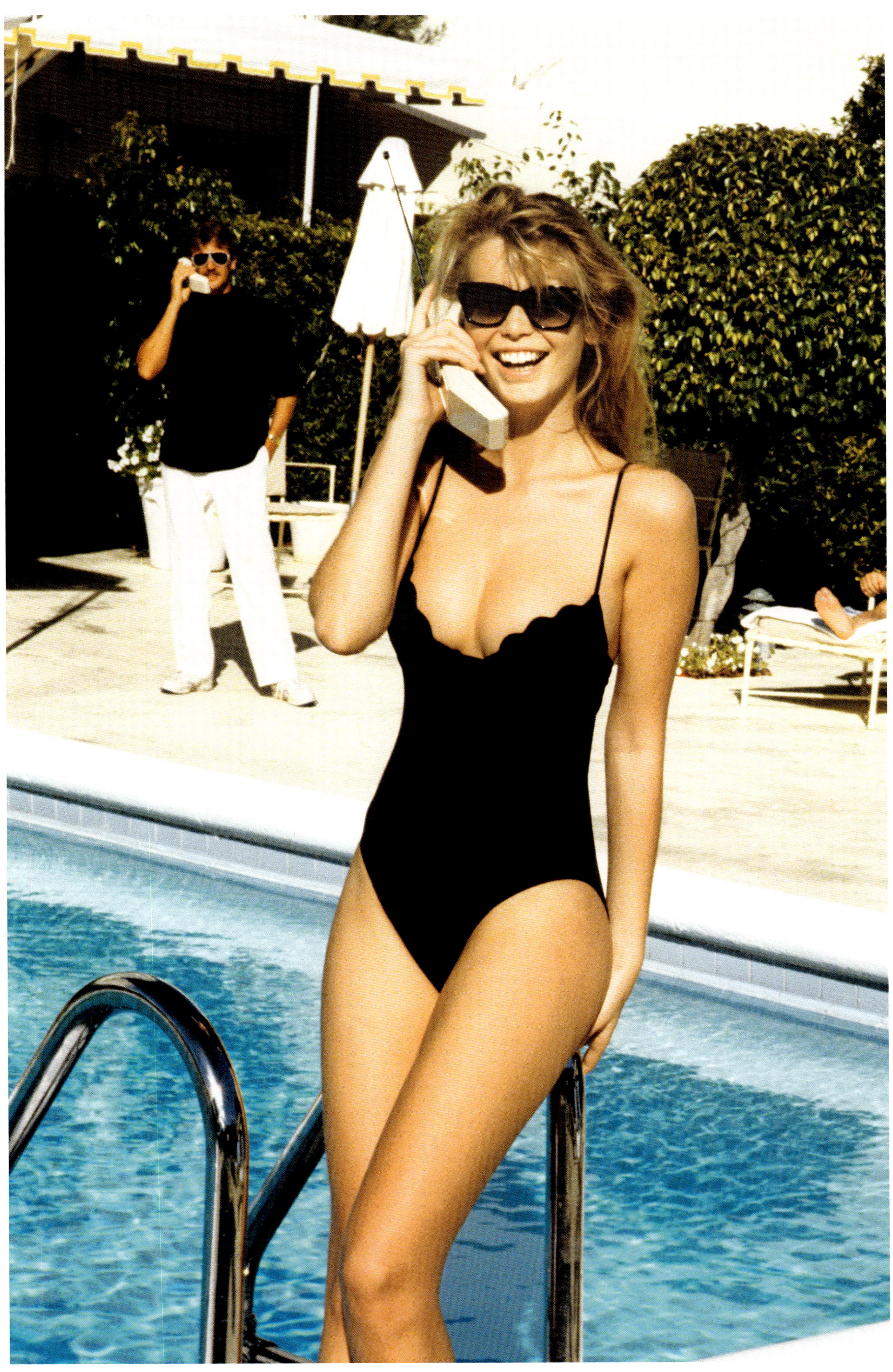

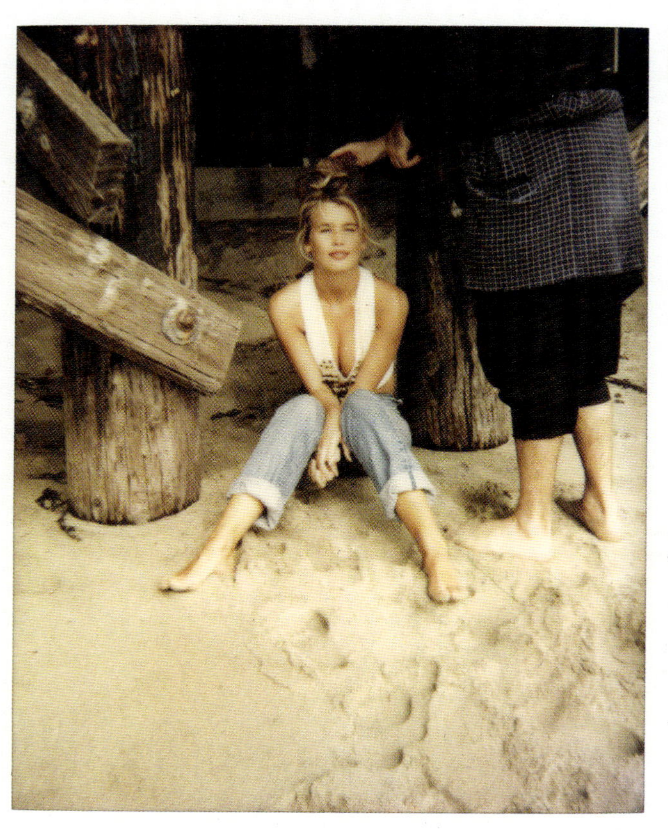

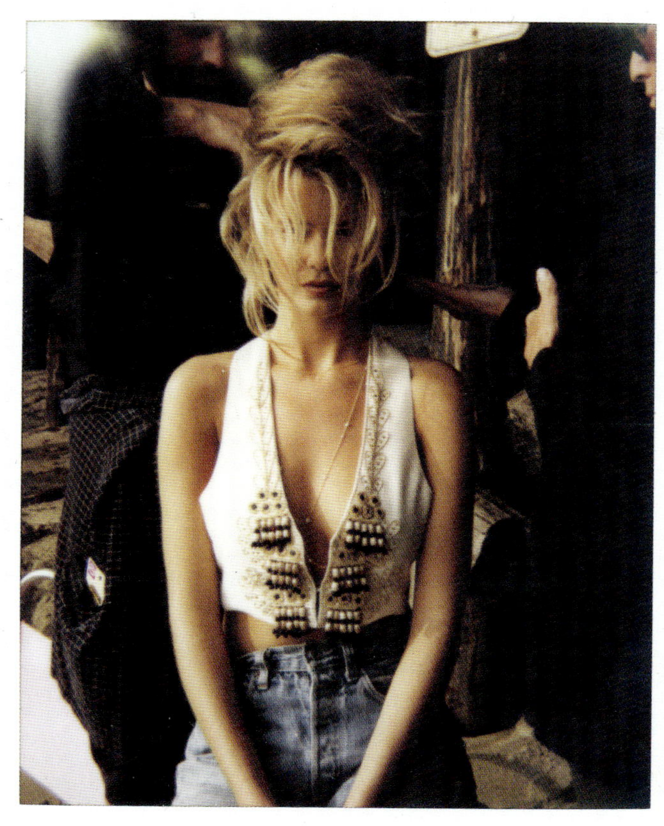

Here I am on set with Herb Ritts for a shoot for *Rolling Stone* in Malibu in 1990. Polaroids taken by a crew member.

Herb Ritts, model: Claudia Schiffer, 1989 for *Vogue* US, published in GQ US 1990

This is Herb Ritts at his best. The cover and story, shot at the beach near Ritts's home in Malibu, was originally made for US *Vogue* but then was sold to *GQ*.

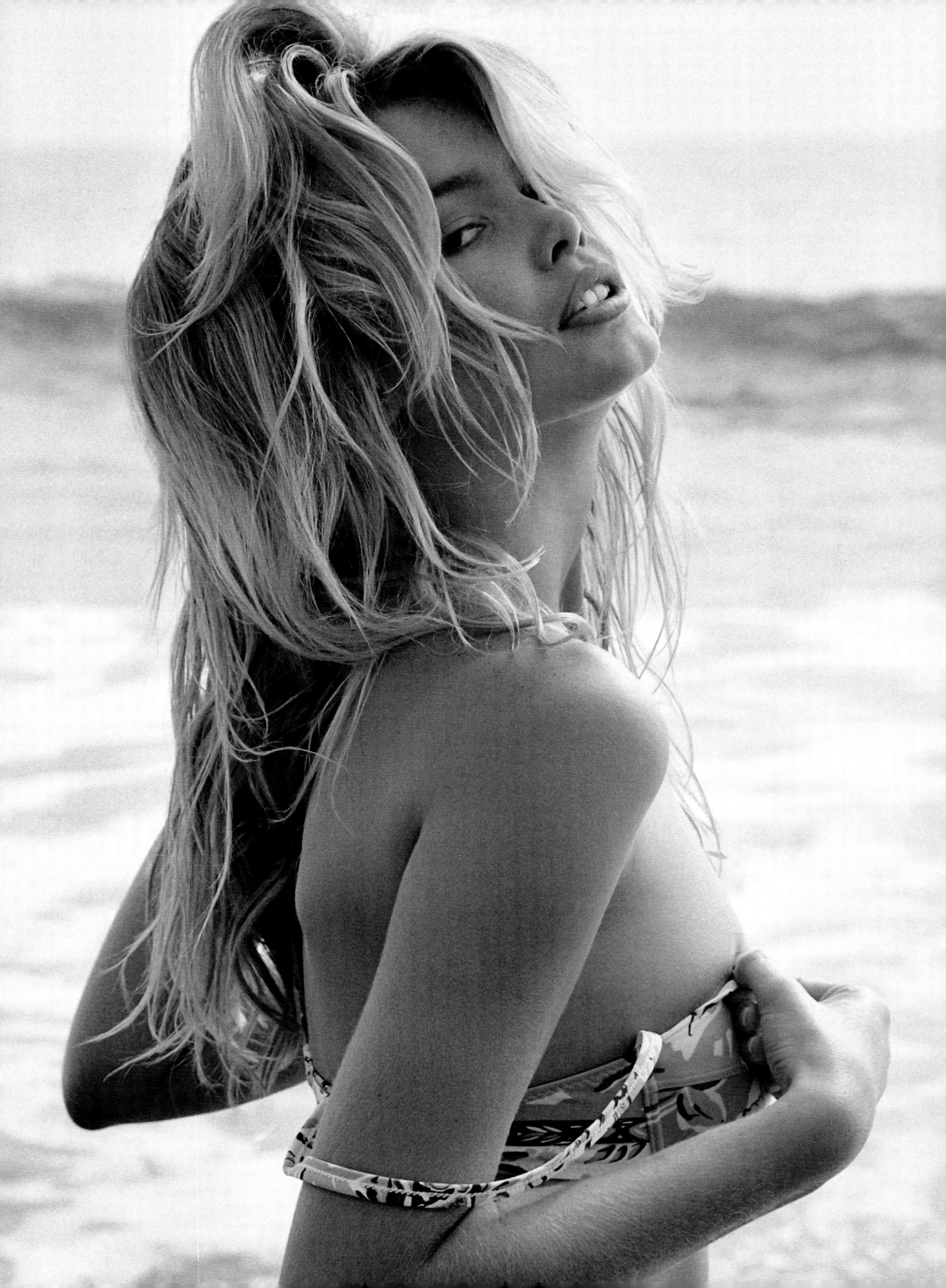

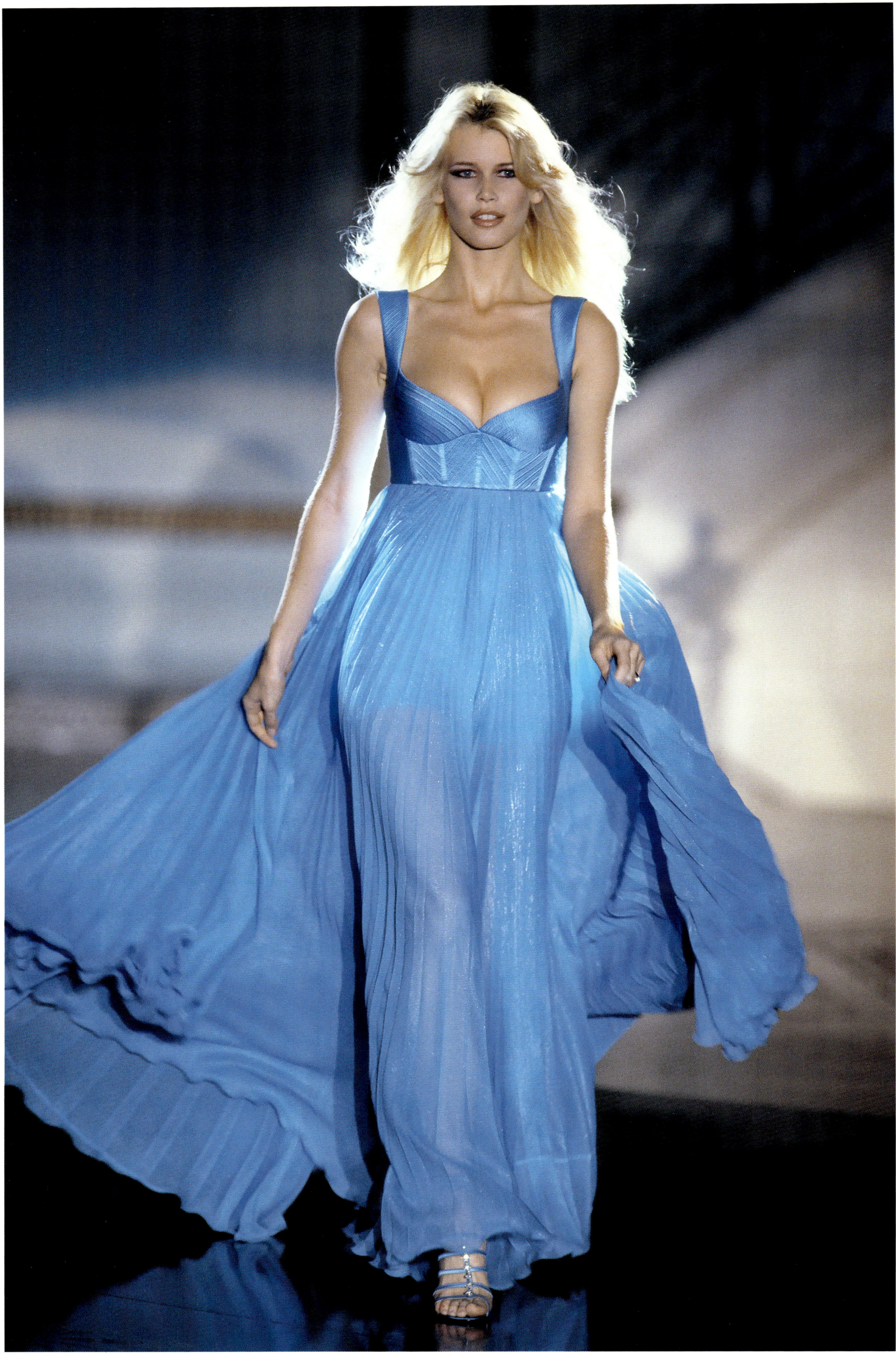

There is no one like Claudia – a woman celebrated for her style, grace and confidence – so there is no better way to celebrate Claudia's first curatorial role than being able to see the blue gown she wore in our 1994 show in this exhibition.

DONATELLA VERSACE

Michel Arnaud, model: Claudia Schiffer, Versace Fall/Winter 1994/1995

One of my favourite fashion moments was on the runway for Atelier Versace's Fall/Winter 1994 couture collection. Fashion, music and art were starting to converge more than ever. I would walk to an amazing track by Prince, with hundreds of photographers lining the runway, only to see the star himself sitting front row.

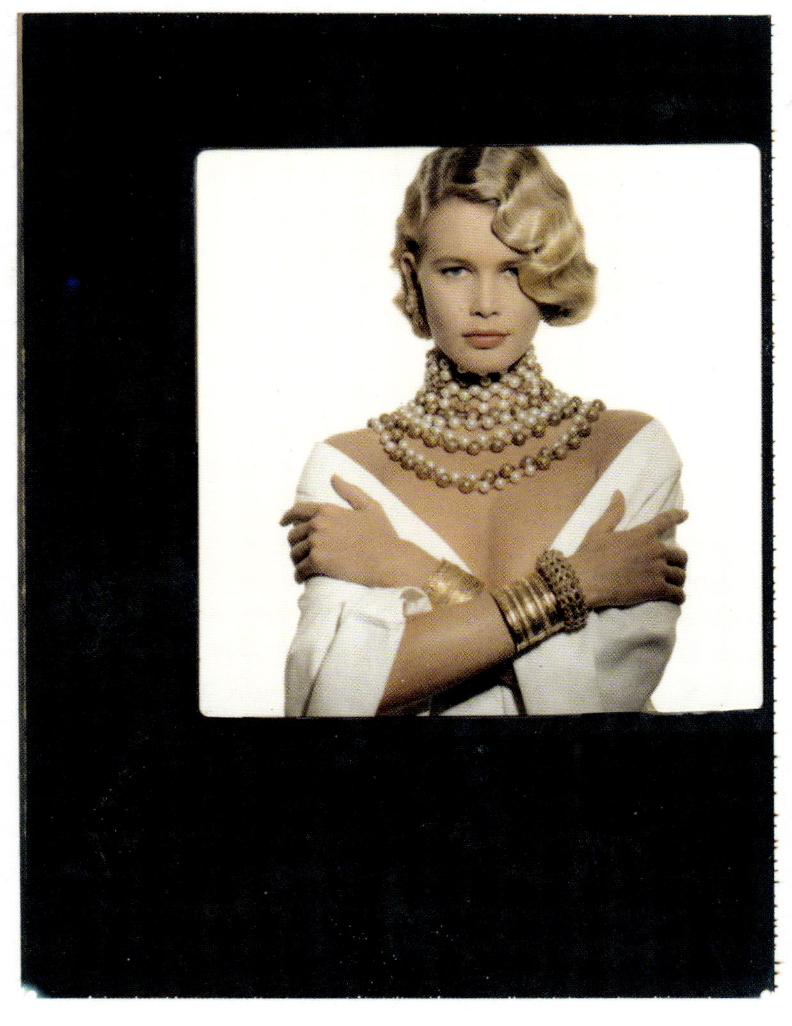

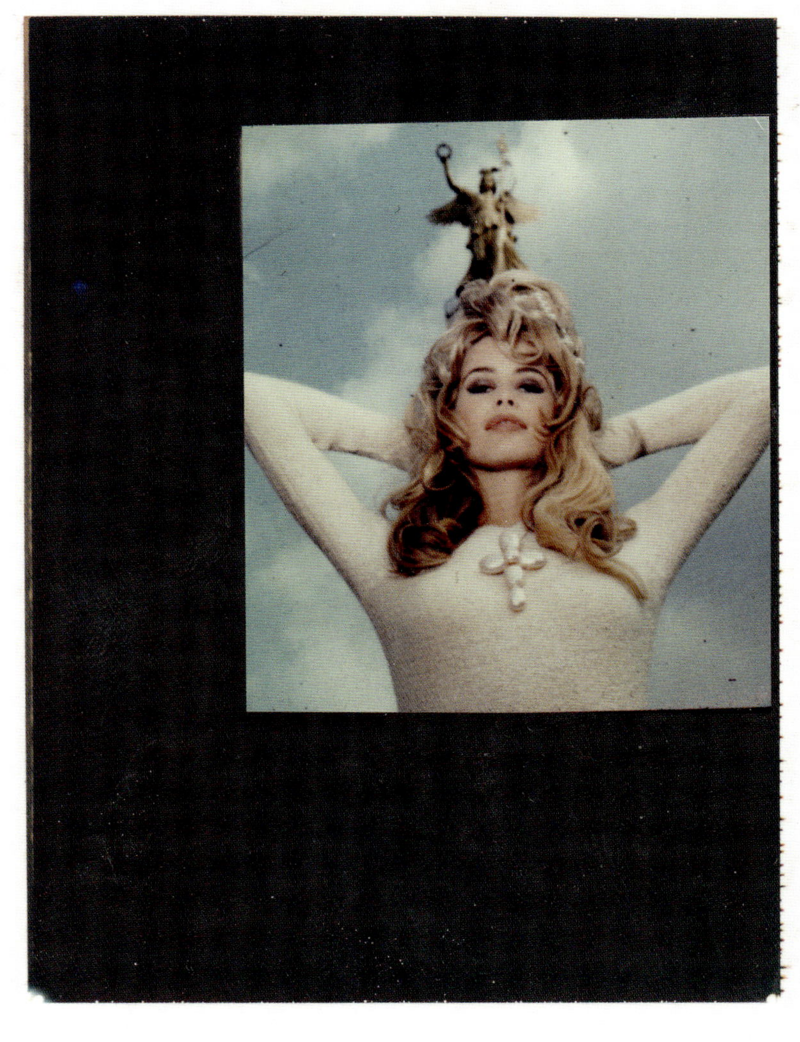

Karl Lagerfeld snapped these Polaroids during two shoots for Chanel. Left, for a Spring/Summer advertising campaign in 1990. Right, for a Fall/Winter 1992/1993 advertising campaign in 1992.

Karl Lagerfeld, model: Claudia Schiffer, Deauville, France 1990 for Chanel

Karl Lagerfeld, creative director of Chanel, was my magic dust. He transformed me from a shy German girl into a supermodel. He shot the campaigns for Chanel, proving to be not only an exceptional designer but also a great photographer. What Andy Warhol was to art, Lagerfeld was to fashion; he was an auteur.

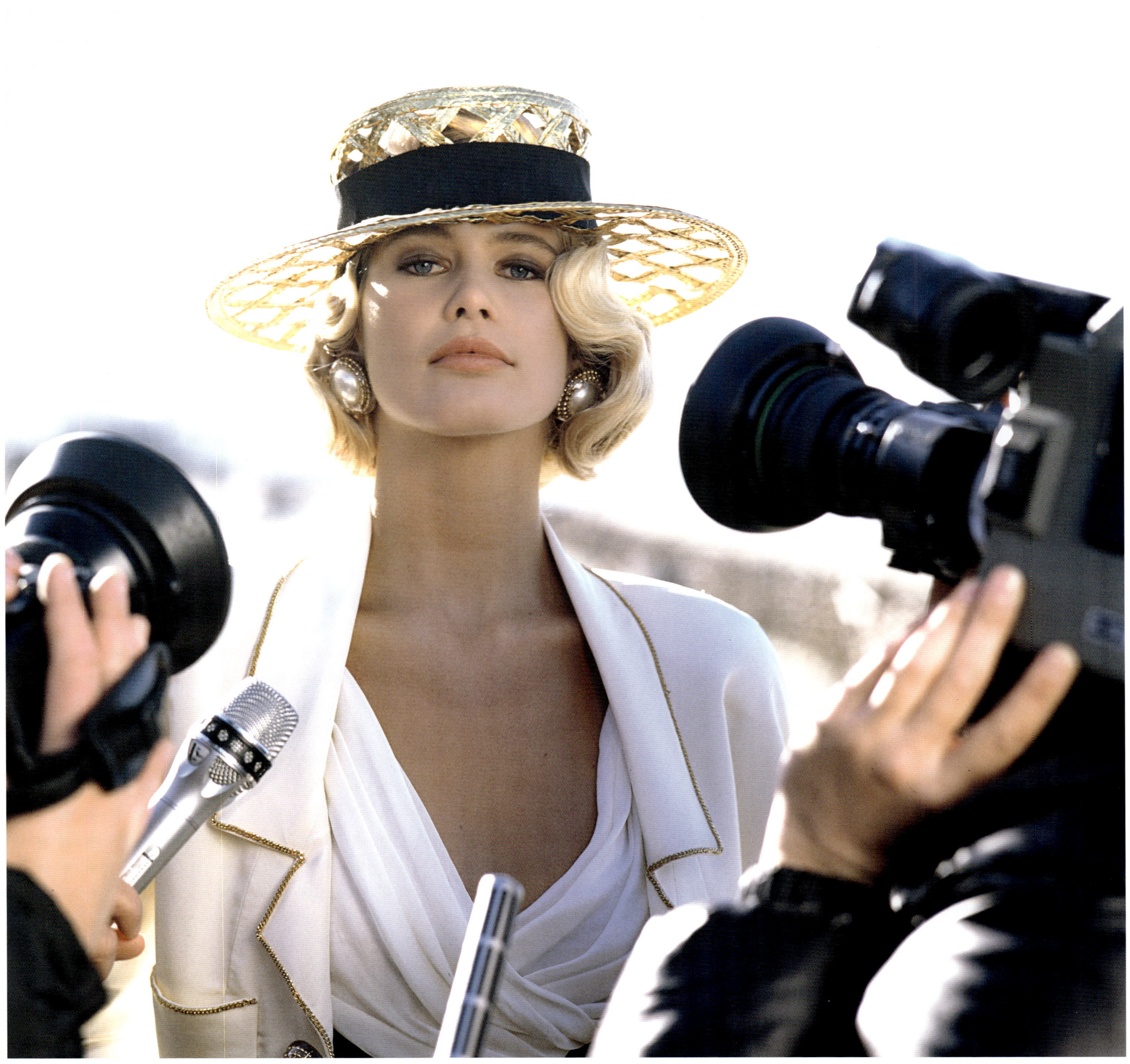

CAM-
PAIGNS

In the 1990s, fashion campaigns started to drive visual culture and became part of the urban environment. New season advertising was anticipated, celebrated and critiqued in the same way as an album release. Advertising appeared across giant billboards, on screens, in stores, in magazines and on taxis.

The stars behind a campaign – the photographers, art directors and stylists – were as important as the talent in front of the lens, and the competition to create 'the' definitive campaign was fierce. Fees rocketed as exclusivity was demanded across the board. Campaigns unlocked huge budgets and suddenly fashion came to be seen as a hot, lucrative, sexy industry.

There was a handful of highly sought-after teams who were masters in creating brand identity. Art directors would often work with designers from the inception of the collection, allowing ideas and inspirations to percolate into every aspect of the brand, from packaging to graphics, logos to perfume bottles. As the decade proceeded, more provocative and innovative campaigns were released, generating headline news. The images may have been created to promote a brand but they became a vital part of pop culture.

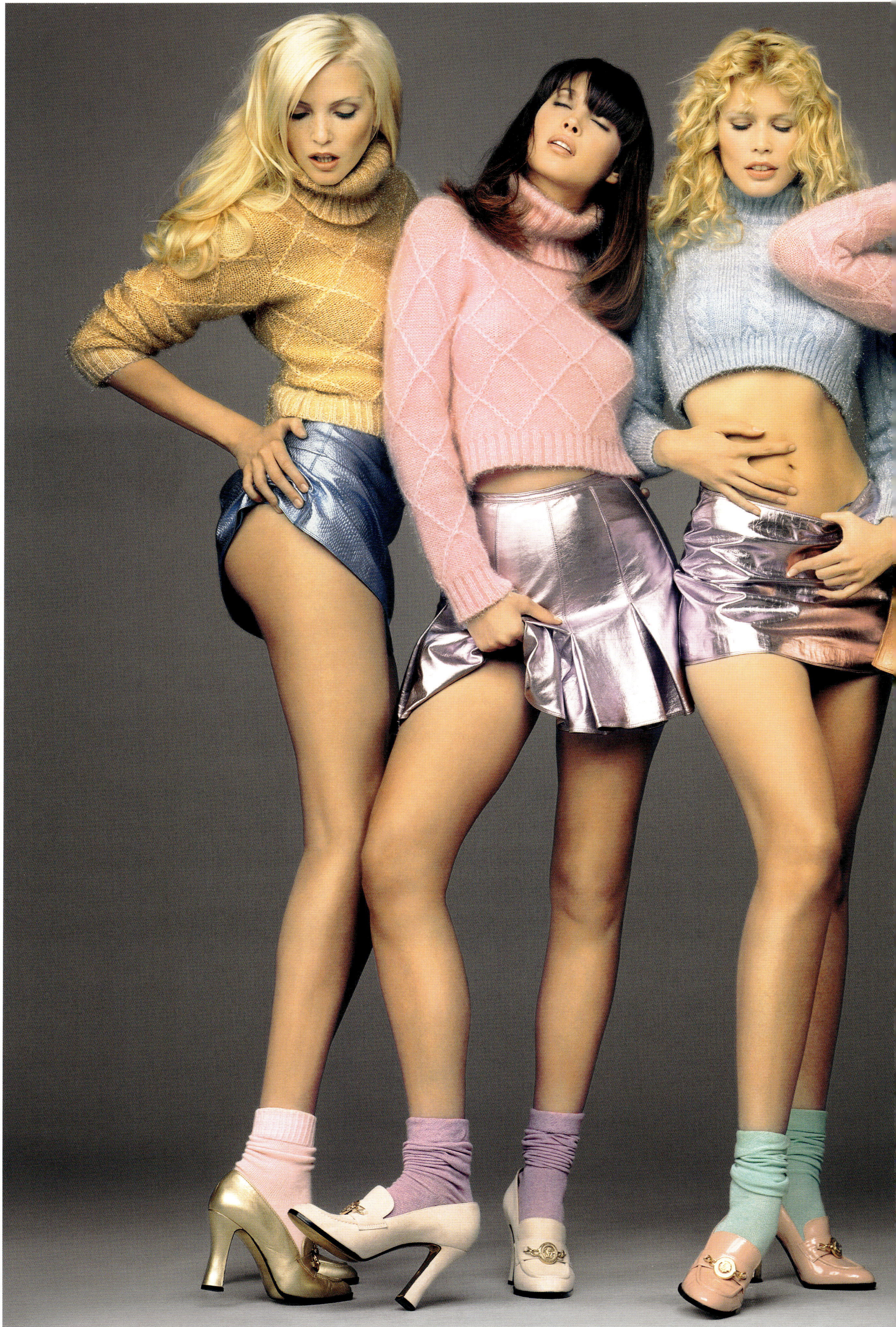

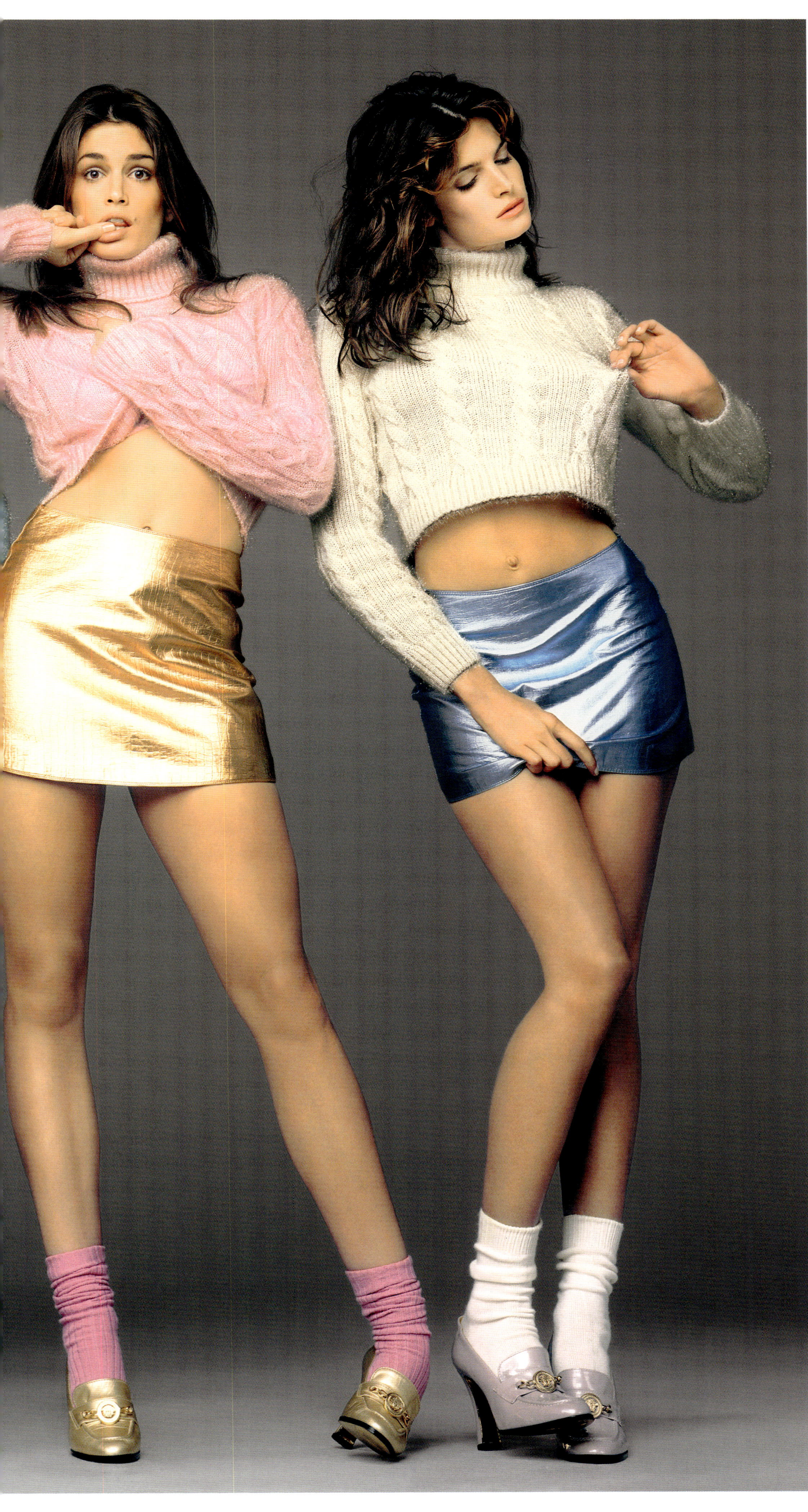

Richard Avedon, models: Nadja Auermann, Christy Turlington, Claudia Schiffer, Cindy Crawford, Stephanie Seymour, 1994 for Versace

This Versace campaign, photographed by Richard Avedon, is iconic 1990s. The image captures Avedon's mastery of a dynamic, choreographed group picture. Avedon was incremental in adding an artistic vision to fashion photography as early as the late 1950s and he was still breaking boundaries and making outstanding work in the 1990s. He was one of the most highly paid and sought-after photographers.

The 1990s was an era when powerful women strode into fashion and brought strength and energy to an industry that had previously relied on sweet young things. Physically, the new female models were as bold and energetic as their male equivalents. Psychologically, they introduced a vigorous attitude that brought in 'woman power' and created for fashion a brave new world.

SUZY MENKES

Mario Testino, models: Ludovico Benazzo, Georgina Grenville, 1996 for Gucci

The campaigns of the 1990s created formidable teams made up of designers, stylists and photographers – for example, this Gucci campaign with photographer Mario Testino, designer Tom Ford and stylist Carine Roitfeld.

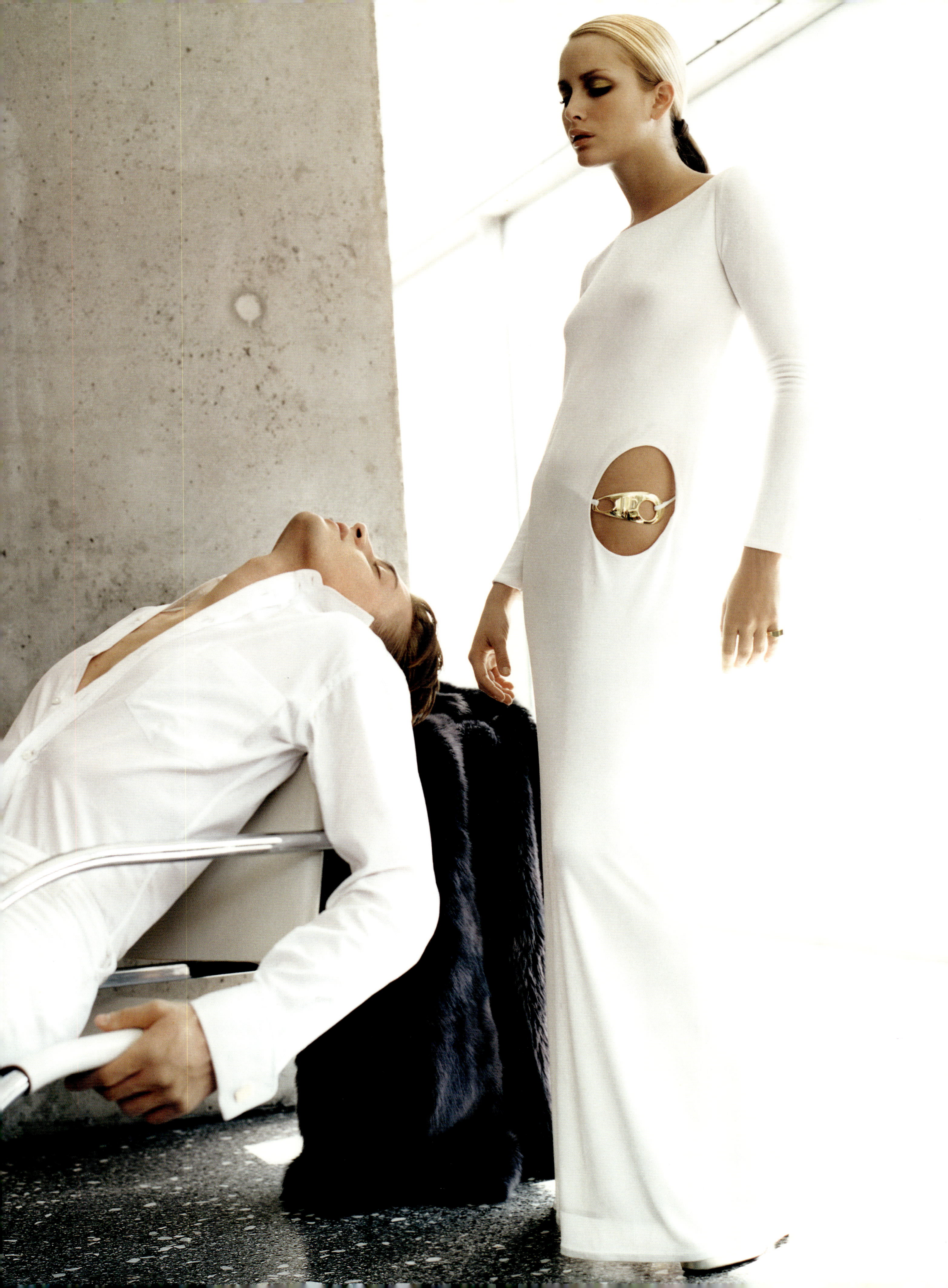

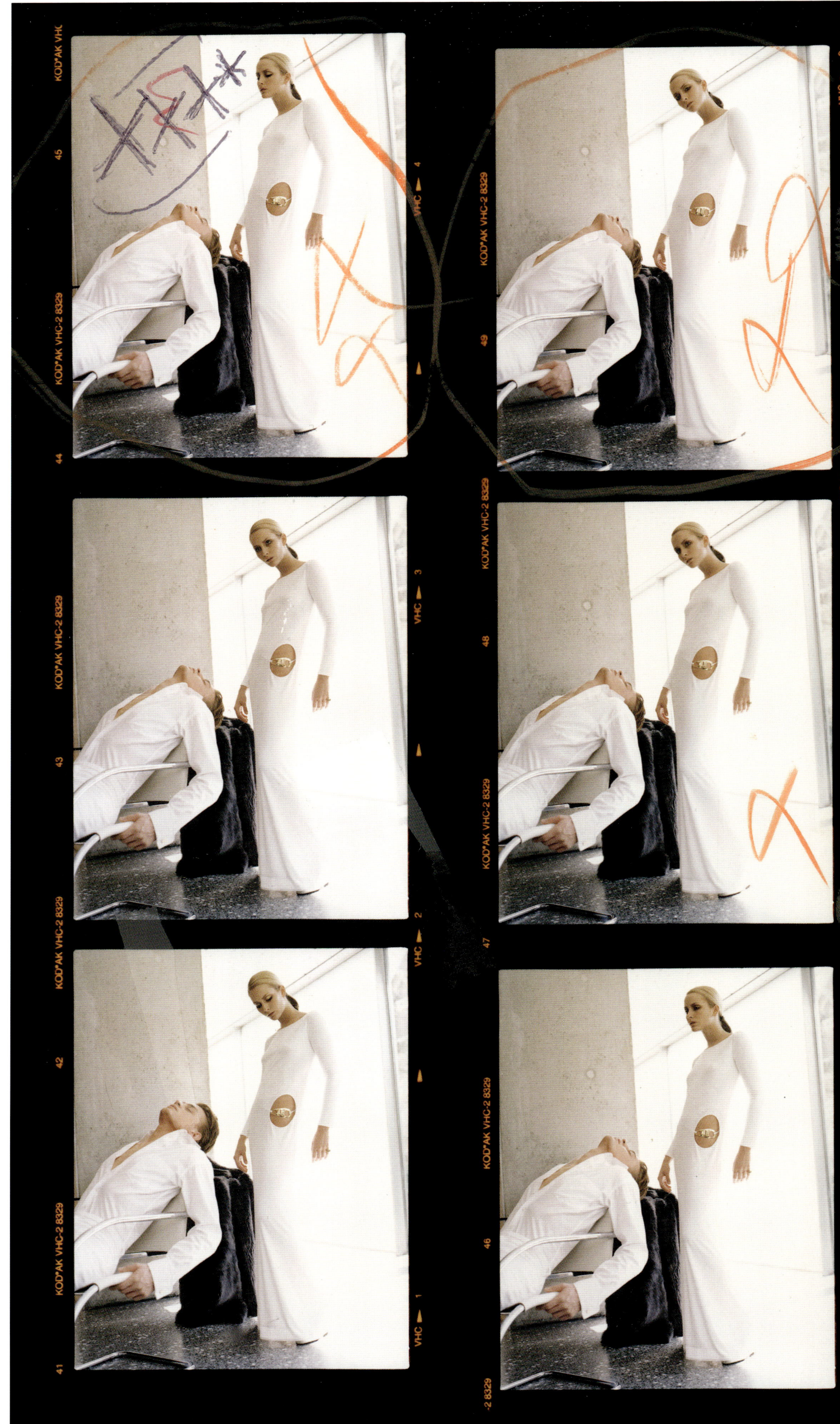

Mario Testino, models: Ludovico Benazzo, Georgina Grenville, 1996 for Gucci (contact sheet)

The contact sheet was an important tool for all fashion photographers in the 1990s analogue world. Made directly from the negative film, it offered an efficient way of editing imagery. Nowadays, the selection process is equally important, but it is done digitally and at speed.

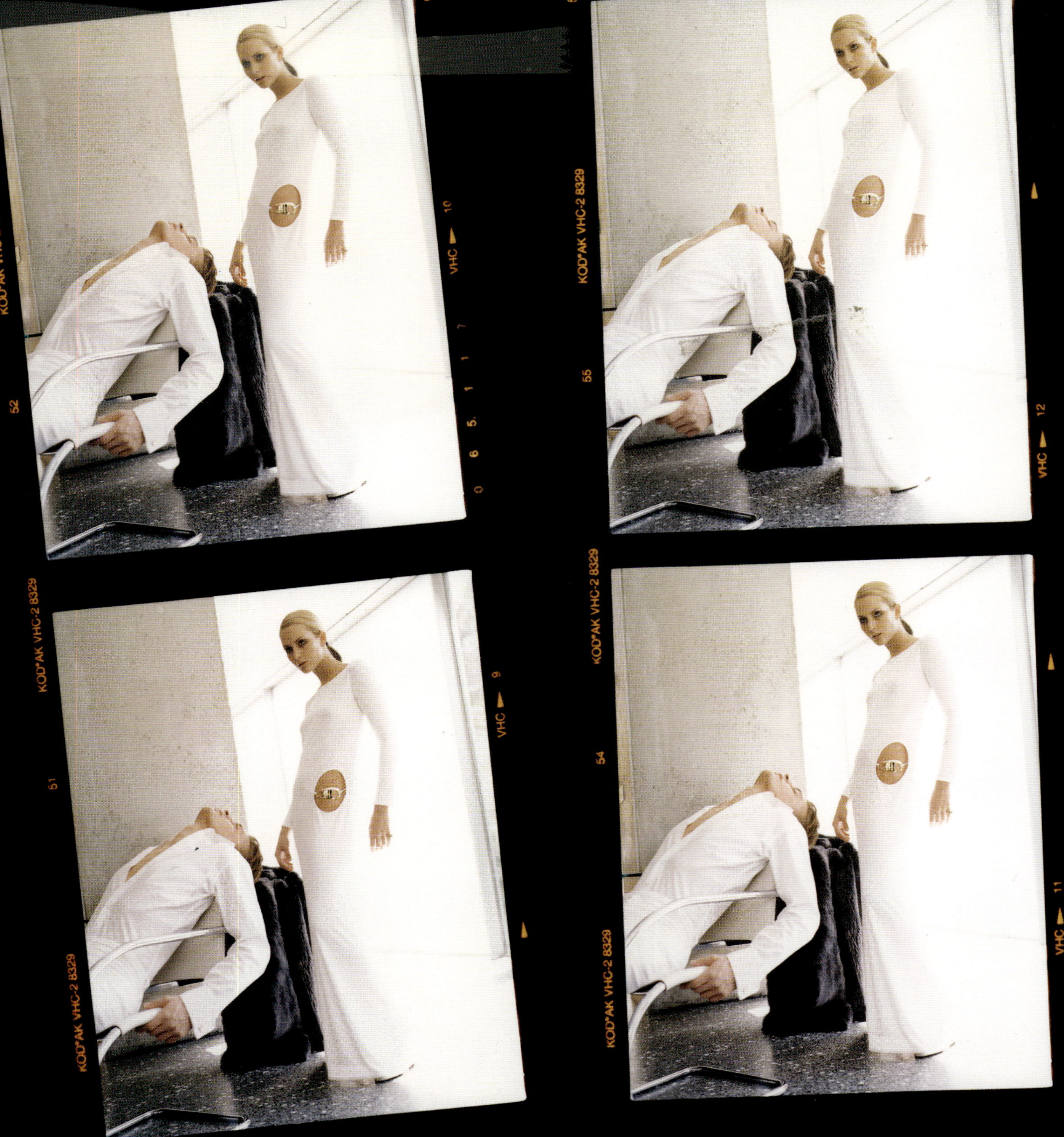

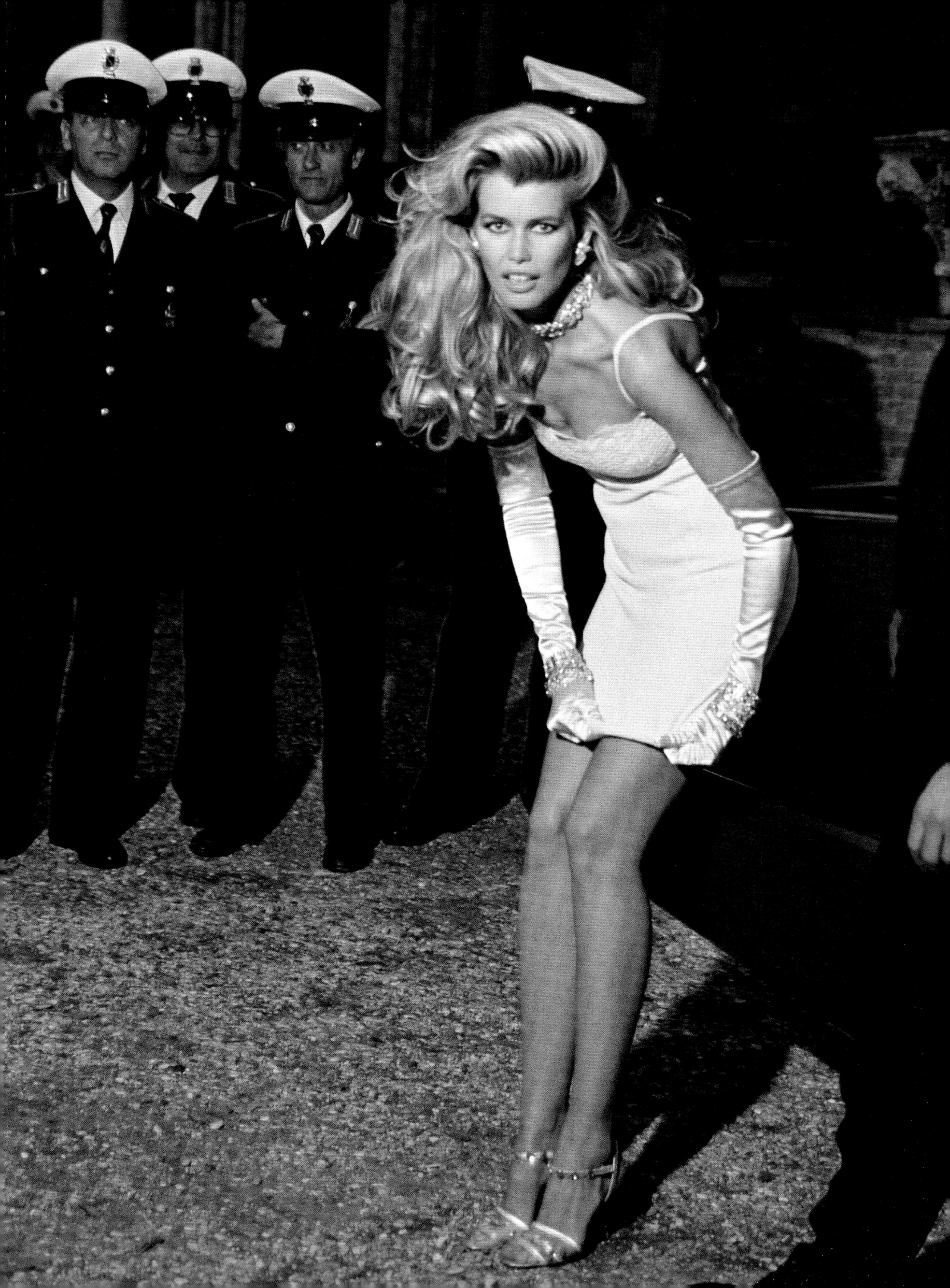

At the height of the 'supermodel' era, in 1994, Arthur Elgort and I took Claudia Schiffer to Rome for a Vogue *fashion story. She was accompanied by two very large bodyguards and her hair and makeup team – Didier Malige and Dick Page. It was hot, hot, hot! Claudia was mobbed wherever we went. At times it was difficult to photograph her without being totally surrounded by a host of paparazzi. But she stood her ground and was totally unfazed by the chaos, which made for really fun pictures.*

GRACE CODDINGTON

It was very emotional for me to see in front of me the re-creation of the time of my arrival in Rome and the start of my career. And having Claudia as an actress and not a model was really inspiring!

VALENTINO GARAVANI

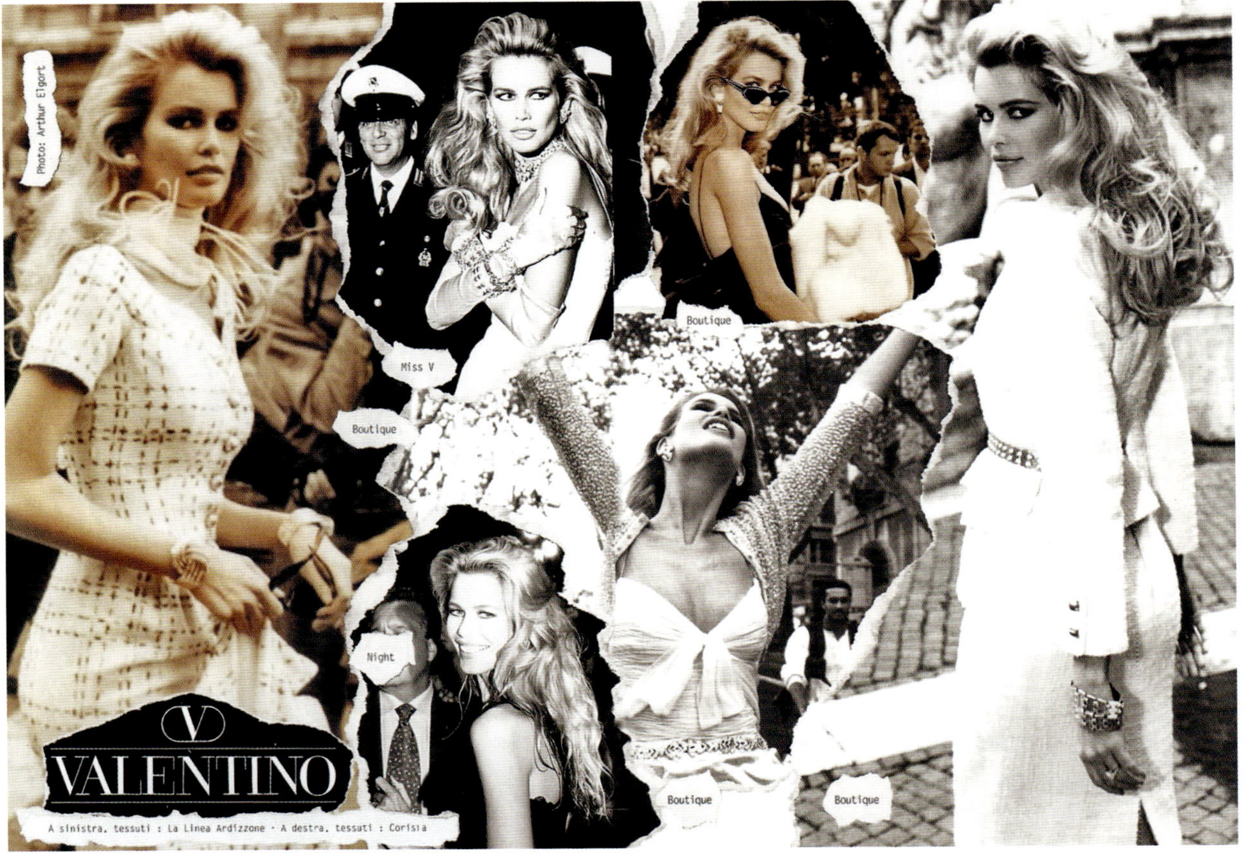

Valentino campaign, 1995

Arthur Elgort, model: Claudia Schiffer, Rome 1995 for Valentino

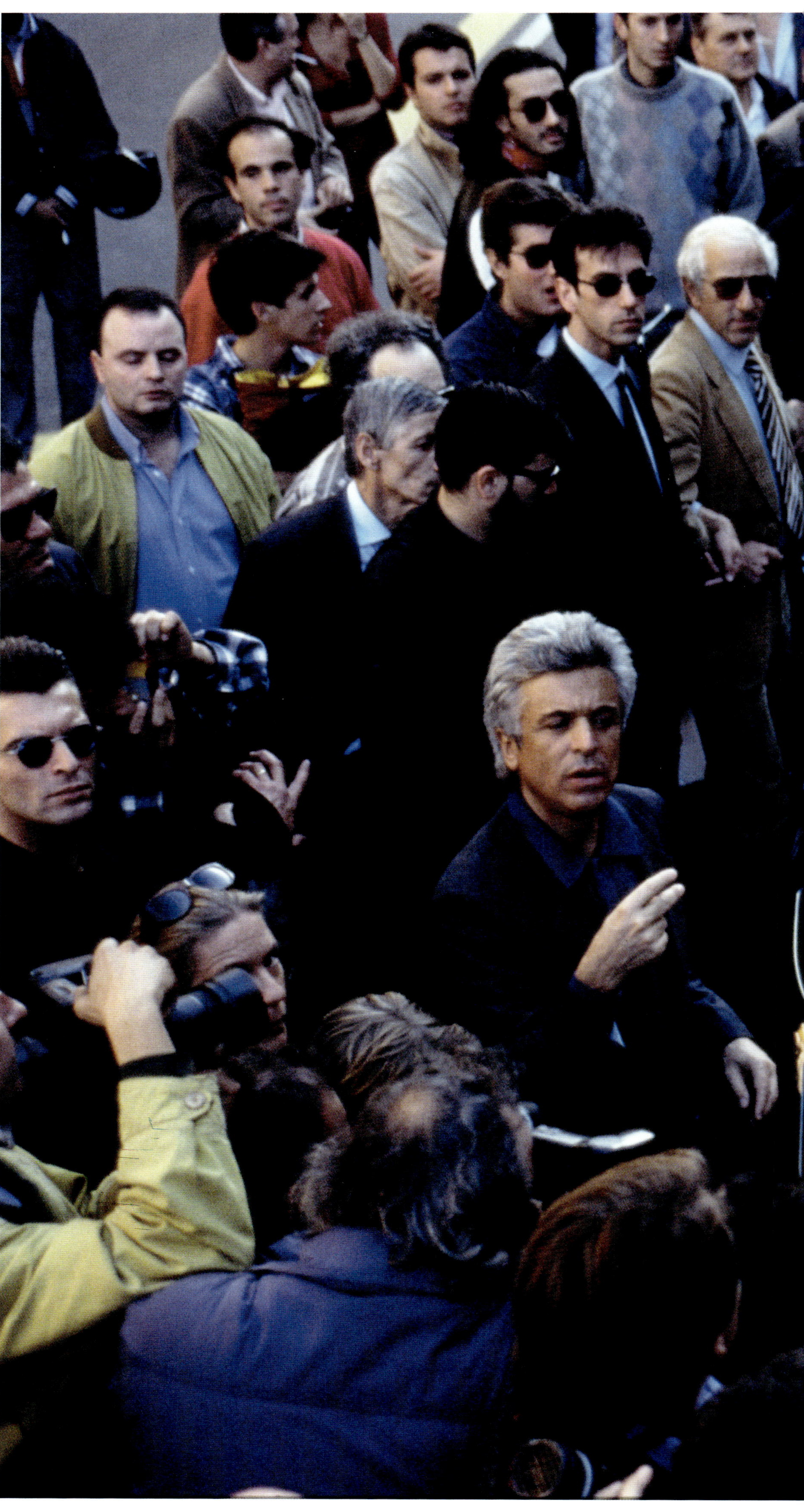

Arthur Elgort, model: Claudia Schiffer, Rome 1995 for Valentino

Arthur Elgort is renowned for his free-spirited, reportage style that liberated fashion photography from the confines of the studio. He allowed stories to unfold in real life and captured the magic of happenstance.

Here, we were in Rome, shooting the Valentino campaign inspired by Federico Fellini's iconic film *La Dolce Vita* (1960). I took on the role of Sylvia, played in the film by Anita Ekberg. Throughout the day, we attracted more and more attention until life finally imitated art: we were chased through the streets by paparazzi and crowds, just like Sylvia in the movie.

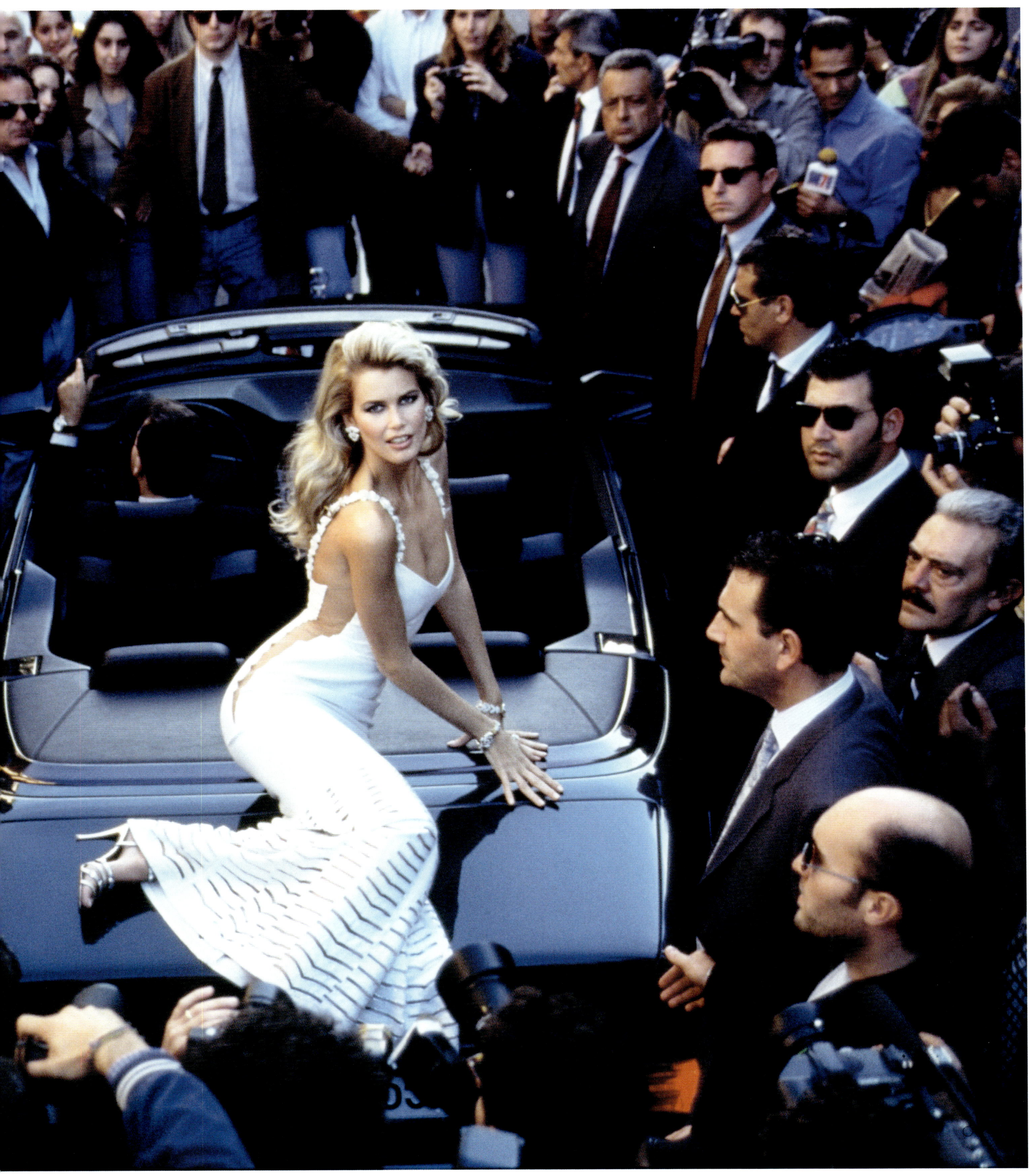

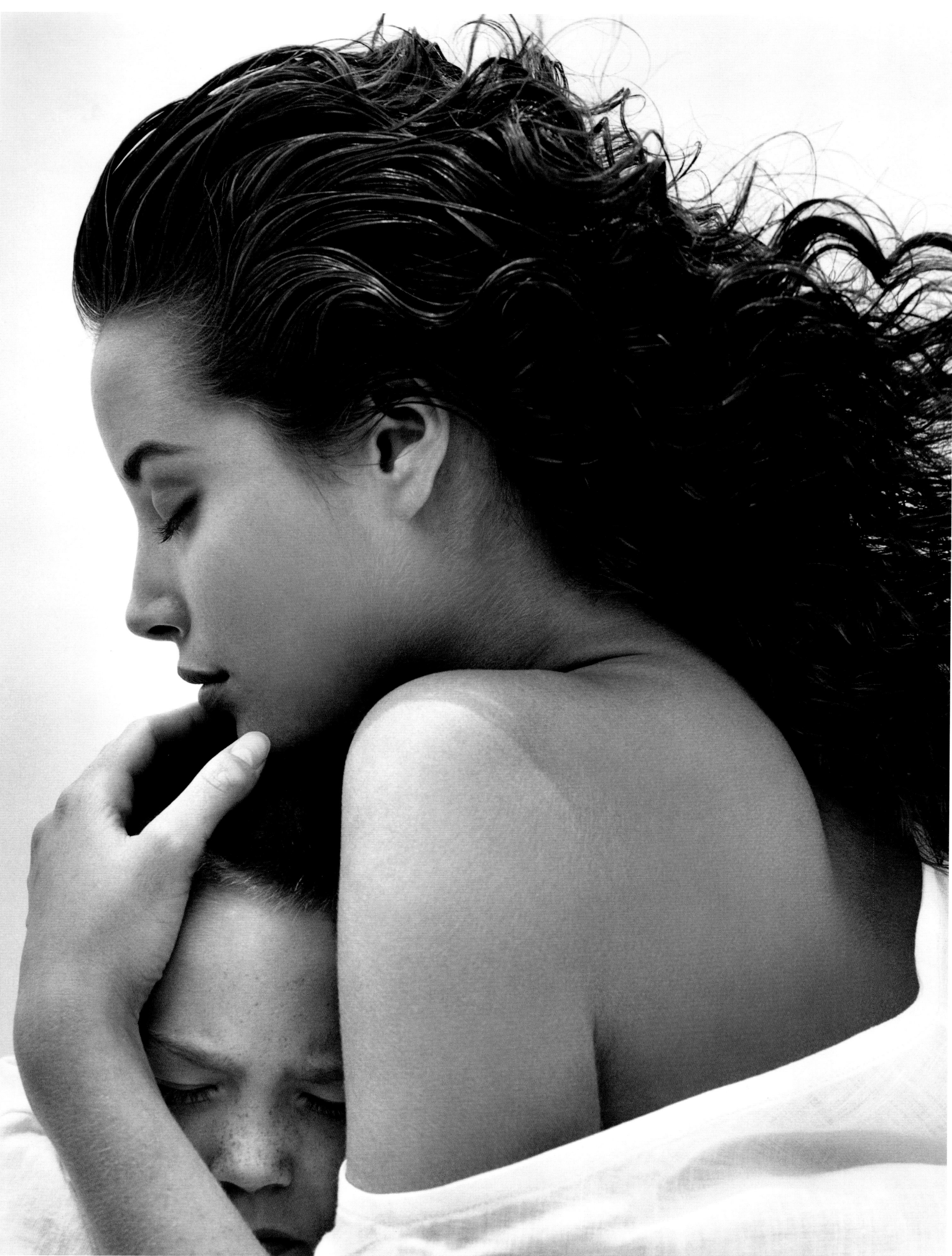

I love the black-and-white Calvin Klein Eternity ads. I still work for the brand today and these images remind me of the start of this long relationship. I started working for CK in 1988.

CHRISTY TURLINGTON

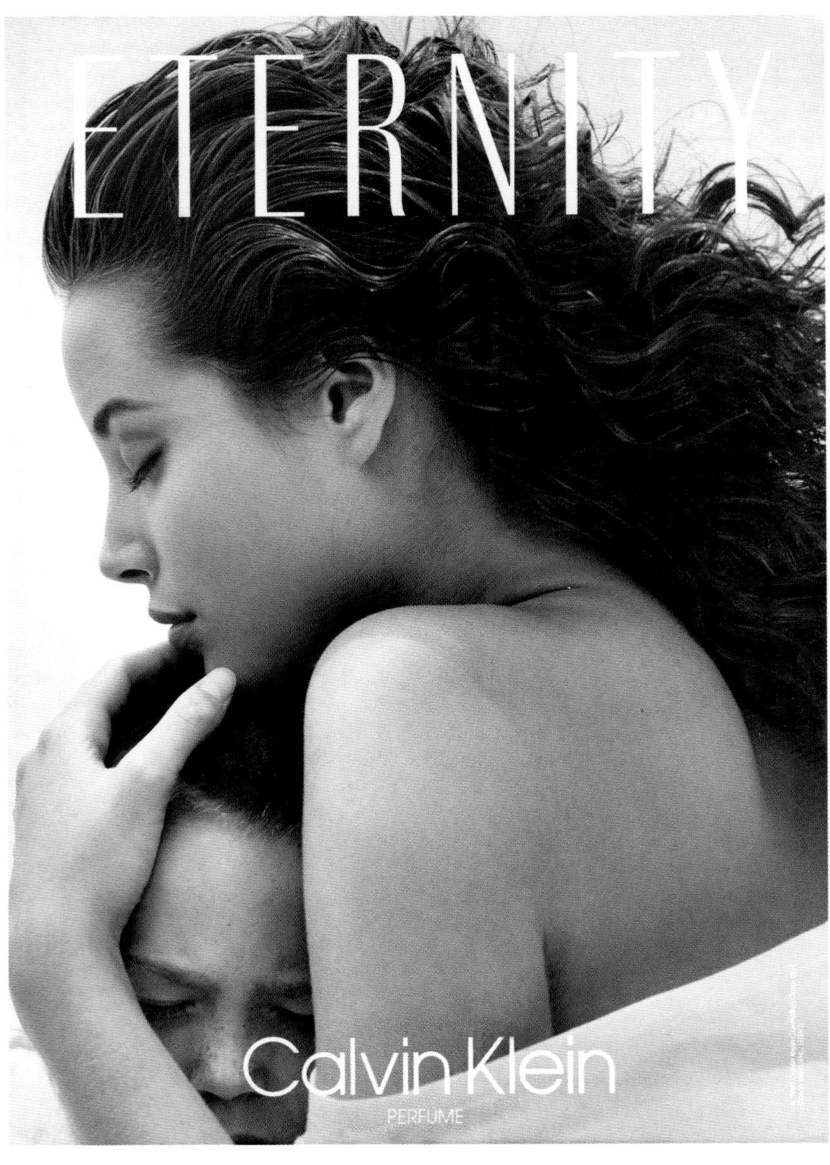

Calvin Klein Eternity campaign 1990

Bruce Weber, model: Christy Turlington, 1990 for Calvin Klein Eternity

106/107
Mario Sorrenti, model: Kate Moss, 1993 for Calvin Klein Obsession

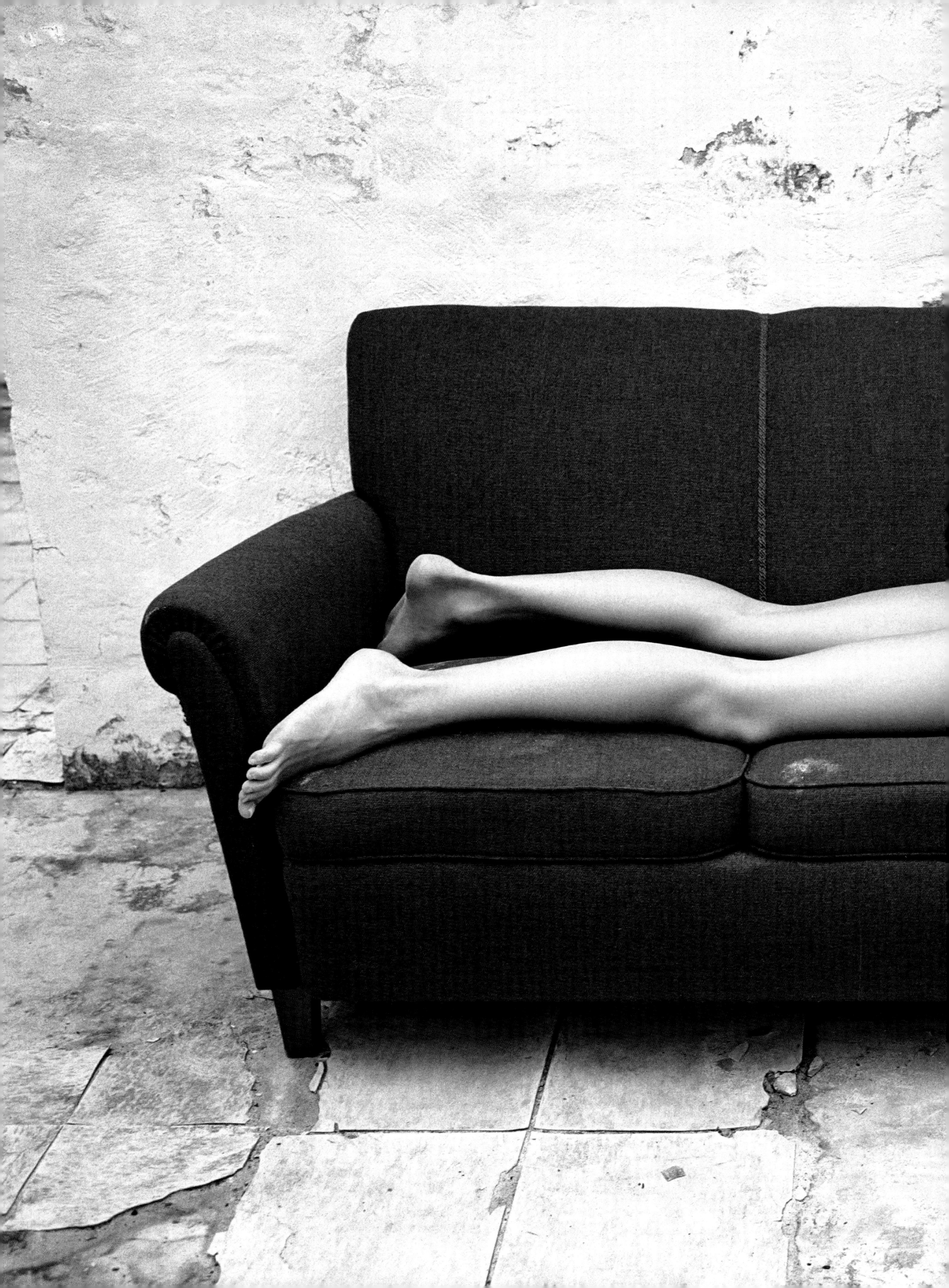

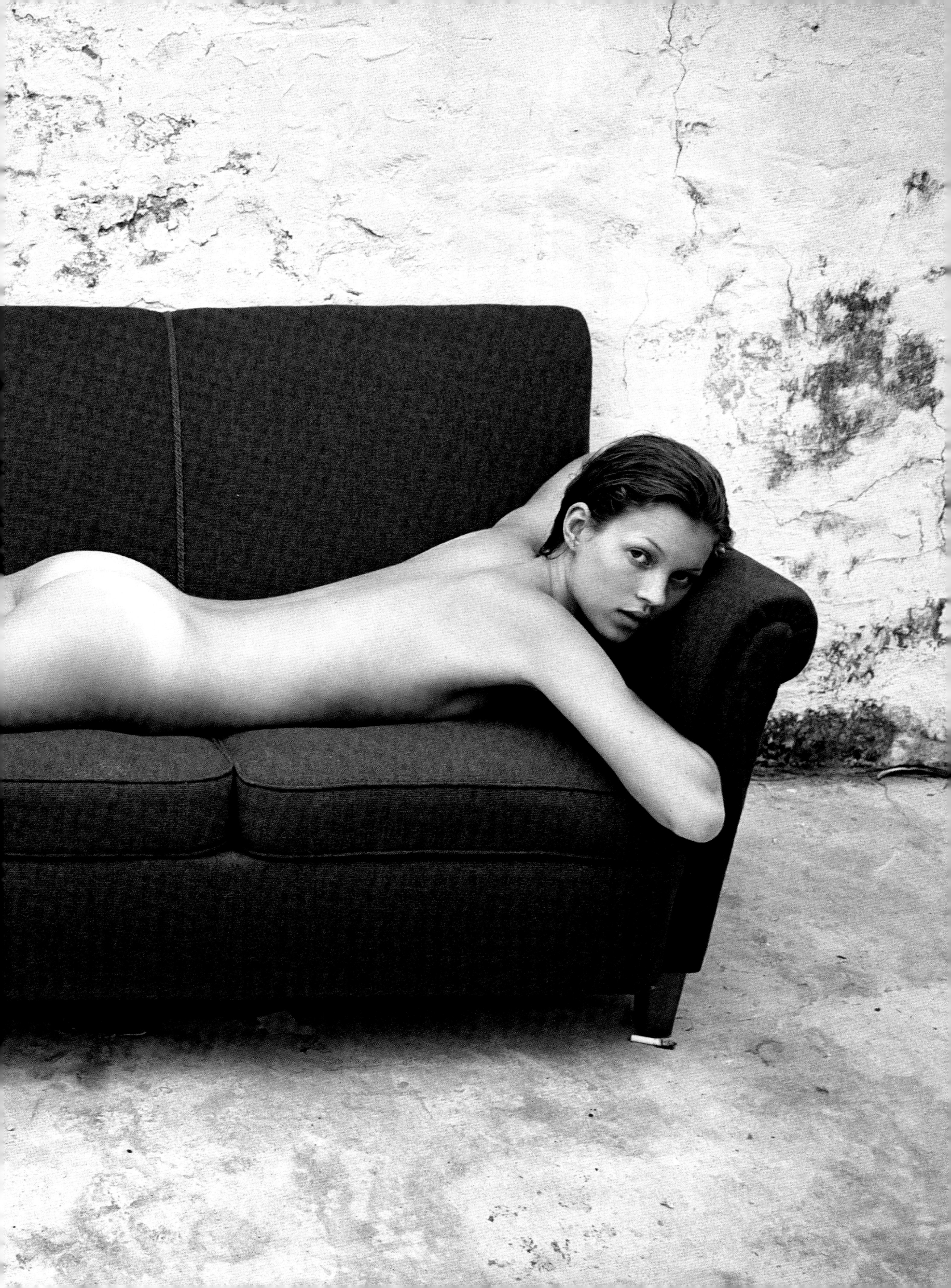

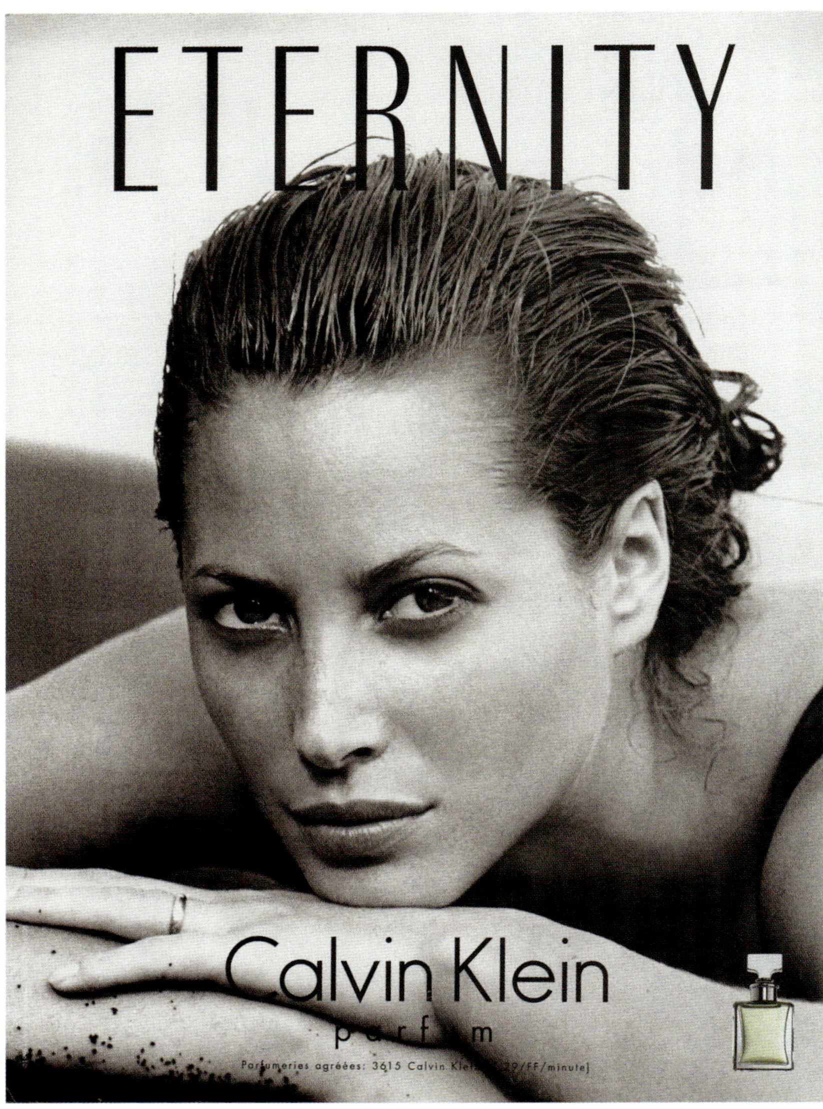

Calvin Klein Eternity campaign 1995

Peter Lindbergh, model: Christy Turlington, 1994 for Calvin Klein Eternity

The fashion industry boomed in the 1990s, as the mainstream market became more aspirational. Advertising budgets grew, with supermodels starring in lucrative campaigns. Christy Turlington became the face of one of the most popular US-American brands, Calvin Klein, in 1988. Peter Lindbergh's series for 'Eternity' perfume, released in 1995 and featuring Turlington, became a classic. Fresh from a dip in the ocean, the model is captured in images that are both evocative and sensual. The brand reissued the campaign in 2014 and Turlington featured in a sequel released in 2020, making this perhaps one of the longest-running campaigns in fashion.

110/111
Mario Testino, model: Kate Moss, 1998 for Calvin Klein Jeans

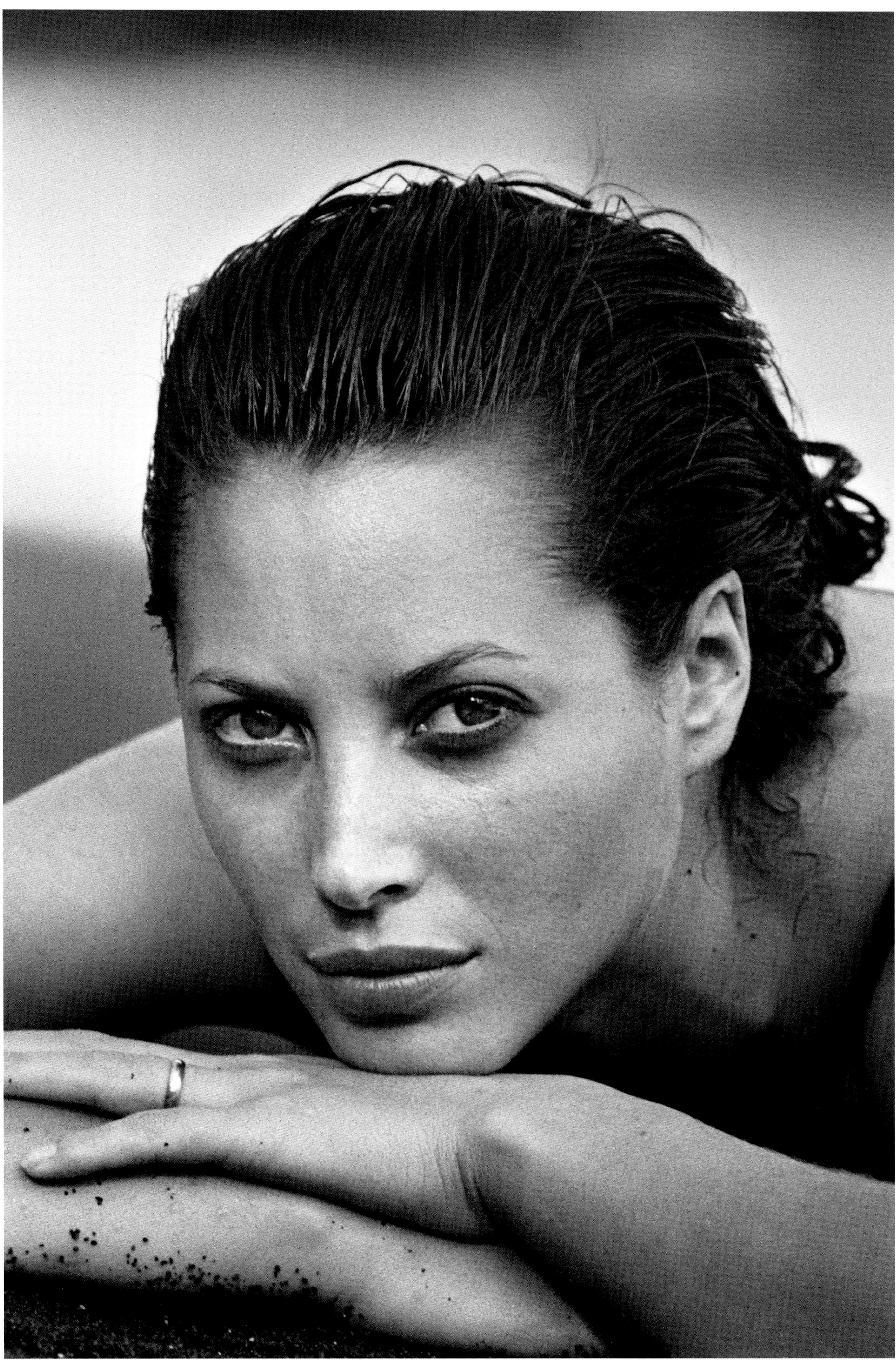

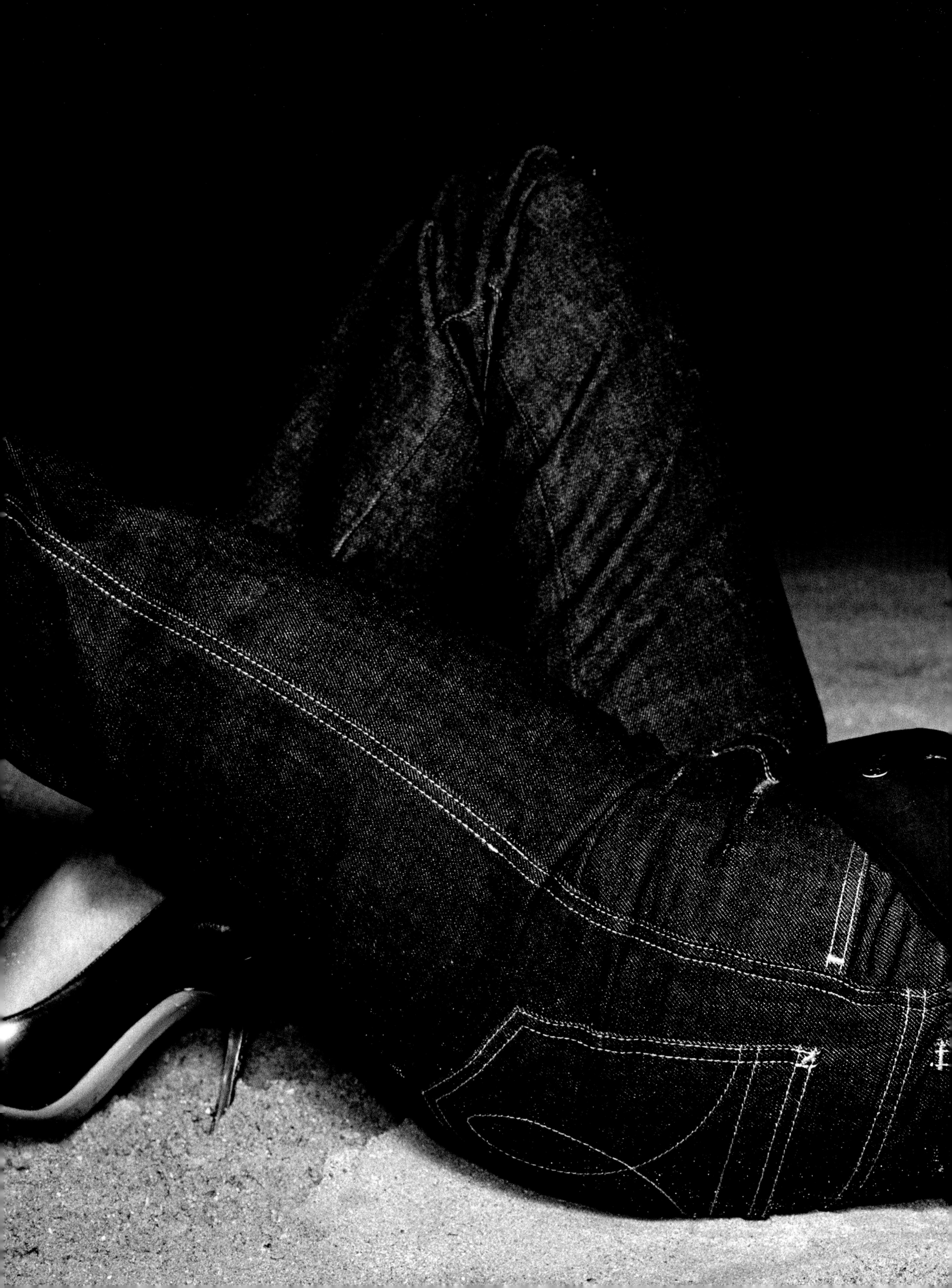

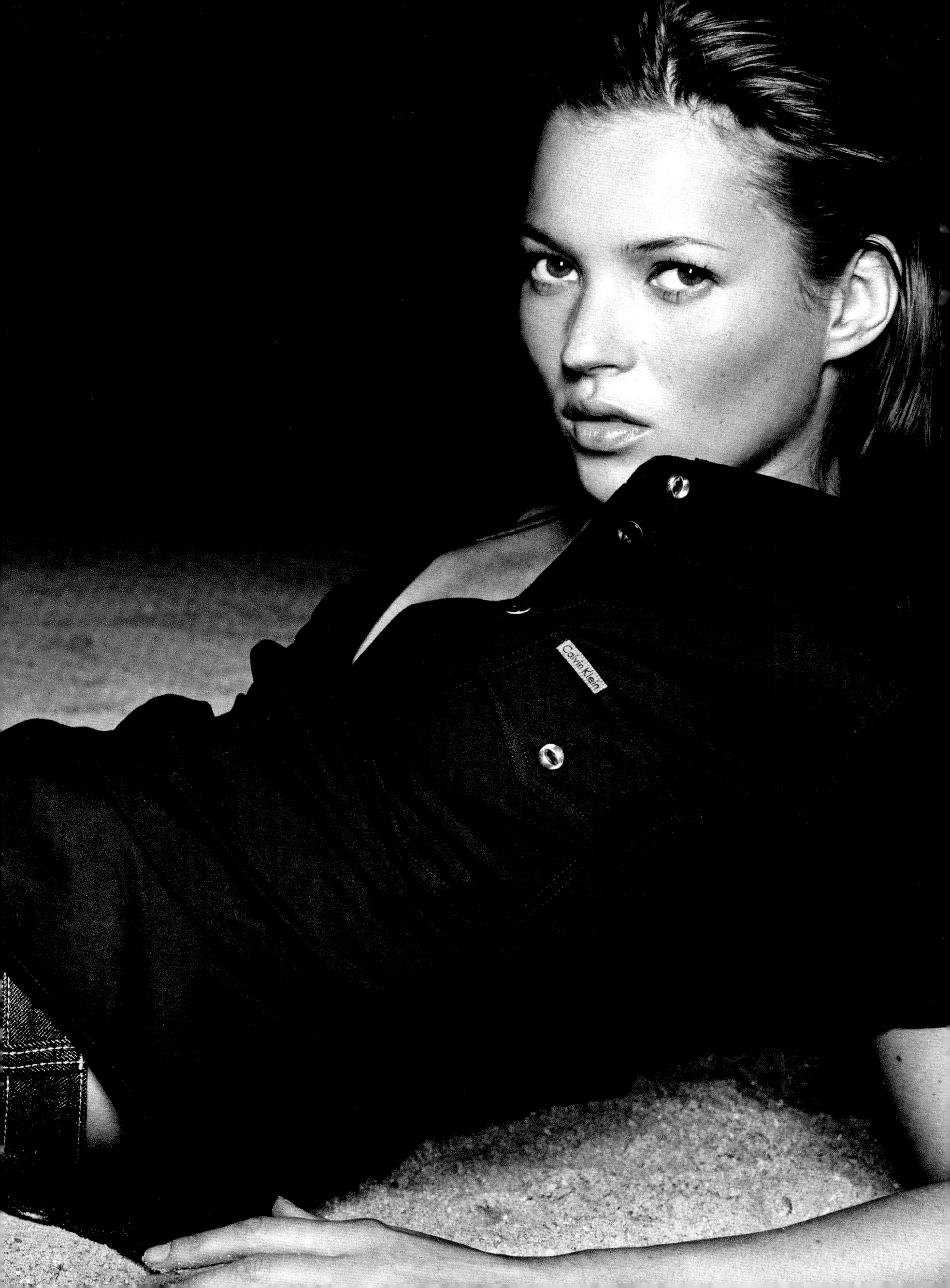
Calvin Klein

COVERS

Before digital technology, the release of a magazine issue was a major event, particularly the new season March and September editions. Sales of each issue pivoted on the cover and in turn drove the magazine's commercial success. The great editors of the era fought for exclusives with photographers, models and celebrities. Fashion and art directors excelled in ever more inventive and compelling cover art that signalled aesthetic shifts, changes in trend and mood. Ultimately, the goal was to seduce the ranks of style fans at the newsstand.

In the 1990s, physical magazines were collected, pored over and dissected, and they became central to the style conversation. Today, we consume and interact with covers in an instant on our devices.

Cover shots require a specific mentality. You have to have strong creativity but also the discipline to understand how the image will appear with design and layout all around it.

RUSSELL JAMES

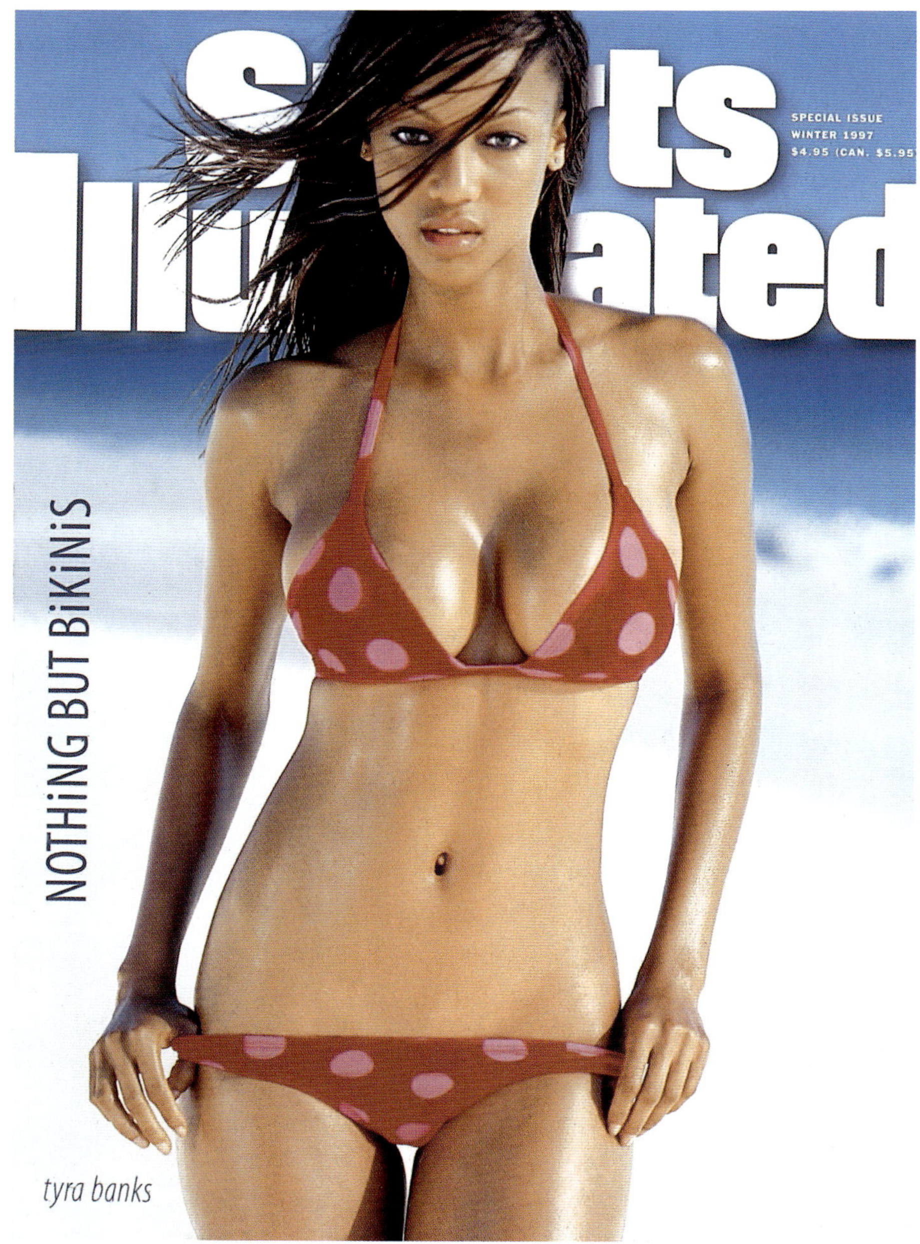

Sports Illustrated, Winter 1997

Russell James, model: Tyra Banks, 1997 for *Sports Illustrated*

Every February, US-American magazine *Sports Illustrated* launches its famous swimsuit issue featuring fashion models, celebrities and athletes wearing swimwear in various locales around the world. With the magazine being sold into thirty-two countries, the cover has always generated huge amounts of publicity. In 1997, Tyra Banks was the first Black model to appear solo on the cover, a historical first and a milestone in mainstream culture.

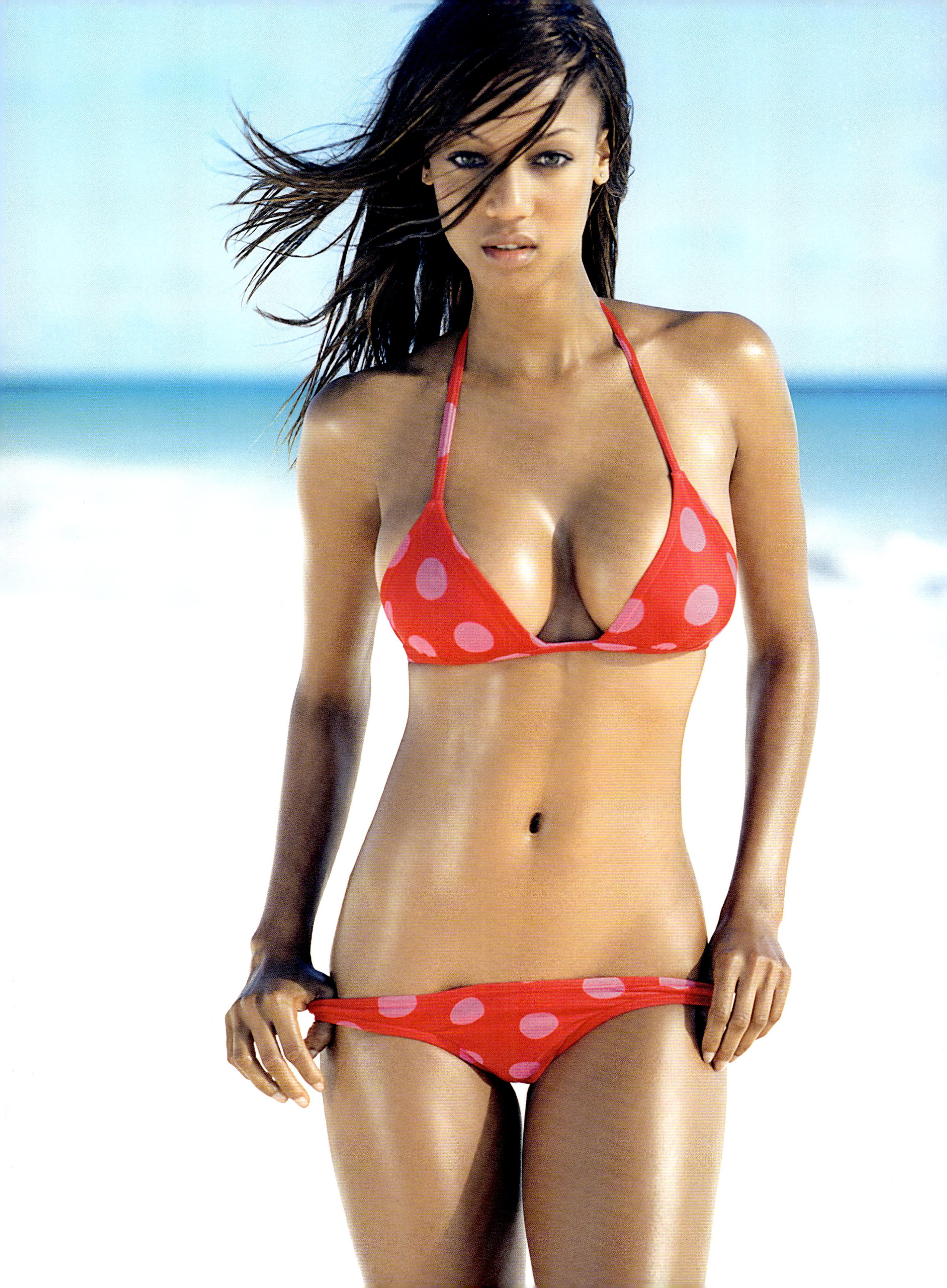

I love how this image showcases different ideals of beauty. The 'no fashion' fashion statement of white jeans and shirts makes this image timeless but it was also a statement that Vogue *understands the modern woman.*

CINDY CRAWFORD

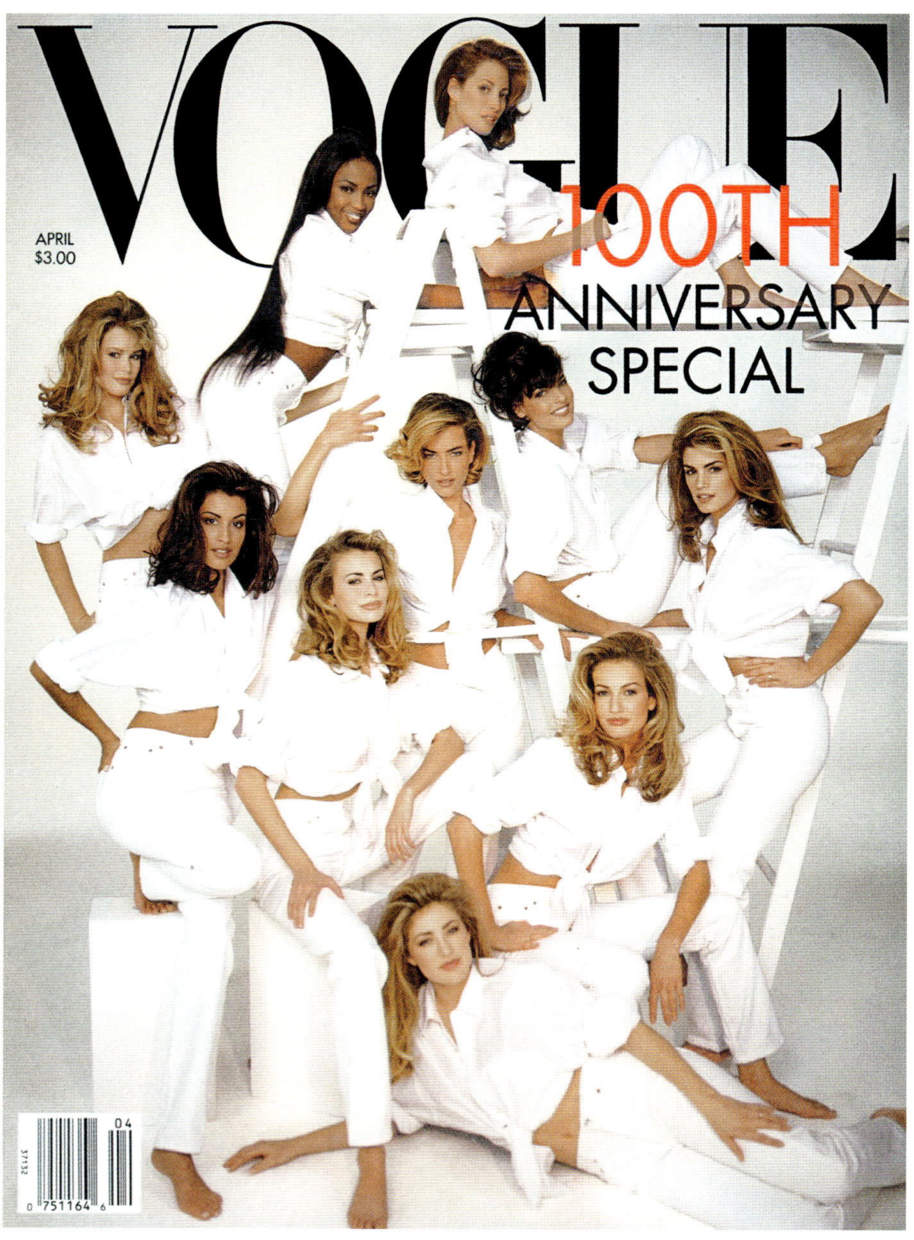

Vogue US, April 1992

Patrick Demarchelier, models: Christy Turlington, Linda Evangelista, Cindy Crawford, Karen Mulder, Elaine Irwin, Niki Taylor, Yasmeen Ghauri, Claudia Schiffer, Naomi Campbell, Tatjana Patitz, 1992 for *Vogue* US

This image was produced for US *Vogue*'s hundredth anniversary issue. Patrick Demarchelier can be credited with a resurfacing of classicism in 1990s fashion photography. There was a refined elegance to his work that appeared so fresh after the excesses of the 1980s.

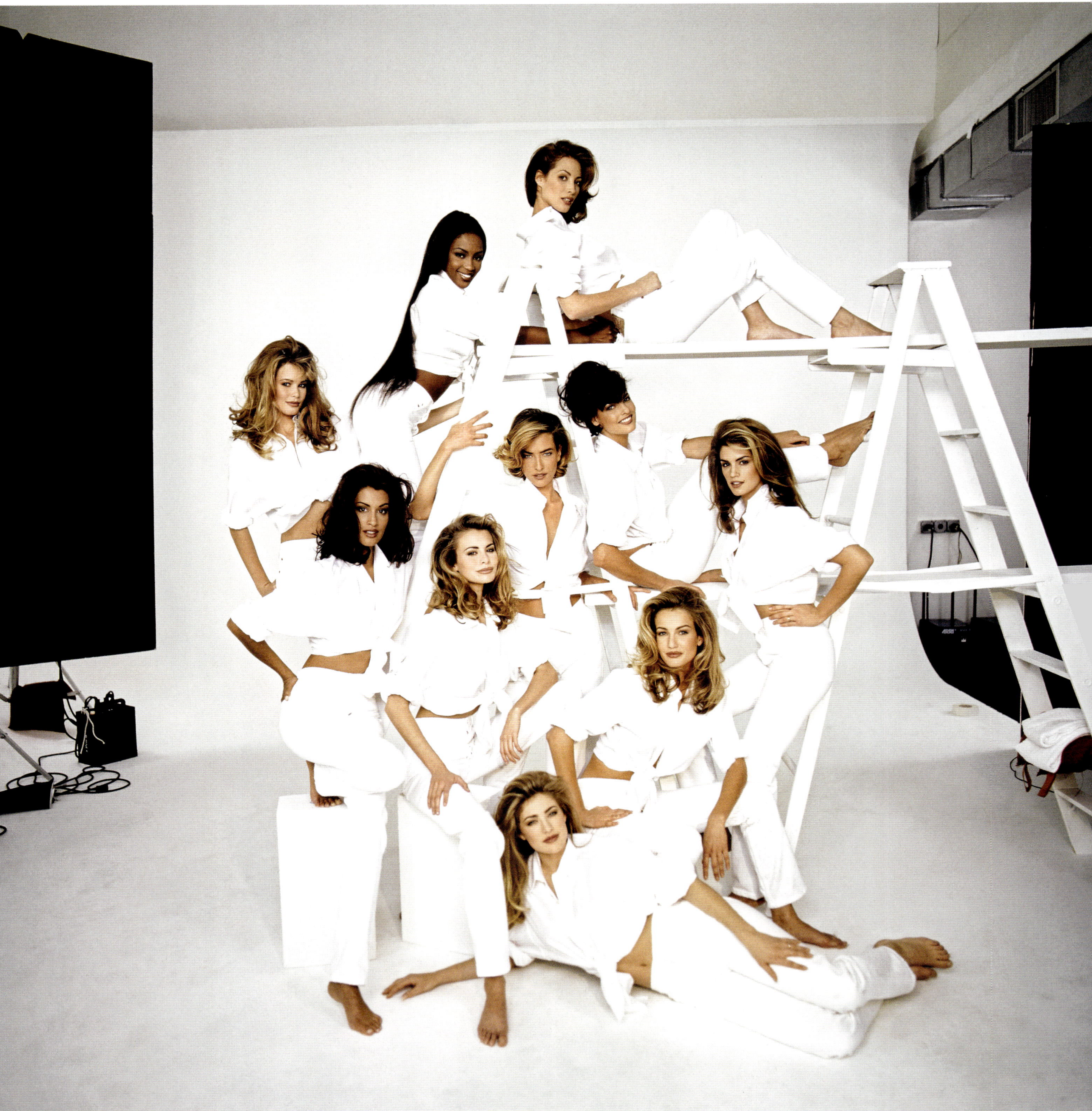

Let's just keep it real.

CORINNE DAY

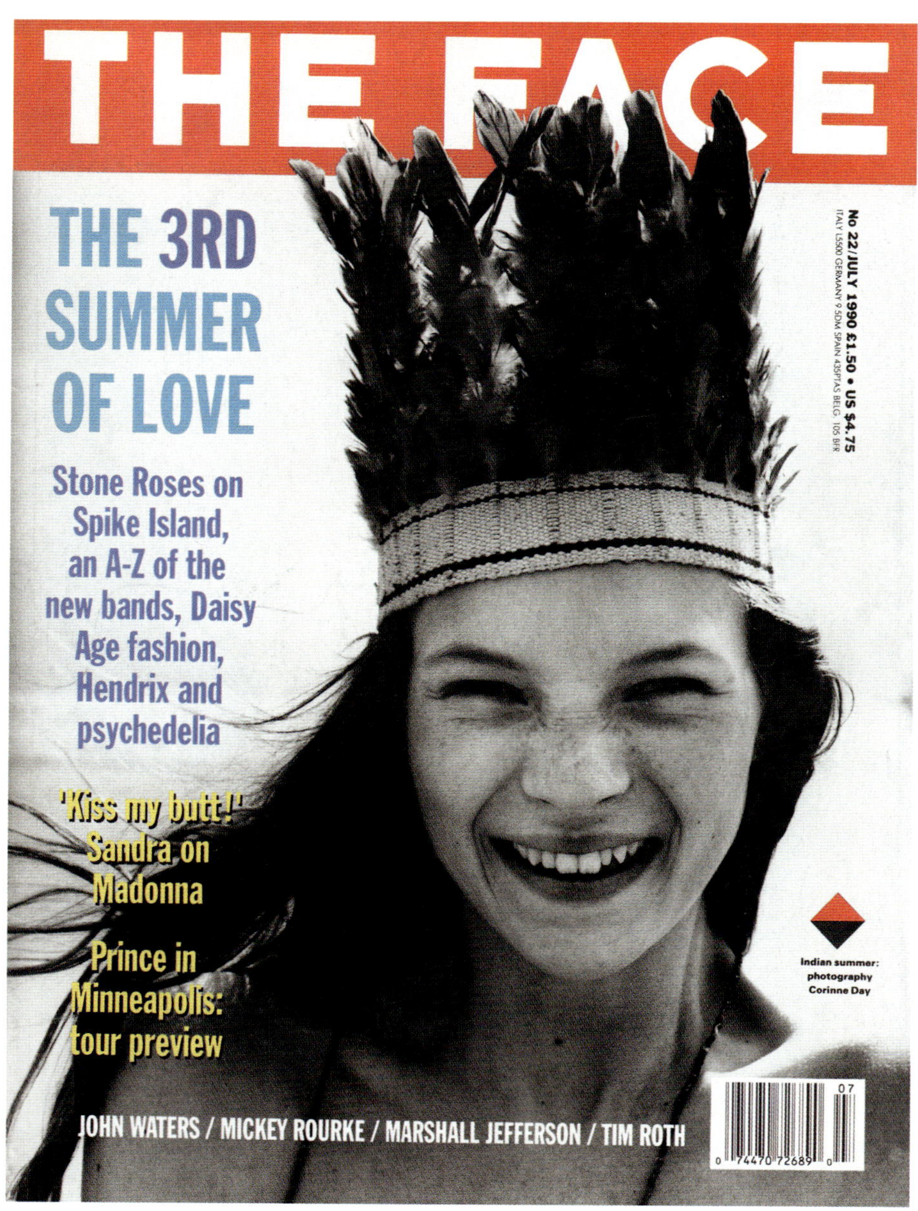

The Face, July 1990

Corinne Day, model: Kate Moss, Camber Sands, England 1990 for *The Face*

There are pictures that have earned iconic status over time. British photographer Corinne Day's and stylist Melanie Ward's images of Kate Moss for British style magazine *The Face* are striking examples of such pictures. Shot in 1990, on Camber Sands in England, for *The Face*'s celebration issue 'The 3rd Summer of Love', Moss, in a feather headdress, became the face of a generation. The authentic images challenged female archetypes of beauty and changed the face of high fashion.

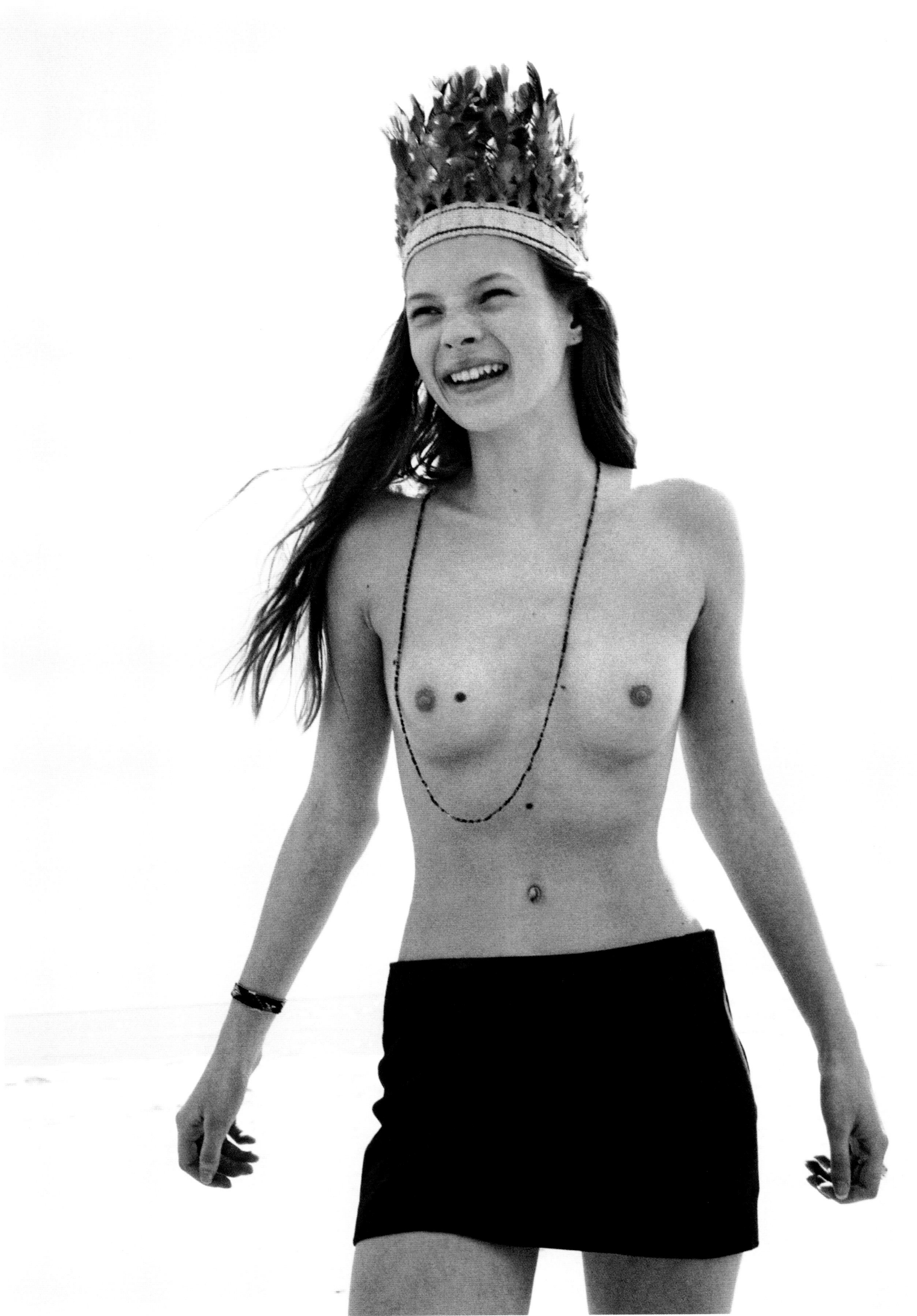

POLAR-
OIDS

The Polaroid camera was a vital part of the shoot process in the pre-digital age. It allowed a photographer to take test shots to judge lighting, look and composition and to see the results within minutes – elements that nowadays are checked digitally. In this section, I present a selection of Arthur Elgort's Polaroids.

Polaroid film does not last well and cannot be reproduced like other photographic techniques. The format is transient, unique to the moment. The square format of the social media platform Instagram, launched in 2010, is arguably the Polaroid's digital successor.

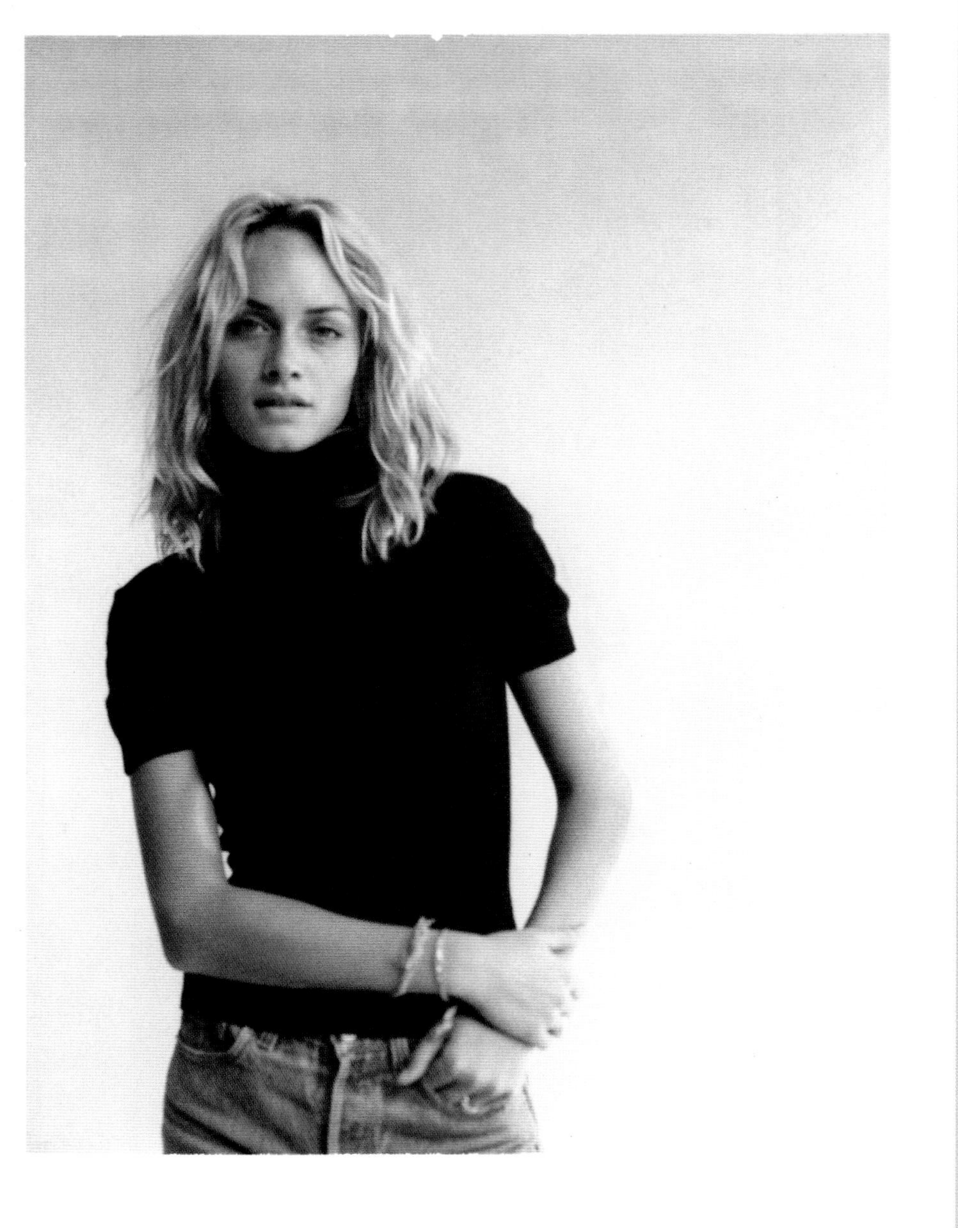

Arthur Elgort, model: Amber Valletta, 1995 for *Vogue* UK

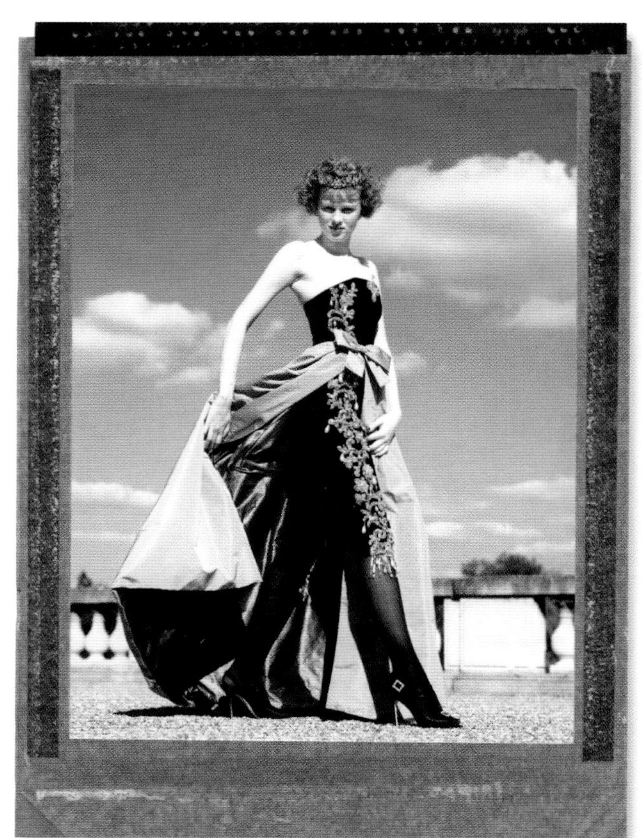

The 1990s were a wonderful time. I had non-stop work all over the world with the best models and the best clothes. With the likes of Claudia, Linda and Christy in China, Russia and Paris, wearing Alaia, YSL and Galliano's Dior, it couldn't get any better.

ARTHUR ELGORT

Arthur Elgort, model: Karen Elson, 1997 for *Vogue* UK

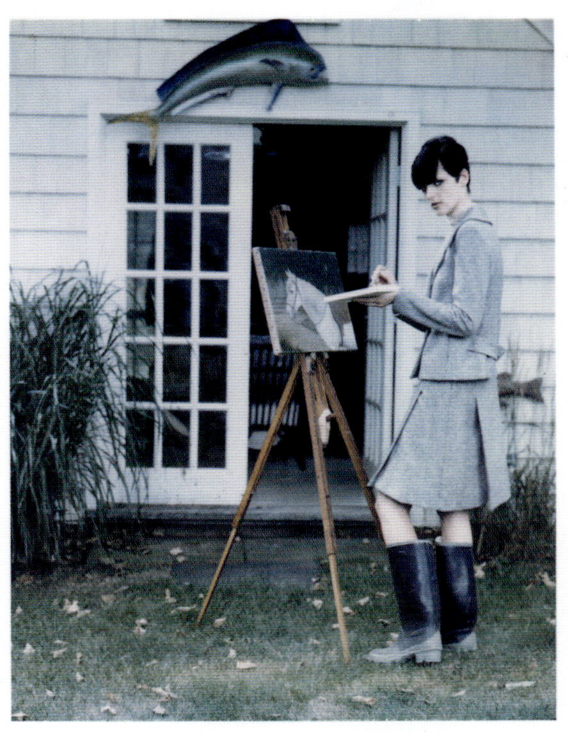

Arthur Elgort, model: Stella Tennant, 1995 for *Vogue* US

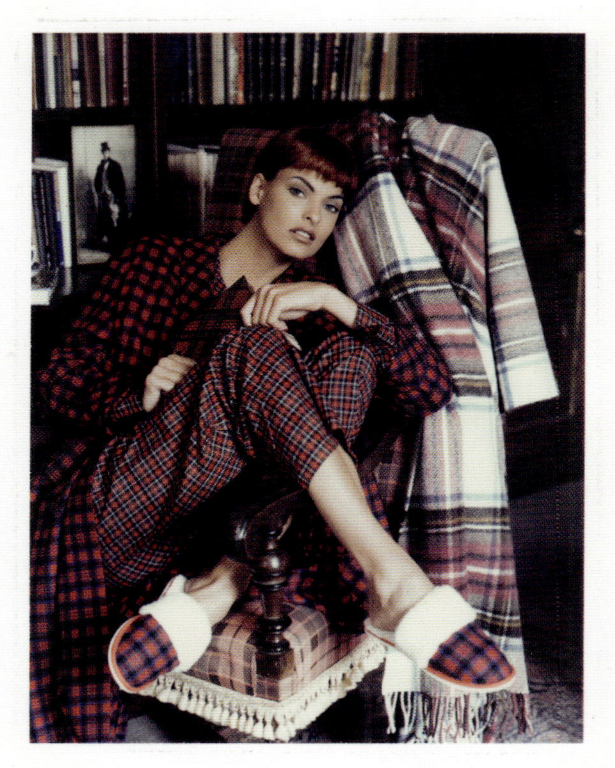

Arthur Elgort, model: Linda Evangelista, 1991 for *Vogue* US

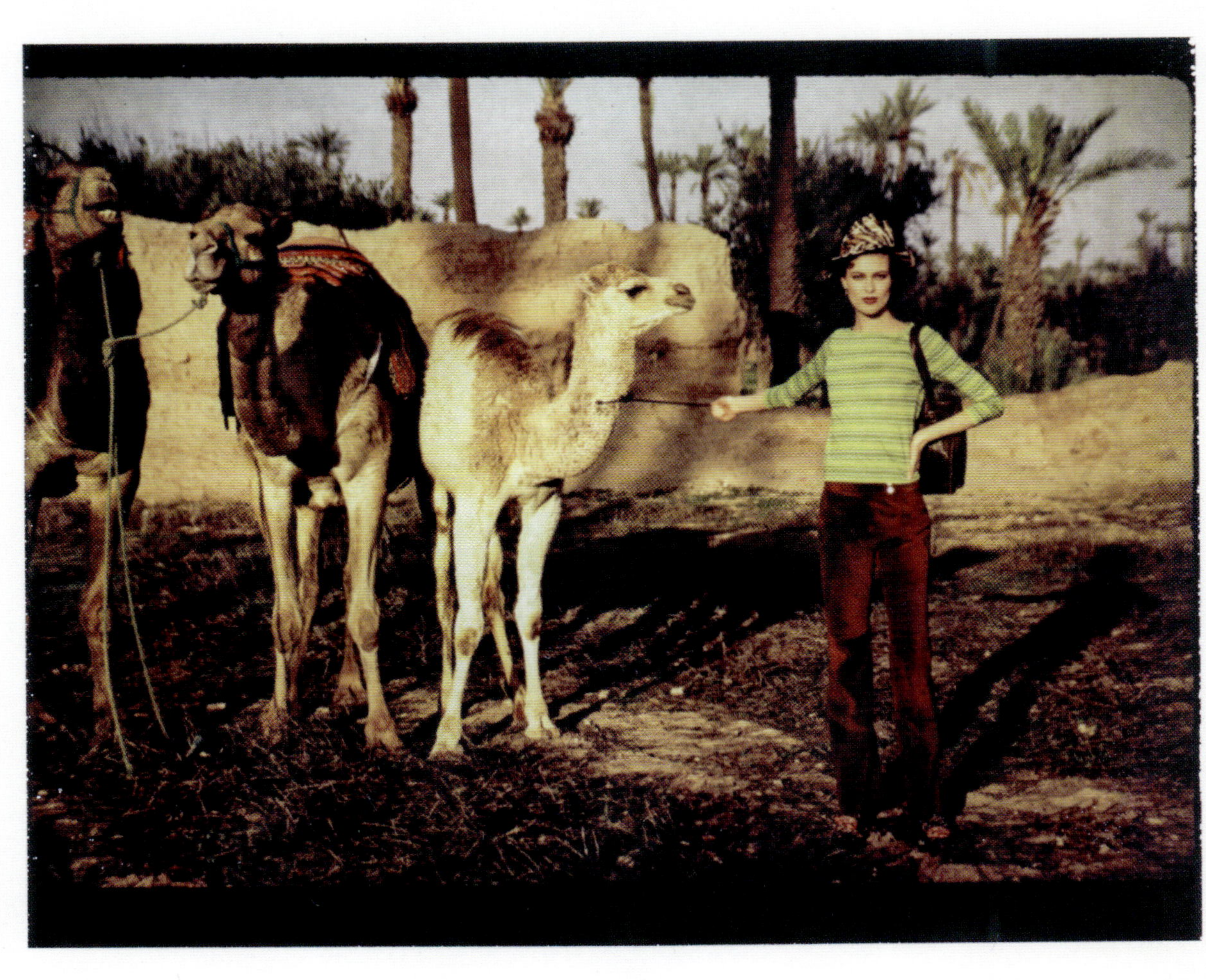

Arthur Elgort, model: Shalom Harlow, 1996 for *Vogue* US

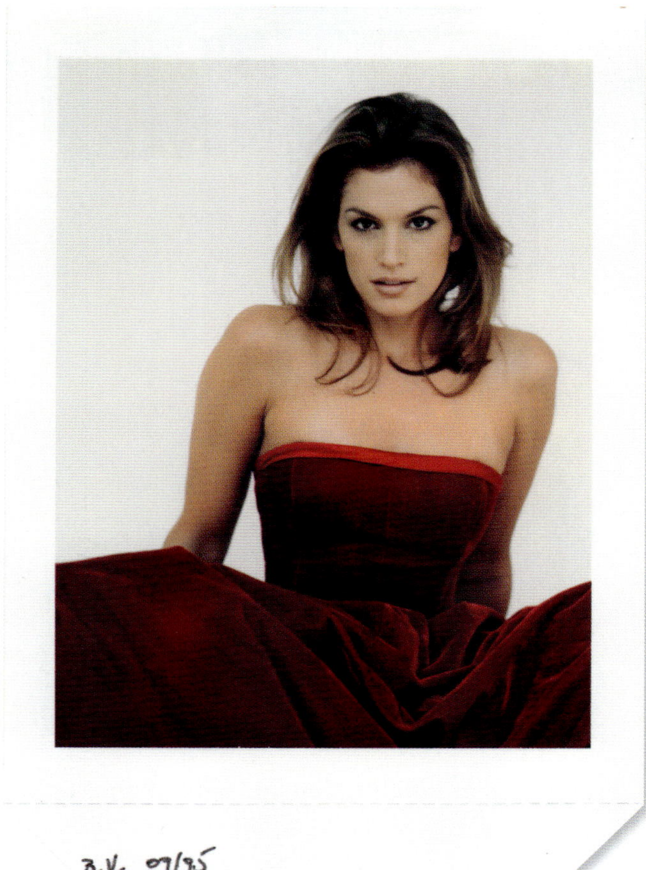

Arthur Elgort, model: Cindy Crawford, 1995 for *Vogue* UK

Because we were not shooting digitally, the crews were smaller and more intimate and there was always anticipation about what the processed images would look like. Sometimes they looked like the Polaroid, but you never knew for sure until you saw the image in the magazine.

CINDY CRAWFORD

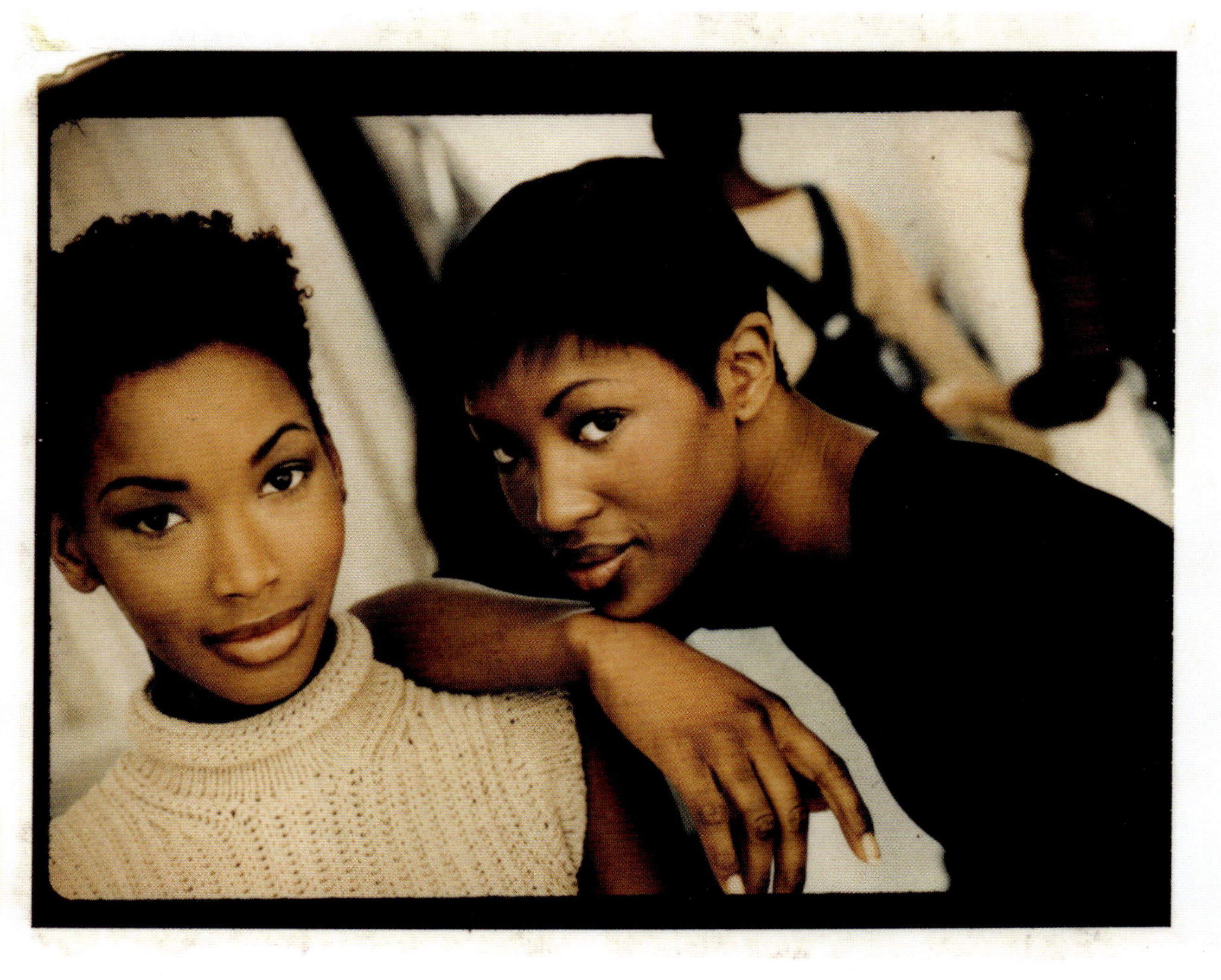

Arthur Elgort, models: Beverly Peele, Naomi Campbell, 1993 for *Vogue* US

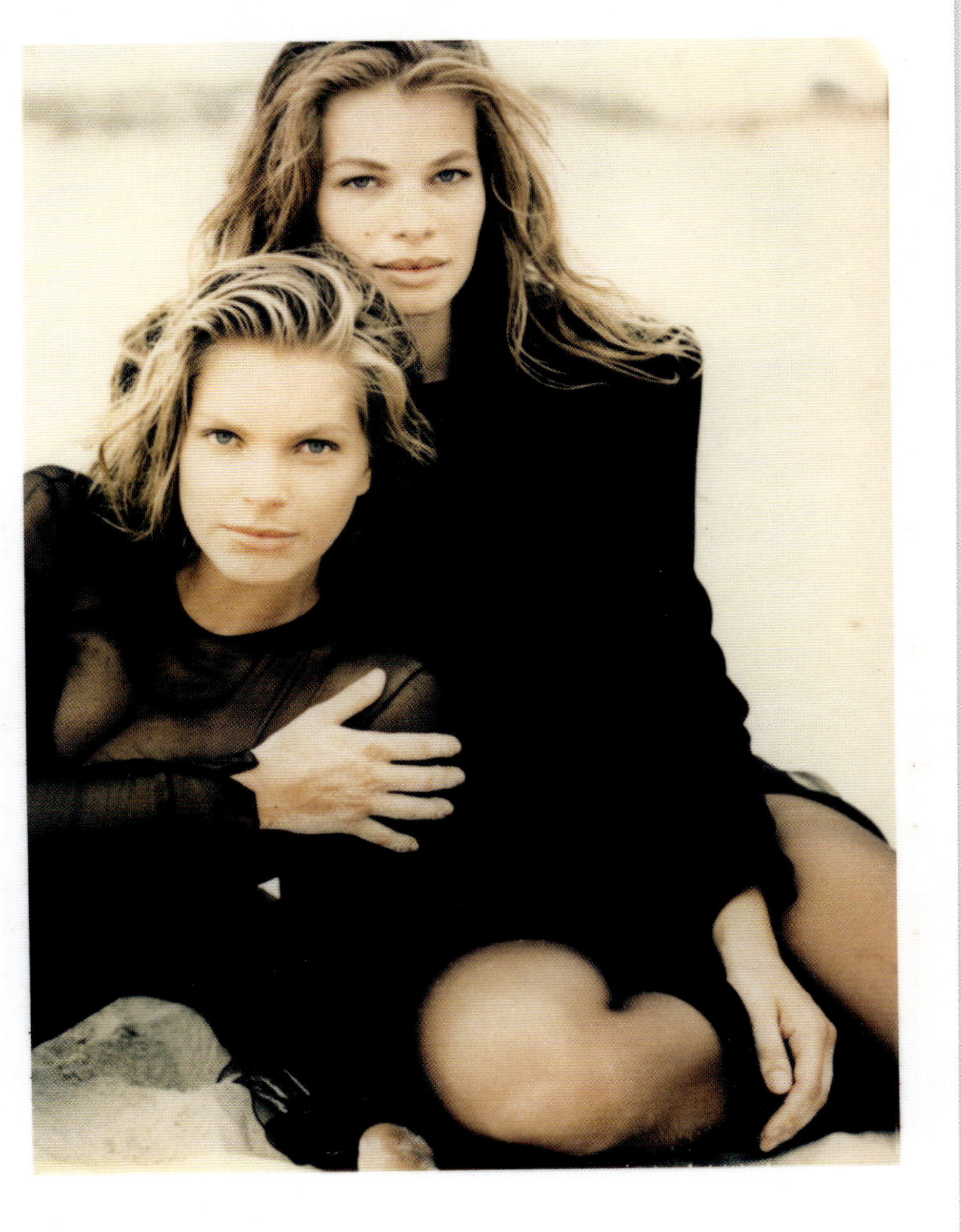

Arthur Elgort, models: Vera Cox, Cordula Reyer, 1990 for *Vogue* UK

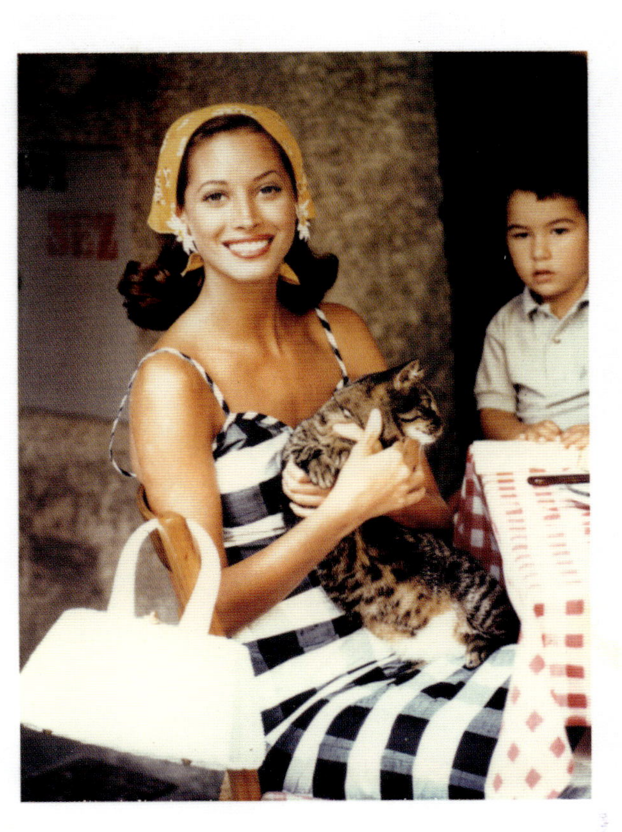

Arthur Elgort, model: Christy Turlington, 1992 for *Vogue* IT

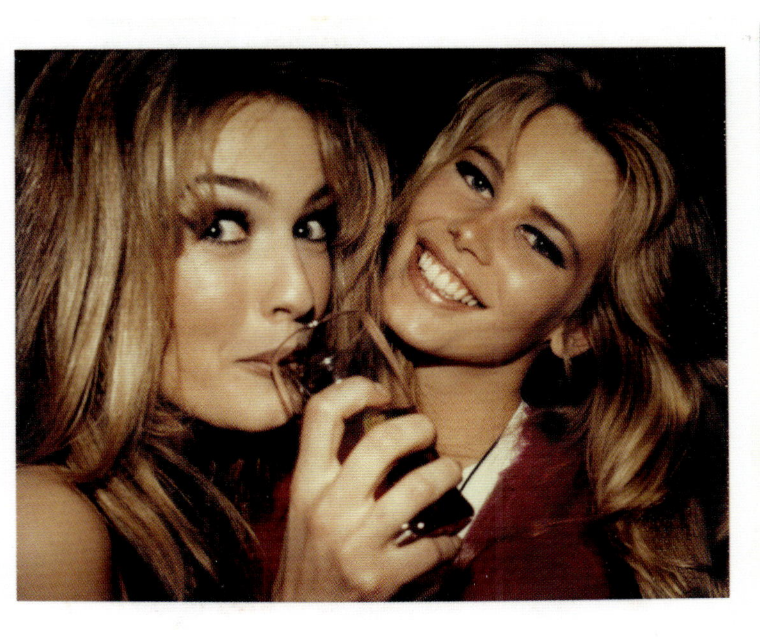

Arthur Elgort, models: Karen Mulder, Claudia Schiffer, 1992 for *Vogue* FR

FASHION STORIES

Editorials or 'fashion stories' were one of the pivotal forms of fashion photography in the 1990s. In collaboration with art directors and stylists, photographers would create whole stories that spanned several pages in magazines. Editorials encompassed a diverse range of work, from incredible story-telling shoots on location to emotive pictorial conversations in the studio. Fashion editors, image-makers, makeup, hair and set designers came together to realise a vision. The creativity on the runway might have been the starting point but inspirations were layered and rich, drawing from art, cinema, nature, science, social observation and the history of fashion photography itself. There was a freedom to explore concepts without the necessary restrictions that often came with advertising campaigns.

Sometimes a shoot lasted a week, with trunks of clothes shipped to far-flung locations. The talented team worked for minimal fees because the final editorial would often attract lucrative advertising clients. Editorial was as important to the industry as it was to the art of magazine-making, and often the most arresting imagery was not a cover or a lead image but lay within the pages.

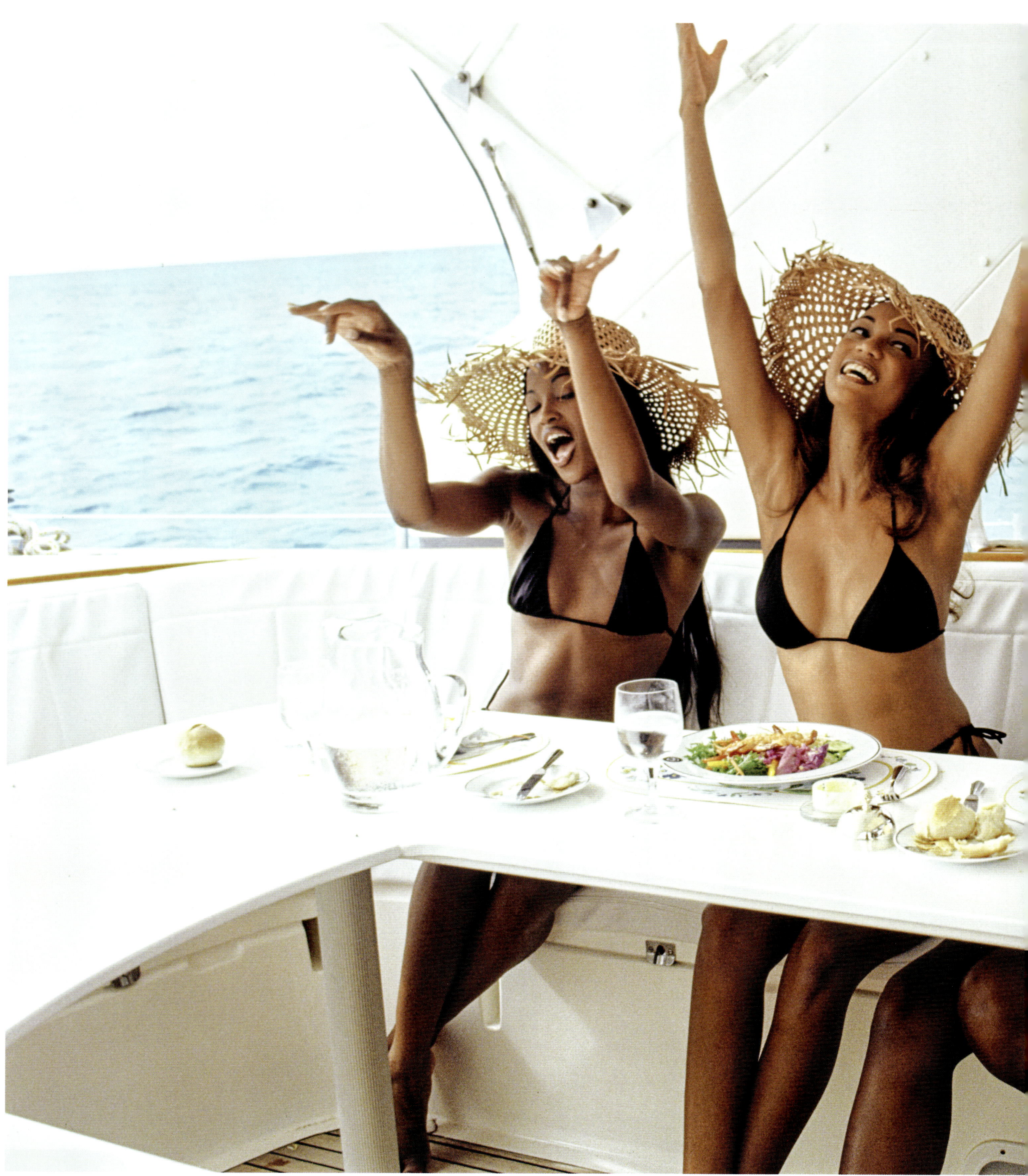

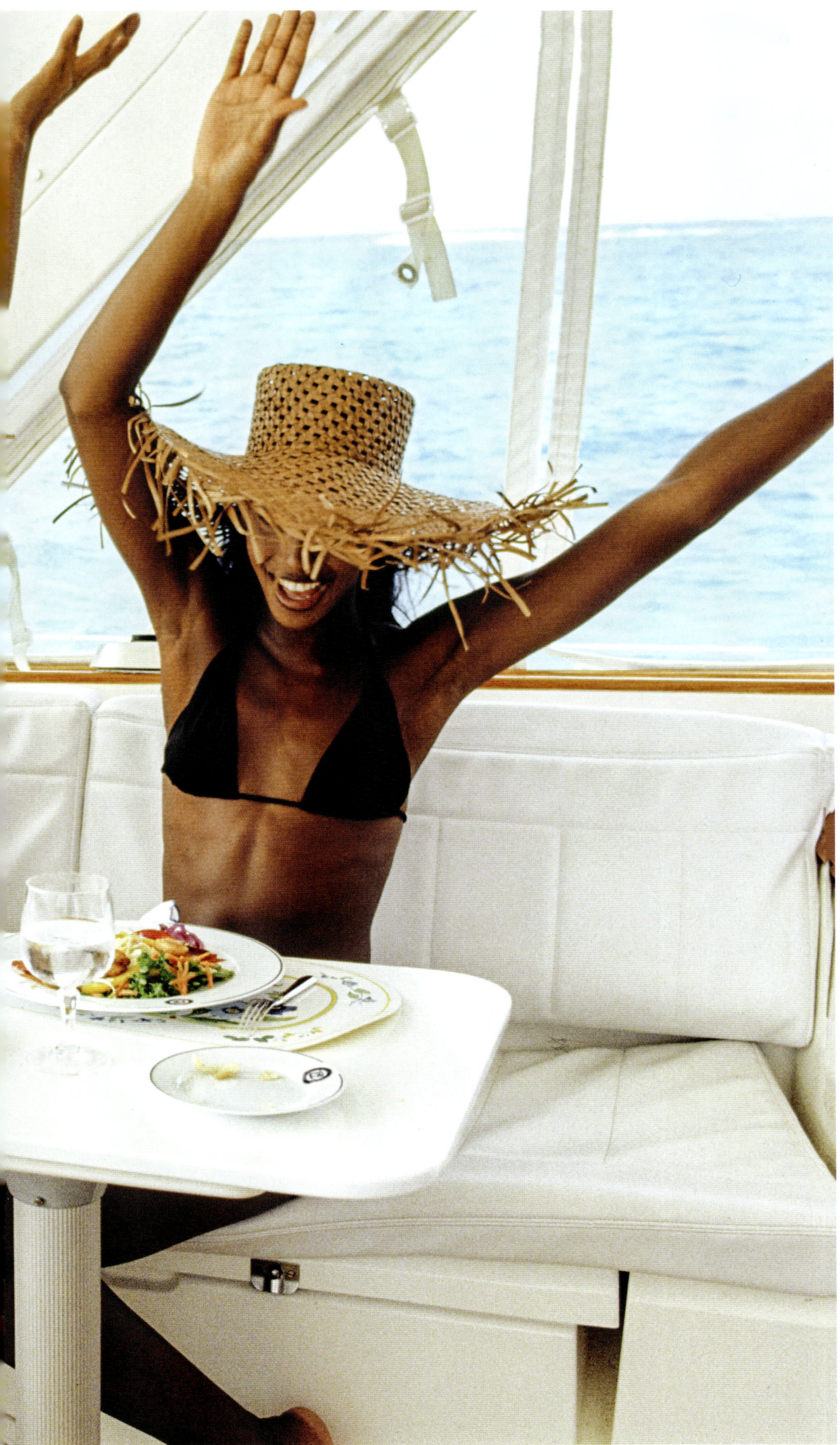

Patrick Demarchelier, models: Naomi Campbell, Tyra Banks, Beverly Peele, 1992 for *Vogue* US

Naomi, Tyra, Beverly – three dancing muses captured by Patrick Demarchelier on a yacht sailing the ocean. The candid style makes this shot so captivating. French-born Demarchelier was one of the superstar photographers of the era, known for his fresh, energetic aesthetic. A master of location and group shots, he helped build the careers of the supermodels as well as stylists, makeup and hair artists. His glamorous but human portraiture was also highly sought after.

Gilles Bensimon, model: Elle Macpherson, 1994

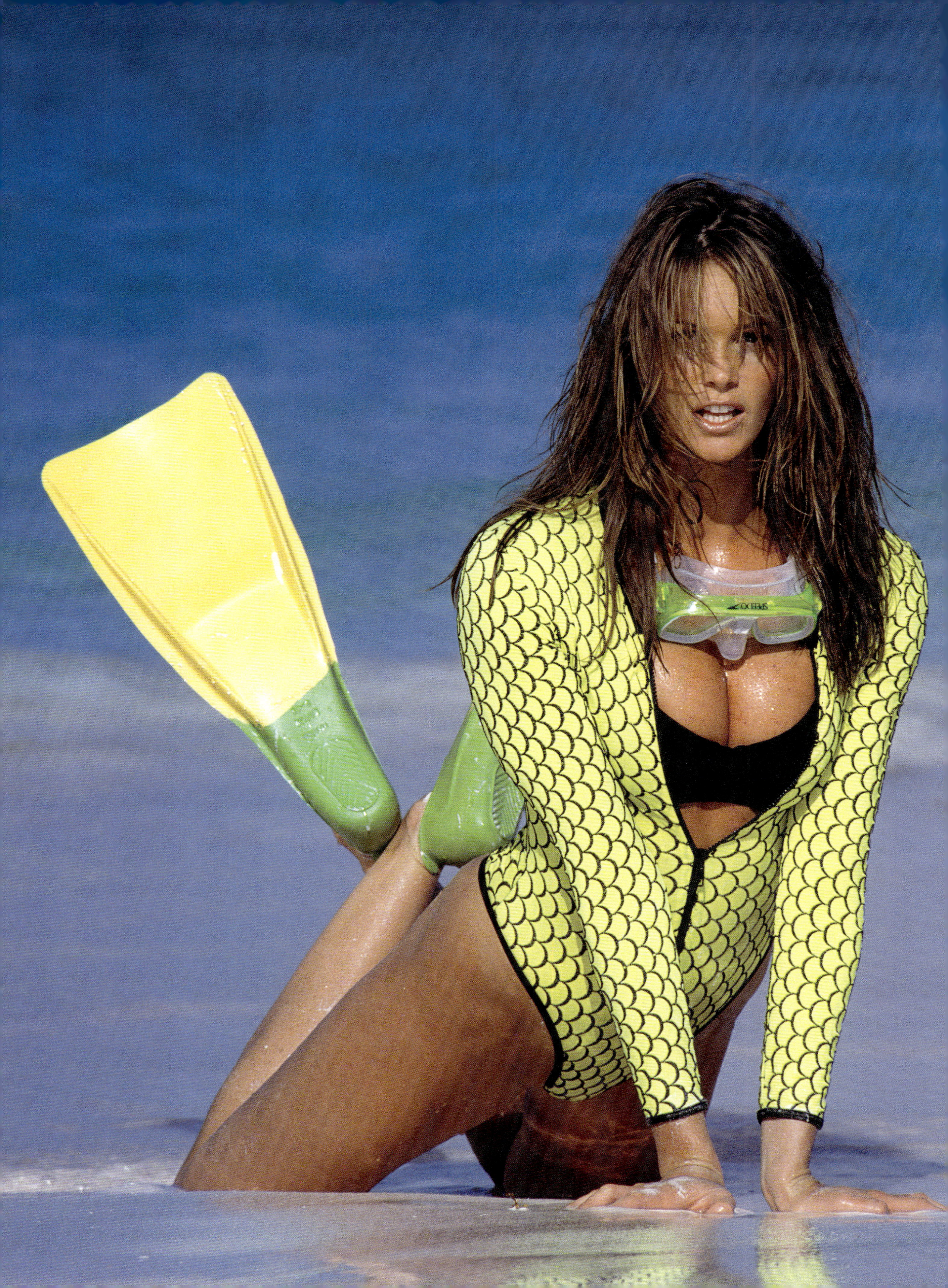

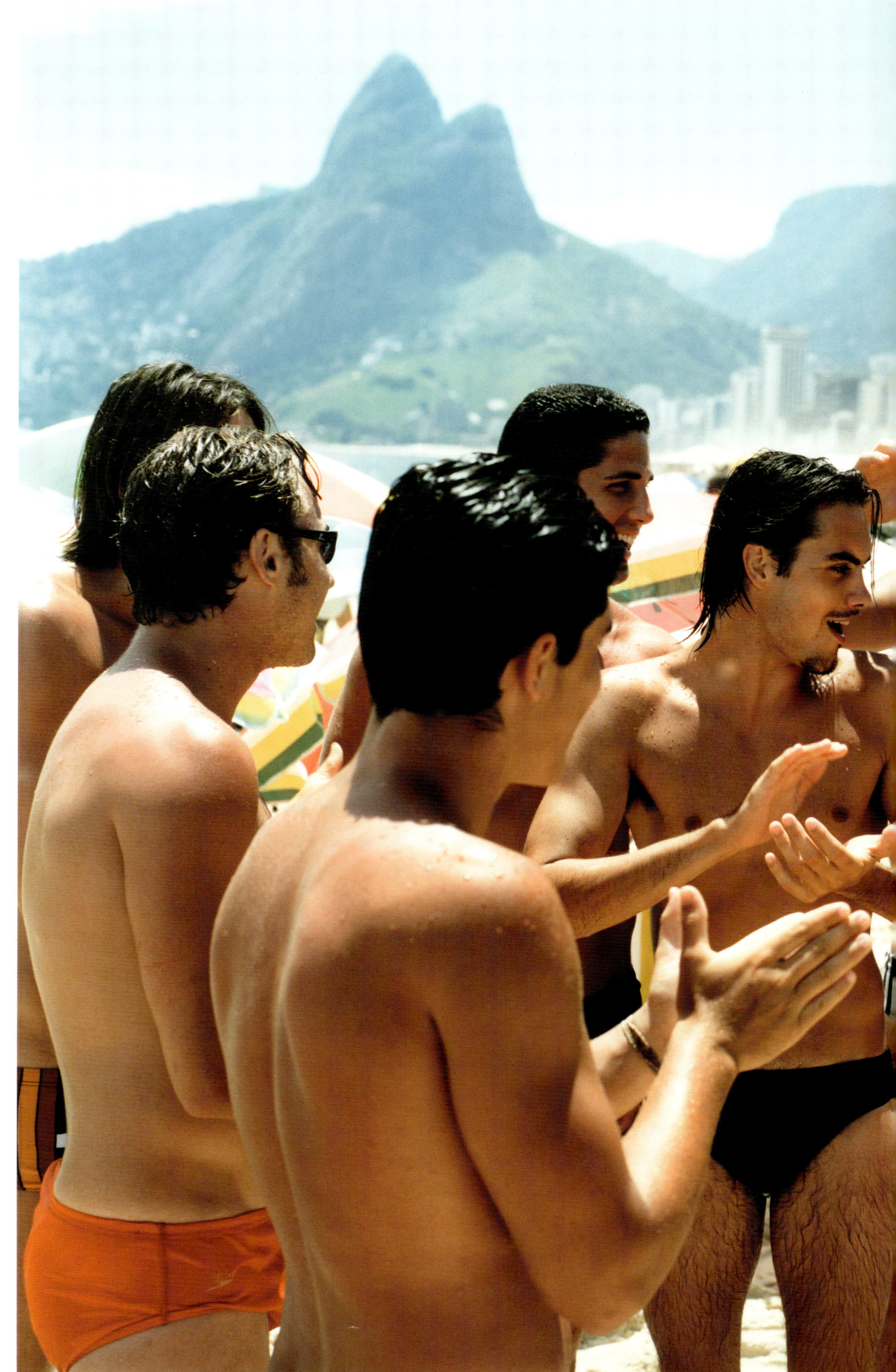

Mario Testino,
model: Amber Valletta,
Rio de Janeiro 1997
for *Vogue* US

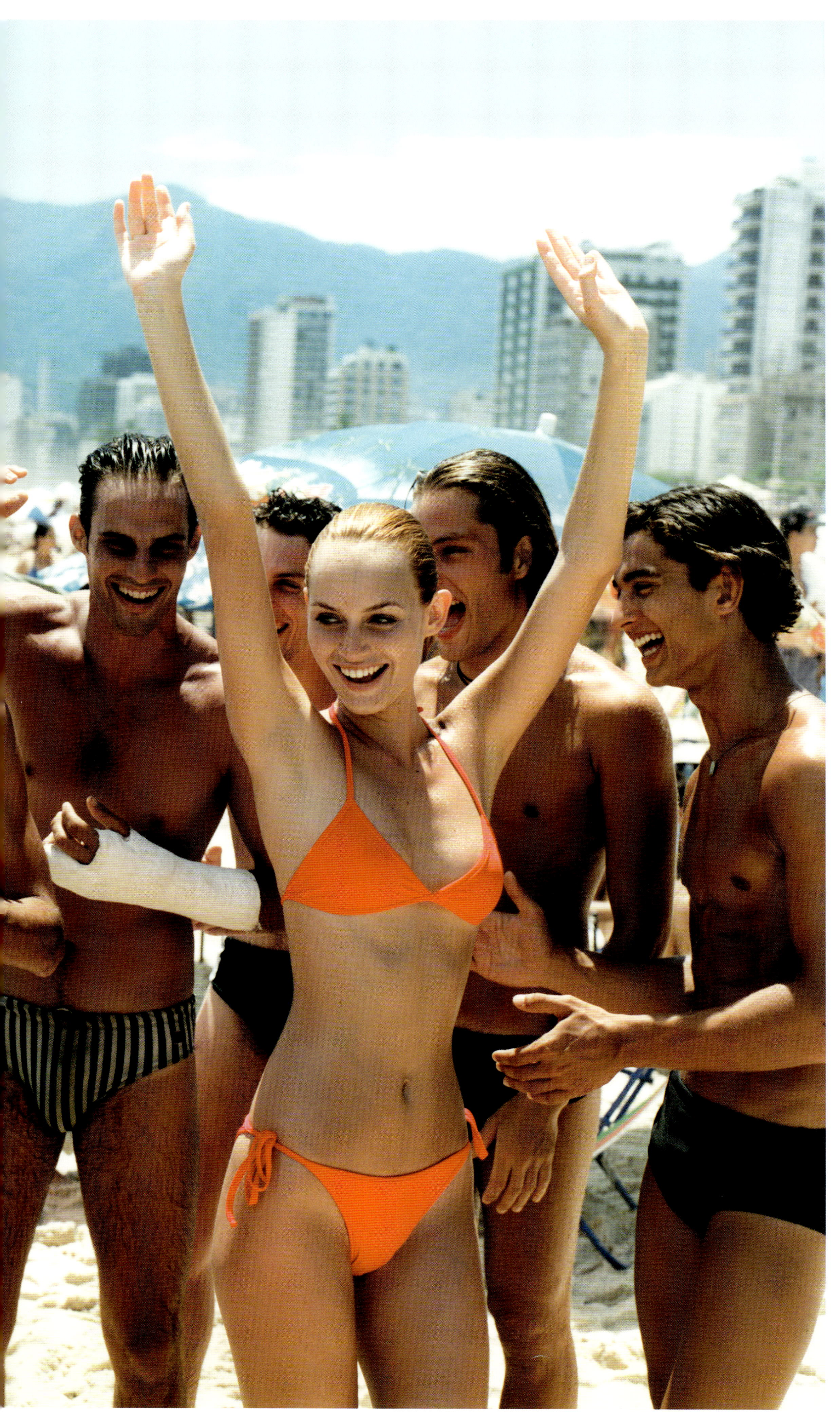

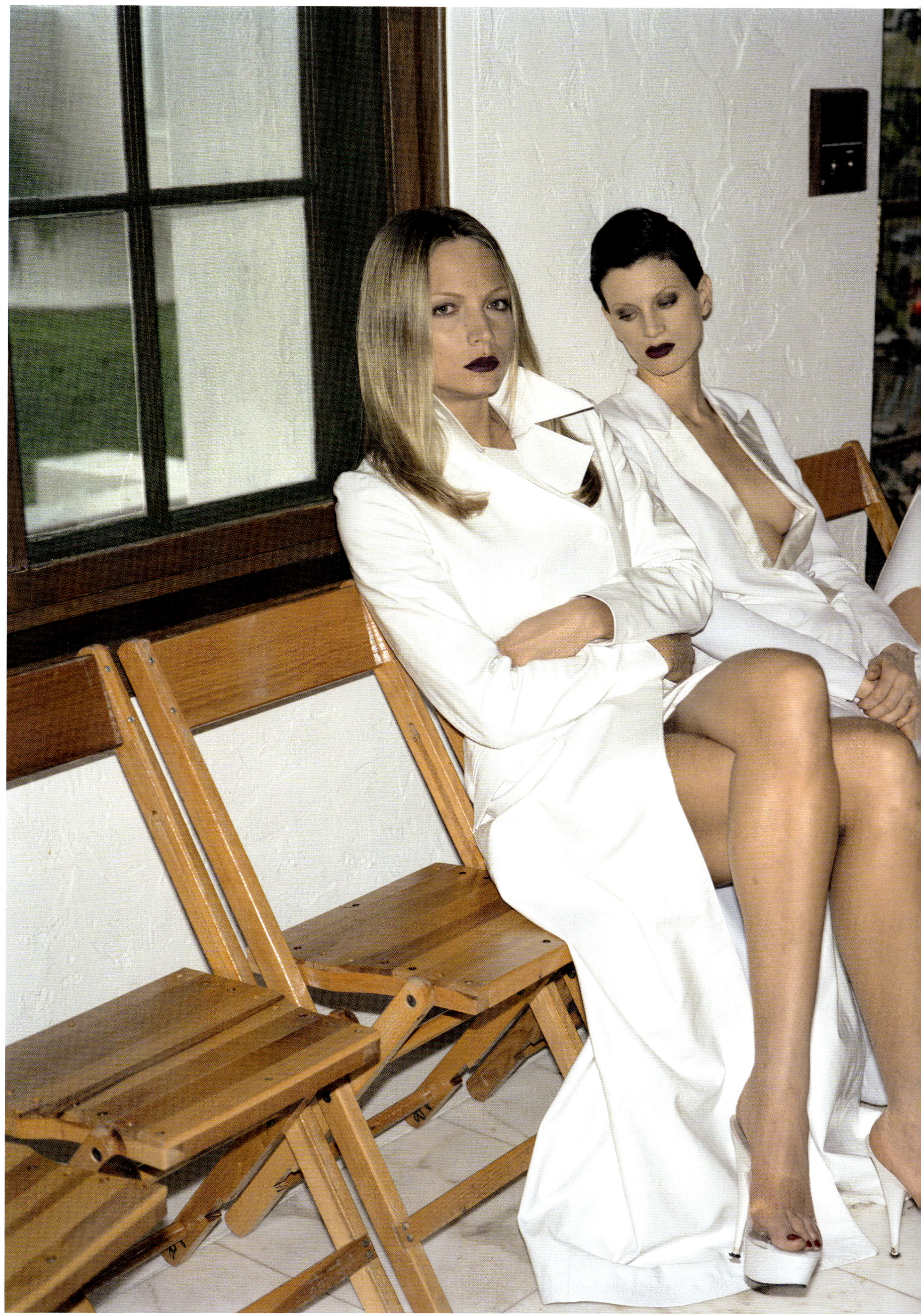

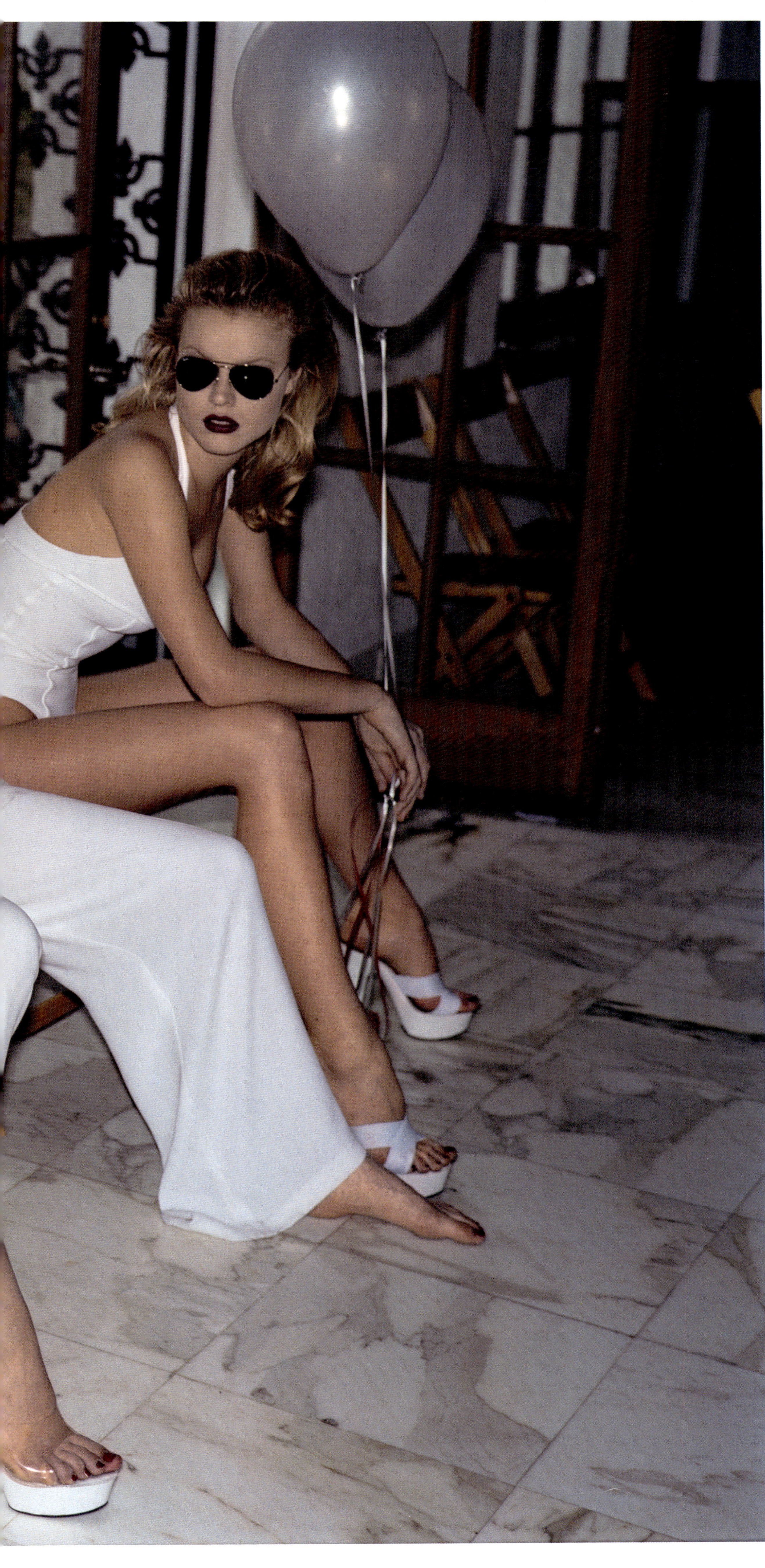

A fashion shoot was more of a story-telling, a movie scripted by the fashion team on location with nobody else being involved. It was an intimate and exhilarating build-up process that belonged to you. And the pleasure, after the longest wait, was seeing the results on the pages of a magazine. That was the whole point…!

EVA HERZIGOVÁ

Helmut Newton, models: Rachel Williams, Kristin McMenamy, Eva Herzigová, Miami 1993 for *Vogue US*

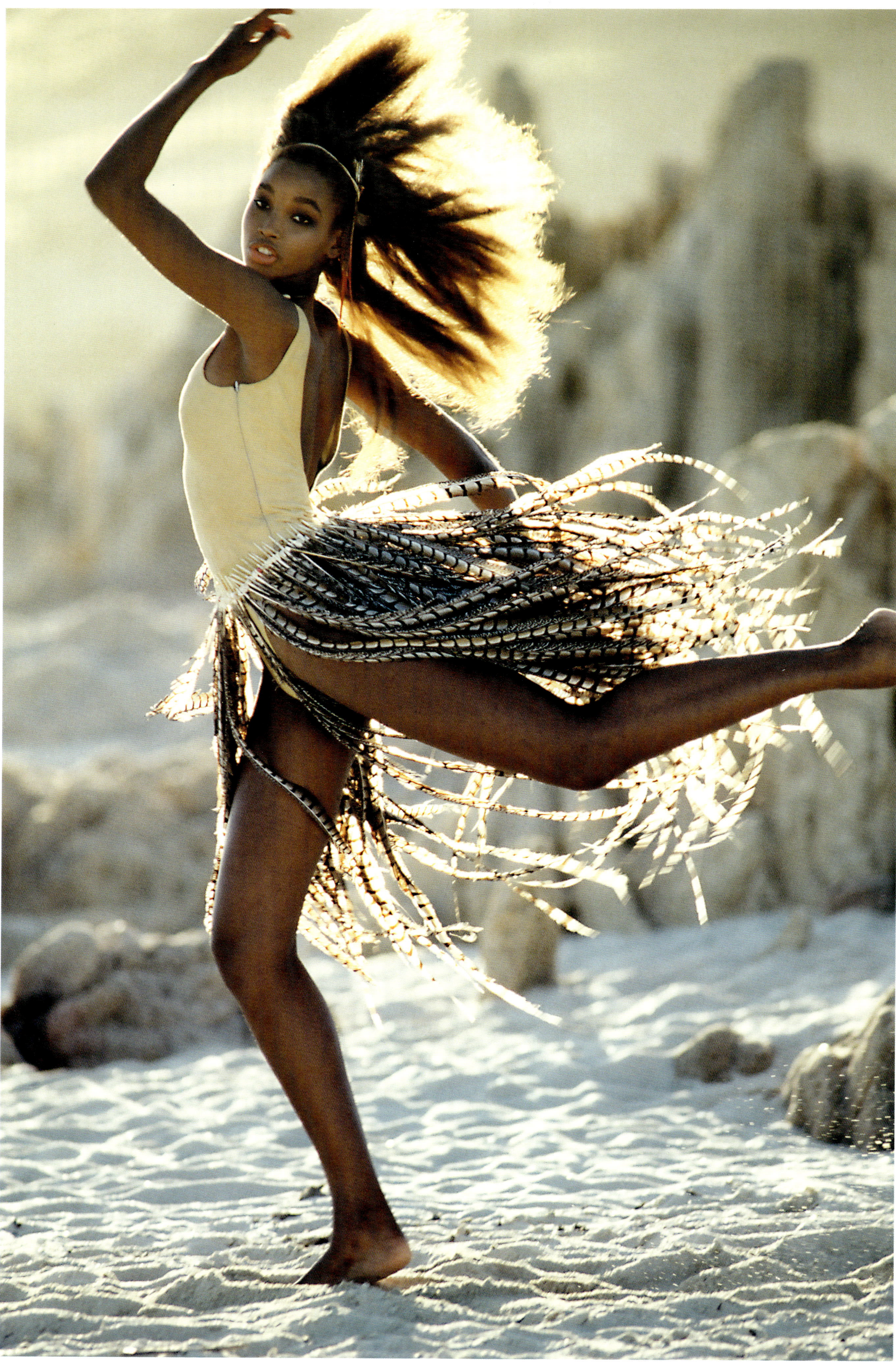

In the 1990s it was still possible to travel to exotic locations with the models and the team, to realise various projects together there. Also at that time print media still had a strong presence, which then increasingly declined.

HANS FEURER

Hans Feurer, model: Beverly Peele, Lanzarote 1991 for *ELLE* FR

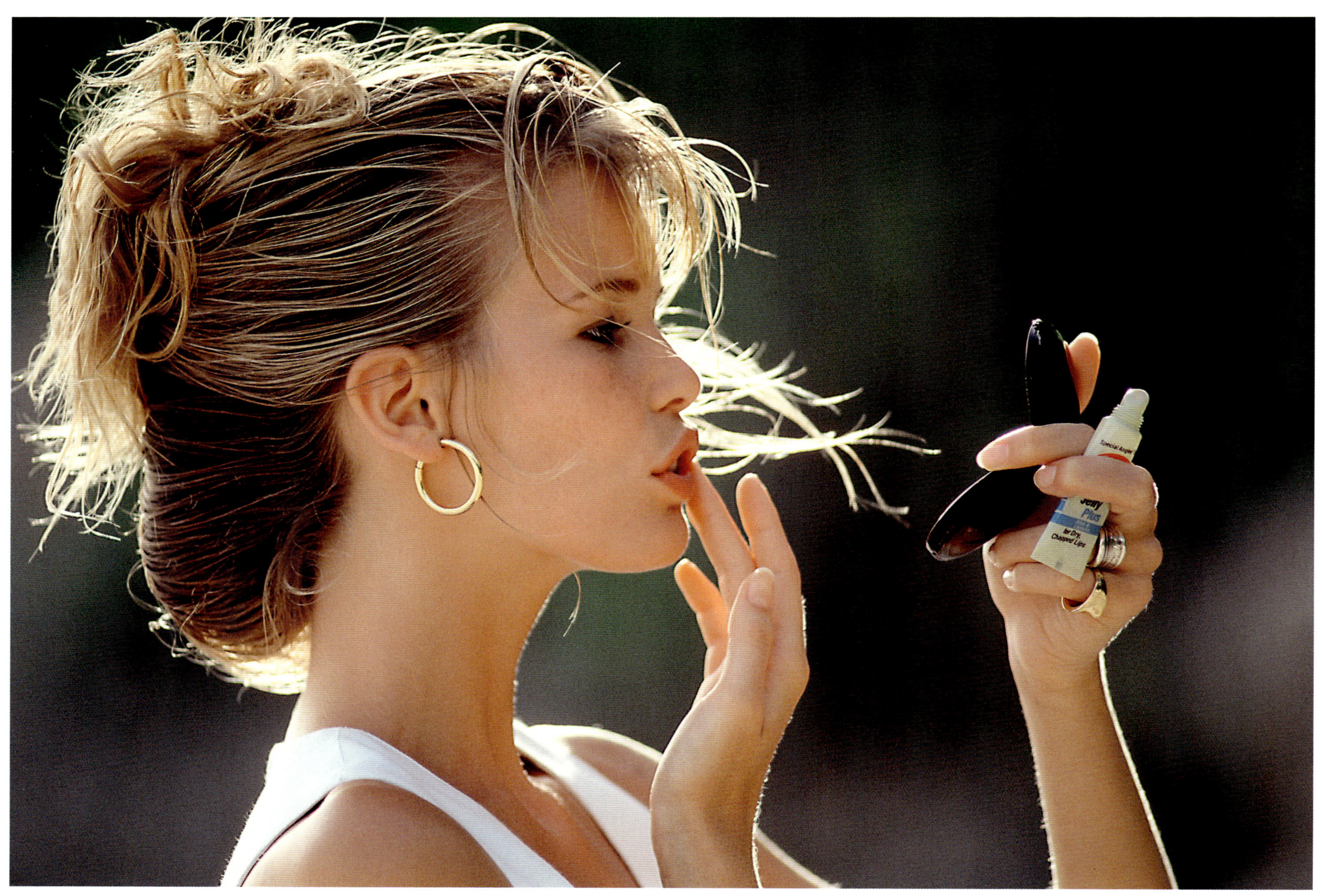

Hans Feurer, model: Claudia Schiffer, 1990 for *ELLE* FR

Swiss photographer Hans Feurer lensed this pretty summer cover for French fashion magazine *ELLE*. Shooting the model in profile and backlit, Feurer ignored conventional cover rules that required eye contact with the reader.

Hans Feurer, Tropical White, model: Christy Turlington, Kenya 1990 for *Vogue* US

140/141
Hans Feurer, model: Yasmeen Ghauri, Panama 1991 for *Vogue* US

142/143
Hans Feurer, model: Claudia Schiffer, Seychelles 1992 for *ELLE* FR

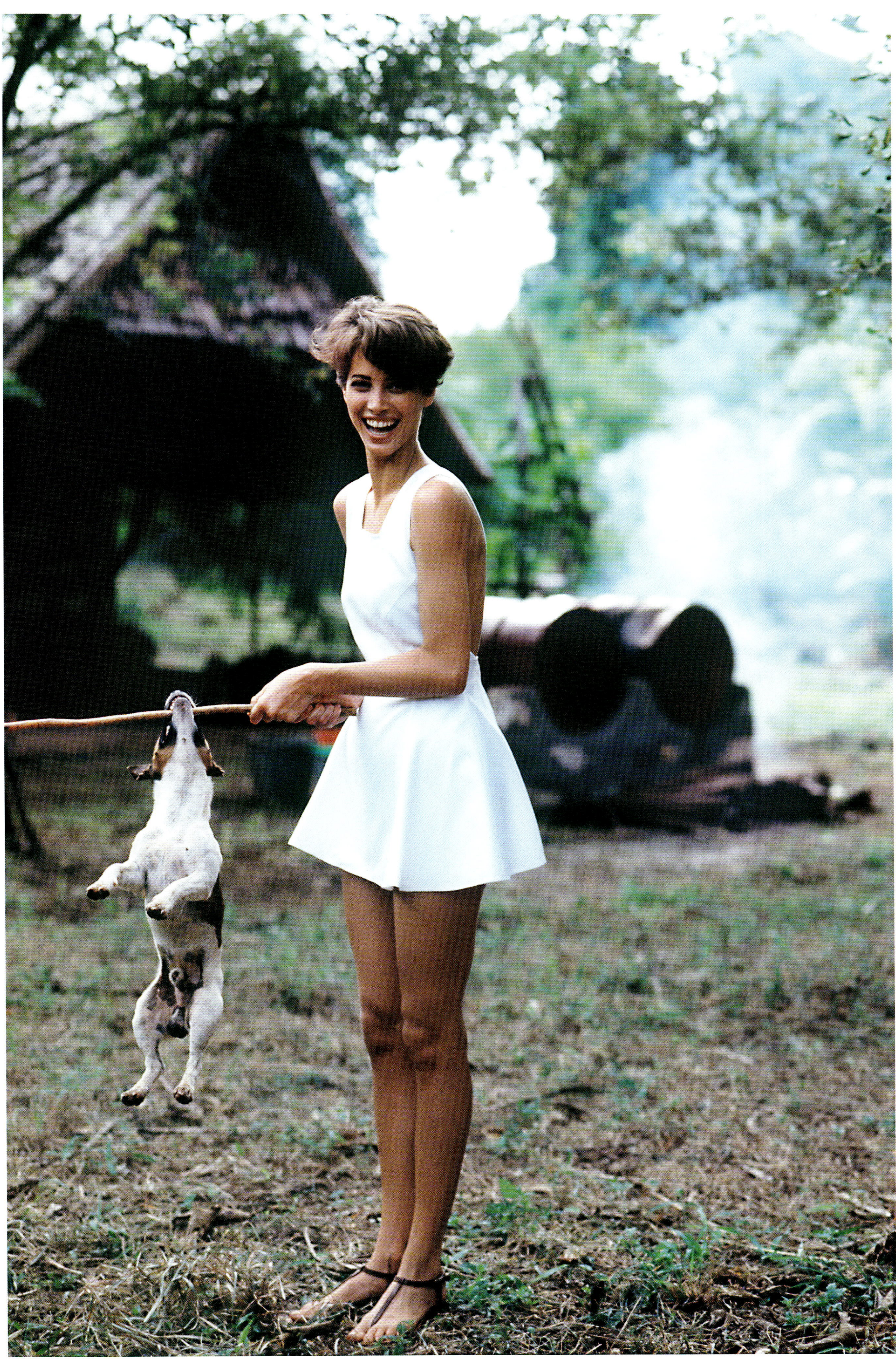

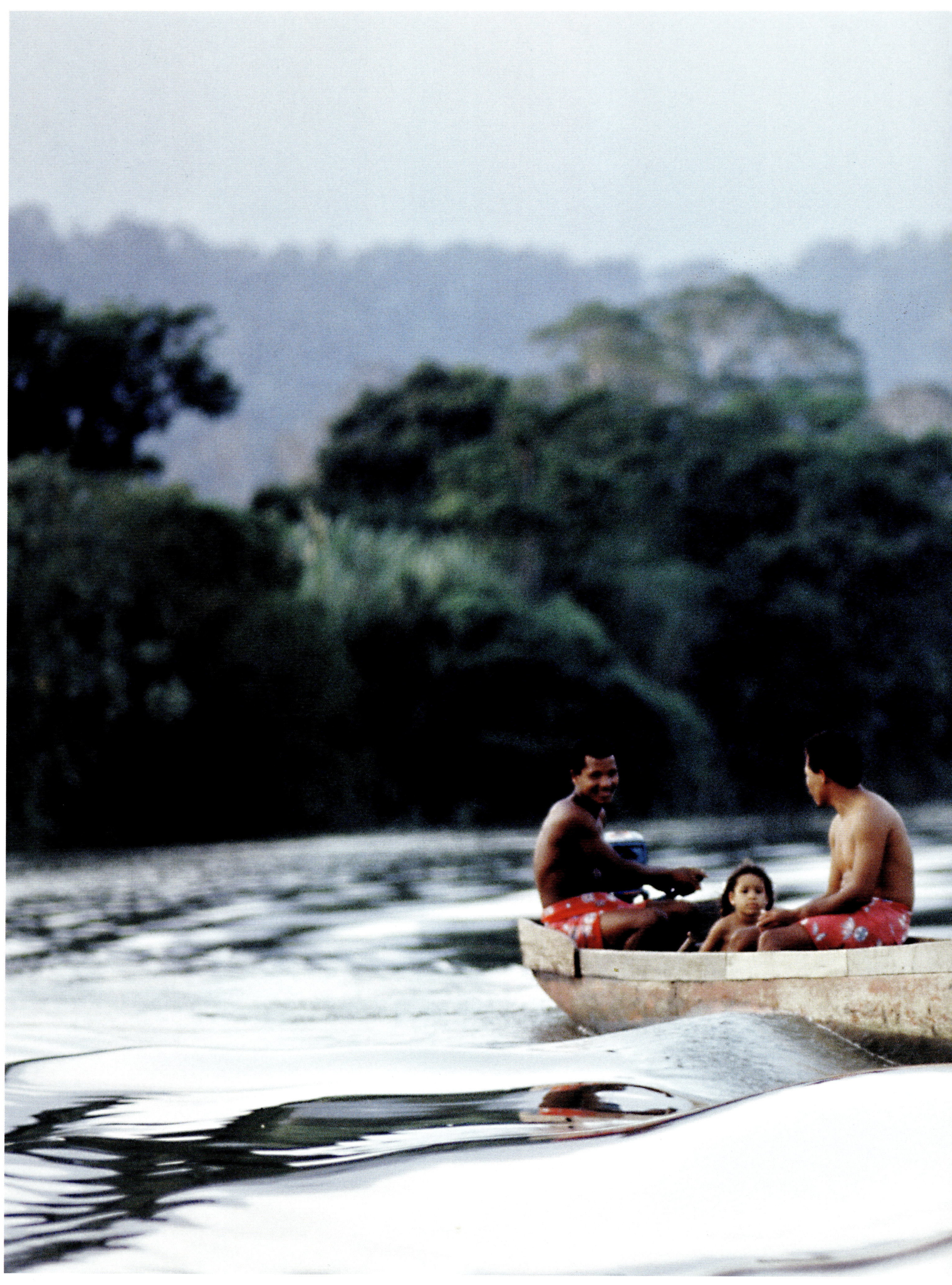

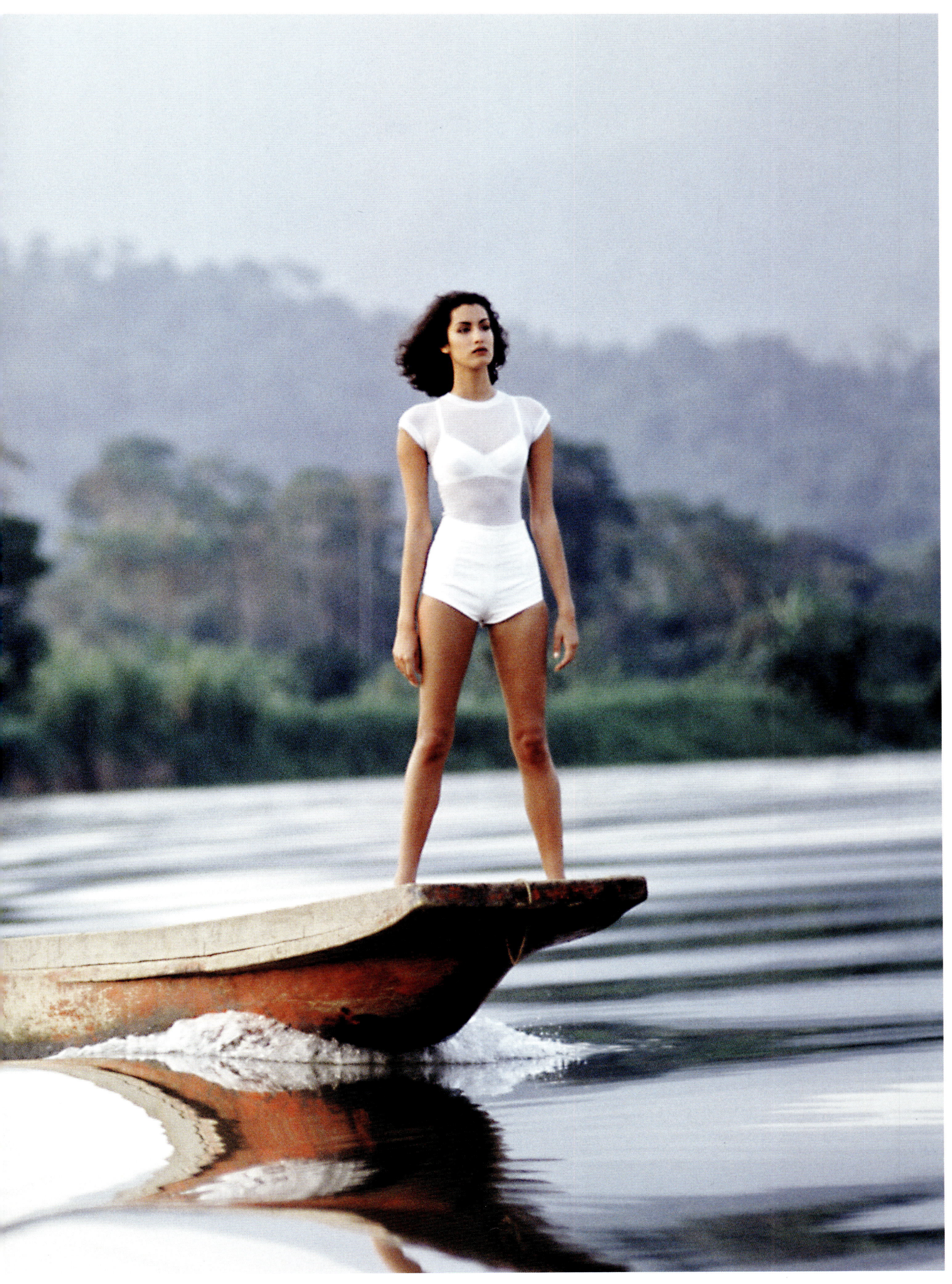

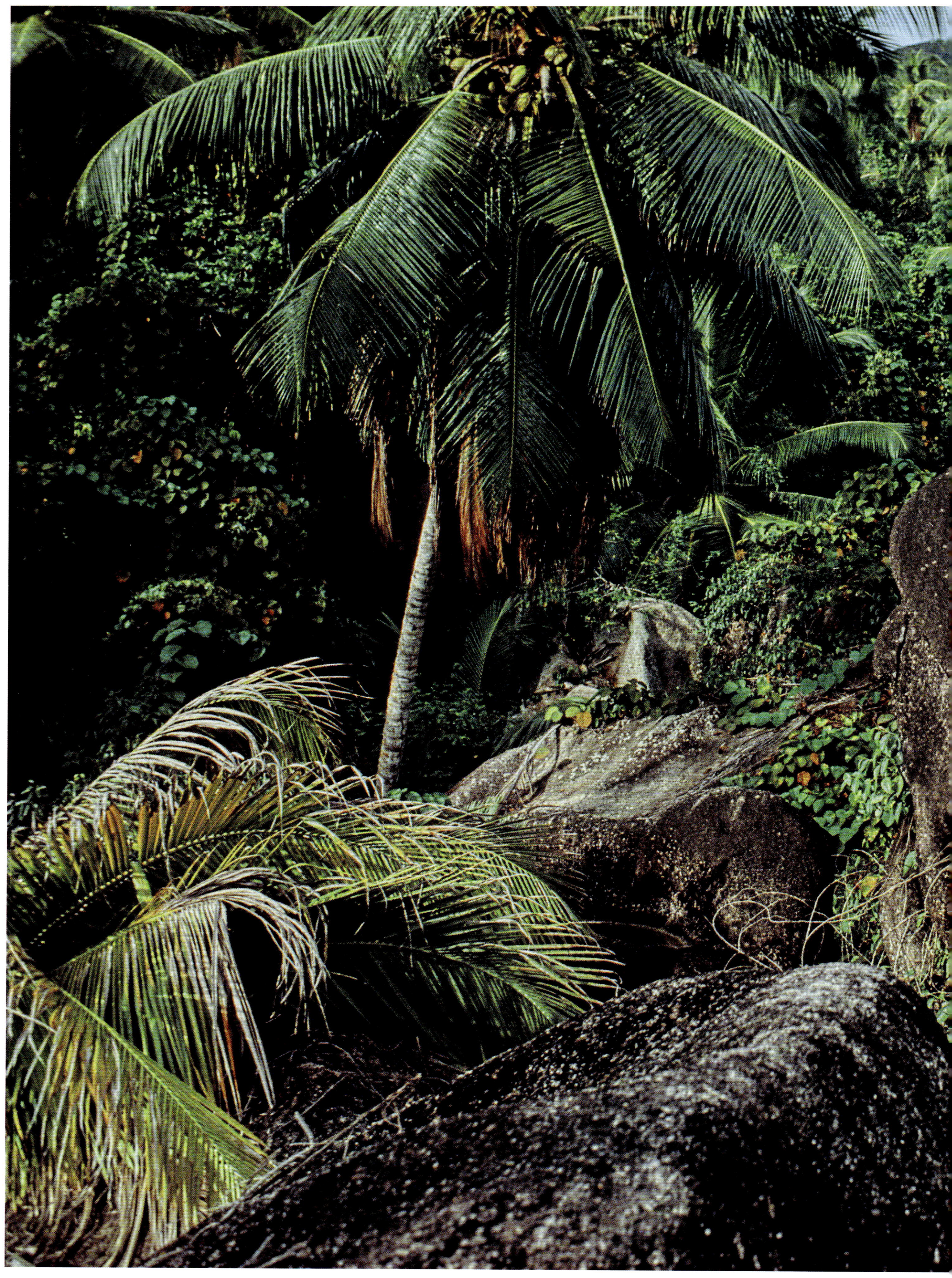

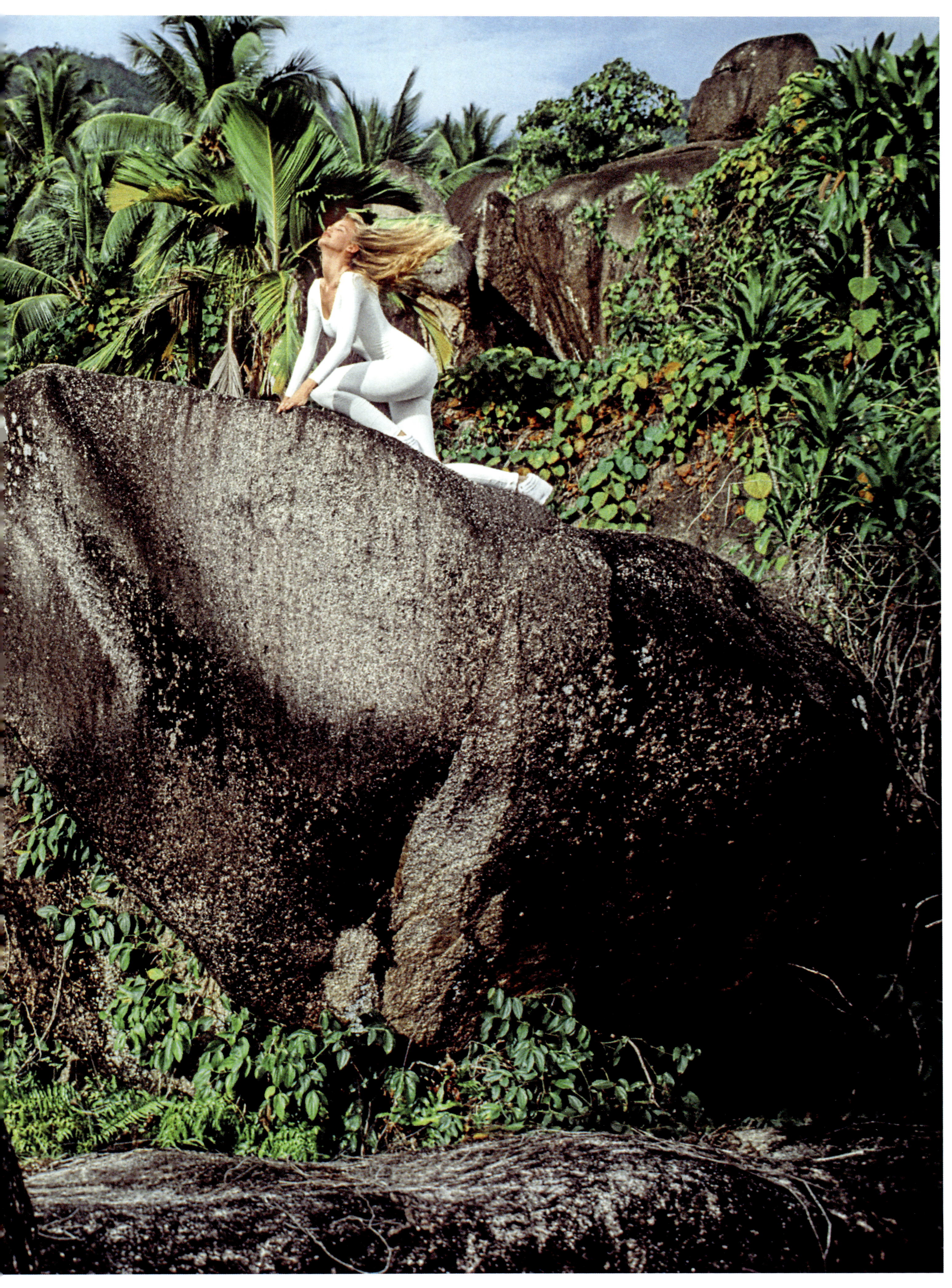

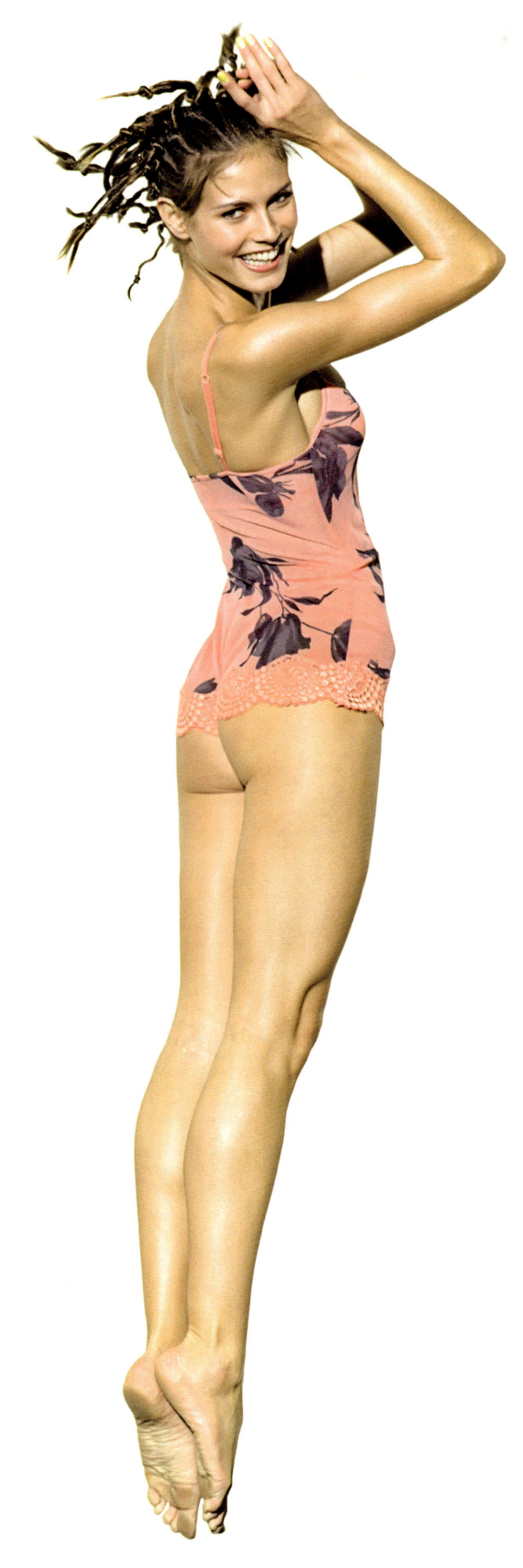

Arthur Elgort, model: Heidi Klum, 1998 for *Vogue* DE

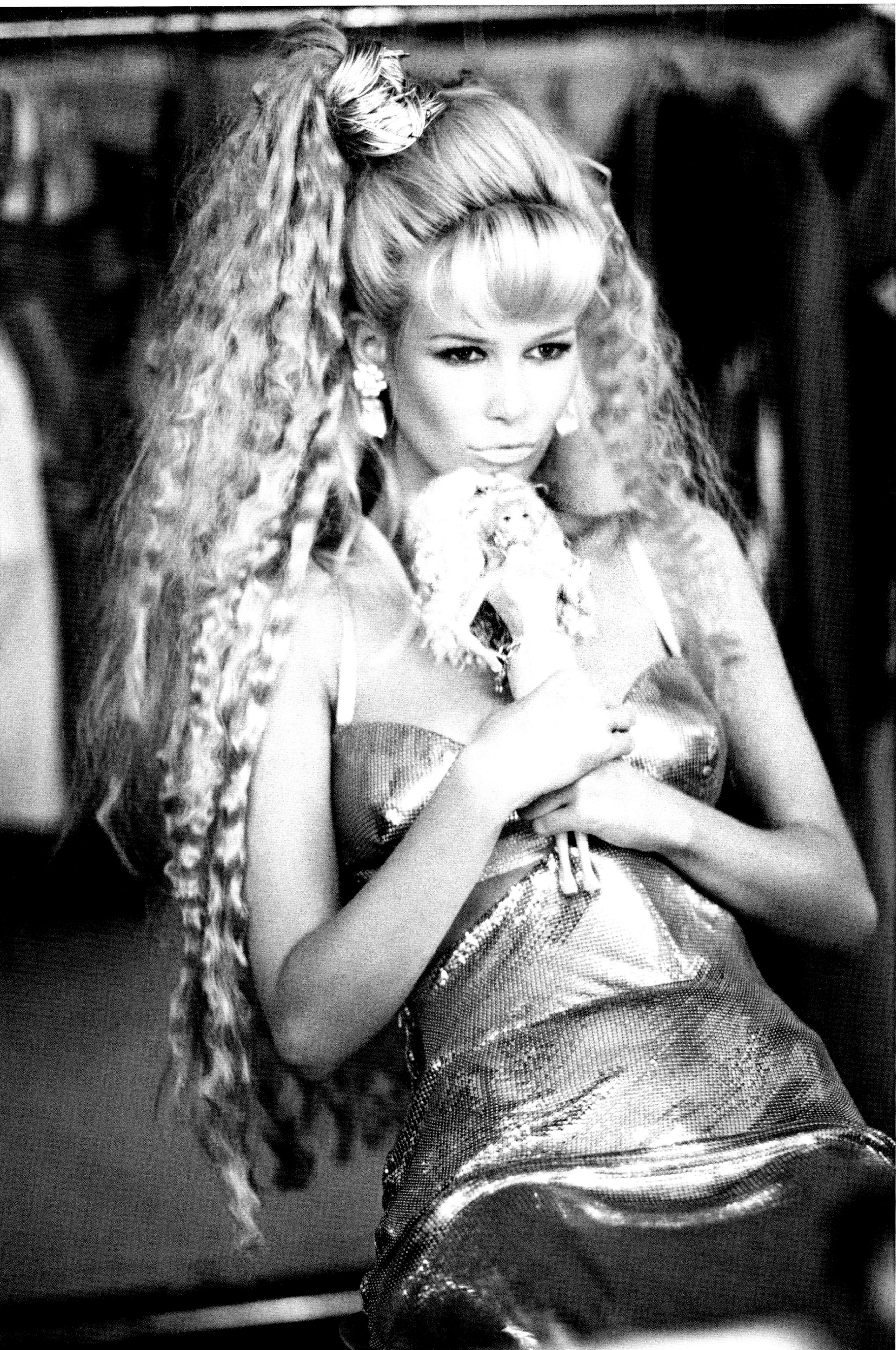

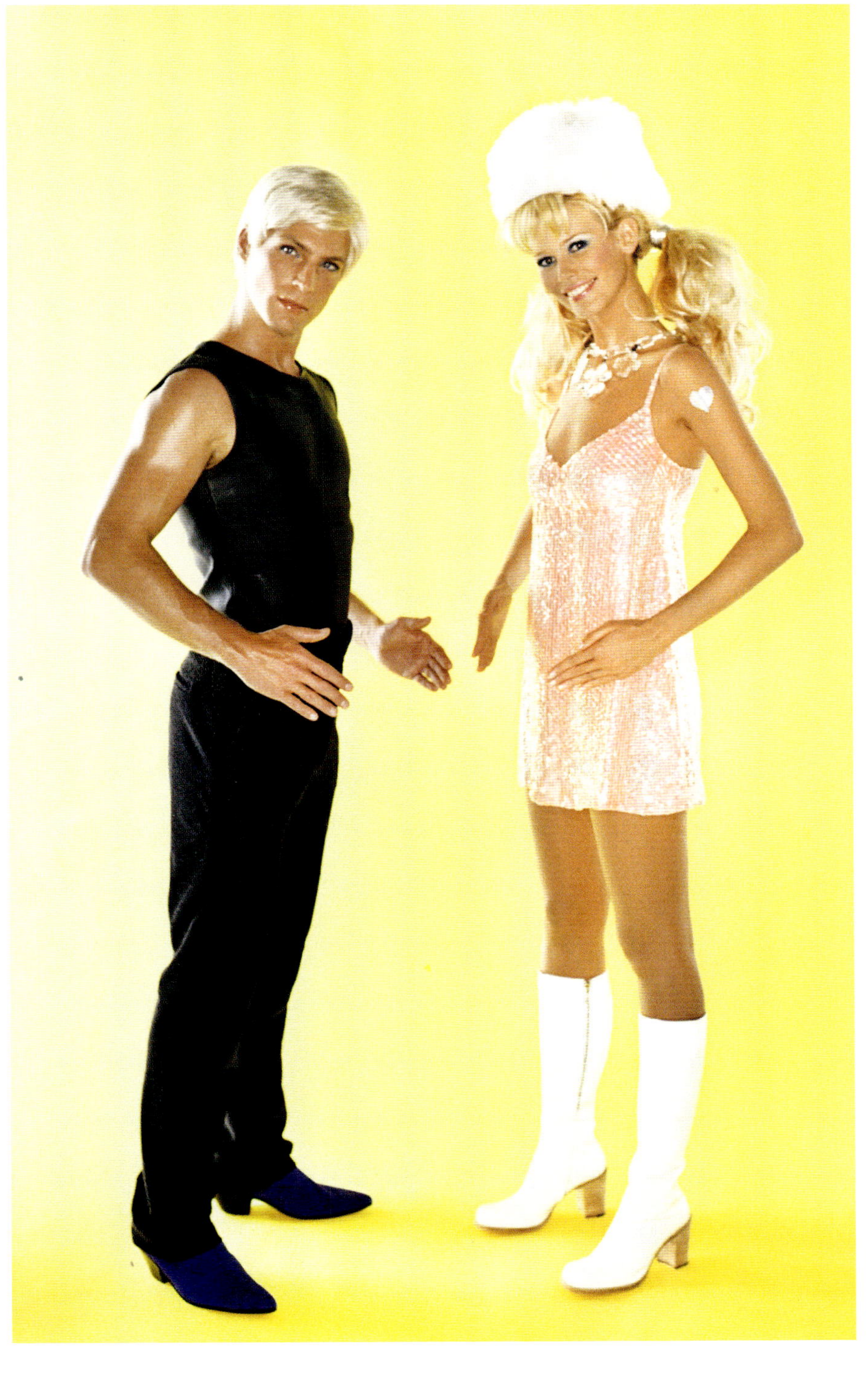

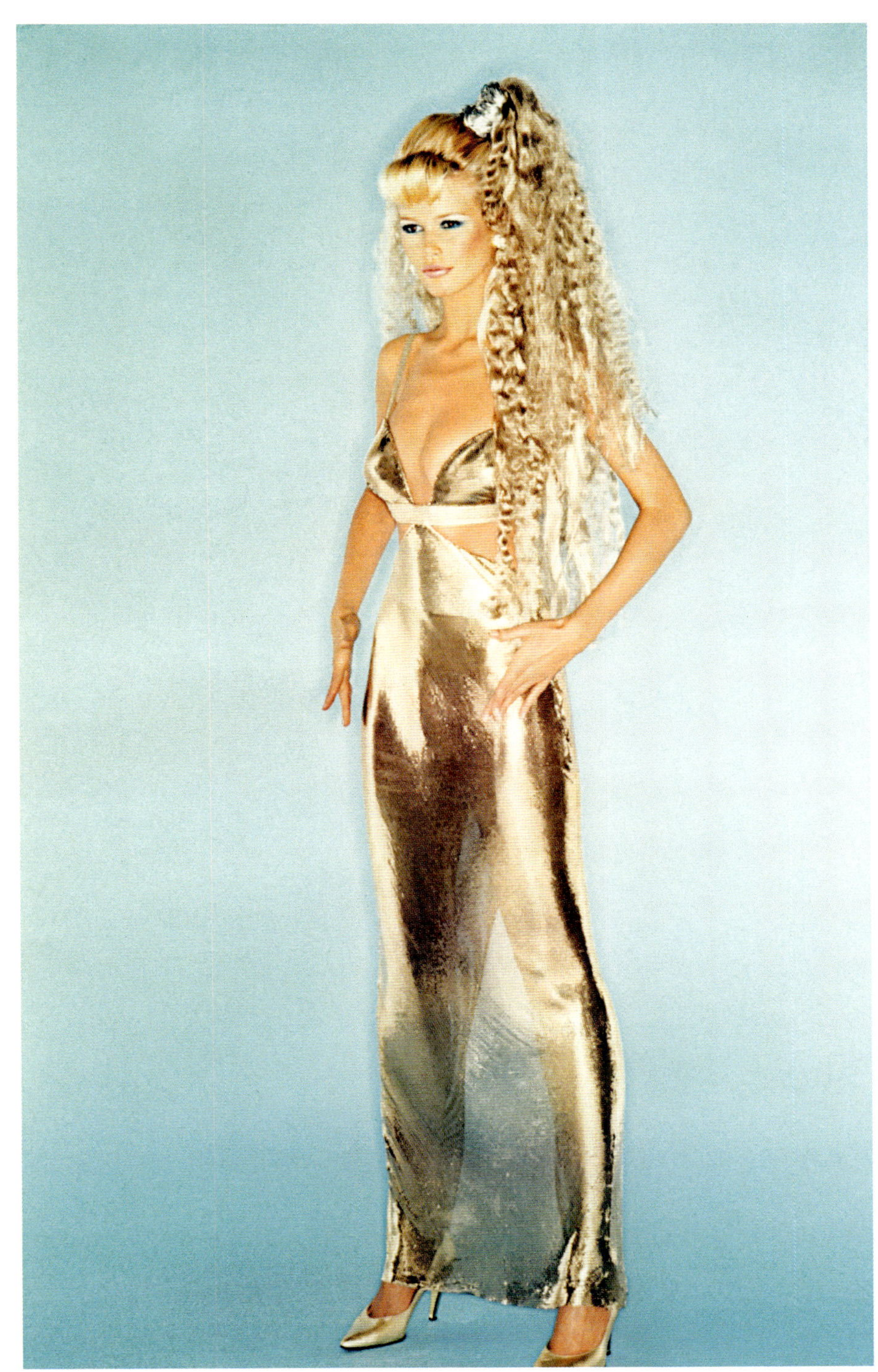

Ellen von Unwerth, The Real Barbie,
model: Claudia Schiffer, Paris 1994 for *Vogue* IT

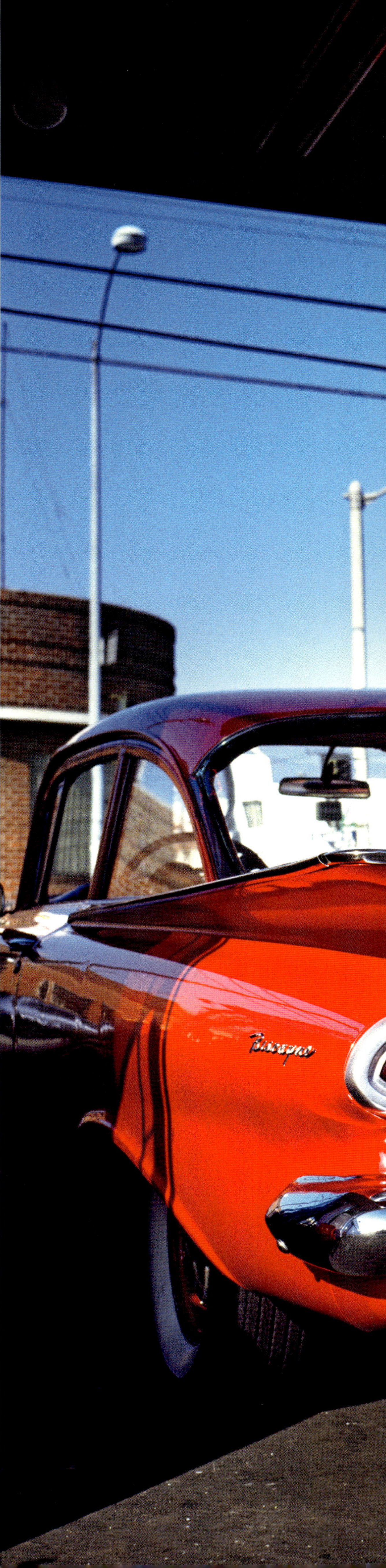

Ellen von Unwerth, model: Claudia Schiffer, Los Angeles 1991 for *Vogue* US

150/151
Peter Lindbergh, Wild at Heart, models: Helena Christensen, Stephanie Seymour, Karen Mulder, Naomi Campbell, Claudia Schiffer, Cindy Crawford, New York 1991 for *Vogue* US

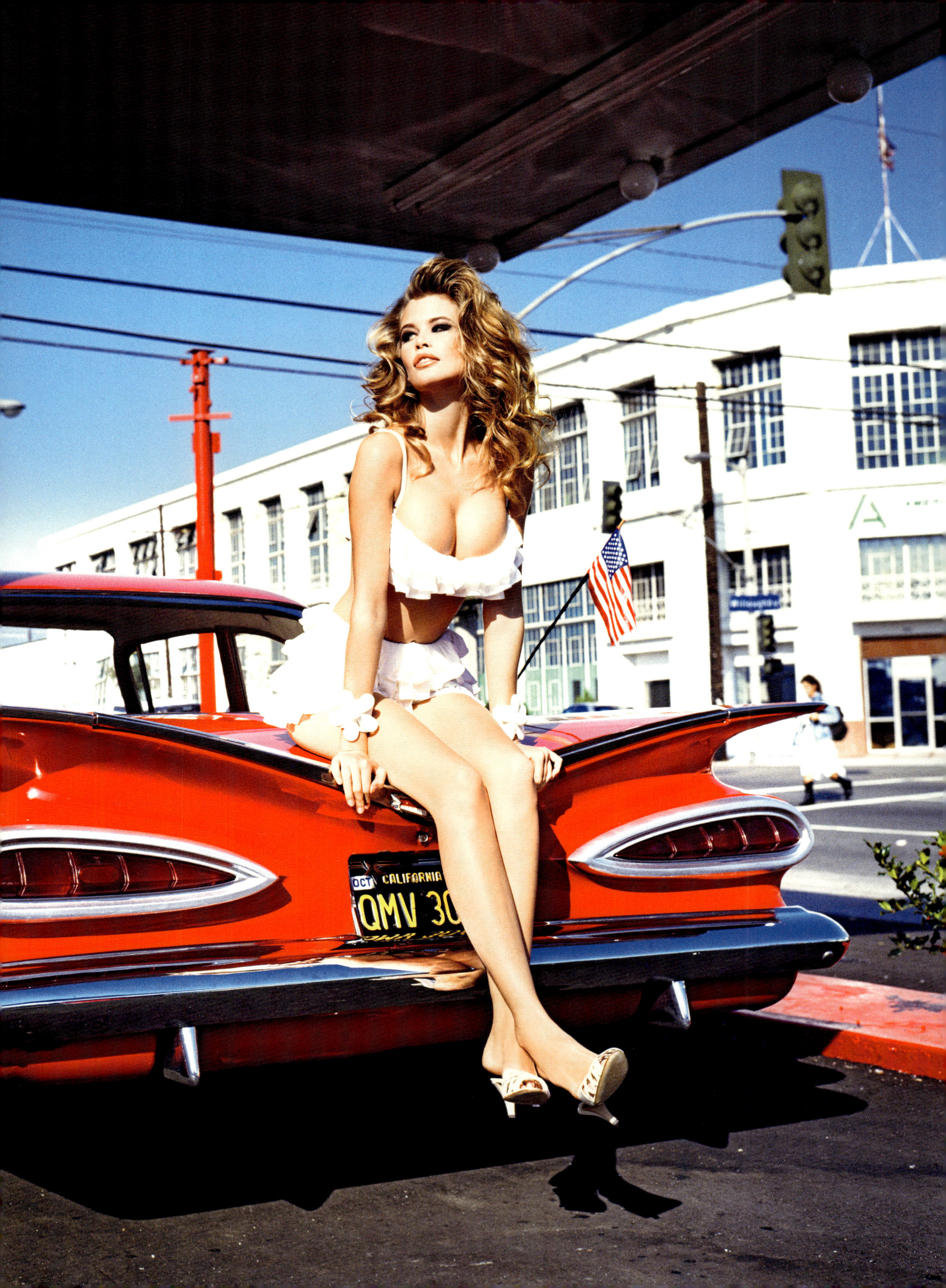
OCT
CALIFORNIA
QMV 30

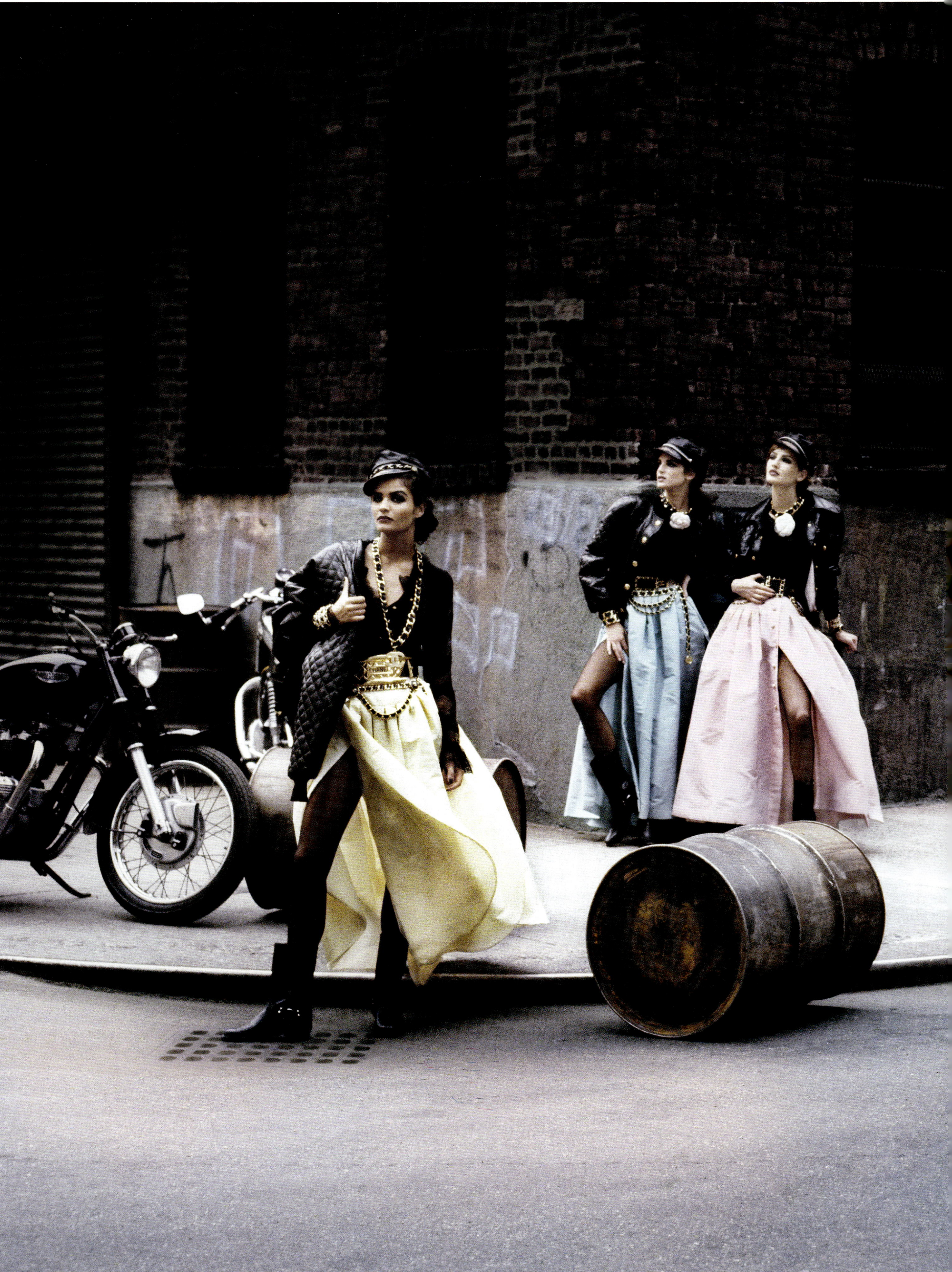

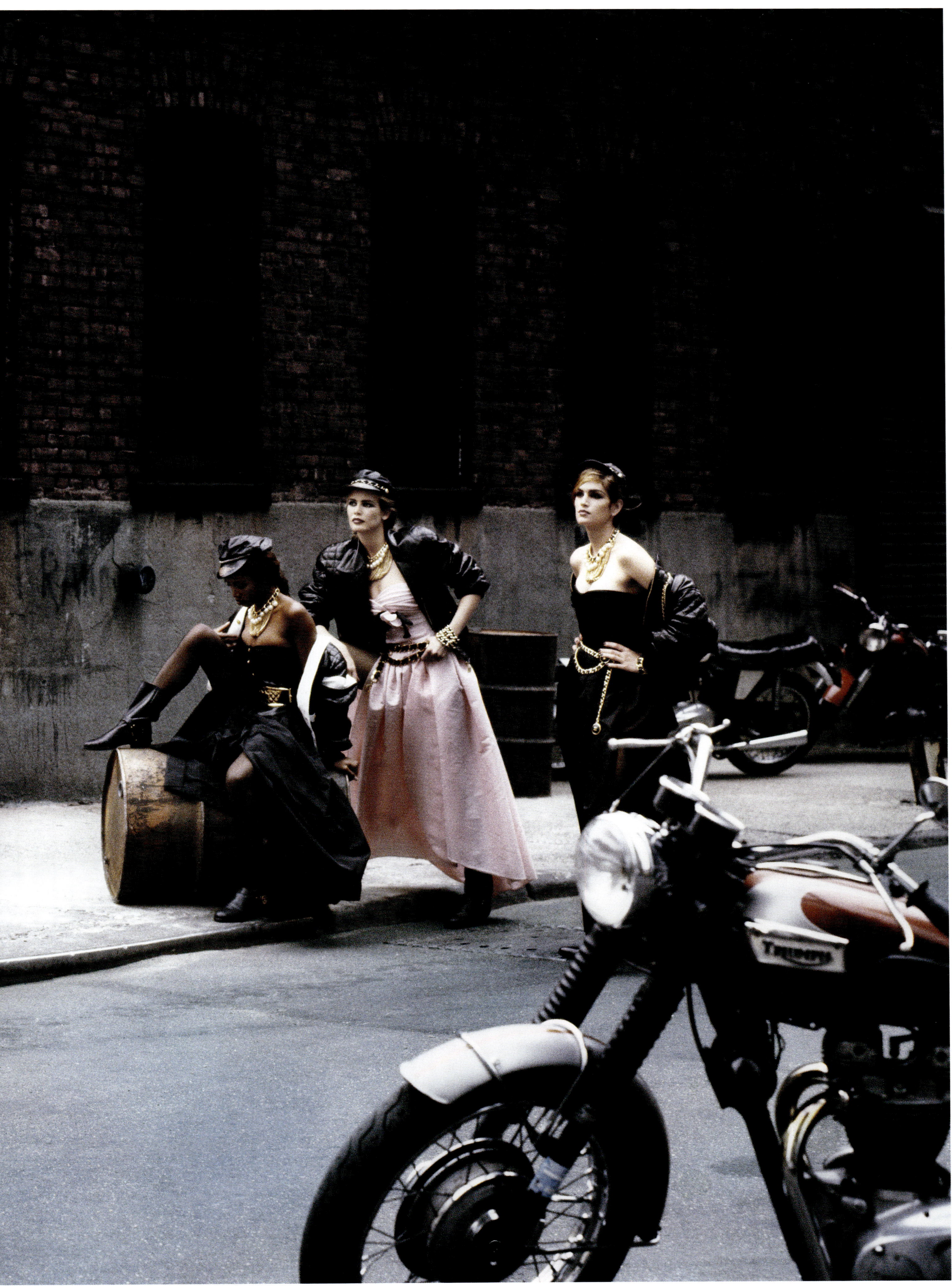

Arthur Elgort, models: Beverly Peele,
Tyra Banks, 1993 for *Vogue* UK

154/155
Ellen von Unwerth, models: Eva Herzigová,
Karen Mulder, Paris 1992 for *Vogue* IT

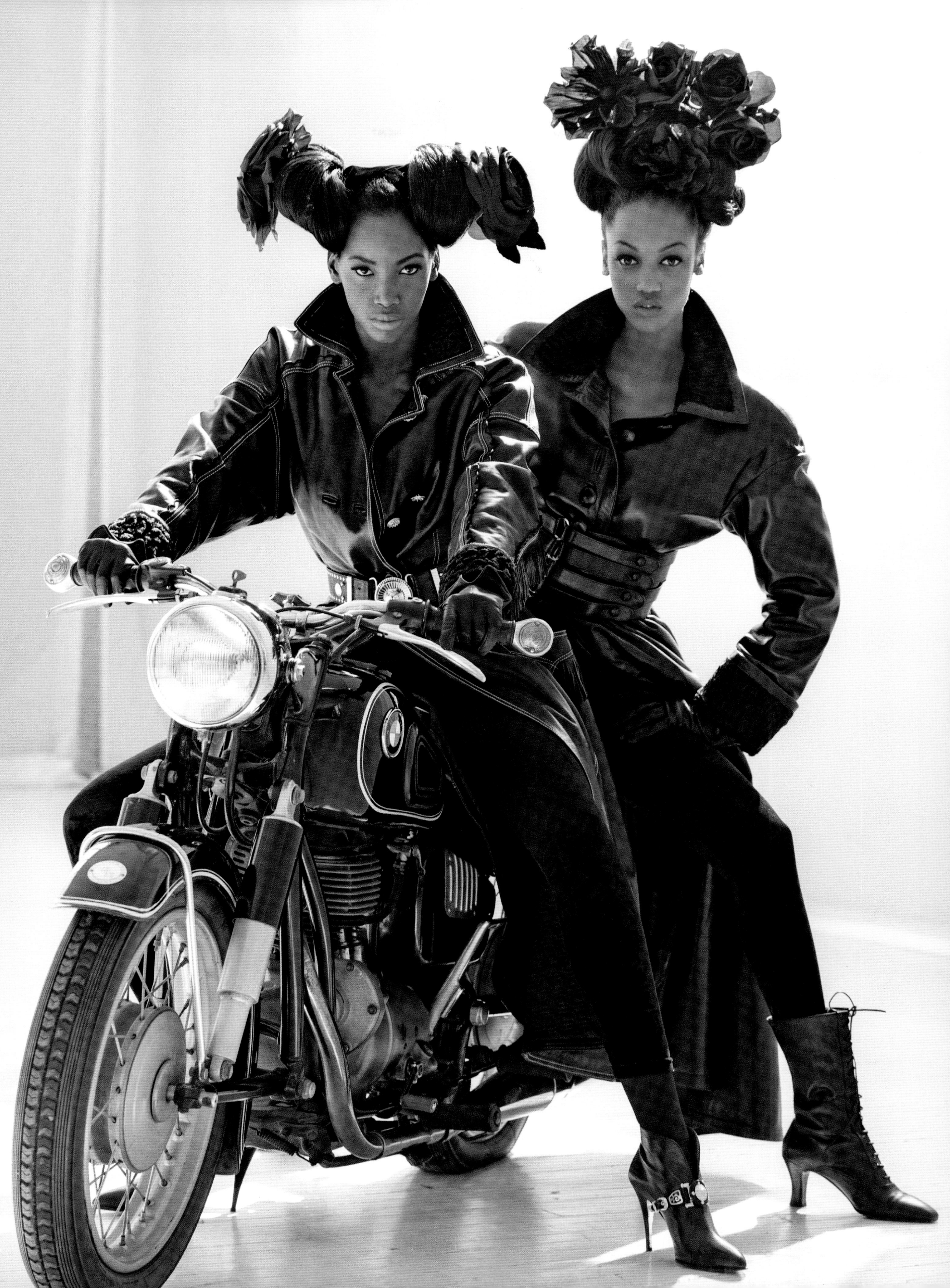

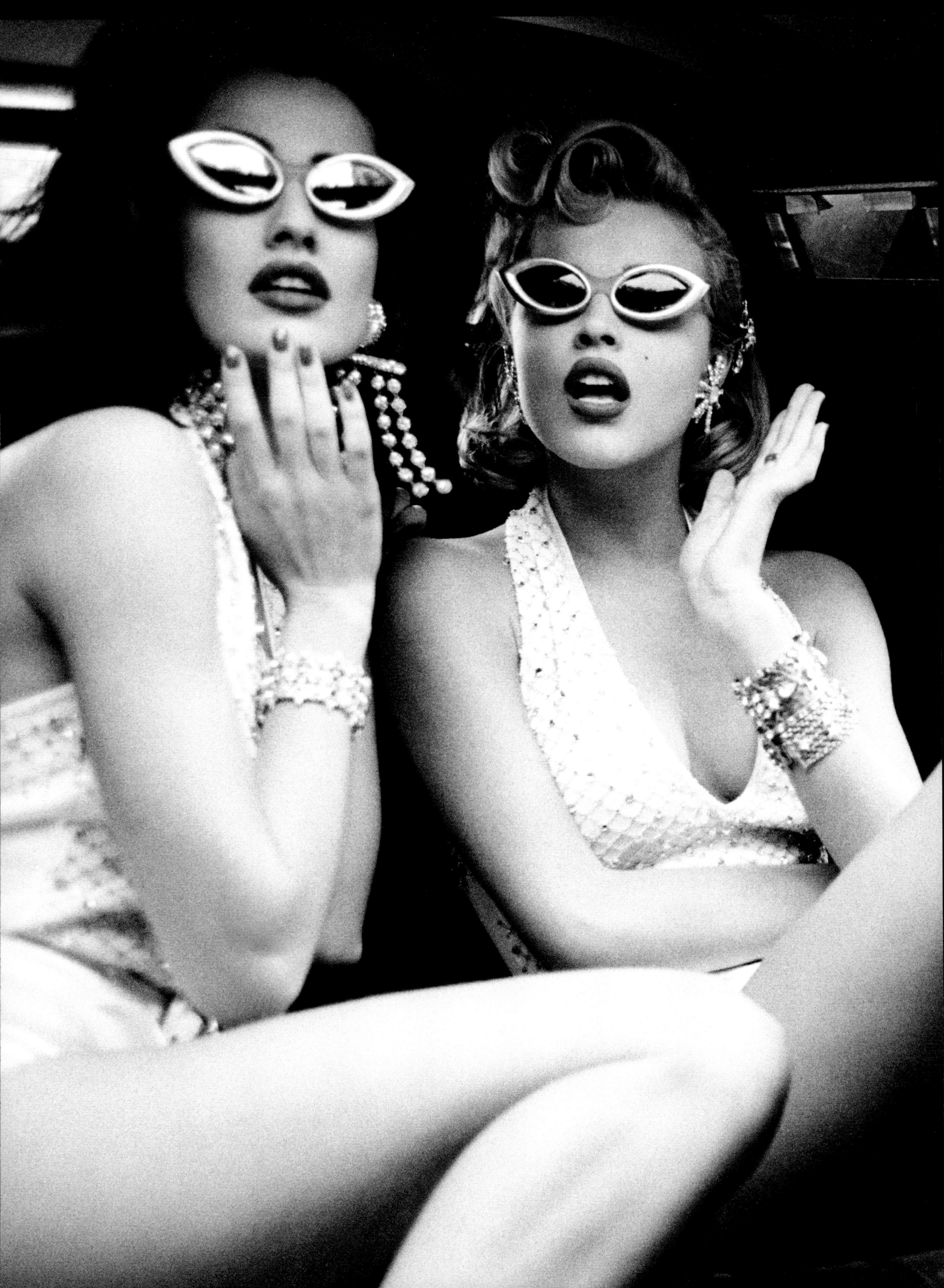

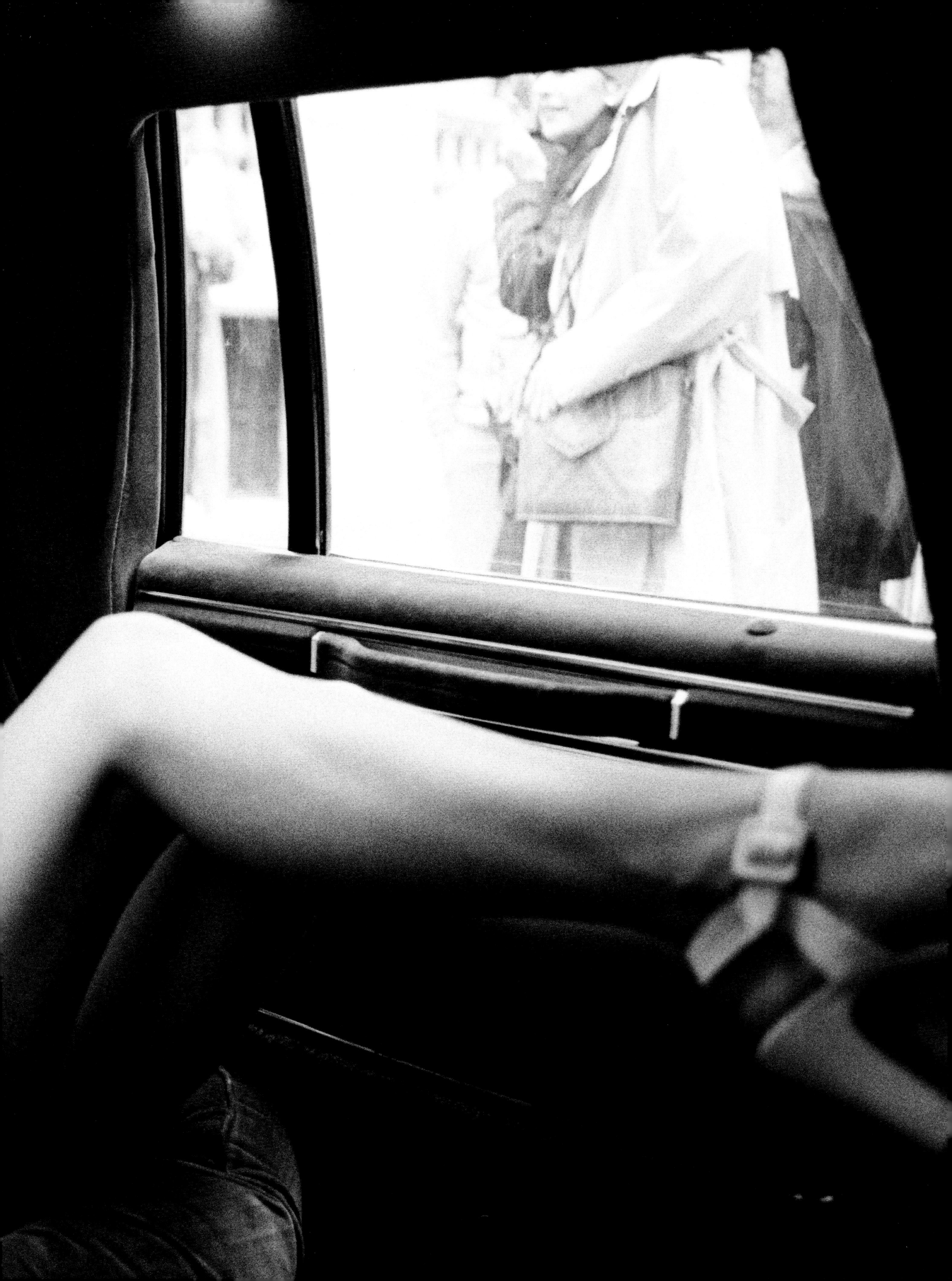

I loved how shooting analogue made the stories seem more documentary / reportage style. They were more like travel diaries than polished fashion shoots.

HELENA CHRISTENSEN

Peter Lindbergh, E.T. Story, model: Helena Christensen, El Mirage, California 1990 for *Vogue* IT

158 / 159
Arthur Elgort, models: Alek Wek, Kirsten Owen, Esther de Jong, Tanga Moreau, 1997 for *Vogue* US

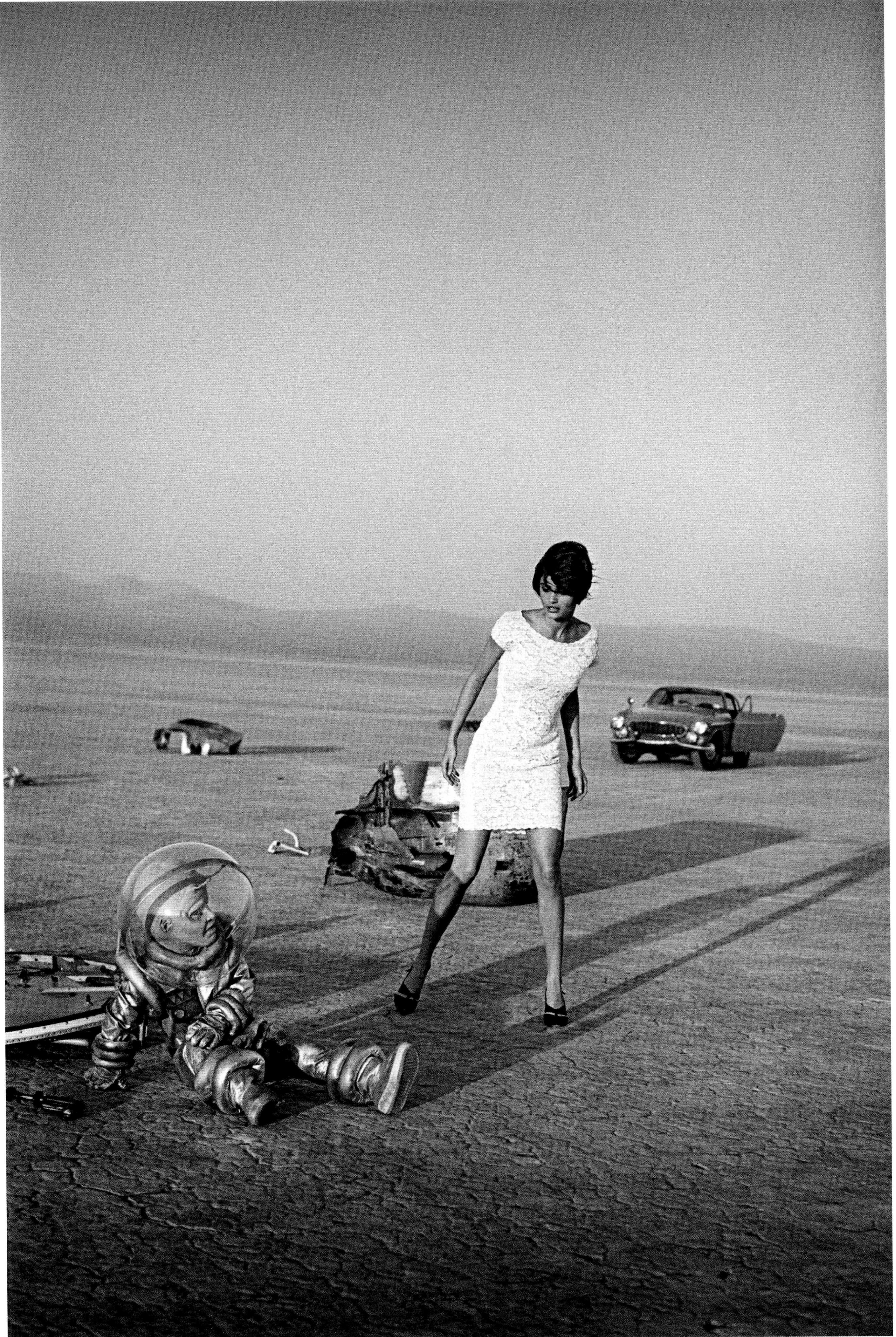

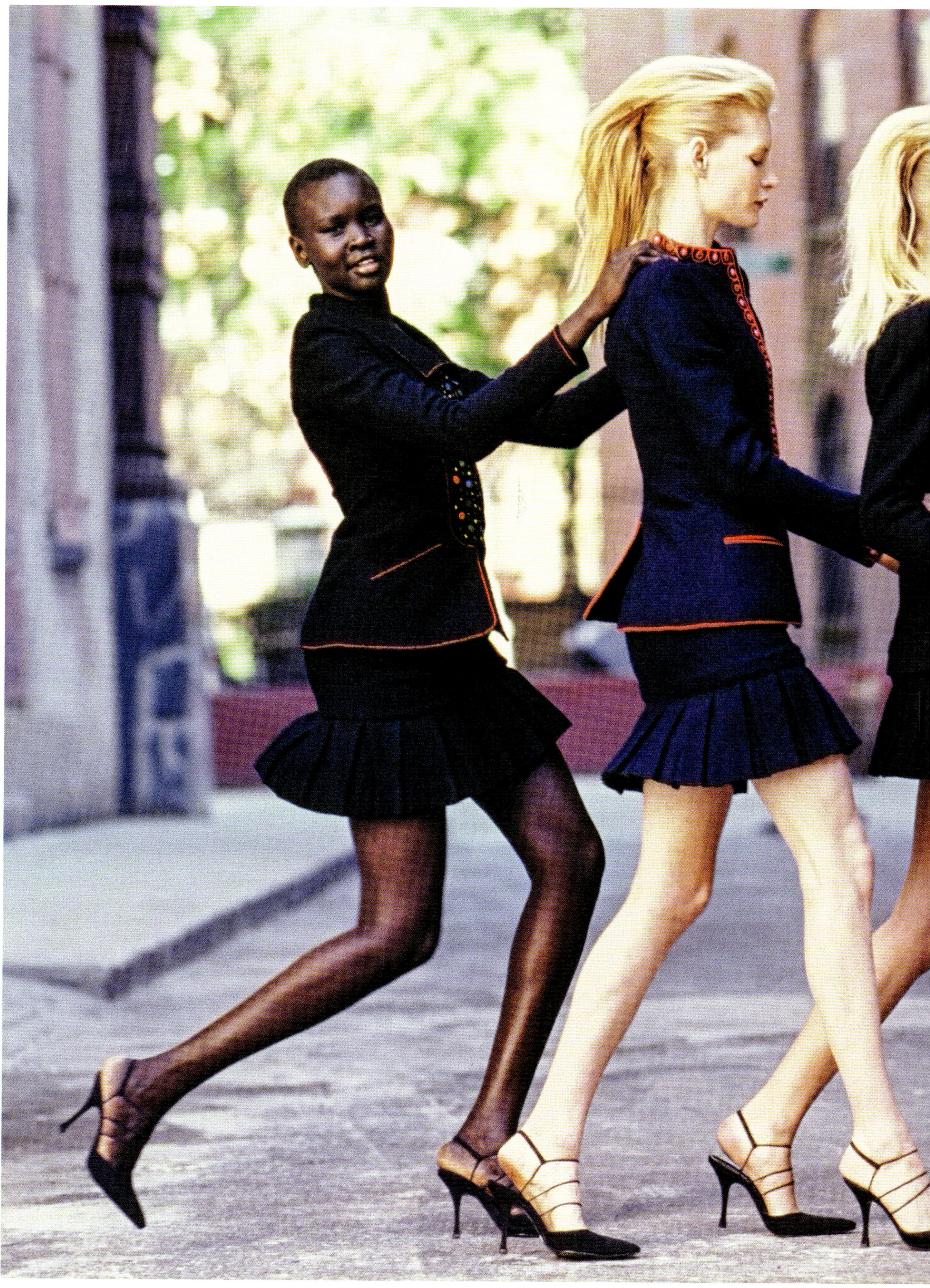

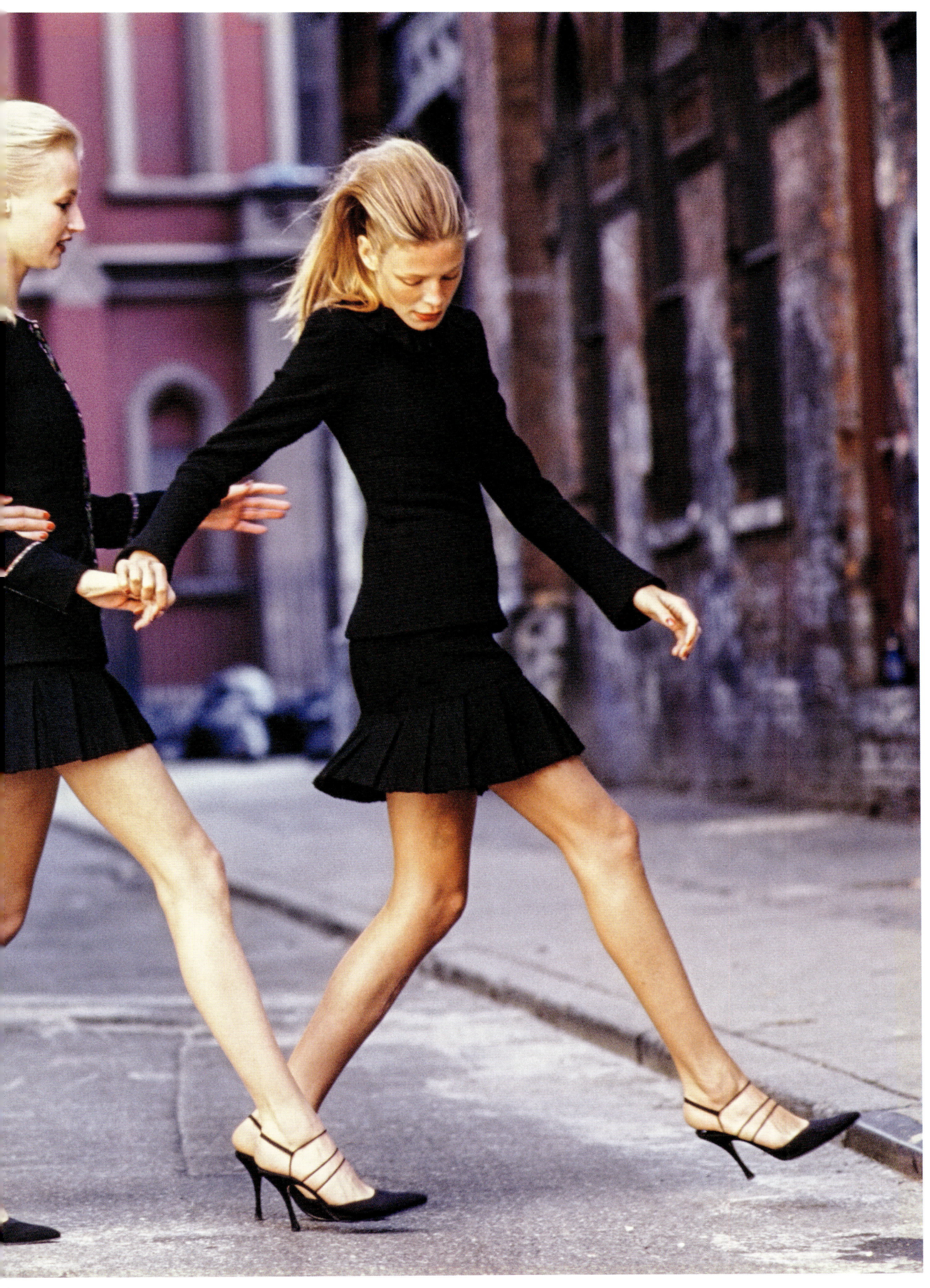

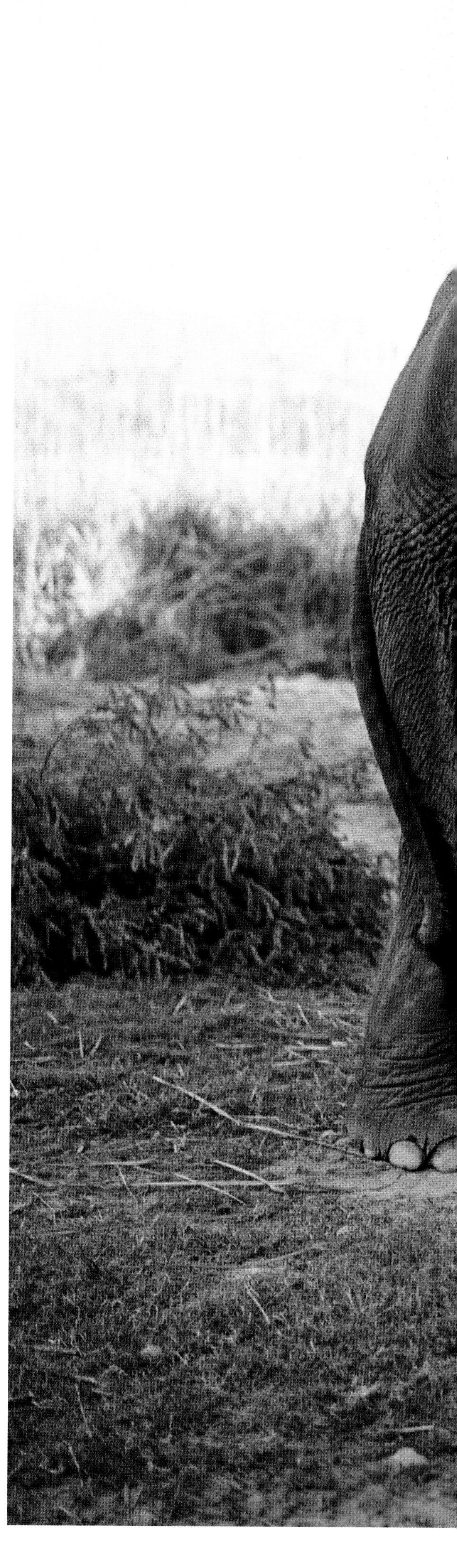

Arthur Elgort, model: Kate Moss,
1994 for *Vogue* UK

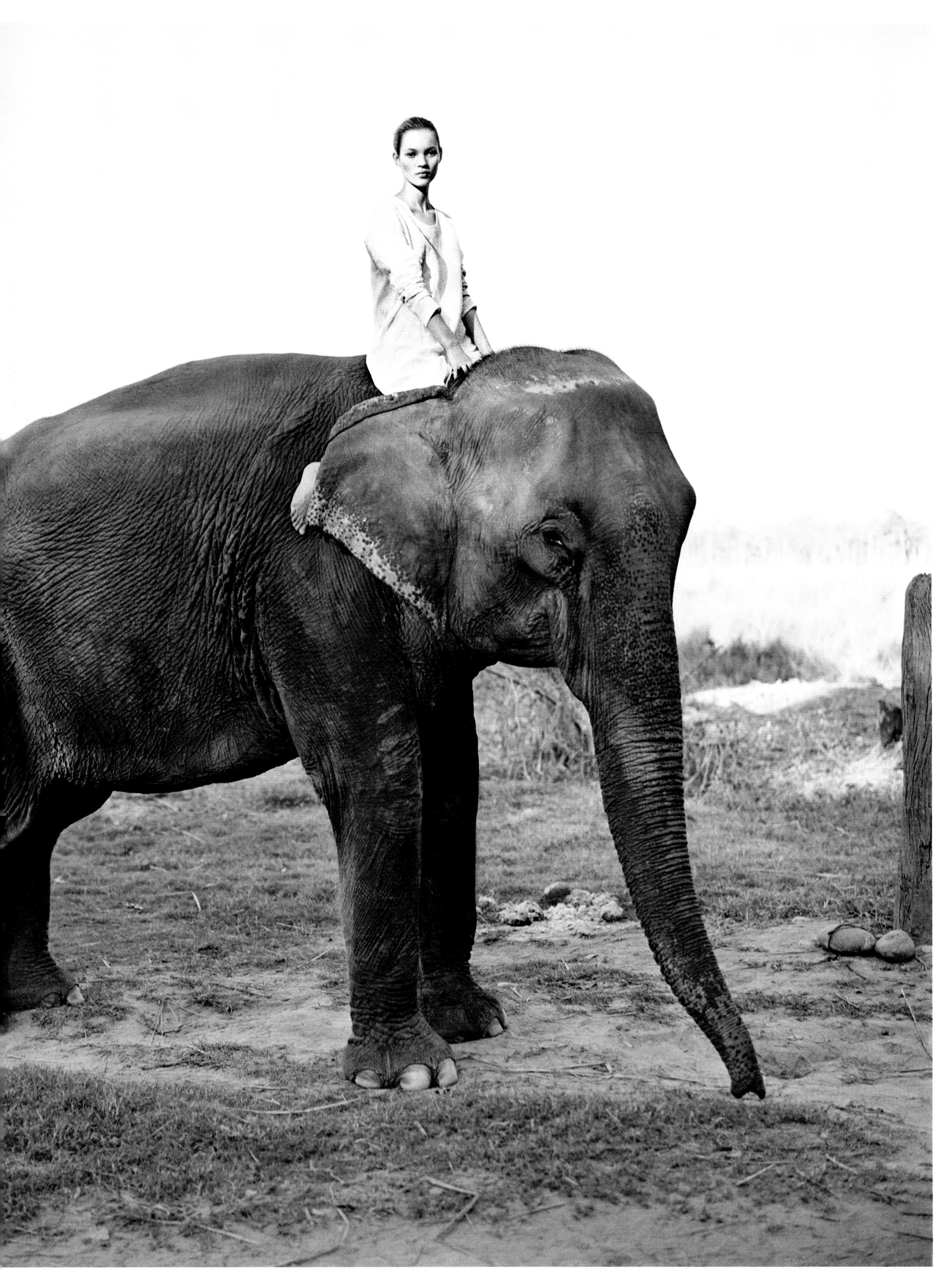

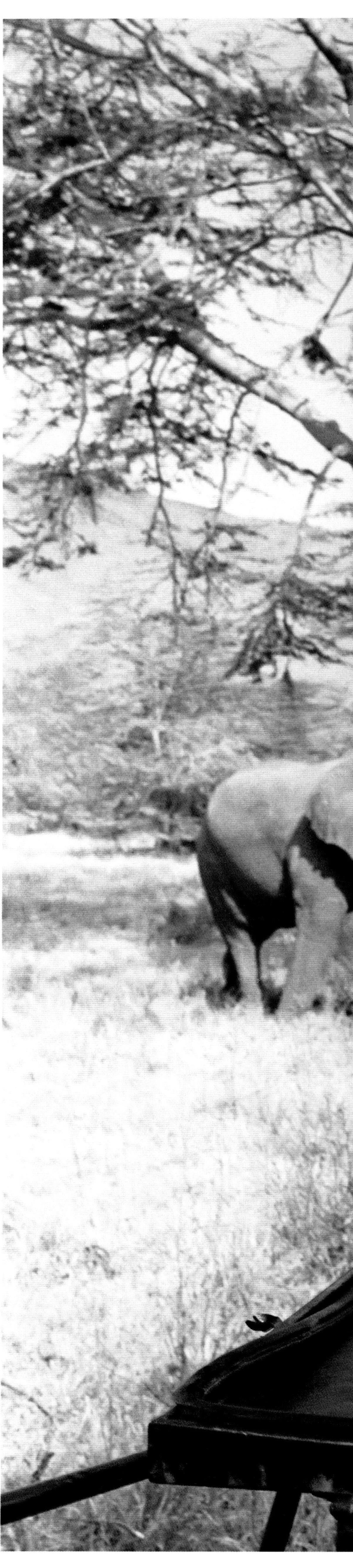

Arthur Elgort, model: Christy Turlington, 1991 for *Vogue* UK

The 1990s were a time of great creativity; shoots took place in closed studios but also in the great outdoors, underlining the new sense of freedom and natural beauty. The productions happened in breathtaking locations all over the world and often lasted for several days, allowing narratives to unfold. That sense of adventure is captured in Arthur Elgort's image of Christy Turlington in Tanzania, for British *Vogue*.

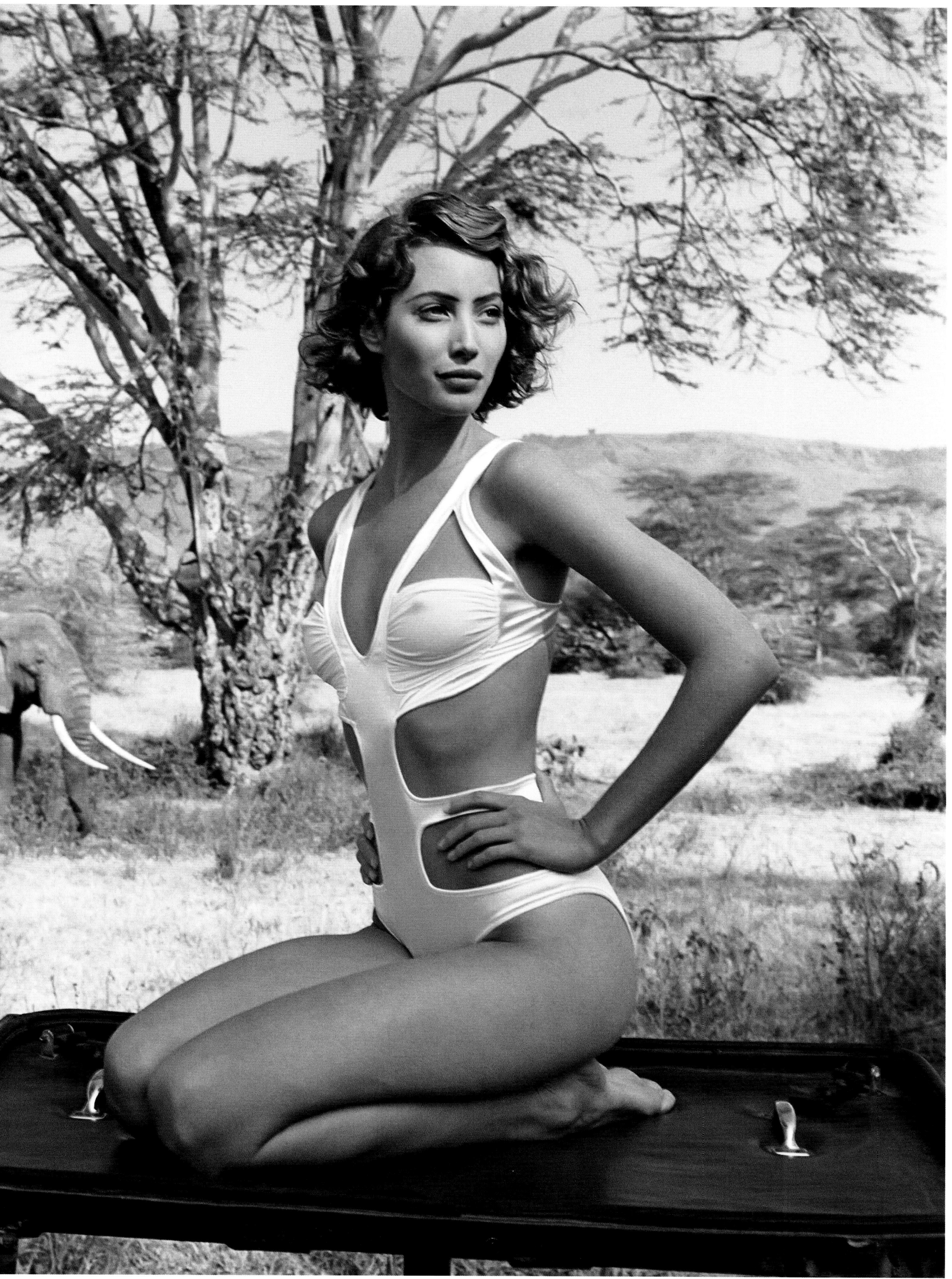

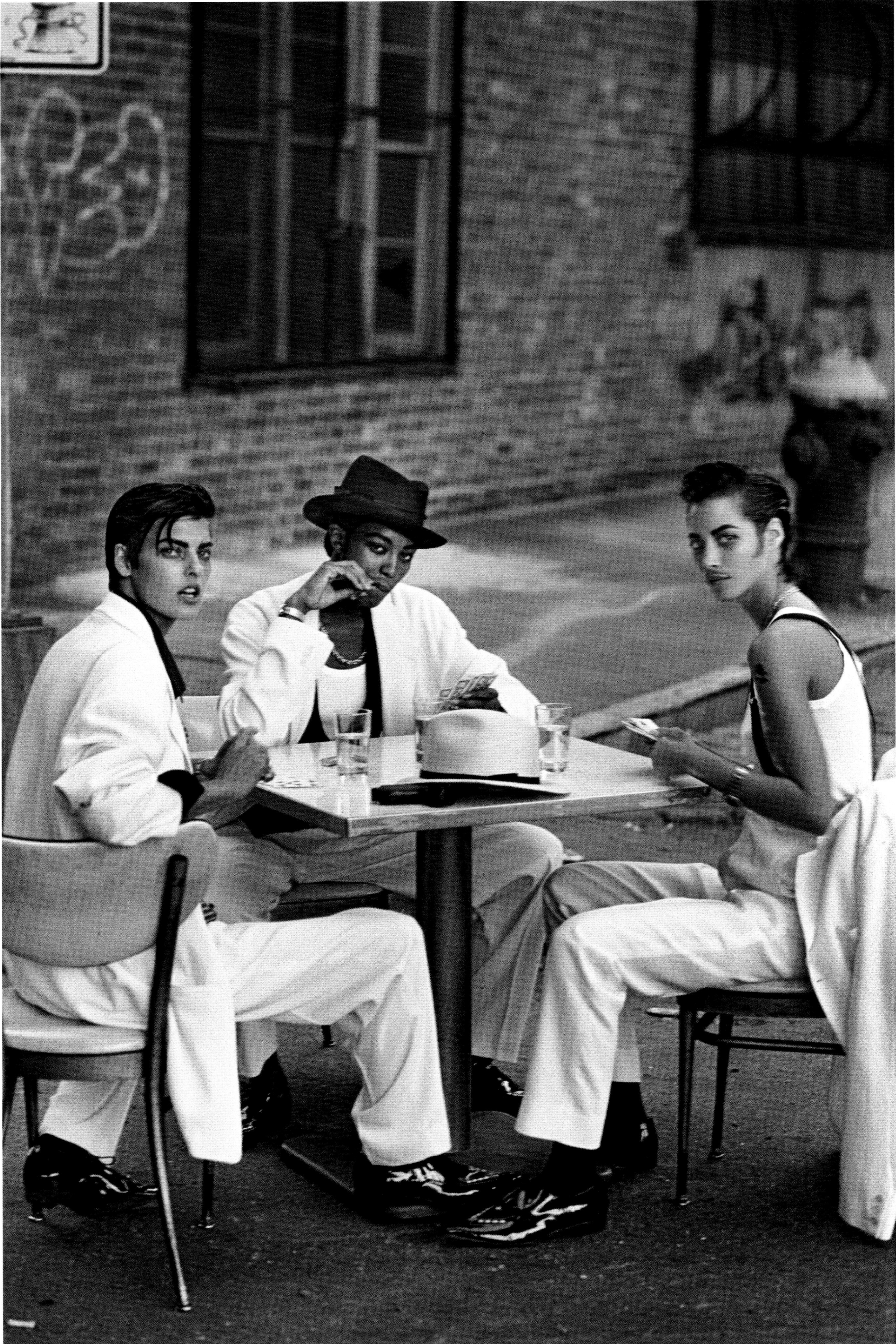

Peter Lindbergh, Gangsters, models: Linda Evangelista, Naomi Campbell, Christy Turlington, 1991 for *Vogue* IT

Arthur Elgort, model: Kate Moss,
1992 for *Vogue* IT

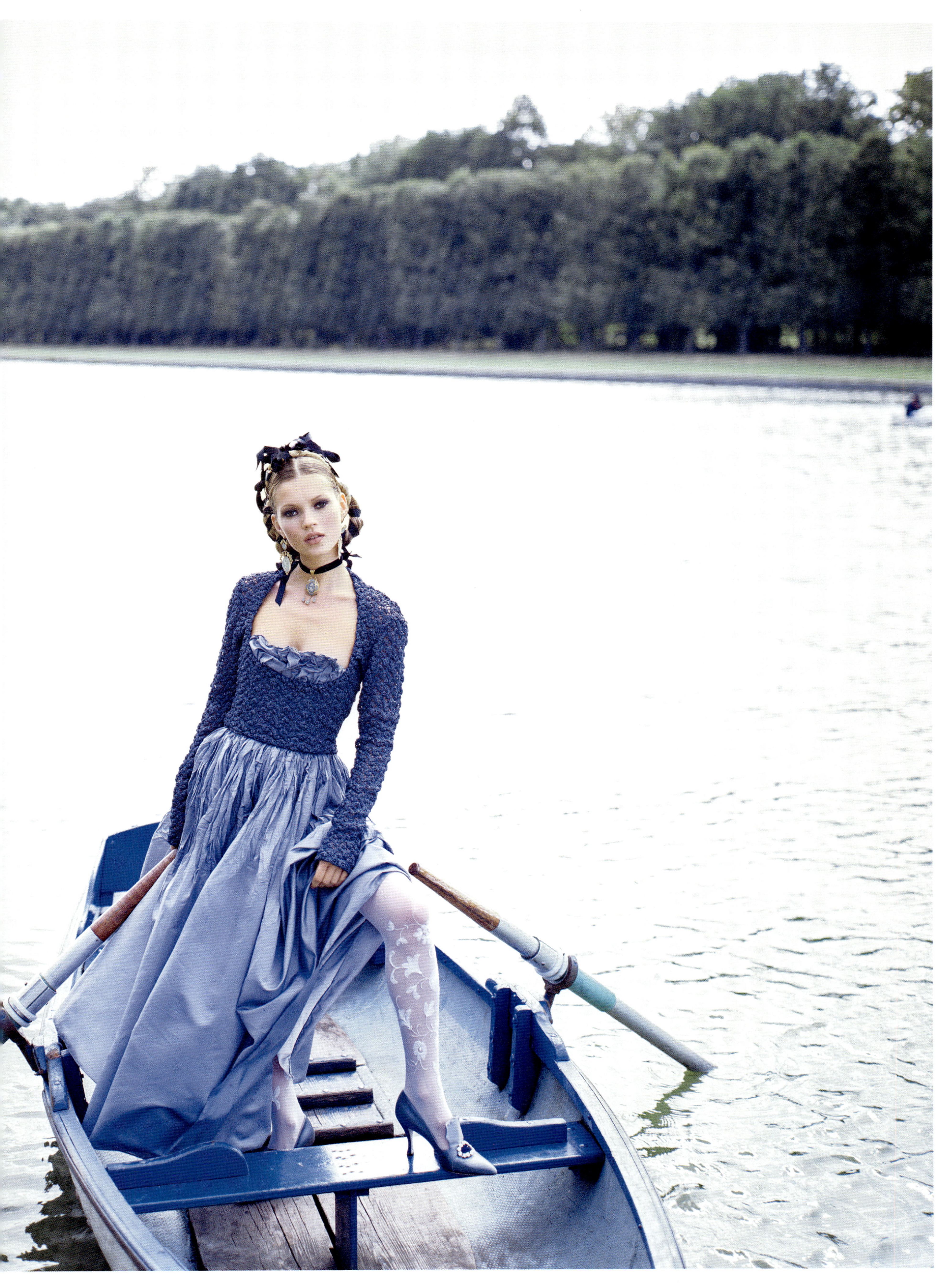

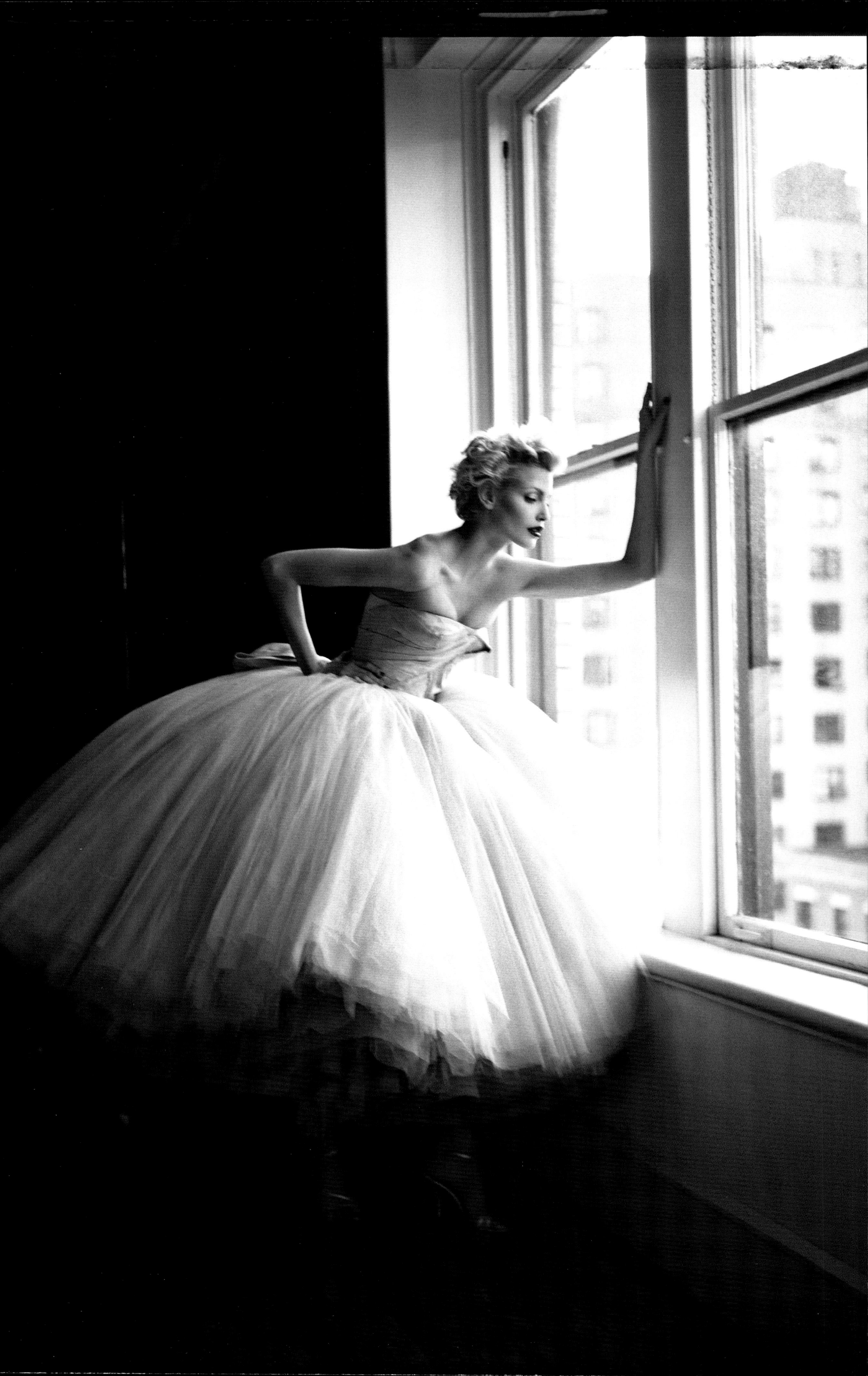

Patrick Demarchelier, model: Nadja Auermann, New York 1995, for *Harper's Bazaar*

There's a refined elegance to this work. This is fashion as art: beautiful, polished and extremely glamorous. Patrick's composition was inspired by Norman Parkinson, the celebrated British portrait and fashion photographer from the 1950s.

I like form and shape and strength in pictures.

HERB RITTS

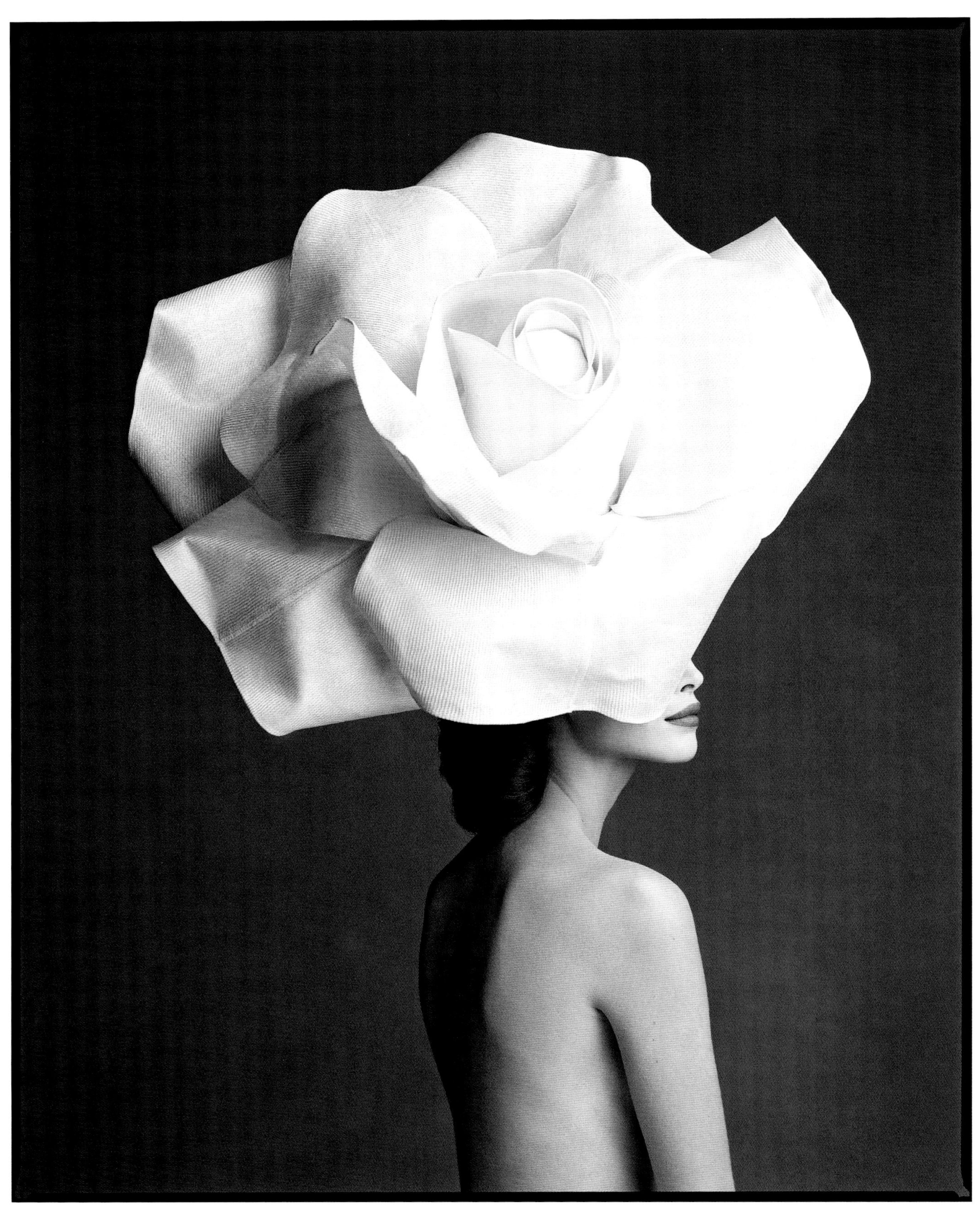

Patrick Demarchelier, model: Christy Turlington, 1991 for *Vogue* UK

Herb Ritts, model: Christy Turlington, El Mirage, California 1990 for Versace

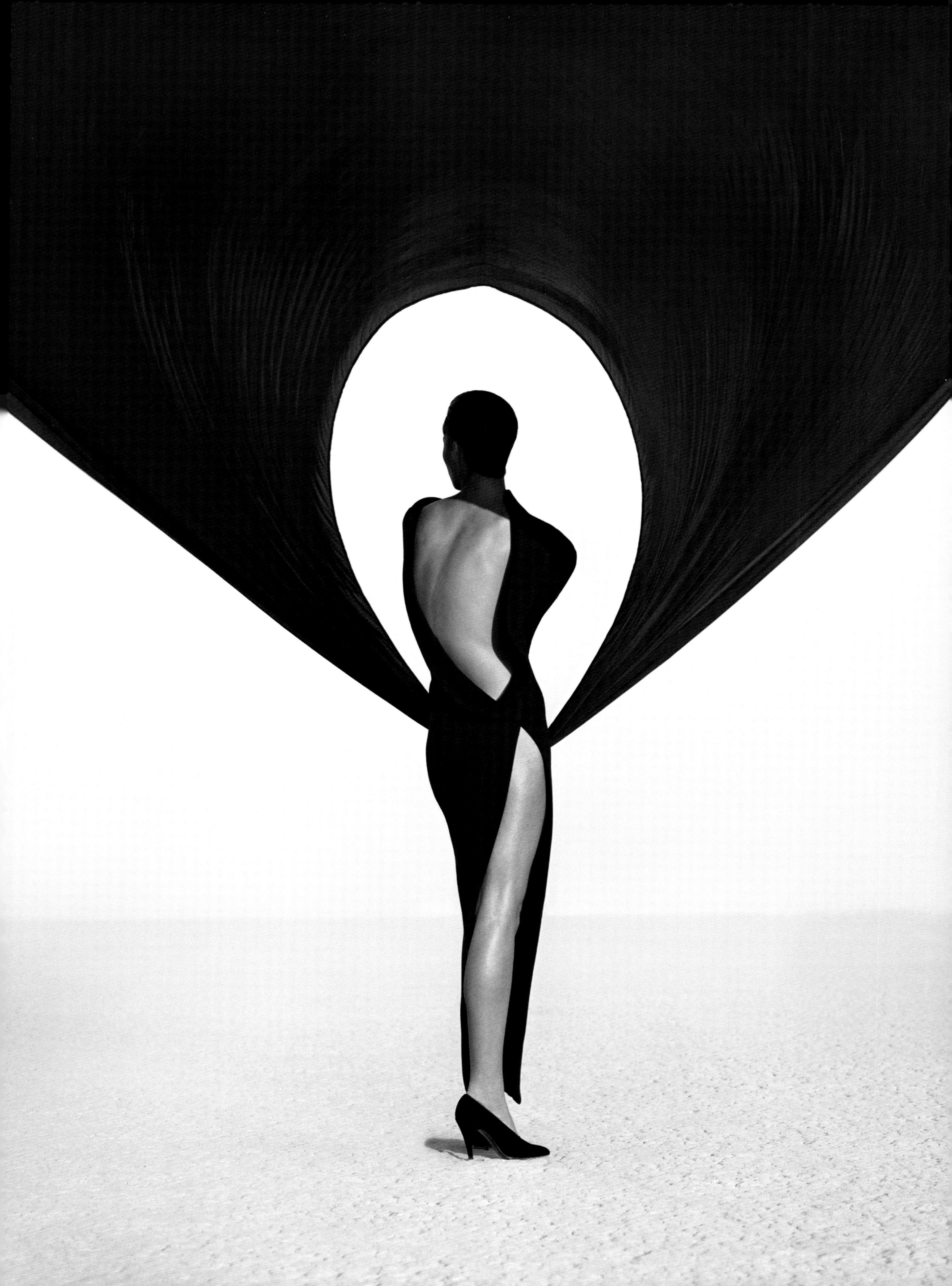

Helmut Newton, model: Claudia Schiffer, Menton, France 1992 for *Vanity Fair*

Helmut Newton pursued his passion for photography from an early age, and in the 1970s he cemented his reputation as one of the most progressive and brilliant fashion and advertising photographers in the world. I remember him as being very 'Teutonic': organised, calm and a complete perfectionist. Every picture took longer, perhaps, than with other photographers because everything was thought through in intricate detail. Newton was incisive. He often shot from ground level, turning the model into a statuesque figure, as in this shot taken for an editorial for *Vanity Fair.*

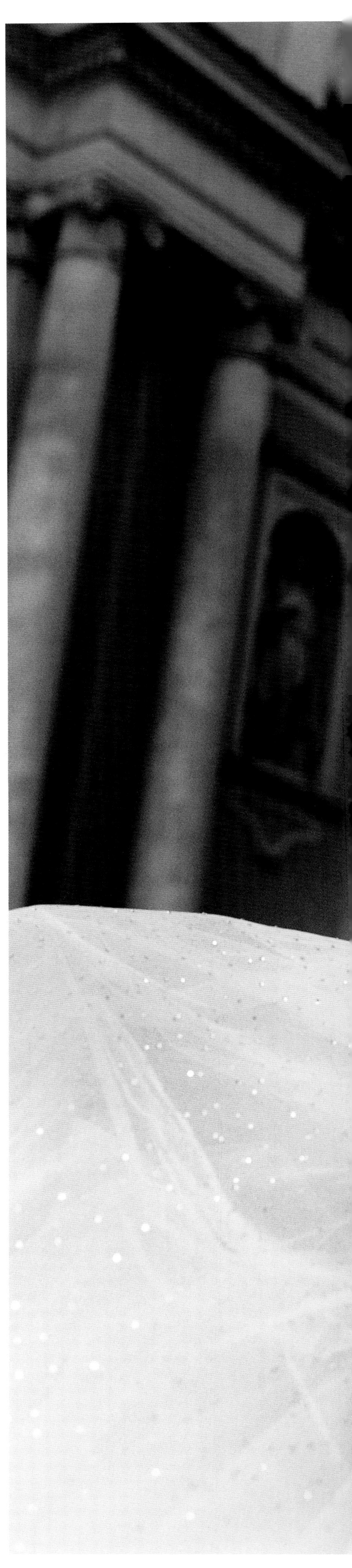

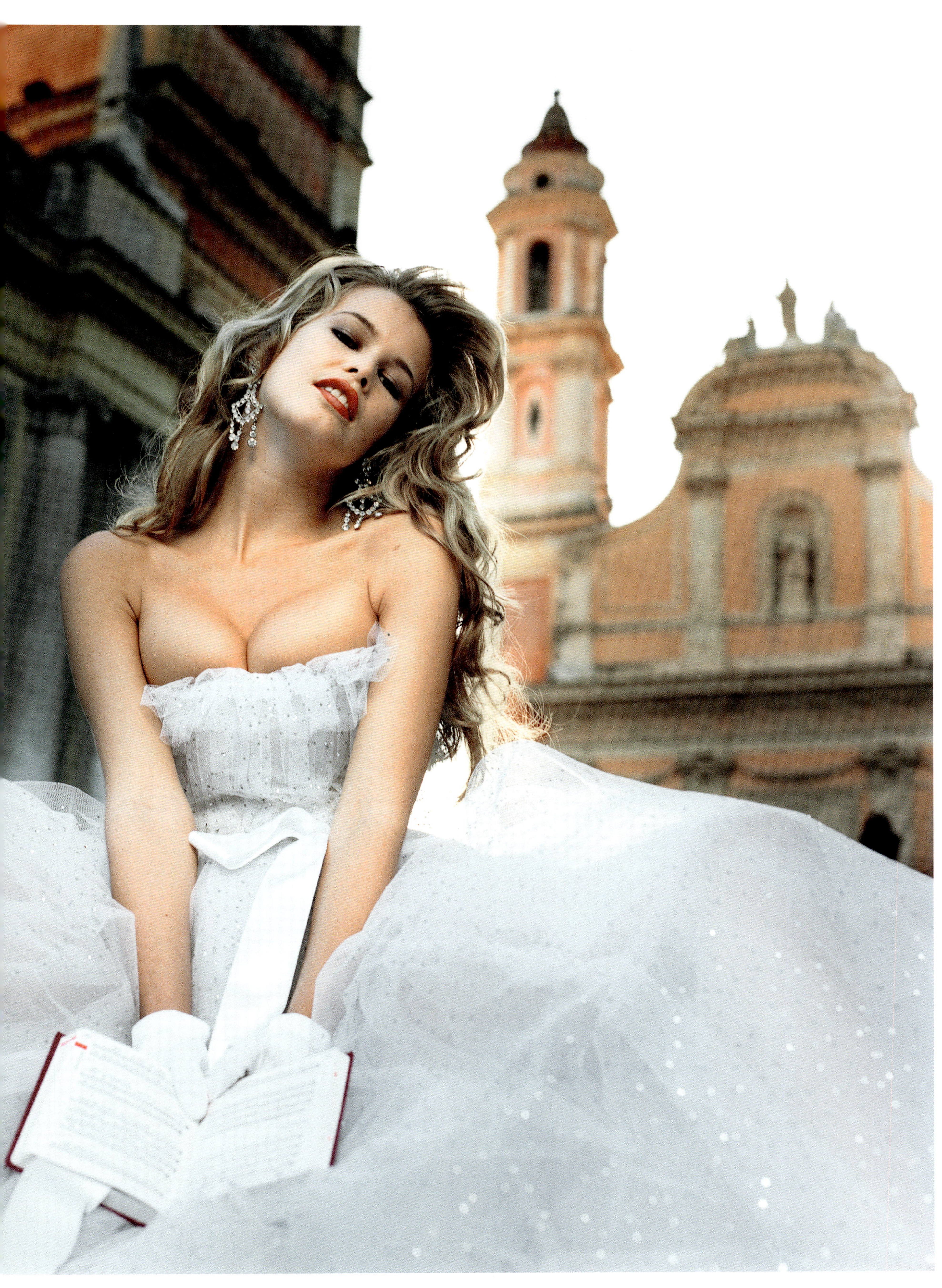

BACK TO REALITY

Glamour and perfectionism represented one side of 1990s fashion photography, but on the other side there evolved a new realism that claimed to present beauty in its unfiltered form. The ‘grunge movement’ swept from music stages into fashion shoots. Photographers started to angle in on raw emotion and feature models without makeup, presenting a fresh, unvarnished vision.

Against this background, two photographers stand out for me: the German photographer Juergen Teller and the British photographer Corinne Day, both of whom are still heavily referenced today. Reflecting a grittier side of fashion, they elevated the ordinary to the extraordinary and championed a ‘take me as you find me’ truth. Diversity and individuality were prized above classical good looks. As a result, the language of modelling changed. The clichéd poses were replaced by idiosyncratic gestures, with photography focusing on ‘off guard’ moments. On the runway, some designers started to remove the raised podium, preferring models to walk at an easy pace on a level with the audience.

In 1991, I was eighteen, living in London and the newly appointed fashion director of i-D *magazine. It was the perfect place to be, and for me, the birth of grunge was about breaking away from the excess of the 1980s and injecting reality into fashion. Our work held a mirror up to our real lives and a new attitude emerged: no makeup, less is more. Alongside fashion, there were bands like The Stone Roses and Happy Mondays, as well as people like John Maybury and Isaac Julien making films. It was a whole cultural movement and when Kate [Moss] was accepted as part of the fashion mainstream, we were accepted as well. We all grew up together, and in many ways, the 1990s was when we came of age, personally and professionally.*

EDWARD ENNINFUL

Juergen Teller, Young Pink Kate, London 1998 (model: Kate Moss)

Juergen Teller brought a raw sexiness to the industry. He used flash and multiple cameras in a way that felt startlingly new. This image of Kate Moss is part of a series that was taken at her house for a personal project. Kate had dyed her hair for a Versace show and when she dyed it back to blonde, it faded gradually through different shades, from red to orange, with Teller photographing each transformation on successive days. With his sense of realness, Teller spearheaded a new wave of photography that questioned and overturned standard ideals of glamour.

178, 179
Corinne Day, model: Kate Moss,
Camber Sands, England 1990 for *The Face*

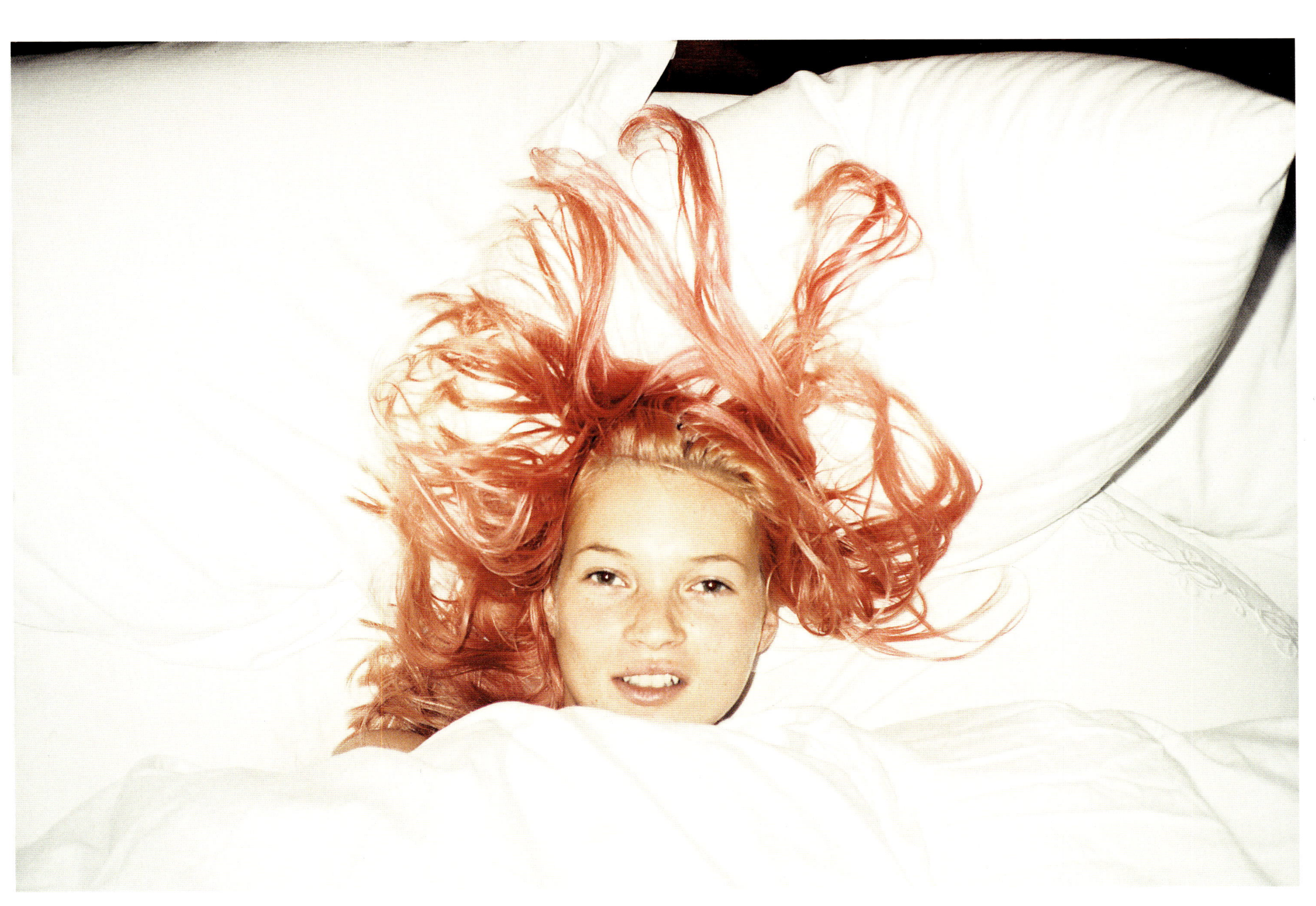

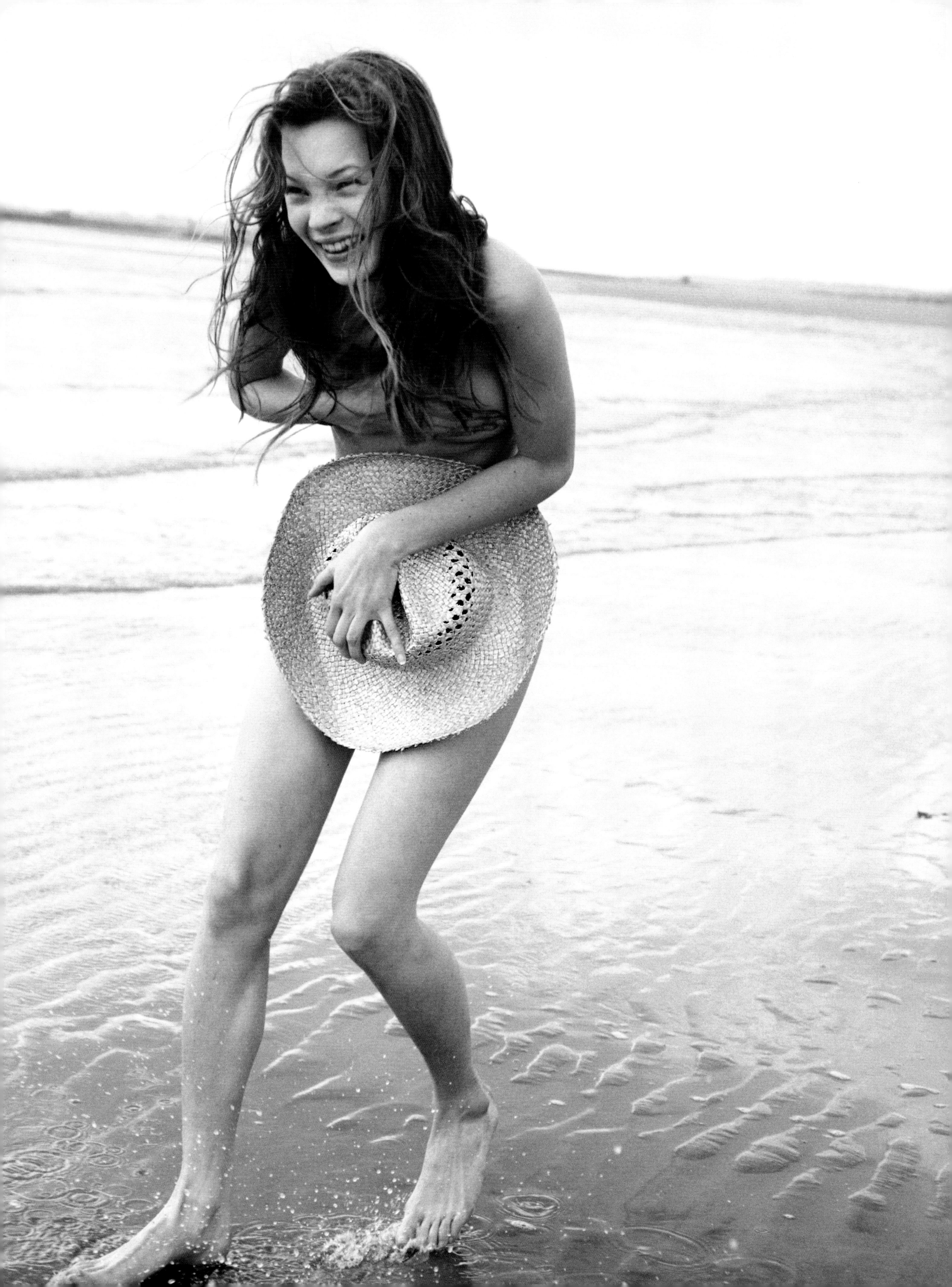

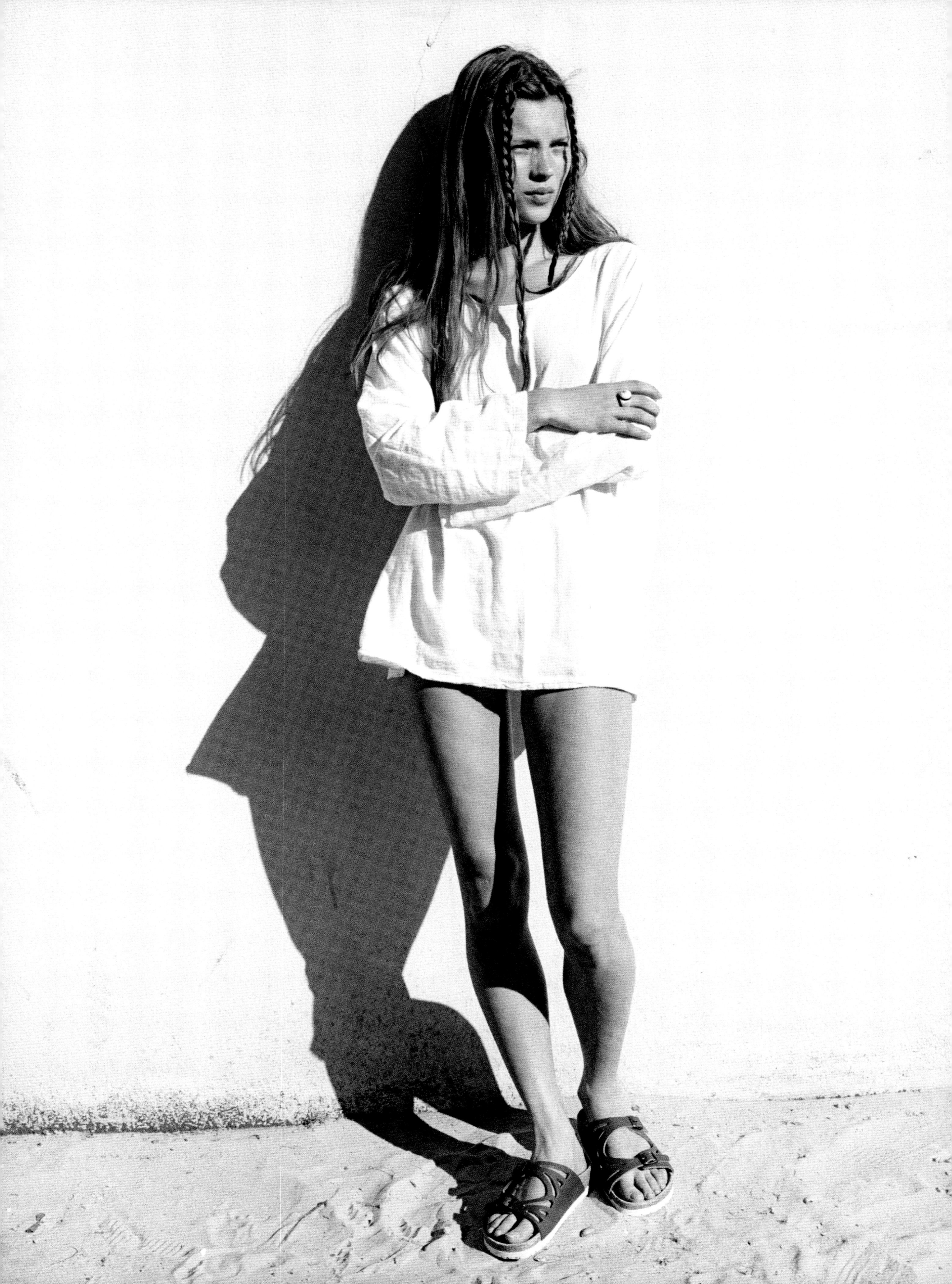

I love this David Sims picture; it was for i-D *magazine and we shot it in London. There was no hair or makeup. I literally was wearing my sweatshirt and it felt like a real portrait of me, exactly the way I arrived there. I love the rawness of the picture, and also the angle Sims shot it at. It felt like I hadn't shot that angle before. I remember it was a really fun day.*

GISELE BÜNDCHEN

David Sims, model: Gisele Bündchen, 1998 for *i-D*

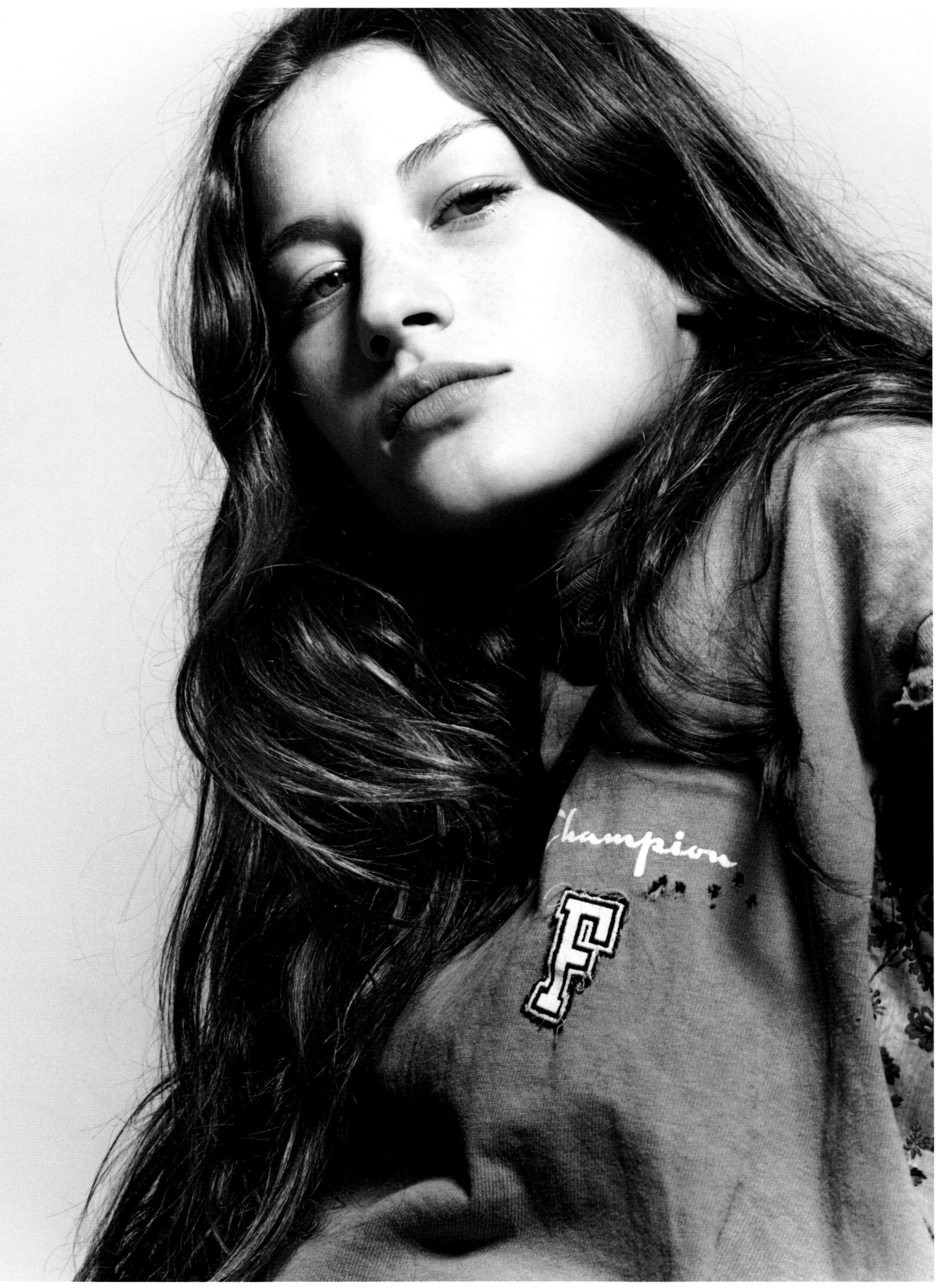
Champion
F

Ellen von Unwerth, model: Naomi Campbell, New York 1994

Ellen von Unwerth brought humour and sexiness to fashion photography – proof of which can be found in this fictional scene with Naomi Campbell as the lead character. It was taken during a shoot for Naomi's debut studio album titled *babywoman*. Ellen is a shining star in an industry that was, back then, largely dominated by male photographers. As a one-time model herself, she was able to develop an intimacy with her female subjects.

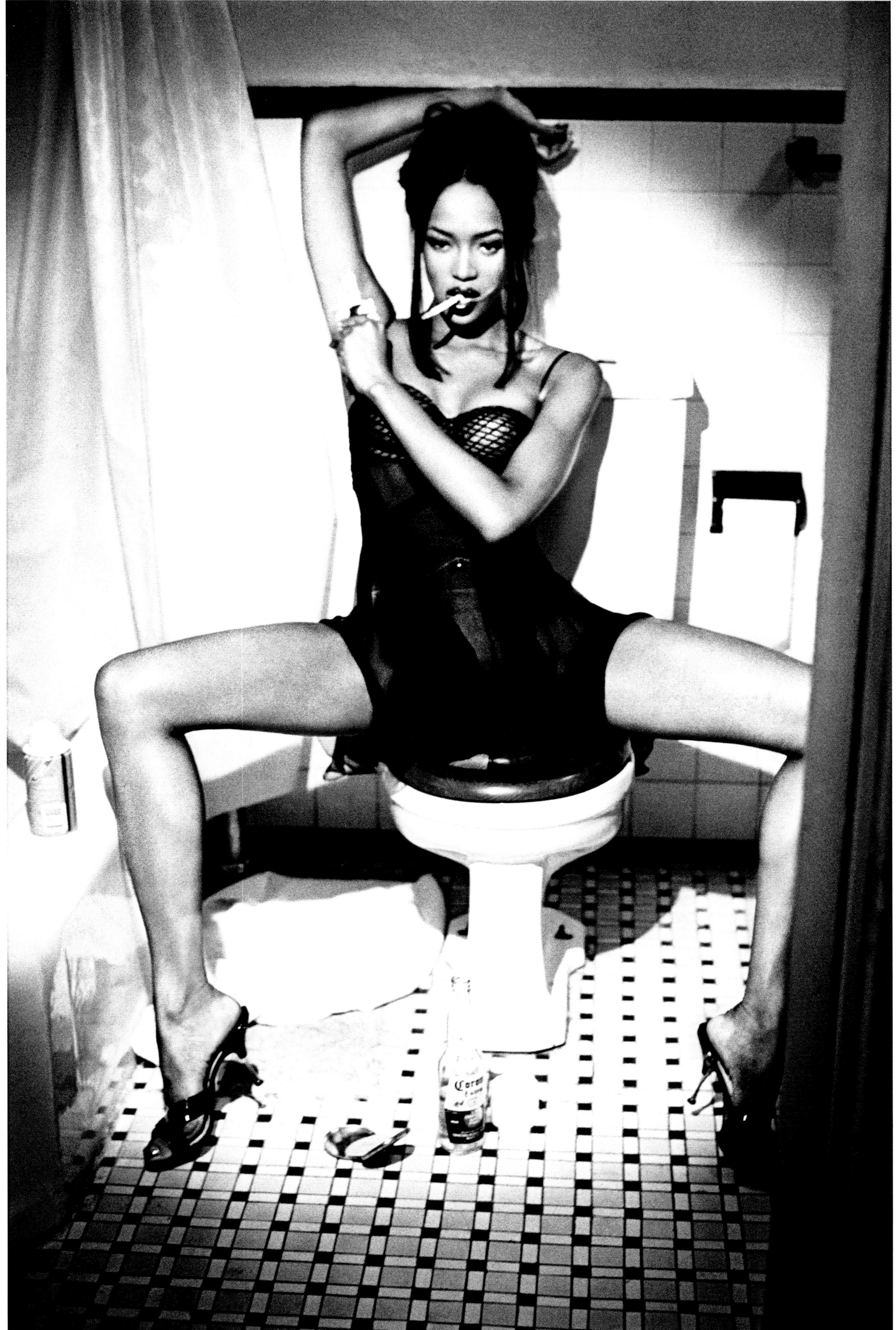

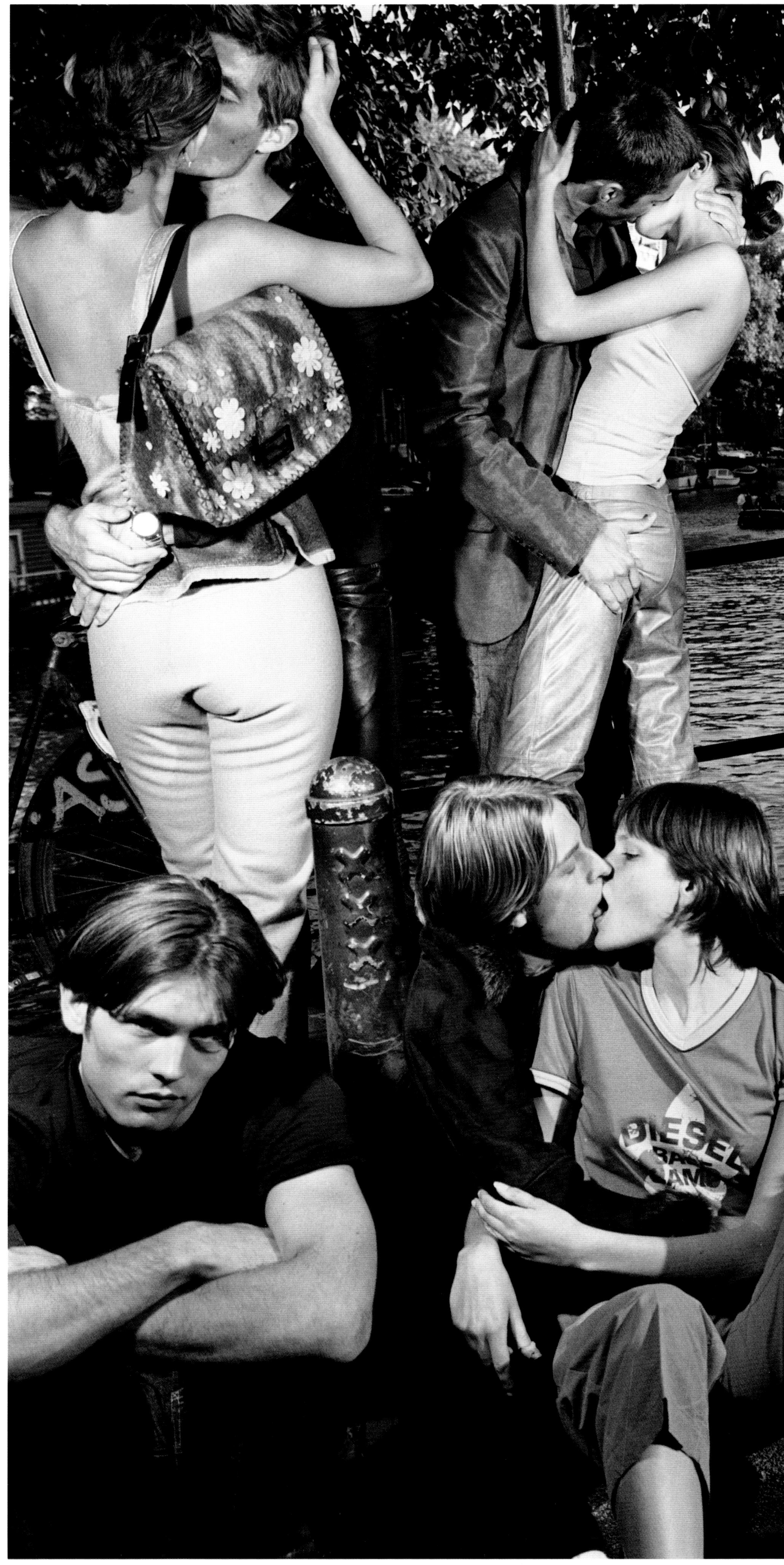

Mario Testino, Brouwersgracht, Amsterdam 1999
for *L'Uomo Vogue*

The mid to late 1990s saw photography take a dramatic turn away from high gloss and opulence towards minimalist, utilitarian design and gritty, raw imagery. Maverick image-makers including Mario Testino refocused their eye on the rebellious 'grunge' spirit.

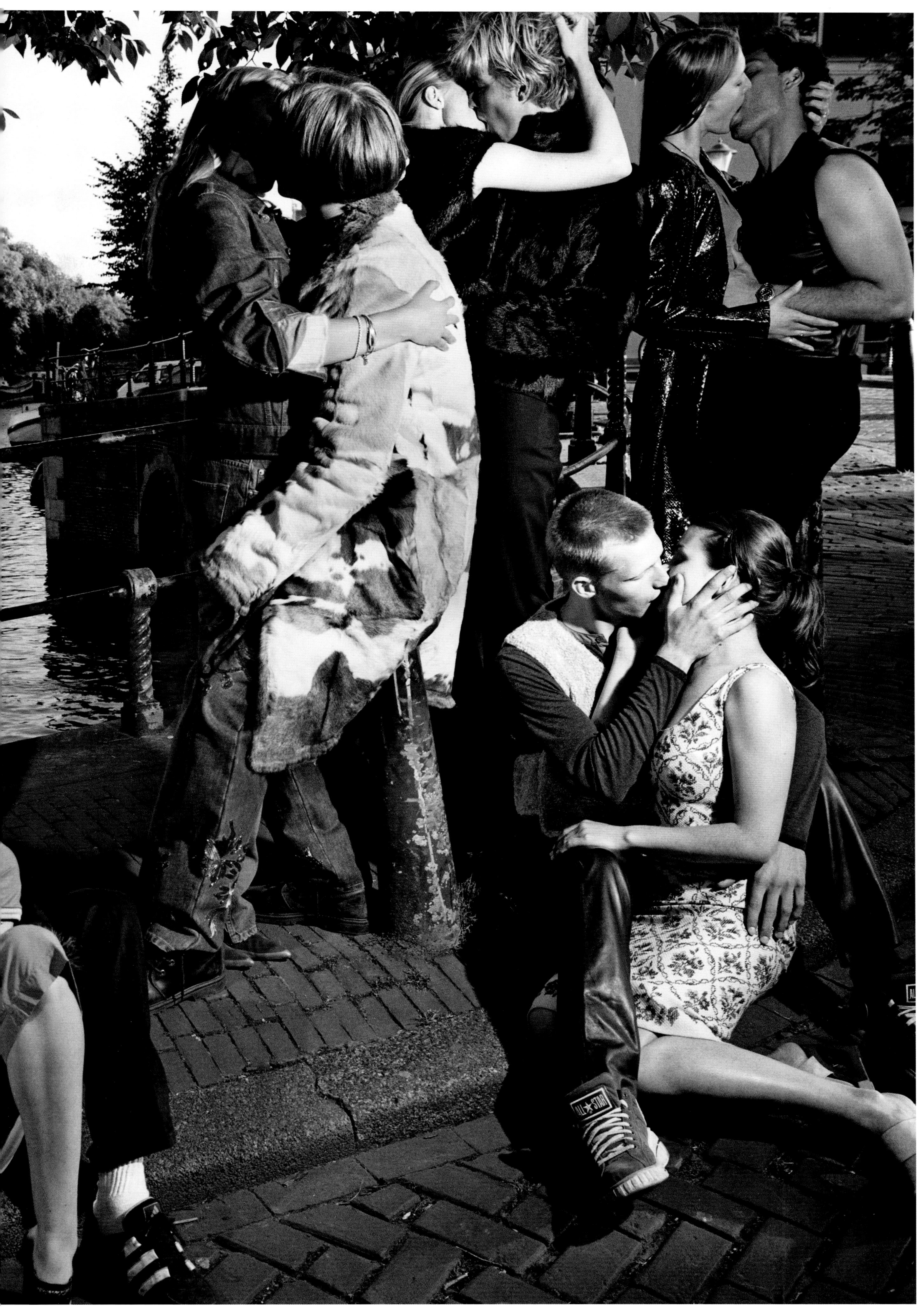
ALL STAR

Mario Testino, model: Eva Herzigová,
Paris 1997 for *The Face*

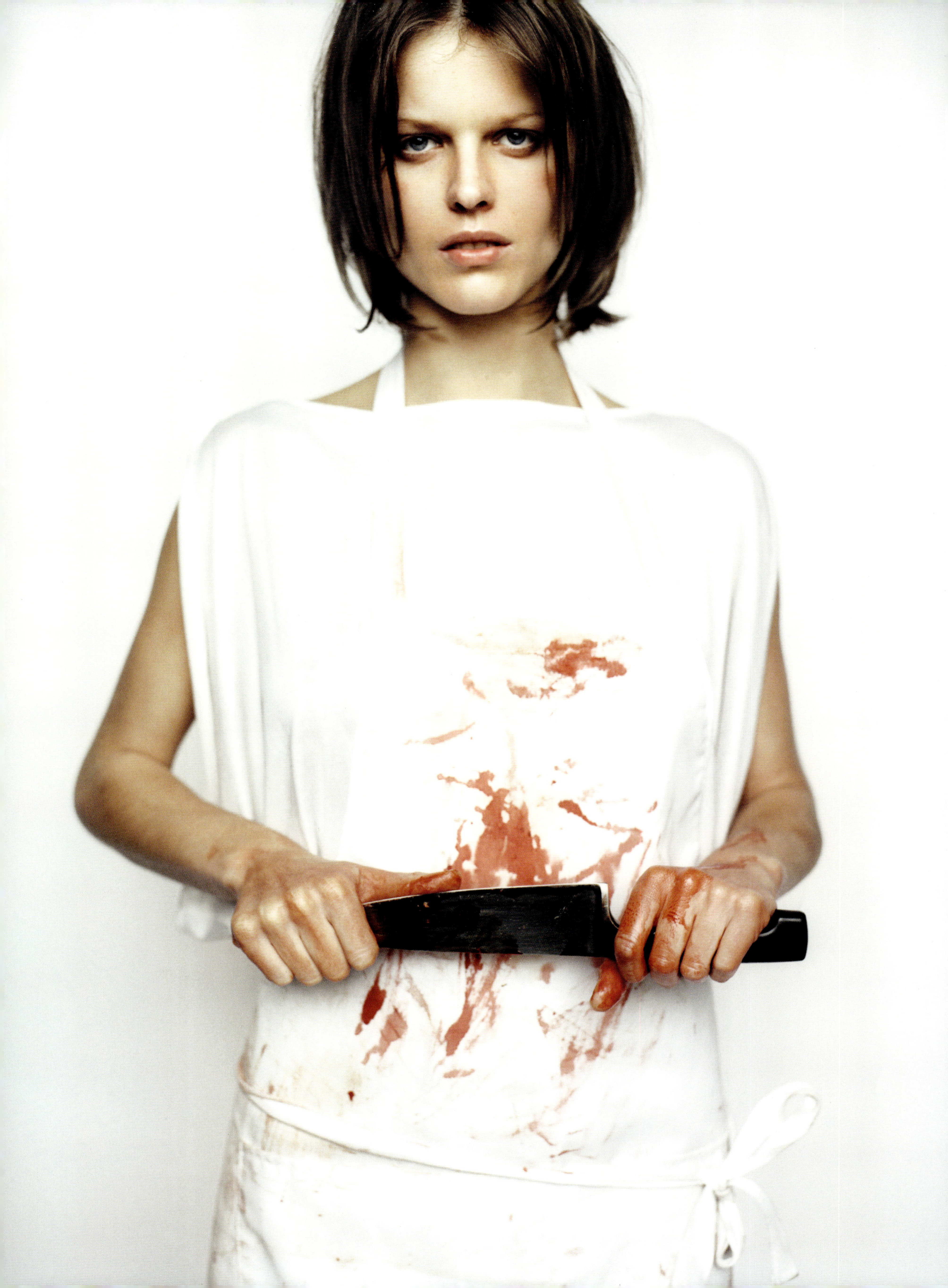

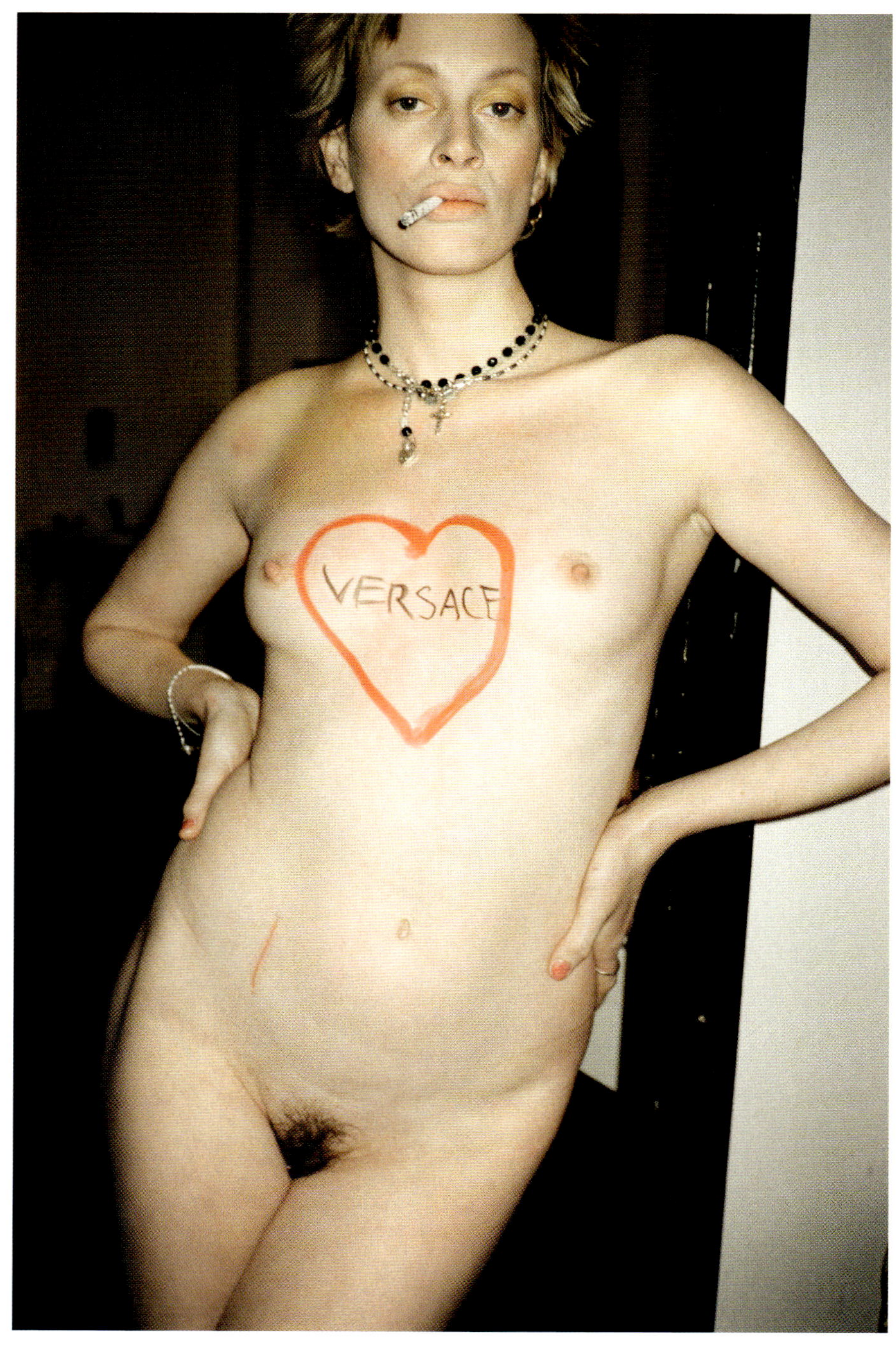

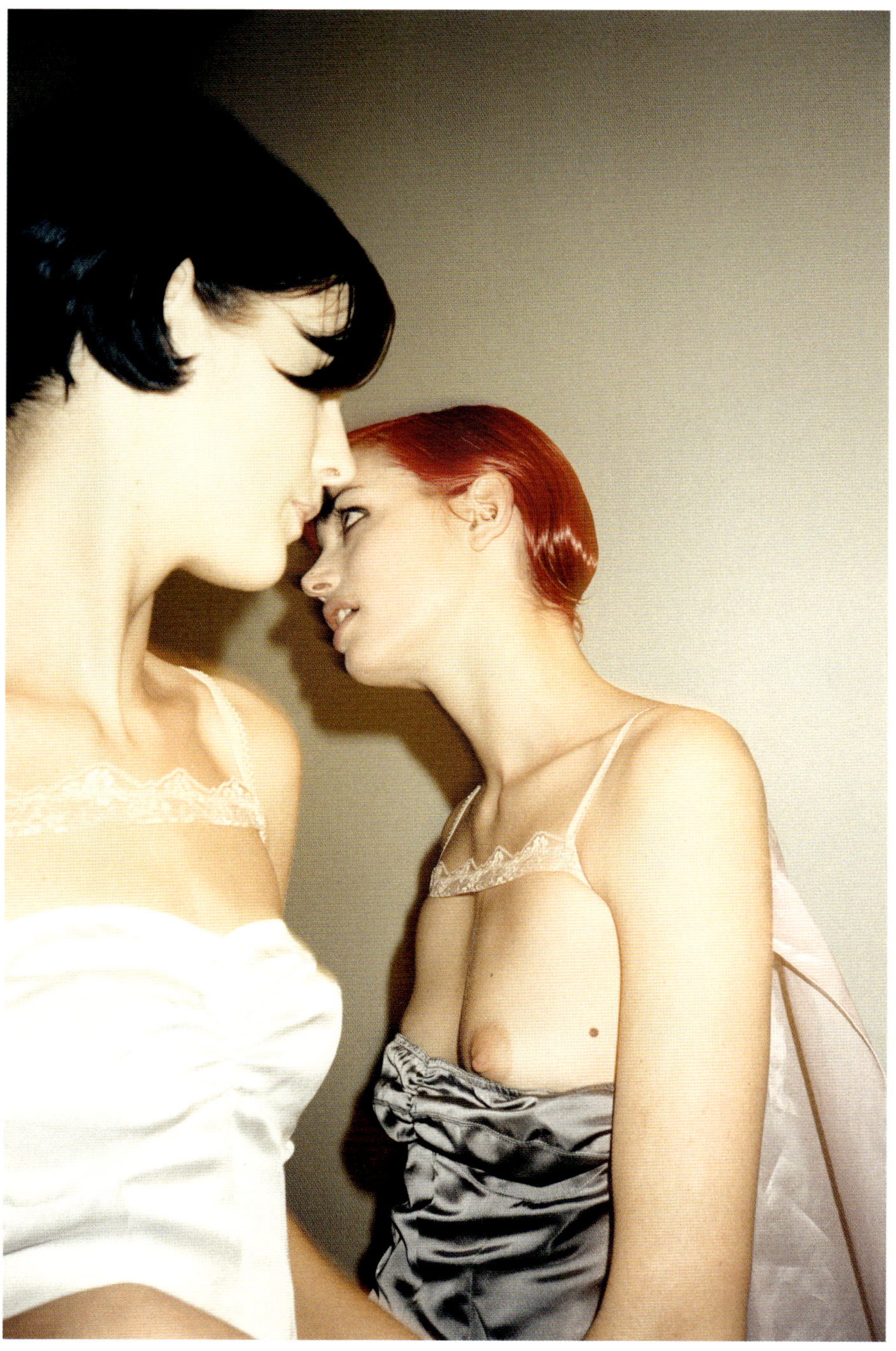

Juergen Teller, Kristen McMenamy No. 3, London 1996 (for *Süddeutsche Zeitung Magazin*)

Juergen Teller, Stella Tennant and Sybil Buck, Helmut Lang backstage series, Fall/Winter 1995, Paris 1995

Juergen Teller, Kirsten Owen, Helmut Lang backstage series, Spring/Summer 1994, Paris 1993

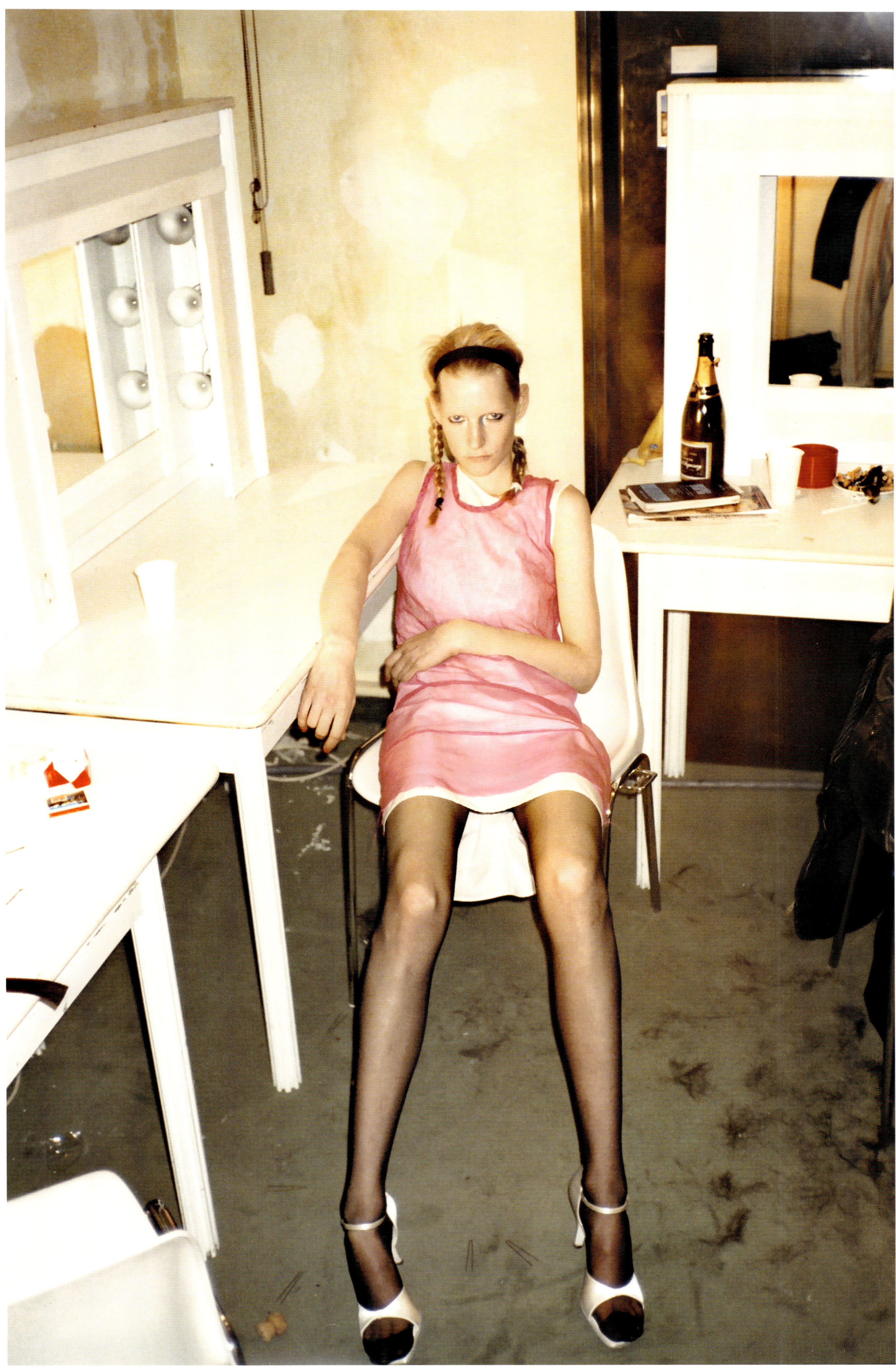

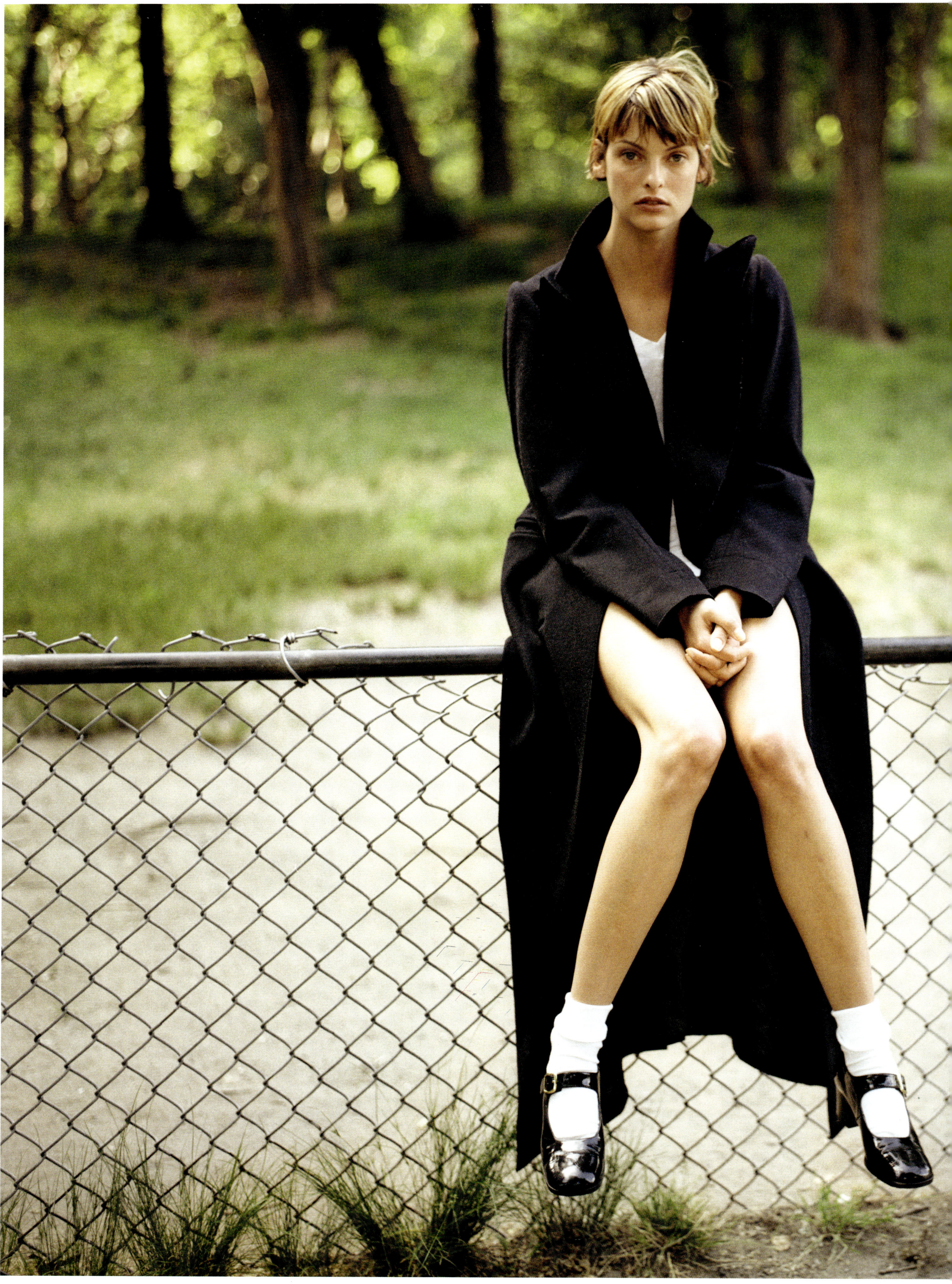

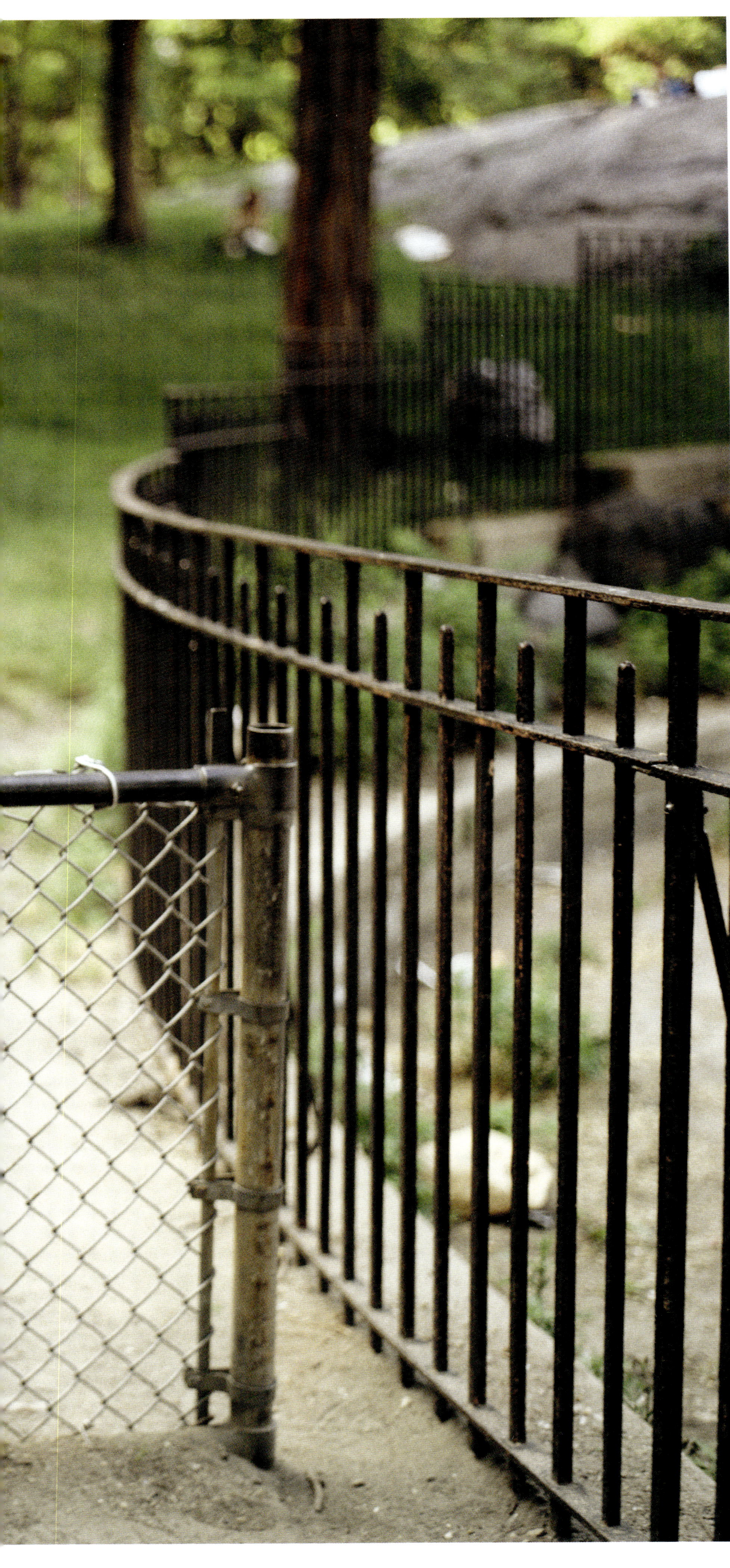

Juergen Teller's radicalism stripped off all artifice, whether in clothing, hair or makeup. Above all, his photos are lived moments. Spontaneity prevails.

CARINE ROITFELD

Juergen Teller, Linda Evangelista No. 3, Central Park, New York 1993 (for *Interview*)

192/193
Helmut Newton, model: Nadja Auermann, Monte Carlo 1994 for Blumarine

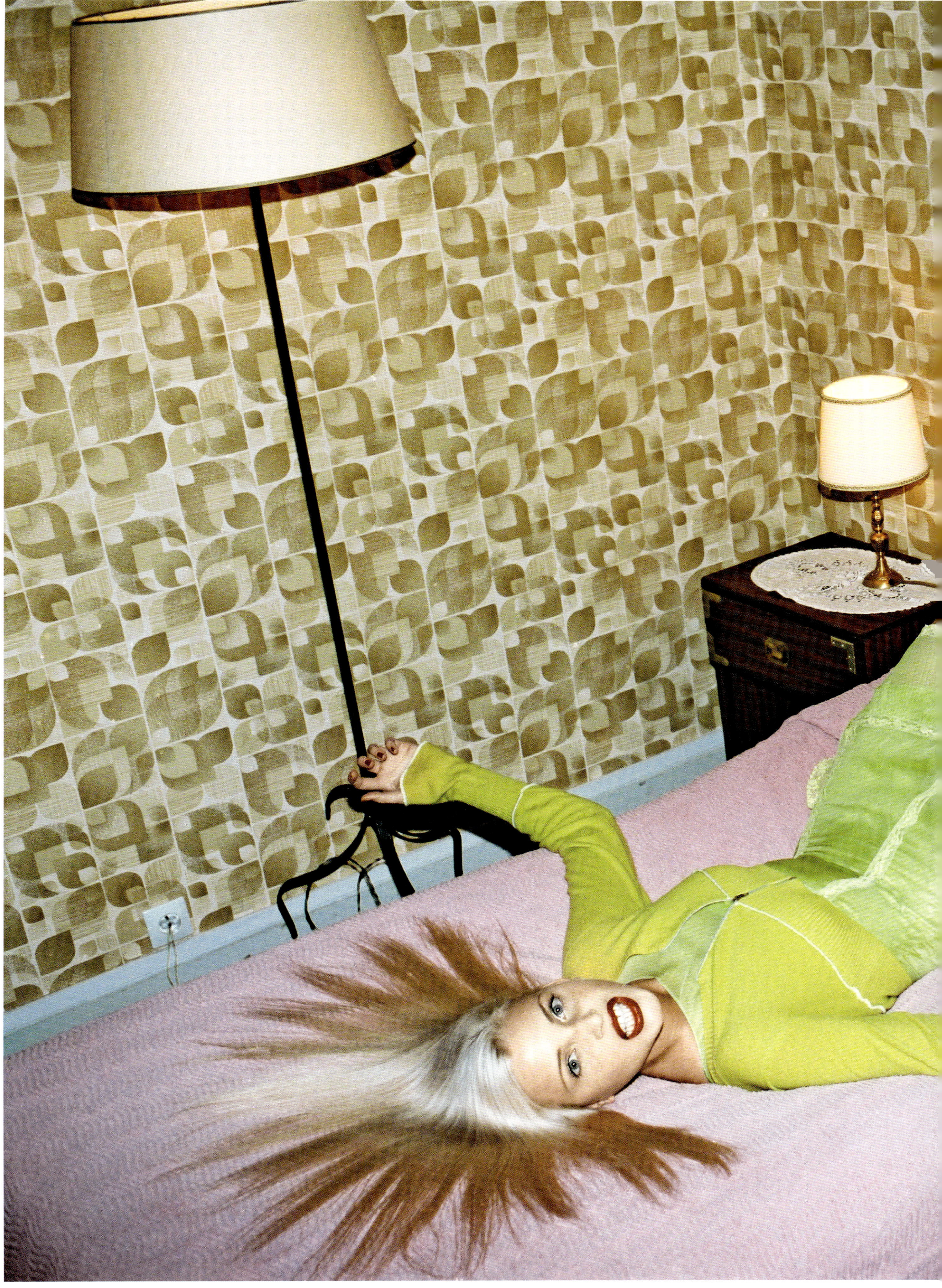

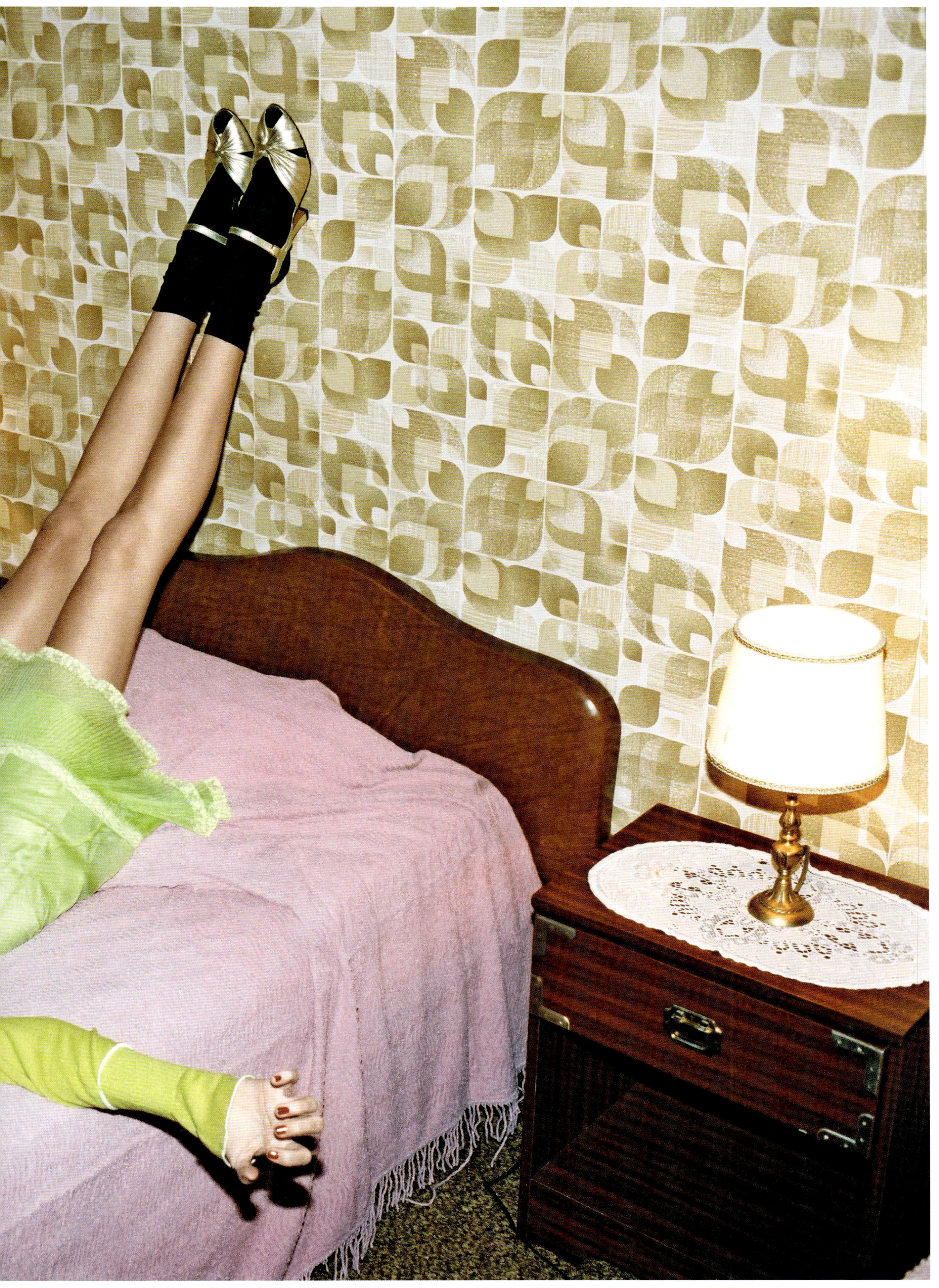

BACK-
STAGE

We are all familiar with the polished finished product that we see on billboards, online, in magazines or in the highly choreographed shows with their high-energy 'theatre'. Yet there is so much that is unseen behind the curtain, that reveals the hard work, the tension and the fun. The fashion season has often been compared to a travelling circus and many bonds are formed between editors, journalists, photographers, designers, hair and makeup artists, stylists and models – all of whom are part of an intricate ecosystem. This section is a tribute and a testament to the invisible talent that makes fashion come alive in the image and in the show.

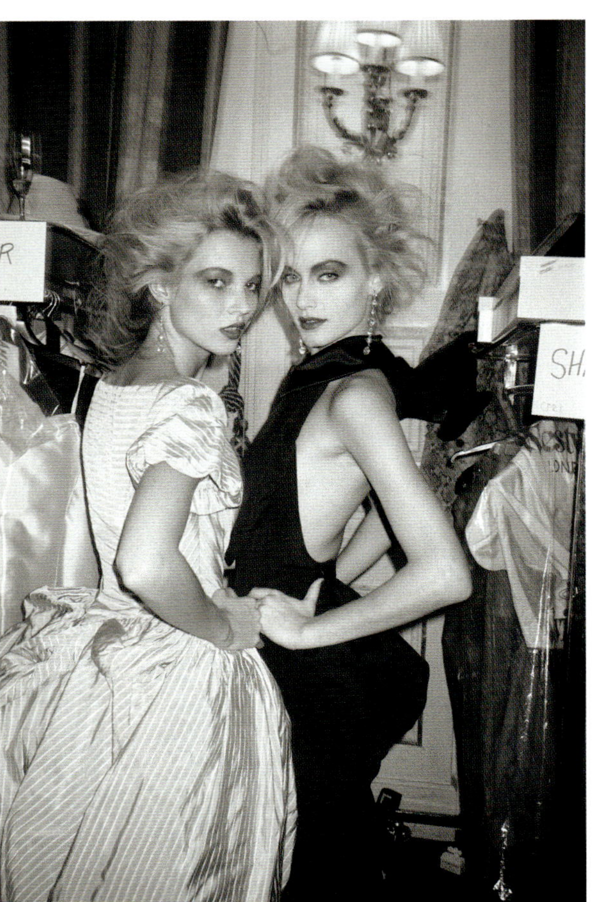

Roxanne Lowit, Kate Moss and Amber Valletta backstage at Vivienne Westwood RTW Spring 1996, 1995

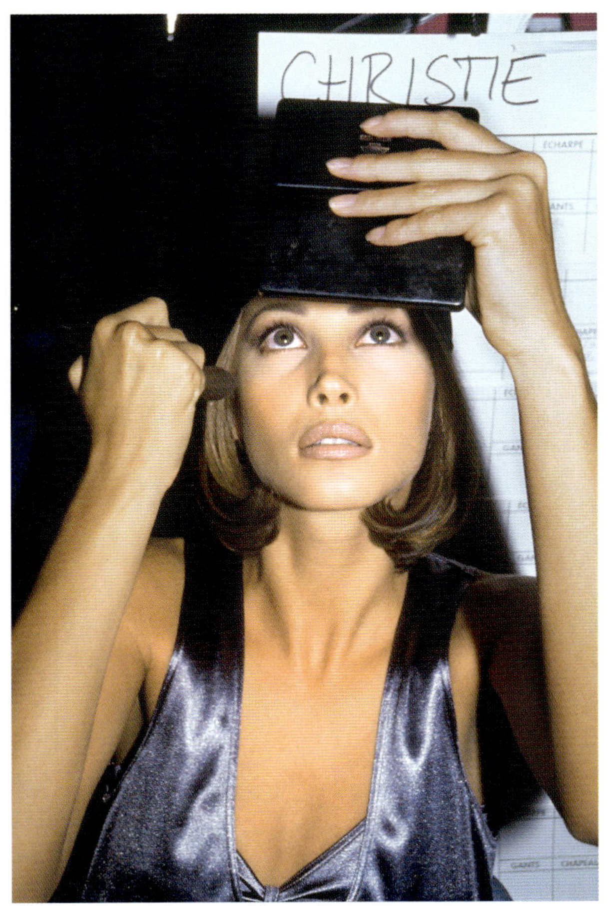

Roxanne Lowit, Christy Turlington, 1992

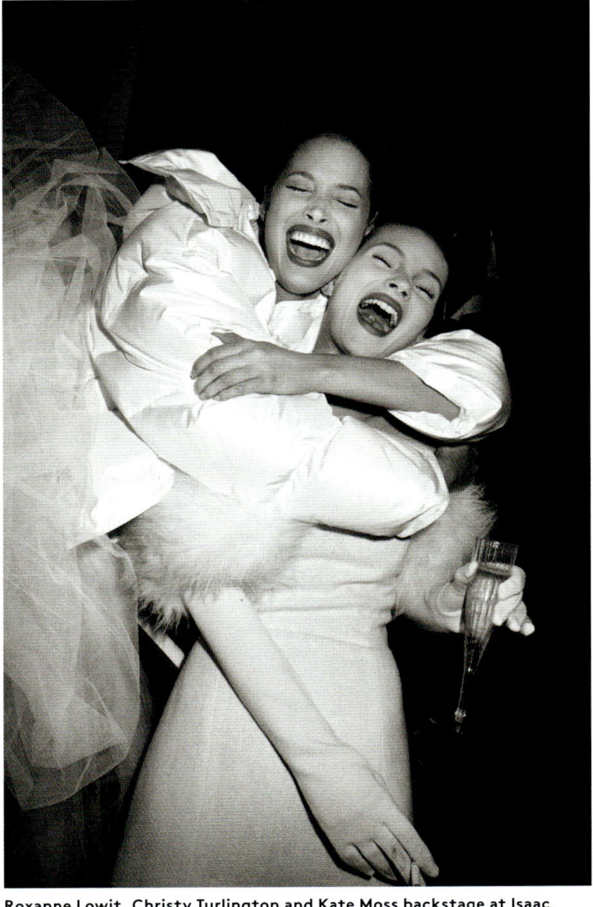

Roxanne Lowit, Christy Turlington and Kate Moss backstage at Isaac Mizrahi, Los Angeles 1994

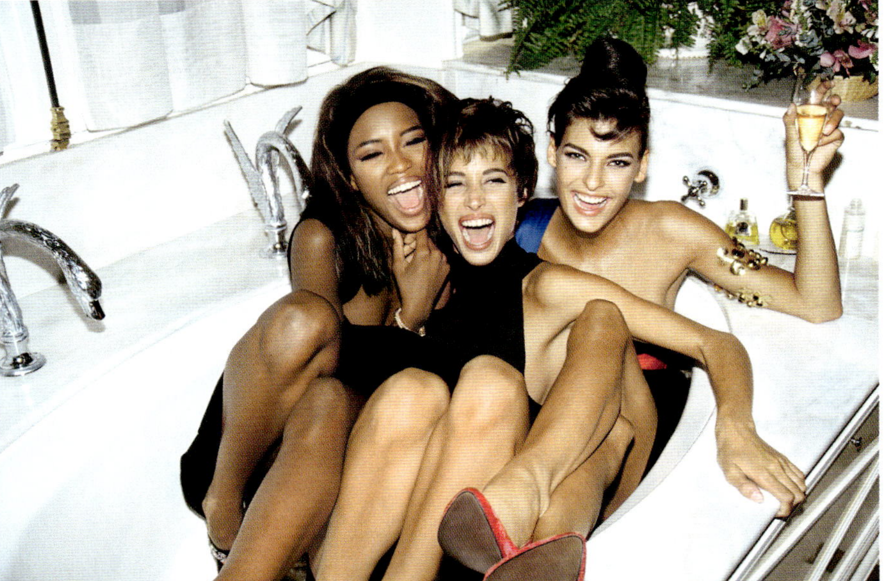

Roxanne Lowit, Naomi Campbell, Christy Turlington and Linda Evangelista, Paris 1990

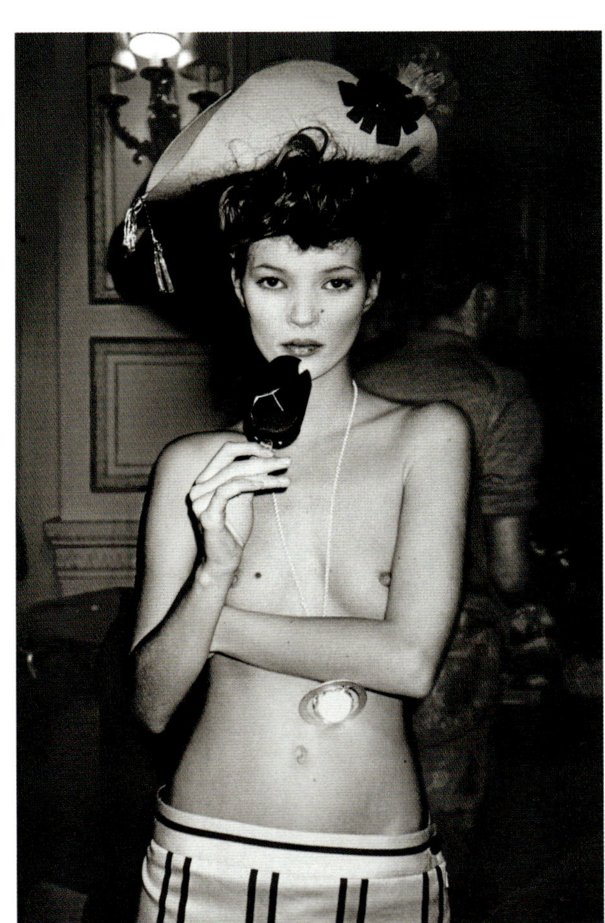

Roxanne Lowit, Kate Moss backstage at Vivienne Westwood, Paris 1993

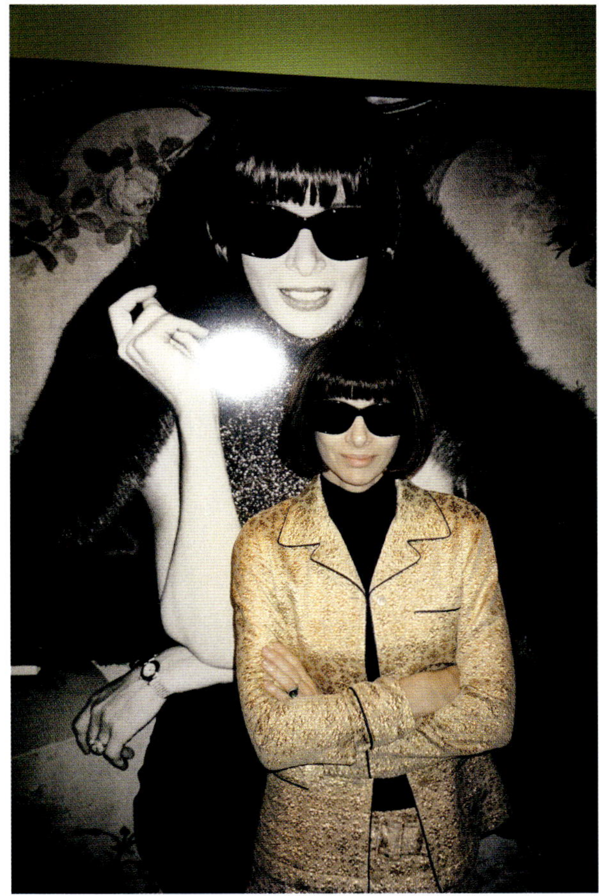

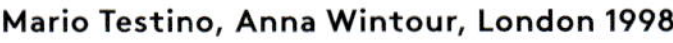

Mario Testino, Anna Wintour, London 1998

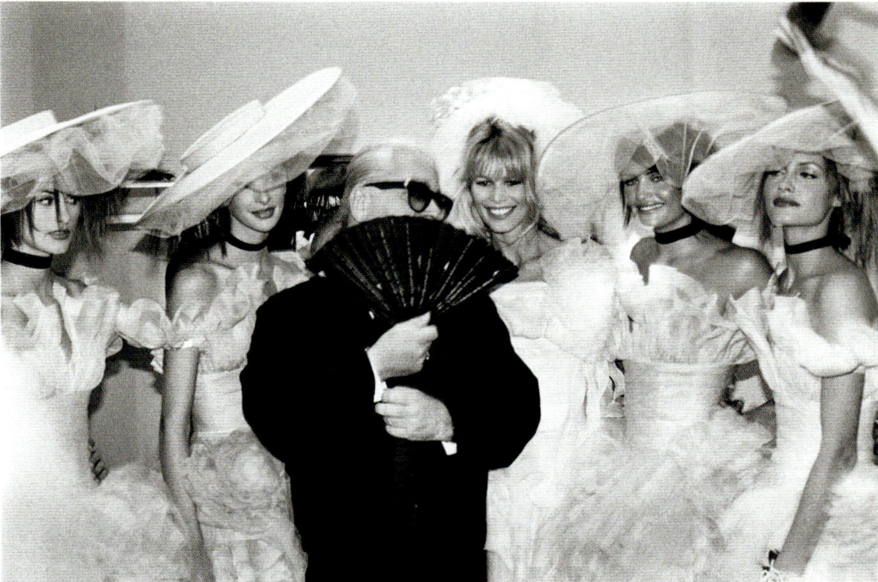

Mario Testino, Karl Lagerfeld surrounded by models, Paris 1994

Photographers document what happens in a moment, but fashion photographers need to do that and more. We capture events, shoots, fashion shows and life in general, but we also interpret what we see to create an interesting story the viewer can respond to. We become the narrator for designers, magazines and viewers alike.

MARIO TESTINO

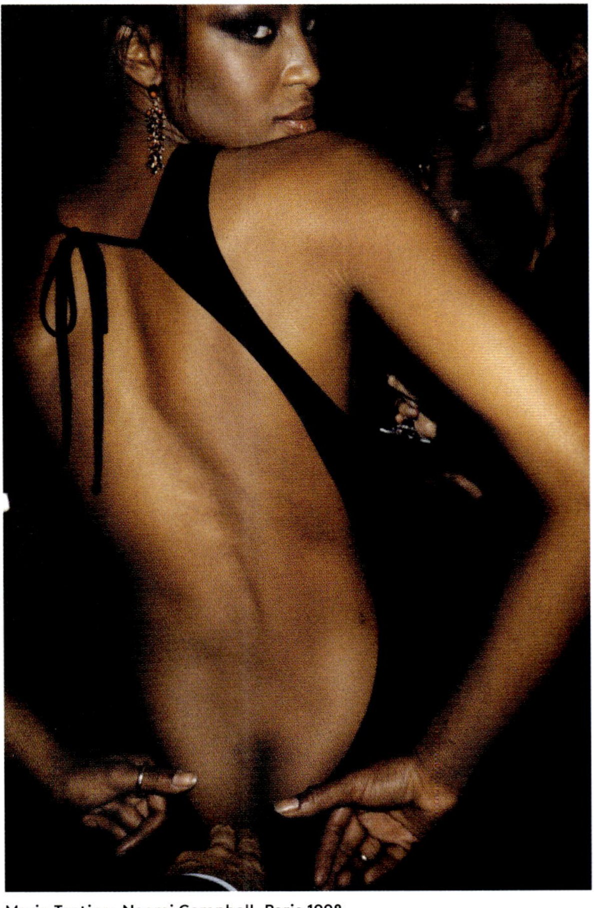

Mario Testino, Naomi Campbell, Paris 1998

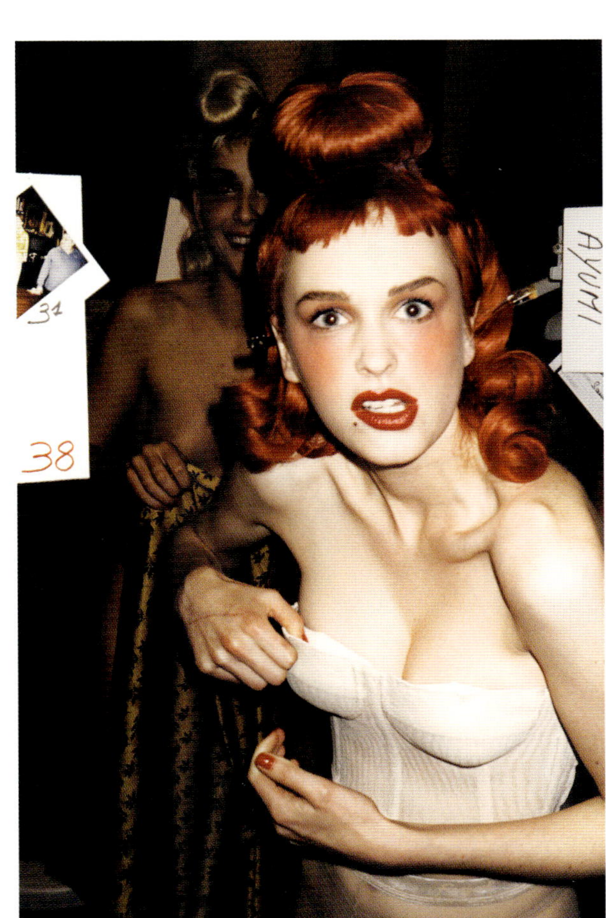

Mario Testino, Kylie Bax, Paris 1997

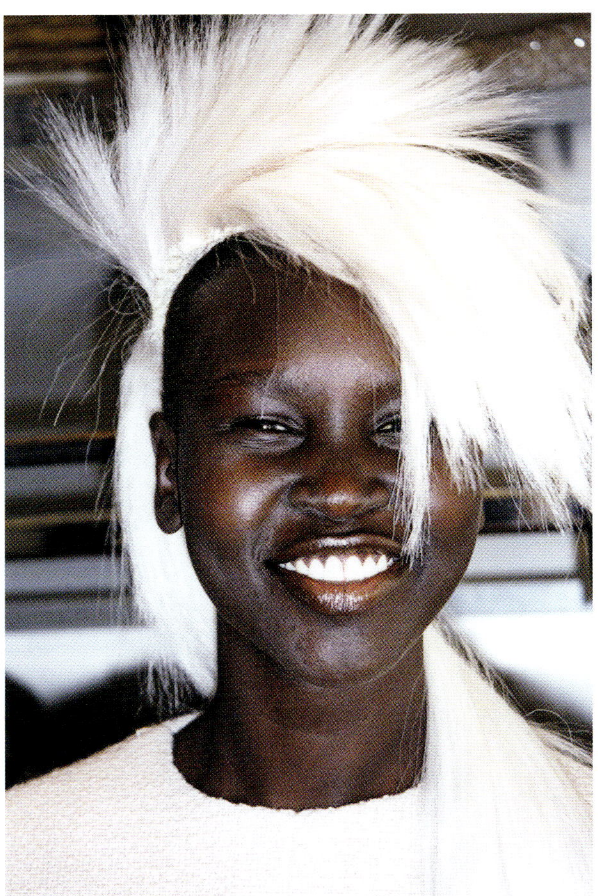
Angelica Blechschmidt, Alek Wek backstage at Chanel Couture Spring/Summer 2000, Paris 1999

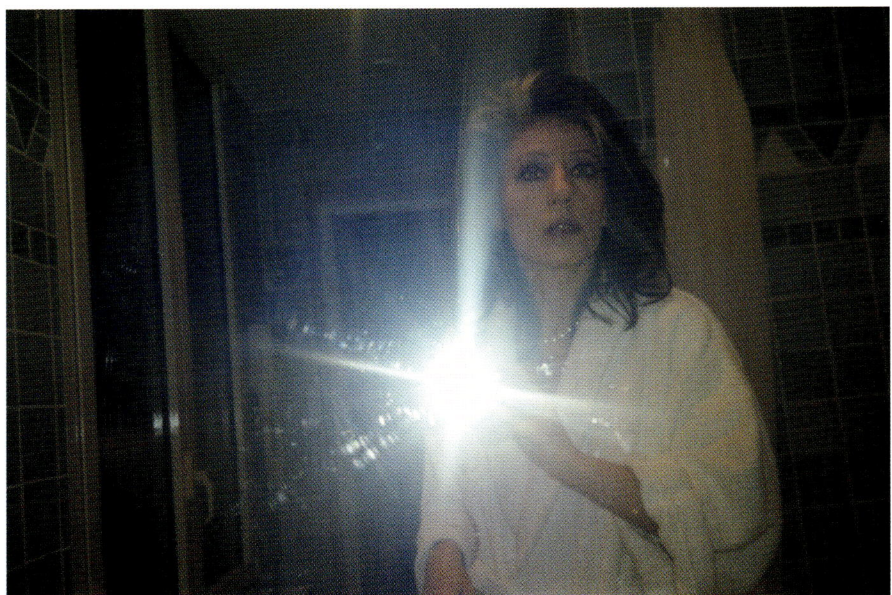
Angelica Blechschmidt, self-portrait at her hotel during the Festival of Photography, Monte Carlo 1993

Angelica Blechschmidt, the former editor-in-chief of German *Vogue*, always had a camera in her hand and snapped from the front row, backstage and at parties. Some of the shots used to appear in her *Vogue* column 'Flash!' She assembled a unique chronicle of an era at a time when street-style and backstage photography were in their infancy. Today, with digital tools, spontaneous snapshots can be edited in an instant. Yet it is the unfiltered edge of Blechschmidt's images that stands out and marks them as typically 1990s.

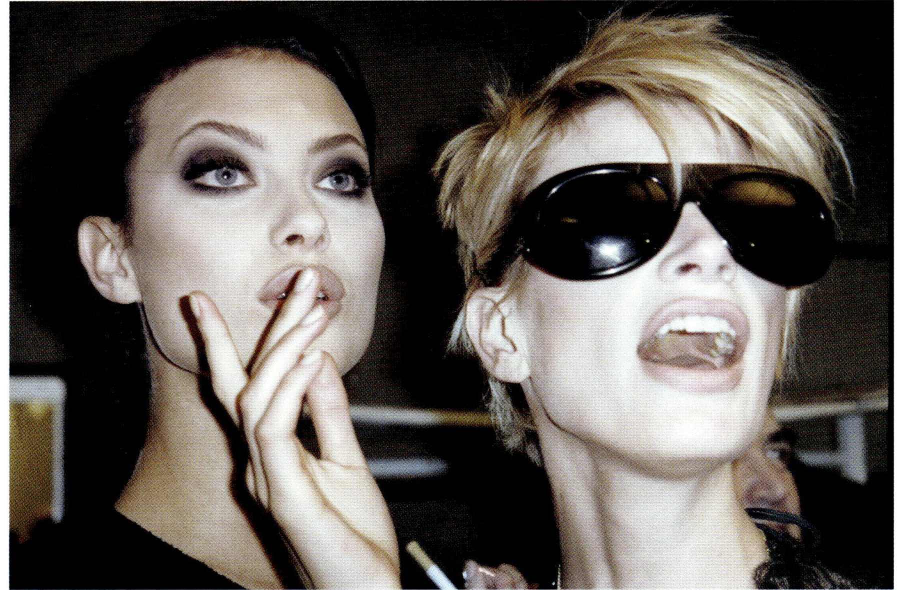
Angelica Blechschmidt, Shalom Harlow and Kristen McMenamy backstage at Chanel Prêt-à-Porter, Paris 1995

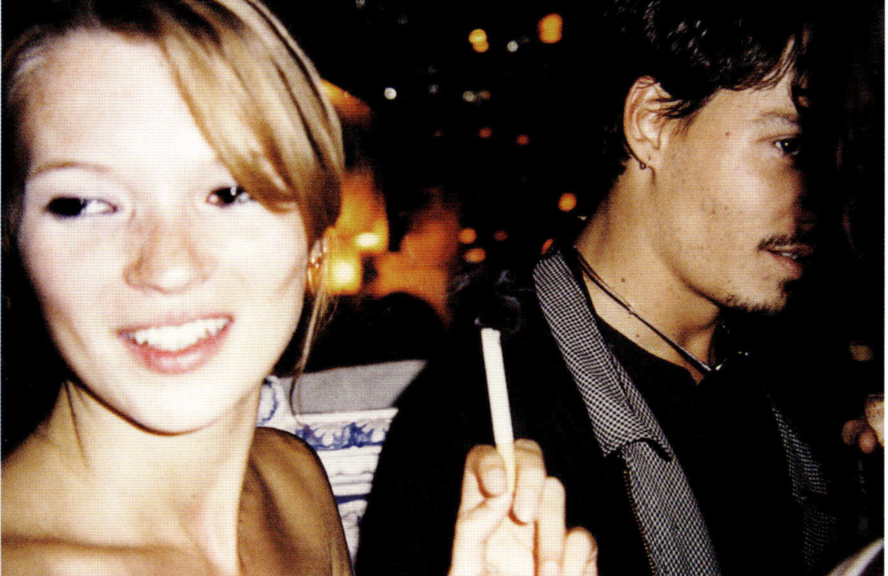
Angelica Blechschmidt, Kate Moss and Johnny Depp at the Atelier Versace afterparty, Paris 1995

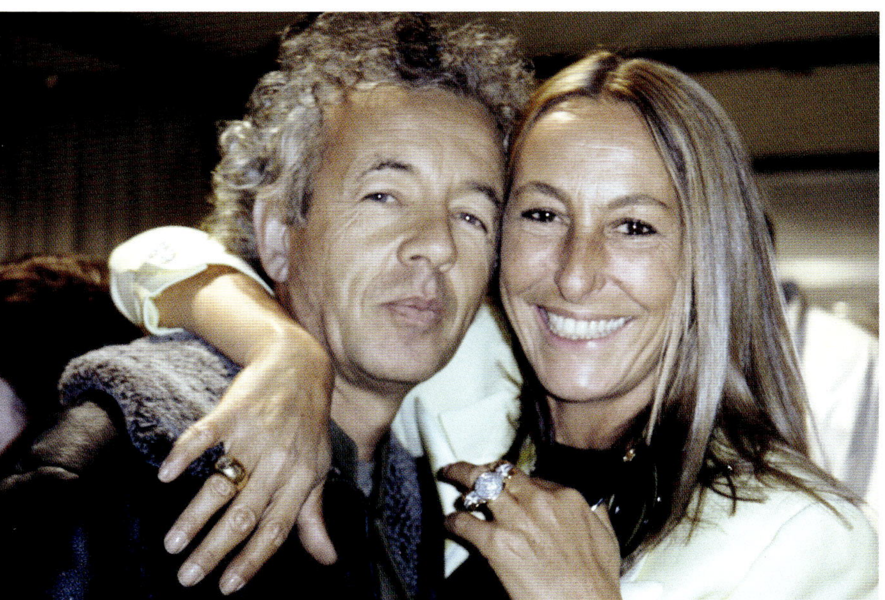
Angelica Blechschmidt, photographer Gilles Bensimon and stylist Carlyne Cerf de Dudzeele backstage at Versace, Milan 1995

BACKSTAGE

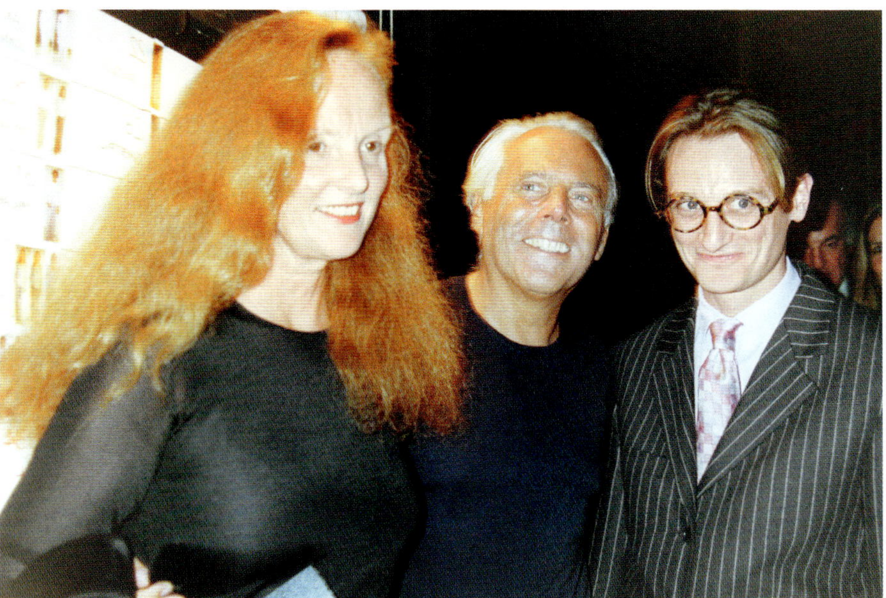

Angelica Blechschmidt, Grace Coddington, Georgio Armani and Hamish Bowles backstage at Armani, Milan 1995

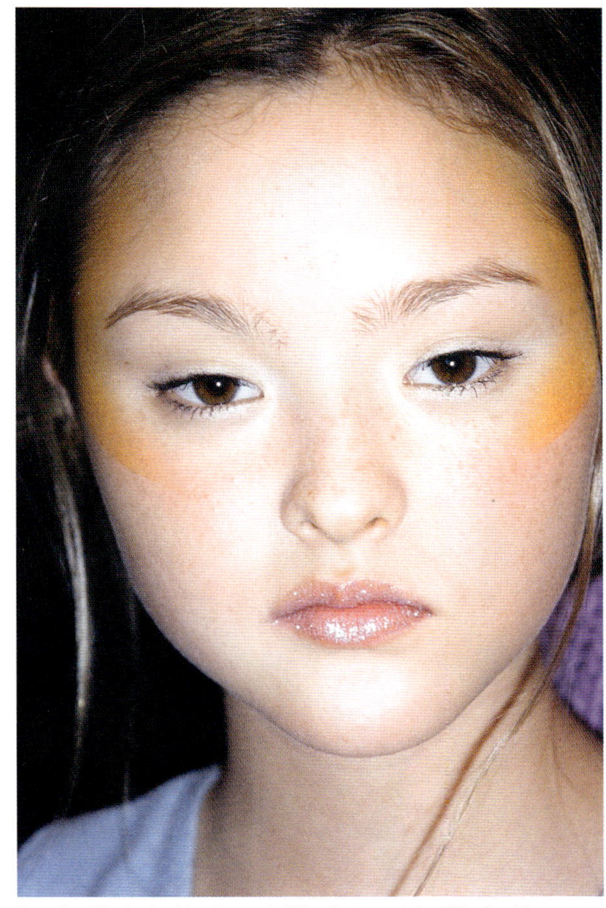

Angelica Blechschmidt, Devon Aoki backstage at Fendi Spring/Summer 2000 by Karl Lagerfeld, Milan 1999

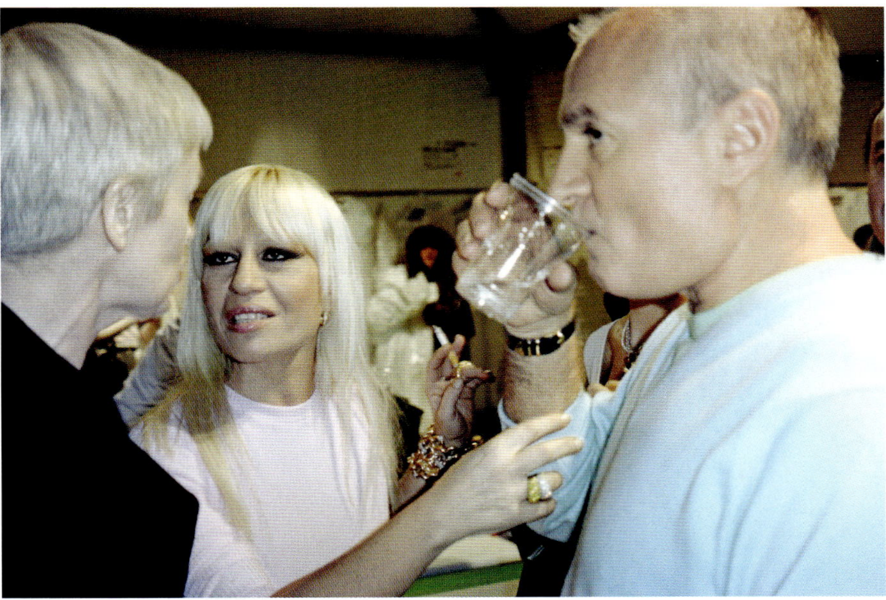

Angelica Blechschmidt, Liz Tilberis, Donatella Versace and Gianni Versace backstage at Versace, Milan 1995

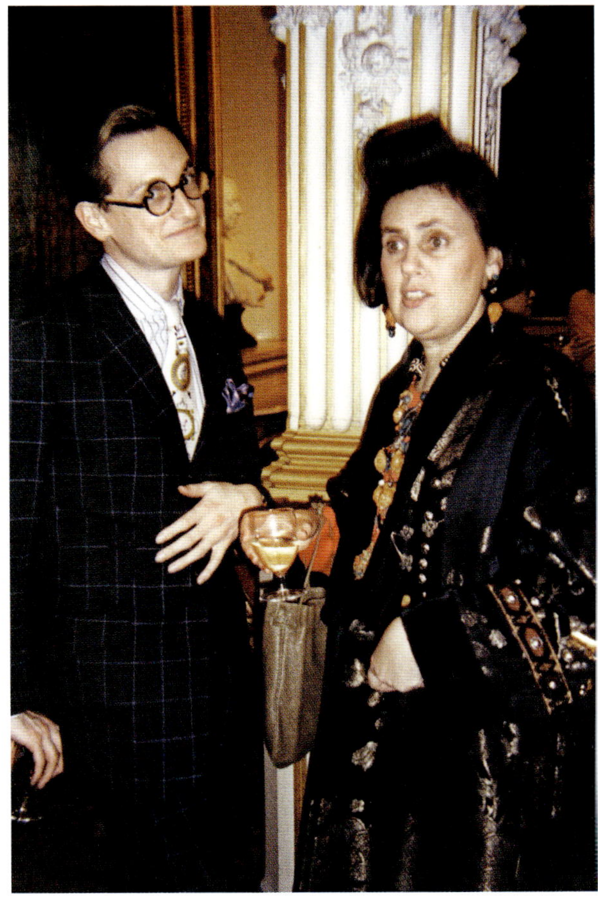

Angelica Blechschmidt, Hamish Bowles and Suzy Menkes at Vivienne Westwood, Paris 1995

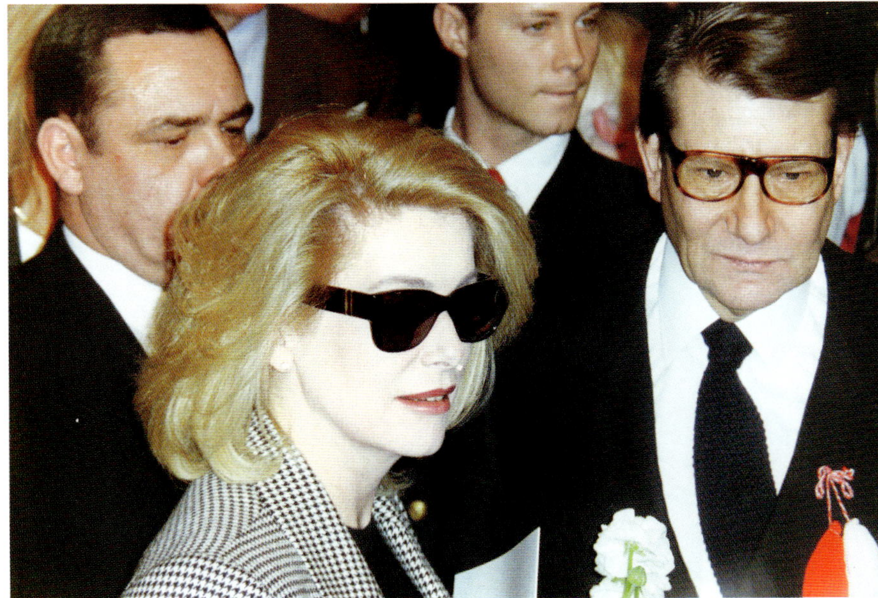

Angelica Blechschmidt, Catherine Deneuve and Yves Saint Laurent backstage at YSL Couture Spring/Summer 1996, Paris 1995

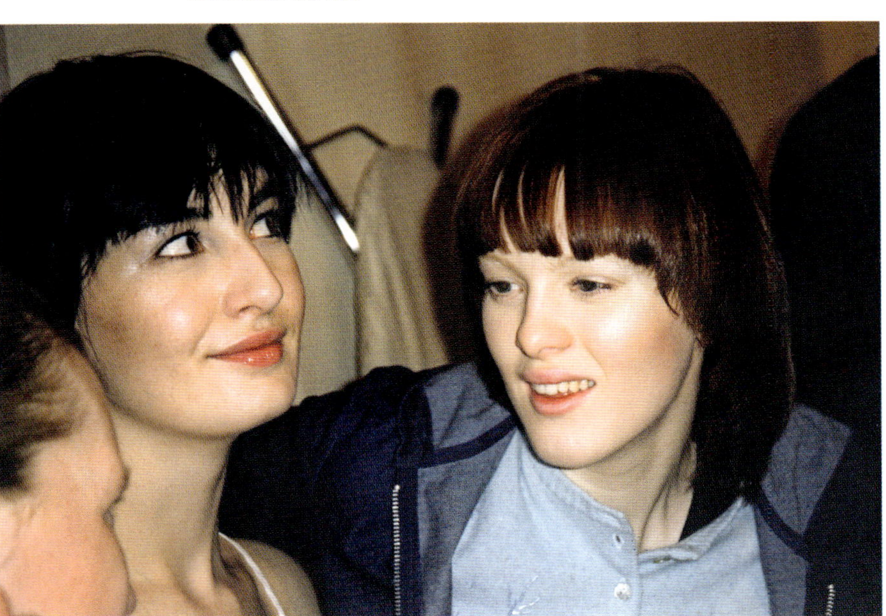

Angelica Blechschmidt, Erin O'Connor and Karen Elson backstage at Chanel Couture Fall/Winter 1999, Paris 1999

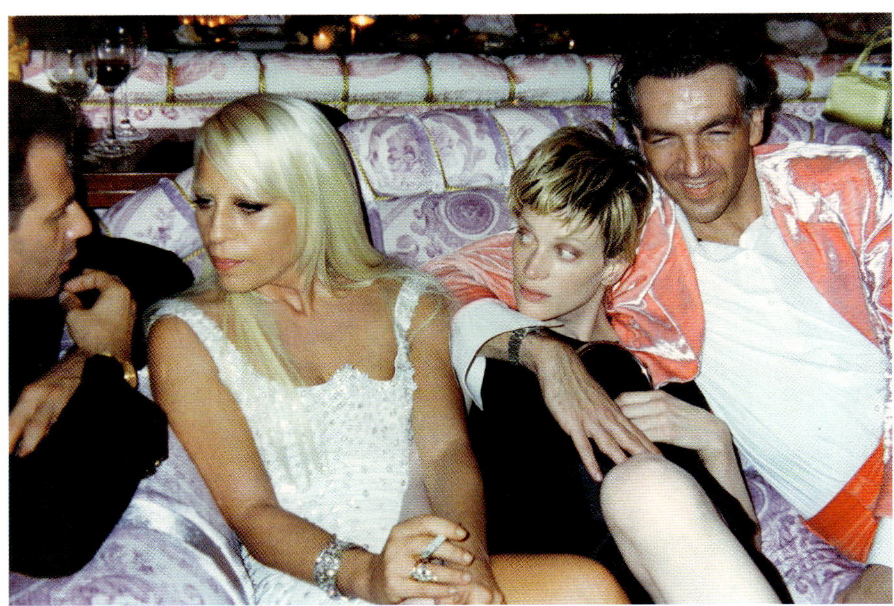

Angelica Blechschmidt, Donatella Versace, Kristen McMenamy and Edgar Otte at an afterparty at Donatella's home, Milan 1996

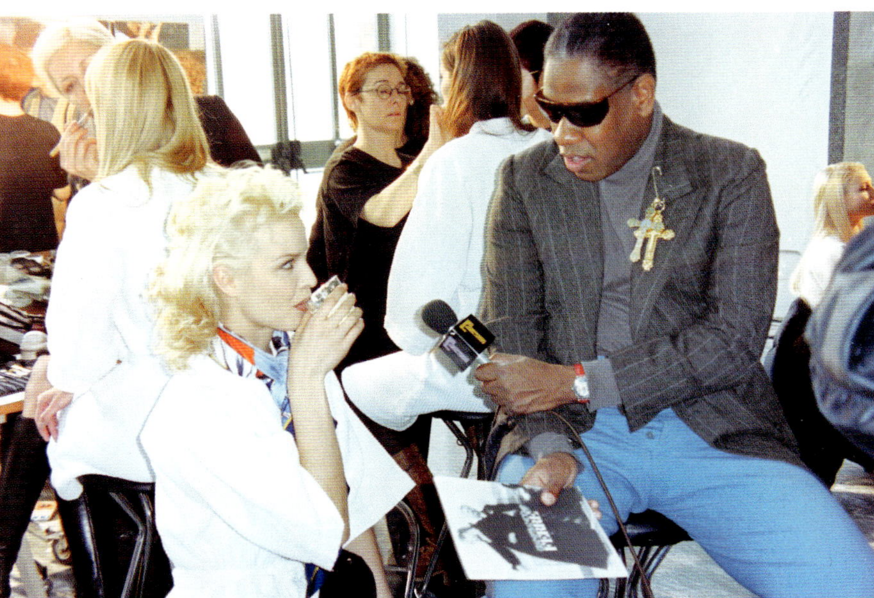

Angelica Blechschmidt, Eva Herzigová backstage at Gianfranco Ferré, interview with André Leon Talley, Milan 1995

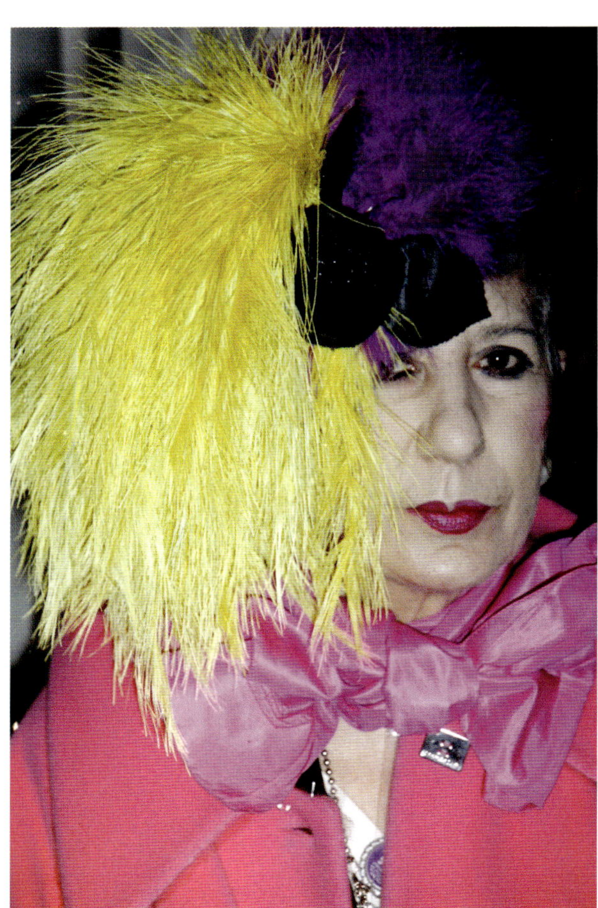

Angelica Blechschmidt, Anna Piaggi, 1995

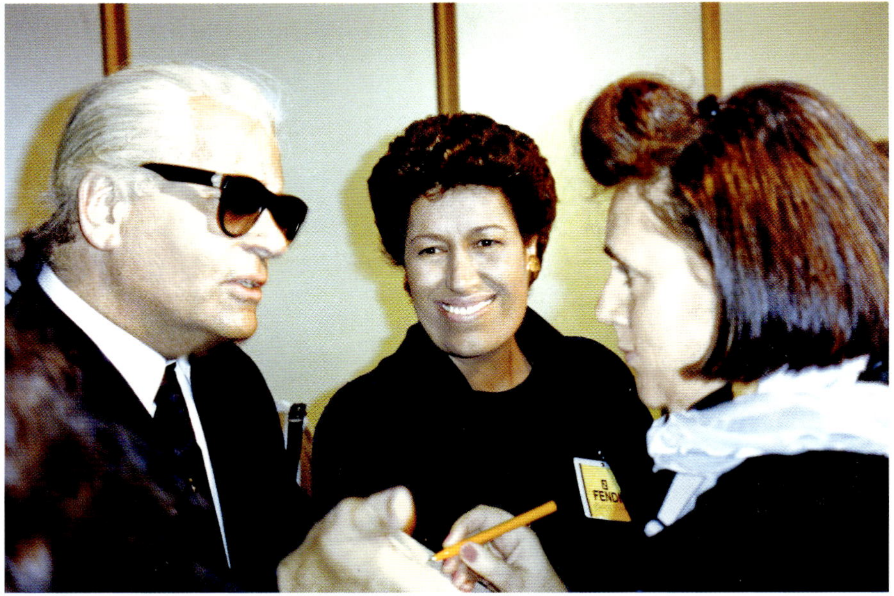

Angelica Blechschmidt, Karl Lagerfeld, Carla Fendi and Suzy Menkes backstage at Fendi, Milan 1995

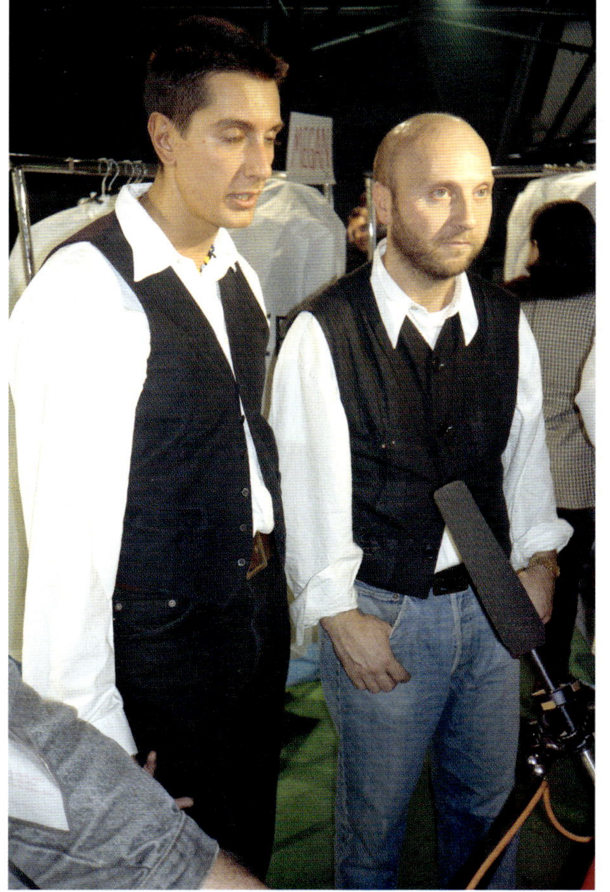

Angelica Blechschmidt, Stefano Gabbana and Domenico Dolce backstage at Dolce & Gabbana Spring/Summer collection, Milan 1993

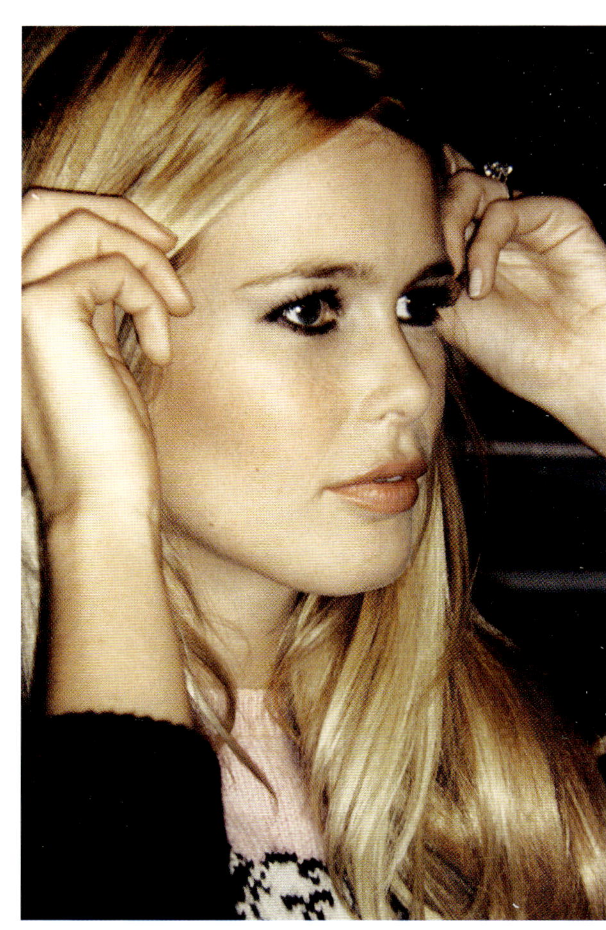

Angelica Blechschmidt, Claudia Schiffer backstage at Chanel Spring/Summer 1996, Paris 1995

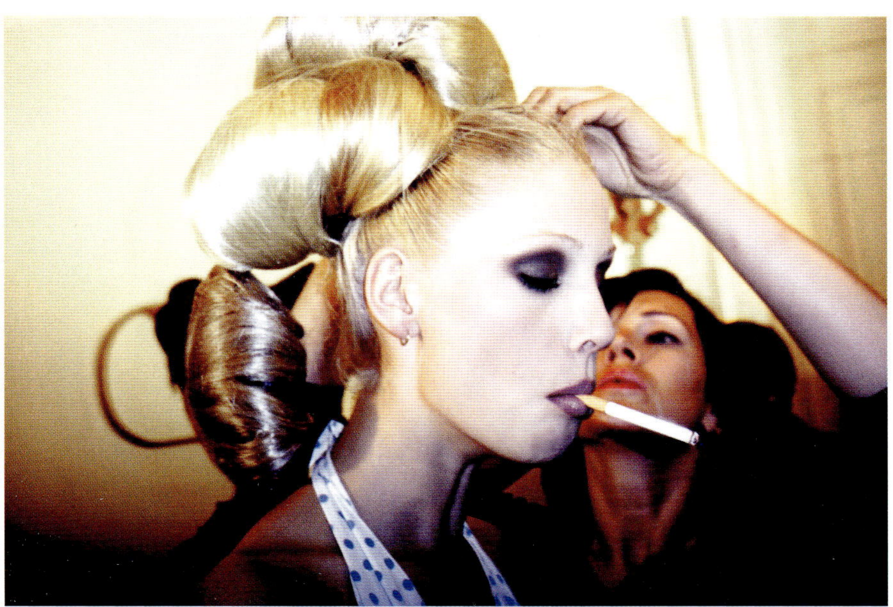

Angelica Blechschmidt, Kirsty Hume backstage at Valentino Spring/Summer 1995, Paris 1995

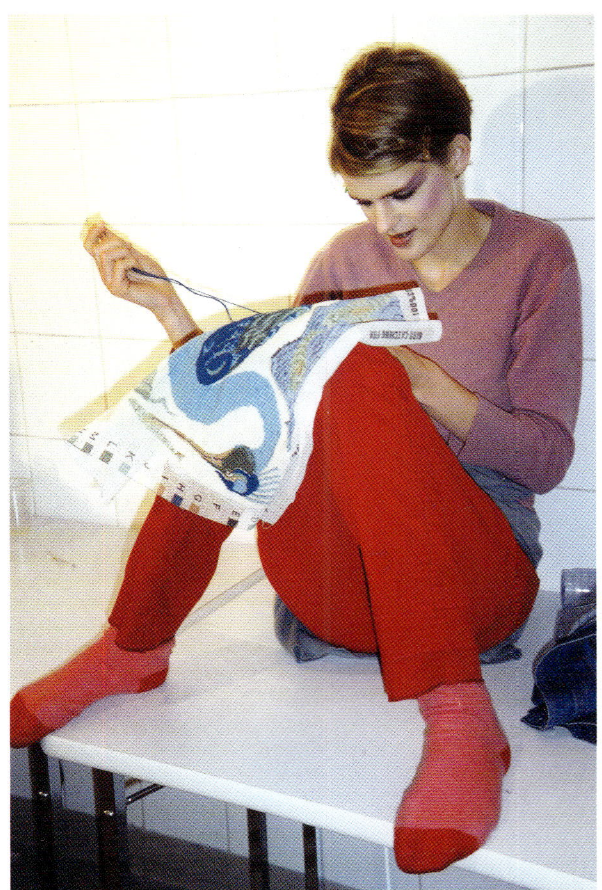

Angelica Blechschmidt, Stella Tennant backstage at Valentino Fall/Winter 1996/1997, Paris 1997

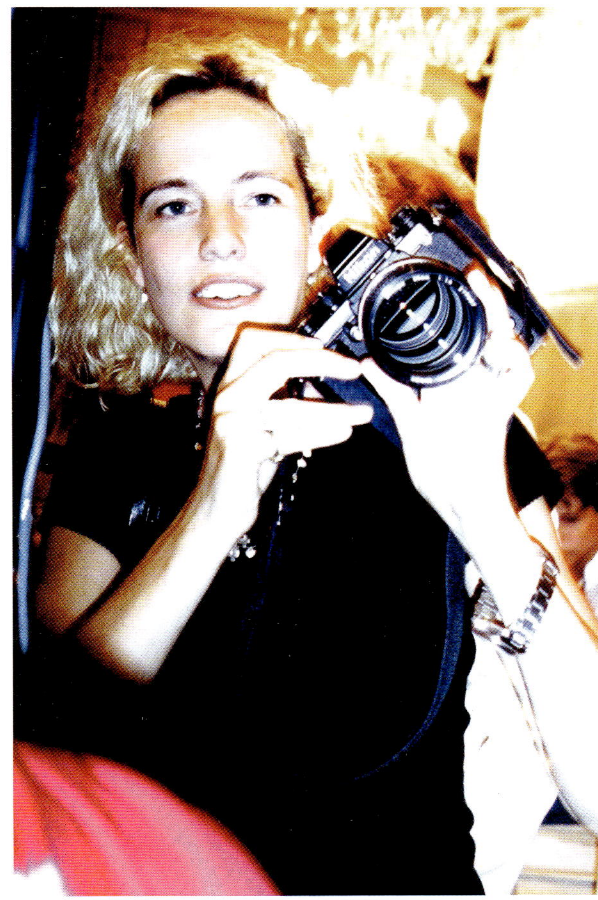

Angelica Blechschmidt, Ellen von Unwerth backstage at Valentino Spring/Summer 1995, Paris 1995

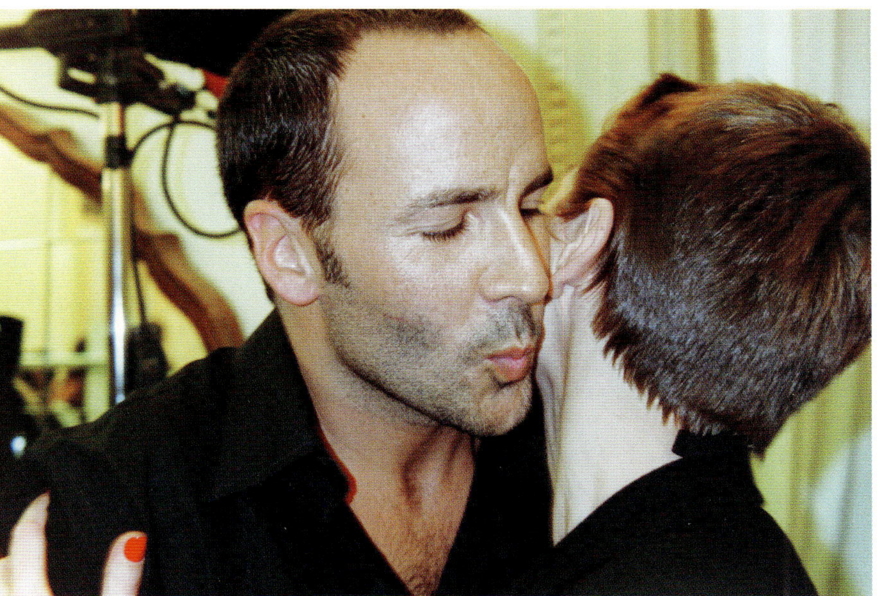

Angelica Blechschmidt, Tom Ford backstage at Gucci Fall/Winter 1995/1996, Milan 1995

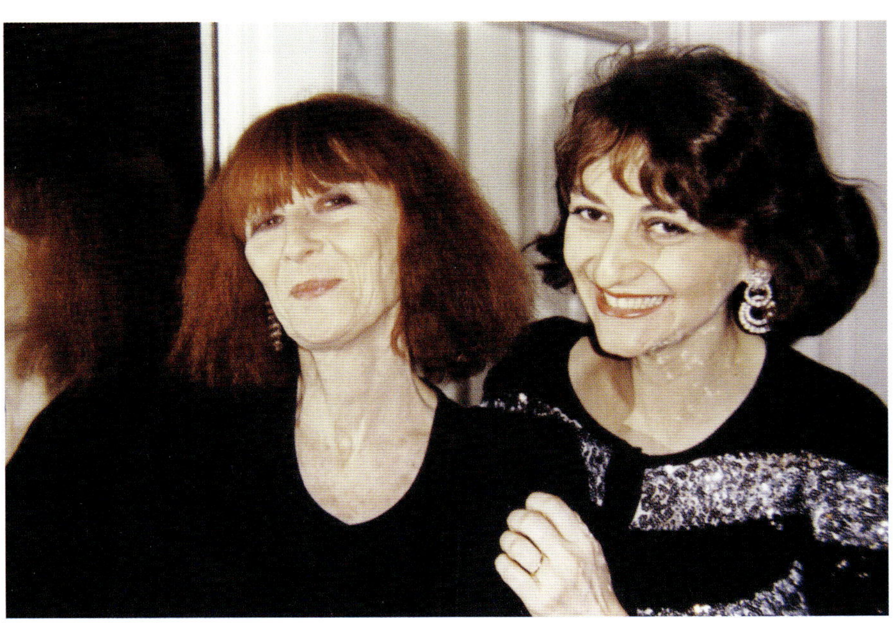

Angelica Blechschmidt, Sonia Rykiel and daughter Nathalie Rykiel backstage, Paris 1995

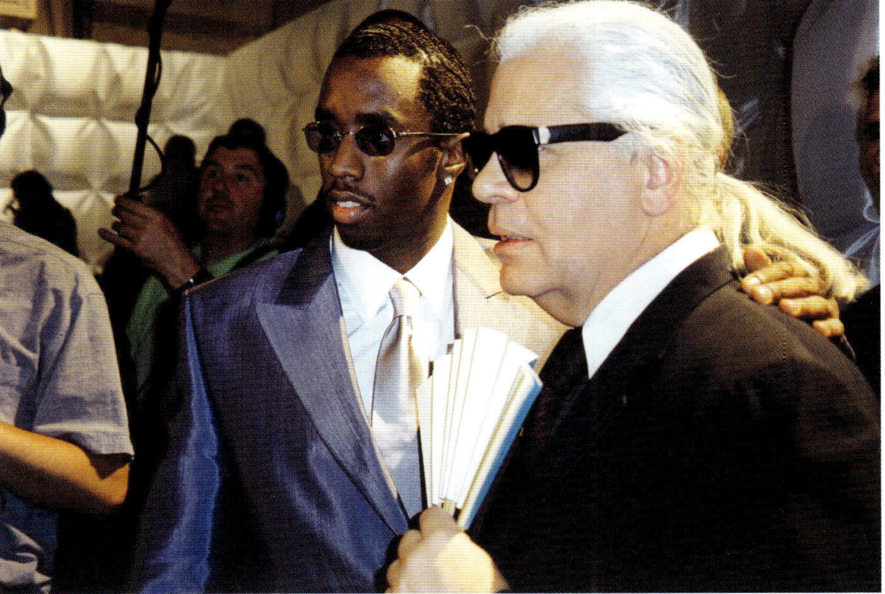

Angelica Blechschmidt, Sean Combs and Karl Lagerfeld backstage at Chanel Couture Spring/Summer 2000, Paris 1999

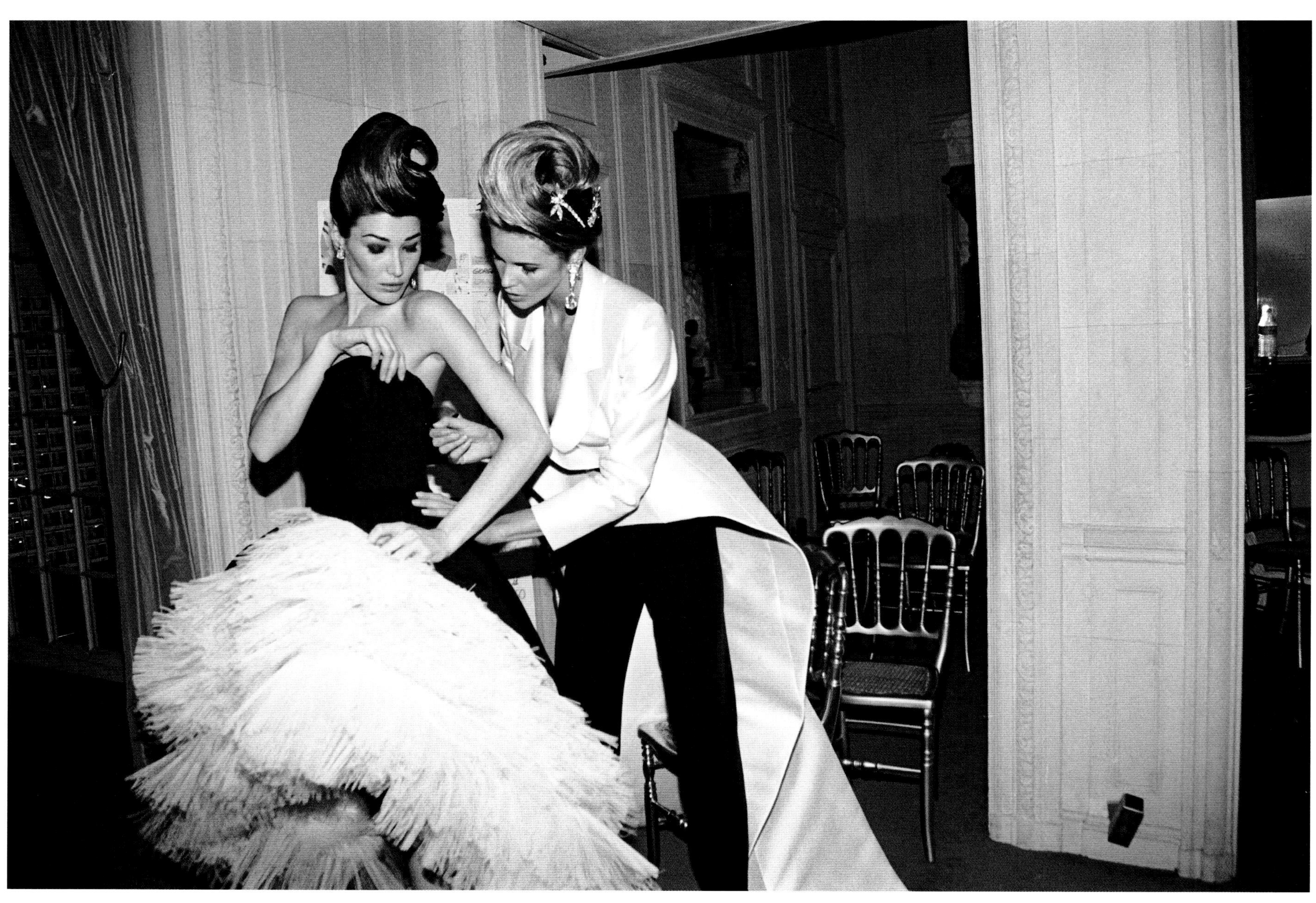

Roxanne Lowit, models: Carla Bruni, Elle Macpherson, 1995 for Dior
Helmut Newton, model: Nadja Auermann, 1995 for *Vogue* IT

In the 1990s backstage photos took on an artistic and commercial value of their own. Inspirations from behind the scenes found their way into campaigns and editorials, as did Helmut Newton's photo for Italian *Vogue* and Roxanne Lowit's Dior campaign. Both depict the process of dressing – the preparation for a fashion show or a photo shoot that is normally hidden from the eyes of audiences or magazine readers. The prominent, public status of these pictures reflects the desire for authenticity that developed in the 1990s.

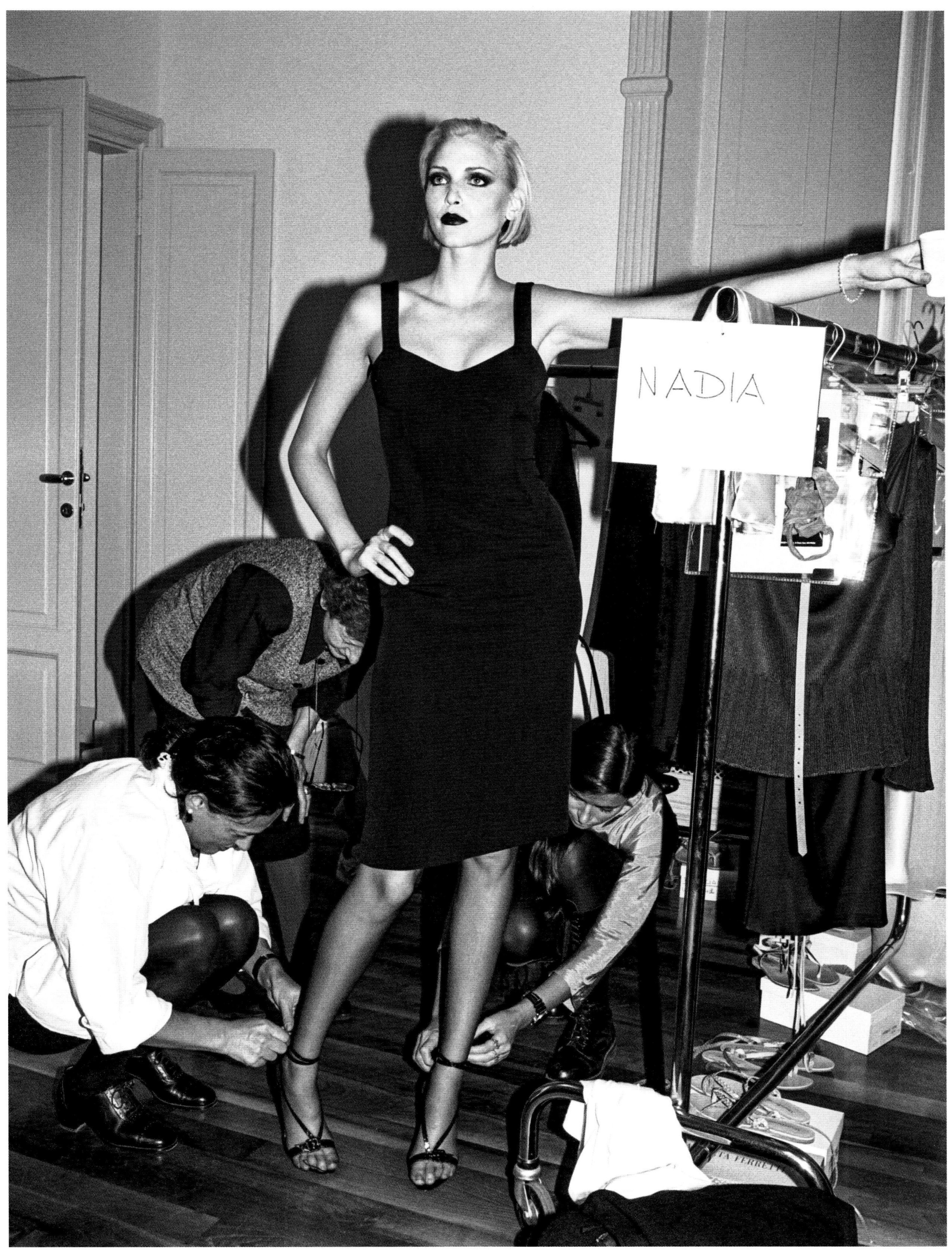
NADIA

WHO IS THE NEXT FASHION ICON?
IT'S YOU.

CLAUDIA SCHIFFER

ESSAYS

BRINGING MAGIC TO 1990S FASHION PHOTOGRAPHY

ELLEN VON UNWERTH

It's moments you cannot ever recreate. The light. Everything. It's just moments.

My photography is a kind of reportage but it's enhanced reportage. It's dramatised. It's exaggerated with the styling and the situation, but I always like to create an image that has a realness to it, something that doesn't immediately look staged, so it could be like a stolen or captured moment on film.

I have an idea of what I want to do. I love to do a storyboard or write a little story, but it's only pictures, not a movie, so I can still be spontaneous. I don't really like to work in studios. I love to work on locations, to have these environments that you play with in your pictures and which sometimes create this unexpected thing. That's what I'm always open to. So, when a dog walks through the picture, or a guy or something, I grab it. And that could be the best picture, because there's always a lot of magic to a spontaneous picture.

A boyfriend gave me my first camera. He said, 'There's a plus, a circle and a minus. When the circle lights up, you start shooting'. That was my crash course in photography.

I grew up in the mountains of Bavaria and then I went to Munich as I was going to study, but I wasn't really into it. On my first day, at the door of the university, somebody asked me if I wanted to model for a hair product. I said, 'Yes', and I turned around and never went back. I never went inside. So I did the job, and after that I joined an agency and they called me to Paris.

I was modelling for ten years. I did runway, too. I did shows for Kenzo and Thierry Mugler and Jean Paul Gaultier. I did Gaultier's first show and he put me in a garbage bag with a belt. That was a really great time, really fun. It still felt like more of a family vibe than being part of a fashion brand. Of course, we did it to make money, but it was friendlier then, and you were closer to the people you worked with – you always worked with the same people. So it was different than it is today.

I had some great experiences. I worked with amazing people, so many great photographers – Helmut Newton, Guy Bourdin, Oliviero Toscani – and I went to lots of beautiful places. It was a very good lesson but I wasn't super happy. I wasn't really enjoying it that much. I always wanted to be creative and do a lot of things, and the photographers would say, 'Look to the left. Look to the right'. So when I started to take photographs, I just did the opposite. I asked the girls to move, to express themselves, to show their personalities. It wasn't only about showing their physiques in the photographs; I also wanted to show what they had inside: if they wanted to laugh, to be angry or sexy. To show their moods and not just their profiles.

That's what's so great about Claudia; she's just so special in that way. She's so playful and always keeps moving. She has this sensuality and is always so charming, and that's why I couldn't stop shooting her.

The first person who gave me a campaign to shoot was the fashion designer Katharine Hamnett. I'd only had my camera for two months, but she gave me her campaign, which was amazing. Then in 1988 I did a shoot for *ELLE* Germany and they wanted me to photograph this German girl called Claudia Schiffer. I thought she was cute. The story was, 'What does a model do when she's not working?' So I went to her home and I shot her brushing her teeth, in her pyjamas with a teddy bear, and walking her dog. Lifestyle pictures. I thought she was so sweet and beautiful, but when I went home and looked at the pictures, I realised there was this really incredible resemblance to Brigitte Bardot, who for me is one of the most iconic, gorgeous women ever. So I called Claudia back a couple of days later and I got a hairdresser and we shot in my tiny apartment in Paris and we made Claudia look like Brigitte Bardot with the hair and makeup. She was brand new. I remember the hairdresser was dancing behind me, showing her how to move. And then I suggested her to Katharine Hamnett, and that was the first campaign we did together.

Then I started to work with Guess. Paul Marciano, co-founder of Guess Inc., called me to come to LA and I did my first campaign with Carré Otis. Then I showed him Claudia and he said, 'Yeah, let's try', and we did a campaign in Nashville (see pp. 27, 30). The story was Brigitte Bardot meets Dolly Parton, the country and western singer from Nashville. We gave Claudia that look with the eyeliner and the poofy hair and it was a big success. To be honest, first of all, I was surprised. You never really know what will touch people. I was excited about working with Claudia, I loved her, but I didn't expect that it would be such a big success for her, for Guess, for everybody. So then we did the campaign many times together. We went to Italy, and Marrakesh, and lots of other places. We did so many shoots together and it basically started our careers. We have so much history together.

I especially love the photographs we did in Greece, and then, of course, the iconic beauty picture of Claudia with her hair over her face and the lace corset (see p. 24). That's one of my favourites; we were in Viareggio, Italy, in 1989, and we were playing this really silly song. We were just goofing around and Claudia was dancing. The sea breeze came in through the window – it wasn't a wind machine – and it was just one of those captured moments. That became the picture that's referenced all the time.

I always love black-and-white photography because you can really see if it's a good picture or not. Black-and-white photography looks better because it's more graphic, it's timeless and it's got that cinematic feeling. In the 1990s that same mood was shared by Bruce Weber, Herb Ritts, Steven Meisel and Peter Lindbergh: all amazing photographers who are featured in this exhibition.

As a photographer you always imagine the story you want to tell or the character you want to create: this kind of girl, in love with that kind of guy. There's always a lot of love and jealousy involved. It's important to have that idea, that narrative, and to work with hair and makeup people who can create that in a realistic way. I've always wanted to create this glamorous girl but to capture her in a very natural way. Shoot her so she doesn't look posed or overly mannered.

That's just the way I see women. I see them as beautiful and sexy, but also strong and in control of their image – liberated and self-assured. That was never even a question for me. They were naughty and daring, but always self-assured and emancipated. Today, this is how women are talked about, but earlier, for me, this was not even a question; it was just how I saw women.

The 'supermodels' were like superheroes. People wanted to know everything about them and they appeared in pop videos like George Michael's 'Freedom! '90'. The supermodels were larger than life. They were so glamorous. Whatever you put on Linda Evangelista, for example, looked like a million dollars. At the fashion shows, it was electrifying when they came out on the runway because often the designers created something really special for them. Every time Naomi or Christy or Claudia came out, you'd be gasping. The supermodels were super professional and so much fun to work with; it was like driving a Ferrari.

And then grunge happened. I think it started with Kate Moss; she was the icon of grunge. I was actually the first one to put her into Italian *Vogue*. Previously she had only done that shoot with Corinne Day for *The Face*. Grunge wasn't so much my thing, but as a photographer you just have to do your thing and not be distracted by what's trendy at that particular moment. Know what you love, what you believe in. It's better to stick with your style than change to what's fashionable because in the end that's what you do best.

I always love my glamorous, slightly bad girls with lots of personality. They have a glossy look, but are also a bit dishevelled. They live. They have experience. They have adventures.

At that time I also photographed so many musicians, like Courtney Love, and fashion magazines would put a lot of these people on the covers. I worked so much for *The Face* and *i-D*, and those magazines also tended to put more musicians on their covers. This change in cover stars was very influential in the fashion world.

And I've shot so many actors. Actually, at one point I was shooting more celebrities than I was models, because that's what magazines wanted. Fashion had moved on from the supermodels, their moment in the spotlight was over; instead editors wanted actresses and musicians on the covers, and it's still the same now. People are more interested in their lives and can identify more with them and what they have to give. As a photographer it's interesting to catch their personalities and bring out their beauty.

A model is employed to do a particular job. With a model the client can say, 'Okay, do this'. Often it's just another job for them, but with actresses you have to be a little bit more diplomatic. You have to coax them into situations. You have to make them feel comfortable because they might not be used to posing for pictures. As they're used to acting, it's great when you give them a role to play, even more so than with models. Actresses become even more beautiful when you see them on the screen, and musicians who might look just okay in real life ooze beauty and animalistic feeling when they're performing. It's interesting to bring out the performer in the photograph.

Before I started taking pictures, and before I started modelling, I was working at the Circus Roncalli in Munich. It was a very special circus founded by André Heller and Bernhard Paul; it was very romantic and special, with lots of young people participating. I did that for a couple of months. The experience was really influential for my photographic career because I loved all the performers, the atmosphere and the glitter and the mystery of it.

I used this inspiration to inform my photography, to inform my approach to making the models move and be expressive, and also for how I wanted the lighting. I felt it was the time to really show their personalities. That was something new for the 1990s. It's the magic that, as a photographer, I'm always looking for.

WHAT REMAINS

CHRISTIANE ARP

In the 1990s foundations were laid and structures created in fashion and photography that we continue to build upon today.

The 1990s may be over, and some of its protagonists no longer active – or, sadly, deceased, like the great Peter Lindbergh and the wonderful Franca Sozzani – but nonetheless, this decade is not yet history. The majority of the most important designers and labels of that time are still on the scene, along with many of the influential fashion photographers and some of their models. However, the structures created and developed in those days for the fashion business and fashion photography remain the foundation of our work to this day.

The most astonishing and enduring phenomena of this decade in fashion is probably that the names of the models became known far beyond the usual fashion circles; they became brands that resonate to this day. When I say Linda, Naomi, Nadja or Claudia, everyone today still knows who I am talking about. Probably the most difficult goal to attain in fashion is to become timeless. Some designers have managed it, as have some fashion photographers. But models? These young women, who supported each other, were not just mannequins; they were 'supermodels'. And they had, or acquired, what it took to successfully follow their own paths, as celebrities and businesswomen – just as Claudia Schiffer did with her film production company, Cloudy Productions, which brought hits like the *Kingsman* series (from 2014) to the silver screen.

What characterised the 1990s? What enabled the supermodel phenomenon, and who contributed to it? What made these women so special? And how does this time period continue to affect our own era?

No one else was, and still is, as often on the cover of German *Vogue* as Claudia Schiffer – she has appeared fifteen times to date. Her first cover was in 1990, and the most recent was 2017. I myself began working more intensively with her after I took over the position of editor-in-chief of German *Vogue* in March 2003. She can be seen on the cover of the August issue along with her first child, who was born in January of that year. It is a photo that is also part of her whole personal history. That such pictures became possible has much to do with a trusting relationship whose foundations were laid in the 1990s.

There was a group of photographers and a group of models who knew each other well, working together over and over, so that they were able to move beyond all limitations by trusting one another. And they knew that the results would be special, and that the pictures they created would become part of their personal histories, not simply a part of fashion history separate from their own existences.

Although new and great talents arrived in the 1990s, it was essentially only a handful of photographers working with no more than ten or twenty models but doing so continually. The teams they worked with and the trust they were able to develop in the process were also of enormous importance. When the models went to the studio knowing that they could expect this makeup artist and that hairdresser to be there, along with a certain stylist, and above all a particular photographer they knew well, then committed teams grew out of that. Together, they were able to create a body of work, for one shoot always built upon the previous one. Without these teams, perhaps the kind of success the supermodels achieved might not have been possible.

There were two women in the background whose influence cannot be underestimated: Franca Sozzani and Anna Wintour, who became the editors-in-chief of Italian and US *Vogue* respectively, in the late 1980s.

Anna Wintour arrived at US *Vogue* in August 1988. Her entirely new concept of fashion manifested almost immediately on the November cover of that year. Peter Lindbergh photographed Michaela Bercu wearing a Christian Lacroix couture jacket and Bercu's own jeans; he believed the picture would be cropped so the jeans would not be seen. But in fact, Anna Wintour included them in the cover image. This was the first time such a combination of streetwear and couture was depicted. It was an apparently simple act, but it led fashion into a whole new world and a whole new time; it was a glimpse of the future. Shortly afterward, Lindbergh's now legendary photo of six white-shirted models, including Linda Evangelista, Tatjana Patitz and Christy Turlington, appeared inside the magazine.

At Italian *Vogue,* Franca Sozzani decided that from then on, all cover photos would be taken by the same photographer, Steven Meisel. For about a quarter of a century, Meisel produced every cover of the magazine: an extreme example of how such an opportunity enabled continuity of work and the development of a specific style. Together Sozzani and Meisel opened up a new dimension in the elaborate narrative possibilities of fashion photography.

Both Franca Sozzani and Anna Wintour contributed to the myth of the supermodel, because, besides the big campaigns, it was their magazines that published so many photo series with them. And the advertising changed, too; ads were influenced by the magazine editorial shoots, and sometimes even derived from them. Richard Avedon's work for Versace, for example, became famous.

Incidentally, it was Gianni Versace – along with the ranks of brilliant photographers from Lindbergh to Ellen von Unwerth to Avedon – who became another crucial person in the creation of the supermodel phenomenon. He no longer wanted to see the perfect, high-stepping models on his runways; rather, he yearned for women with radiant, vivacious spirits and personalities to represent his fashion. In those days there was still a distinction between runway and print models. And so Versace's eye fell upon the women being photographed in the studios: the future supermodels. Even then, they were highly individual personalities. Naomi Campbell, Linda Evangelista, Tatjana Patitz, Christy Turlington, Claudia Schiffer and then Kate Moss – they were inimitable and enormously versatile. When Versace put them on his runway, he made their images come alive. There they were, no longer caught in a camera lens but present in the real world, ready to become stars.

Versace was also one of the first to turn his campaigns into books and send them to fashion journalists. Advertising became as important – and, for the first time, as creative – as magazine photography. Claudia once told me that she wanted to be a canvas for the photographers, transforming herself for each story and theme, just as she had in Von Unwerth's famous Guess campaign, with Claudia in the role of Brigitte Bardot.

The 1990s was not just the era of the supermodels, though. It also witnessed styles such as grunge and dirty realism, and the arrival of Photoshop, the massive image-processing program, which has now found its way into the private sector in the form of filters used for social media pictures. Women who were already the most beautiful in the world were being photographed, but suddenly they all looked as if they had undergone cosmetic surgery and had large shots of Botox: that was Photoshop. They all looked the same. Such unrealistic images put pressure on everyone and they continue to do so on the Internet. Still, even back then, both consumers and models began to oppose it. The former felt subordinated to a supposed ideal that was hardly attainable, and the latter were confronted with artificial images of themselves – and this at a time when the first phase of their youth, in which everything was taken for granted, was slowly coming to an end, and the choices of adult life had to be examined. At the same time, the fashion world was also changing.

The pioneers among the supermodels began exploring their options. They became 'influencers' before this term even existed. Nearly all became successful (business)women, each in their own way. The solidarity that existed among them certainly helped them achieve this. They had always appeared together earlier, and to this day they can be seen on social networks, greeting each other, wishing each other luck, and celebrating each other's projects. At the same time, many of them have remained active as models. Ten of the fifteen German *Vogue* covers featuring Claudia Schiffer were shot since 2000.

During this period, Claudia Schiffer became a mother. While she was pregnant with her third child, we collaborated with her on an entire issue, which, among others, included a portrait of Karl Lagerfeld. Perhaps today she appears less frequently in front of the camera than she once did, but nothing has changed regarding either her professionalism or her sense of fashion, nor of the story that we want to tell.

Supermodels like Claudia Schiffer, and their credibility, authenticity and personal style, have hugely contributed to altering our view of fashion and, above all, of ourselves. We wear the dress; the dress does not wear us.

GEORGE SAID FREEDOM

CARINE ROITFELD

The rise of the supermodel, a minimalist dogma and the hippy resurgence. The 1990s mark a major turning point in the design, presentation and embodiment of fashion. Its sole ideal: freedom. More than a happy decade.

I first meet Claudia in the 1980s, my *ELLE* France years. It is Odile Sarron, the magazine's casting director, who first believes in her and propels her to the top. The other girls also currently adored by the world are called Linda, Cindy, Naomi, Christy, Stephanie, Carla, Nadja, Yasmeen, Tatjana… We just use their first names.

For the fashion world, at the time, everything seems possible. A sense of frivolity is back in the air. The times are upbeat. Music sets the tone. And as George Michael says: 'Freedom!' Freedom is the watchword on the runway, on the sets of advertising campaigns, on the covers and in the contents of magazines.

Alongside Mario Testino, our most iconoclastic ideas know no obstacles. Now is the time for experimentation; it is welcomed and celebrated. Fashion is still not an 'industry', accessories are no central to the growth of brands, and the visibility given to the clothing in the images created is of little importance. What matters is image, beauty and emotion. A utopia with hippie aspirations, which I try to recapture today as it fascinates, stimulates and inspires me.

This freedom, which is crucial to the 1990s, is manifested particularly in the depiction of sexuality. It is a paradigm shift. Women take control of their sexuality. They become the masters of it. No more 'male gaze' – now women are equal to men, who appear in fashion imagery for the first time. In the Versace campaigns by Richard Avedon, it is men who are often deprived of their clothes; their bodies are sexualised, they are shown as being sensitive, more vulnerable, a position hitherto reserved for women.

At Gucci, where we've joined forces with Tom Ford, just arrived from the US, the looks scream 'SEX'. A liberated approach missing from the runways since the late 1970s and the AIDS epidemic, which plunged the world into a state of anxiety and robbed the fashion industry of some of its most promising talent. Tom proposes a hedonistic fashion. The girls in white dresses inspired by Halston are 'Newtonesque' (see p. 97). They tread to the rhythm of 'Killing Me Softly' by the Fugees.

At the time, men's fashion is almost non-existent on the runway. But at Gucci, diversity reigns. Each gender and all skin colours are represented on Tom's runway who sees in his models the embodiment of potential customers. Feminine looks are adapted for men, and vice versa. Men and women wear the same red velvet suits and the same thongs with the double G. The era loves provocation – and so do we!

The ascent of Kate Moss occurs at the same time. She is fourteen years old when she is discovered, and she does not meet the standard criteria of beauty. She is smaller than the other girls, doesn't have much of a bust, more 'girl next door' than 'bombshell'. Although her beauty is not obvious, it is imposing.

She becomes the face of Calvin Klein underwear. Fixed firmly in the collective imagination of today, David Sims's photographs mark a break with the past. Even more than youthful sexuality, it is boyish femininity that shocks. In 1994, Steven Meisel shoots the perfume campaign for cK one inspired by Avedon's images of Andy Warhol and members of The Factory.

These tableaux tell of a young multicultural generation that questions heteronormativity and gender. The wardrobes of women and men are interchangeable. The definition and depiction of 'sexy' is evolving. The models are not those found in calendars with their extreme physiques. The bodies presented are less 'perfect' than those from before, more accessible, more real. They become desirable role models for young people, who identify with them more easily.

Now is the time for minimalism, dictated by the collections of Helmut Lang, who transforms the silhouette of a whole generation. Calvin Klein and Martin Margiela in turn make their contributions. 'Less is more' is now the mantra. The styling in fashion photography is simple: a pair of jeans and a white T-shirt, effortless but formidably effective.

This minimalist wave is captured by Juergen Teller, whose photography, in my opinion, remains among the most representative of the spirit of the 1990s (see pp. 177, 188–191). His gelatin silver prints show the models of the time as we've never seen them before. He publishes *Go-Sees*, a collection of images shot before casting calls. Mariacarla wears a cardigan and a pair of Birkenstocks, Adriana arrives in jeans and a white tank top, Devon is in an extra-large college T-shirt.

This raw realism contrasts sharply with the sweetness of the images from the previous decade. Spontaneity prevails, and Juergen captures the moment and the intimacy. This radicalism stripped of all artifice, whether in clothing, hair or makeup, has a major impact on 1990s fashion photography.

The image embraces movement and is accepting of blurriness. Digital photography does not exist. The pictures are rarely if ever retouched. The beauty of the girls is never the subject. Above all, the photos are lived moments.

These are shared behind the scenes, where families are formed. Photographers, stylists, hairdressers, makeup artists, casting directors, models… the designers are loyal to their teams both on the set and in the high life that cements their fame. I spend my first time at the Met Gala alongside Helmut Lang, Stella Tennant and Melanie Ward. I wear a dress that Helmut made to measure for me. It is one of the rare pieces I have kept. There was no Instagram yet. You had to make people dream. It was enough.

SPECIAL THANKS

I am grateful to all the photographers who have contributed their iconic works to this exhibition. It is their work, created during a monumental decade in fashion and photography, that we are celebrating.

I want to thank Ellen von Unwerth, Christiane Arp and Carine Roitfeld for their insightful essays and support for the show.

To the editors, designers, stylists and models who have shared their points of view and memories of the time – thank you. What fun we had!

Thank you to everyone at the Kunstpalast, Dusseldorf, especially Felix Krämer, Linda Conze and Svenja Schütte, for their support and dedication to *Captivate!*, and Mathias Beyer for his graphic design work.

And finally, thanks to my creative team Lucie McCullin, Erin Graham and Oscar Humphries for spending many hours helping me put it all together.

Claudia Schiffer

Richard Avedon (1923–2004)
At the age of twenty-two, Richard Avedon began working for *Harper's Bazaar*. He photographed on the streets, in nightclubs, at the circus, on the beach and at other unusual locations. In 1966 Avedon joined US *Vogue*, where he worked for more than twenty years. Throughout, he ran a successful commercial studio and is widely credited with erasing the line between 'art' and 'commercial' photography. His brand-defining work and long associations with Calvin Klein, Revlon, Versace and dozens of other companies resulted in well-known advertising campaigns. Solo exhibitions of his work have been held, among others, at the Smithsonian Institution, Washington, D.C., and the Metropolitan Museum of Art, New York.

Gilles Bensimon (*1944)
The career of photographer Gilles Bensimon began in 1967 at *ELLE* magazine in France. In 1969 the Frenchman moved to New York, where he was the creative director of US *ELLE* for many years and made considerable contributions to its development. His incisive images had a lasting influence on the magazine's look. Aside from his extensive work as a fashion photographer, Bensimon also produced numerous iconic portraits of pop culture celebrities. Beyond his commercial work, he has always pursued his own independent, artistic approach to photography, and regularly exhibits in galleries.

Angelica Blechschmidt (1940s–2018)
Angelica Blechschmidt became the editor-in-chief of German *Vogue* in 1989. She knew how to combine fashion with intellectual and artistic aspirations, turning the German offshoot of *Vogue* (founded in 1979) into a magazine that people did not simply leaf through but also read. With her Olympus compact camera, Blechschmidt photographed everything that happened in the fashion world. Out of this emerged the column 'Flash!', a mix of analogue motives of current trends and snapshots of parties as well as all the relevant figures on the fashion scene from the 1980s to the early 2000s. In 2003 Blechschmidt retired from her position as editor-in-chief, and in 2005 she moved out of the former Castle Weyhern, near Munich, to Potsdam, where she spent her twilight years. To the last, she was active in following the fashion scene with her camera.

Walter Chin (*1955)
Walter Chin was born in Jamaica to a Chinese family and grew up in Toronto. There, he received his Bachelor of Arts from Ryerson University. After his graduation, Chin moved to Paris, where he worked for French *ELLE*, before relocating to New York in 1990. His work has been published in many magzines, including *Allure*, *Mademoiselle*, *Vogue*, *Glamour*, *GQ*, *Interview* and *Vanity Fair*. He has also photographed advertising campaigns for fashion houses such as Chanel, Valentino, Tommy Hilfiger and Missoni. His works have been represented in several exhibitions, including at the International Center of Photography, New York, and the National Portrait Gallery, London.

Michel Comte (*1954)
The Swiss photographer and filmmaker Michel Comte is a master of spontaneity and transformation who is always on the lookout for new challenges. Over the course of his more than forty-year-long career, he has photographed movie stars, supermodels, the greats of the jazz and art scenes, and people in crisis situations around the world. Although he was educated in modern art restoration, he turned to photography in the late 1970s and moved to Paris. In 1979 his work was noticed by Karl Lagerfeld; as a result, he received commissions from prominent fashion labels such as Chloé, Armani, Dolce & Gabbana, Nike, Versace and Chanel throughout the 1980s and 1990s. Comte also regularly worked for Franca Sozzani at Italian *Vogue* and has created a variety of projects for museums and galleries.

Corinne Day (1962–2010)
Corinne Day was a self-taught British photographer who brought a documentary look to fashion imagery, in which she often included autobiographical elements. She was known for forming long and close relationships with many of her muses: a way of working which resulted in candid and intimate portraits. With her unique approach Day transferred 'grunge' to fashion photography and thus shaped an international style. She worked with magazines associated with youth and counterculture such as *The Face* and *i-D*, as well as established fashion publications such as *Vogue*. Her work has been exhibited in the National Portrait Gallery, the Victoria & Albert Museum, Tate Modern, the Saatchi Gallery and The Photographers' Gallery, all London, and the Whitney Museum of American Art, New York.

Patrick Demarchelier (*1943)
Patrick Demarchelier grew up in France. His enthusiasm for photography was kindled by a camera given to him by his stepfather. As well as working in photography labs, he studied the aesthetics of famous photographers in leading fashion magazines. Subsequently, he enjoyed increasing success, ultimately becoming one of the most famous fashion photographers in the world. A move to New York in 1975 coincided with his international breakthrough. From the 1970s onwards, Demarchelier's photographs have appeared in magazines such as *ELLE*, *Vogue*, *Glamour*, *GQ*, *Mademoiselle* and *Rolling Stone*. His visual vocabulary has had considerable influence on the genre of supermodel photography. He lives in New York.

Arthur Elgort (*1940)
Born in New York, Arthur Elgort went on to study painting at Hunter College. Finding the medium too lonely, he decided to try his hand at photography. In 1971 he debuted in British *Vogue*. With just one shoot he created not only a sensation but a permanent place for himself in the arena of fashion photography. His relaxed and easy snapshot style was a breath of fresh air in a scene where staged and stiff studio shoots were the norm. Taking his models outside into the 'real world' became a signature of his. From his *Vogue* covers to his luxury-brand ad campaigns, Elgort became one of the best-known photographers in the world and has been a major influence for over fifty years.

Ross Feltus (1939–2003)
The American photographer Ross Feltus achieved fame largely through his portraits of children; in Germany he was even considered the most well-known photographer of children. His photographs appeared in *Stern*, the *Sunday Times Magazine*, *People* and international syndications. His calendars were published by UNICEF, Verkerke, the Lübbe Verlag and many other renowned publishing houses. Feltus was also a commercial photographer and worked on advertising campaigns for various firms such as Henkel, Colgate-Palmolive, Horten, Ford, Steiff, Miele and Rodenstock. Feltus practised his profession in Dusseldorf until just before his death. He died in Miami on 18 January 2003. He and his wife Ursula were the parents of Barbara Feltus, who was married to the tennis player Boris Becker from 1993 to 2001.

Hans Feurer (*1939)
After studying art in the 1960s, Hans Feurer worked as a graphic designer, illustrator and artistic director in England. During a trip to South Africa, he discovered a passion for photography, which he proceeded to turn into a profession, making his international breakthrough in 1967. Subsequently, his work was published in magazines such as *Vogue*, *Numéro*, *ELLE* and *Twen*. To this day Feurer works in fashion photography, travelling to some of the most remote countries in the world for his profession. His pictures are infused with a period atmosphere, which, depending on the decade, can be recognised primarily by the colour palette and recurring stylistic features. Hans Feurer lives in Switzerland.

Russell James (*1962)
Russell James worked as a policeman and a model before achieving his international breakthrough as a photographer in New York in the late 1990s. He has established himself as an artist who combines the classic aesthetics of late twentieth-century fashion photography with contemporary elements and a formative style. He is regarded as someone who has continued to develop upon the work of photographers such as Herb Ritts and Patrick Demarchelier, and hence has had a substantial influence on supermodel photography in the twenty-first century. His photographs also reflect the culture of his home country, Australia. Unusual landscapes and spectacular lighting also contribute to his individual style. He lives in Australia.

Karl Lagerfeld (1933–2019)
Karl Lagerfeld was born in Hamburg. His ascent to the position of one of the most renowned fashion designers in the world began in the mid-1950s in Paris, where he worked for fashion houses including Balmain and Chloé. In 1983 he became the creative director at Chanel. In 1987 Lagerfeld photographed his first press kit for the House; from then on, he produced all the company's campaigns himself. His extensive photographic oeuvre, which has been shown at various institutions including the Museum Folkwang in Essen and the Kunstmuseum Moritzburg Halle, reveals artistic references to the paintings of Lyonel Feininger, Edward Hopper and Florine Stettheimer, as well as to the films of Fritz Lang and the photographs of Edward Steichen.

Peter Lindbergh (1944–2019)
Born in Duisburg, Peter Lindbergh became known for his cinematic black-and-white images, and pioneered a form of new realism by redefining the standards of beauty. In the late 1980s, he photographed a new generation of barely made-up models in white shirts, and soon afterwards shot them on the streets of New York for the January 1990 issue of British *Vogue* – a shoot considered by many as the 'birth of the supermodels'. His genuine form of storytelling was influenced by early German silent cinema as well as by his industrial hometown. He collaborated with multitudes of major fashion brands and magazines including *Vogue*, *Vanity Fair*, *Harper's Bazaar*, *Interview* and *W*. His work is held in prestigious museum collections and has been exhibited in institutions such as the Victoria & Albert Museum, London, the Centre Pompidou, Paris, MoMA PS1, New York, and Düsseldorf's Kunstpalast.

Roxanne Lowit (*1942)
For over four decades Roxanne Lowit has captured the faces and personalities of contemporary culture from a unique perspective. A native New Yorker, Lowit was originally a textile designer but found her true calling crafting imagery of a different kind, creating a new genre of photography shooting backstage at fashion shows. She transformed fashion photography forever, elevating it to the ranks of fine art. Lowit has published four books. and her photographs, which are inscribed in cultural memory, have been exhibited at the Metropolitan Museum of Art and the Whitney Museum of American Art, both New York, the Victoria & Albert Museum, London, and the Moscow Museum of Modern Art. Her photographs are part of the permanent collection of the prestigious Kobe Fashion Museum.

Helmut Newton (1920–2004)
Helmut Newton was born in Berlin. His interest in photography was sparked during his childhood; he received his first camera at the age of twelve and, as a teen, was apprenticed to the renowned photographer Yva. As the son of Jewish parents, he was forced to leave Berlin in 1938 due to National Socialist persecution. After a circuitous journey he finally arrived in Australia, where he opened a small photography studio in Melbourne. In 1961 he moved to Paris and from then on worked for French *Vogue*, creating some of the magazine's most renowned fashion photographs. Aside from fashion photography, he was soon in demand around the globe for advertising images, portraits and nude photographs, whose aesthetic interplay of power and seduction remains polarising to this day. Newton's work has been presented in countless exhibitions and today it is shown not only in international museums but is also on

display in regularly rotating exhibits at the Helmut Newton Foundation in Berlin.

Doug Ordway (*1962)
After graduating from New York's Germaine School of Photography in 1983, Ordway became assistant for the renowned photographer Bruce Weber, igniting a lasting passion for fashion and travel. In 1989 he moved to Milan to pursue his own career as a fashion photographer. Here, he was introduced to the Versace family, which led to a long-term professional relationship with Donatella Versace. Beginning with shooting backstage for fashion shows, he gradually received commissions for catalogues and advertising for a wide variety of projects. He lives and works between New York, Milan and Savannah, Georgia, working for a number of clients from the fashion and travel industries.

Herb Ritts (1952–2002)
California-born photographer Herb Ritts began his career in the late 1970s, and quickly gained a reputation as a master of artistic and commercial photography. In addition to producing portraits and fashion work for editorials in *Vogue*, *Vanity Fair*, *Rolling Stone* and *Interview*, he also created successful advertising campaigns for Calvin Klein, Chanel, Donna Karan, Gianni Versace and Valentino, among others. In both his life and work, Ritts was drawn to clean lines and strong forms. His images often challenged conventional notions of gender or ethnicity. Ritts passed away in 2002 from complications of AIDS. The Herb Ritts Foundation continues his longstanding engagement with HIV/AIDS charities and also promotes his great passion for photography through offering assistance to institutions with educational programmes that advance the art of photography.

David Sims (*1966)
The renowned British photographer and director David Sims is known for constantly pushing the boundaries of fashion photography with his incomparable approach, setting a benchmark for a new generation of photographers. Sims has exhibited widely, including a solo exhibition at the Institute of Contemporary Arts, London. His work is held in the permanent collections of the Victoria & Albert Museum, London, The J. Paul Getty Museum, Los Angeles, and the Palais Galliera, Paris.

Mario Sorrenti (*1971)
Mario Sorrenti has been an important part of contemporary fashion photography since he came onto the scene in the early 1990s. Born in Naples, Sorrenti grew up in New York and as a young adult quickly developed a love of experimenting with image-making, predominantly through photography but also through painting. Sorrenti's photographs are characterised by confident, experimental compositions and a sophisticated use of colour and light. He has shot for *Vogue*, *W*, *The New York Times*, *Self Service Magazine* and *i-D*, among other publications. His clients include Calvin Klein, Ferragamo, Chanel, Jil Sander, Tom Ford, Yves Saint Laurent, Bulgari and Revlon. Sorrenti has published several books. His work is held in the permanent collections of the Victoria & Albert Museum and the National Portrait Gallery, both London.

Juergen Teller (*1964)
Juergen Teller was born in Erlangen, and studied at the Bayerische Staatslehranstalt für Photographie (Bavarian State Institute for Photography) in Munich, before moving to London in 1986. Navigating both the art world and the world of commercial photography, he has shot campaigns for brands such as Celine, Louis Vuitton, Marc Jacobs and Vivienne Westwood, and editorials for magazines including *Arena Homme Plus*, *Pop*, *Purple*, *System* and *W*. Major solo exhibitions of his work have been held at the Fotomuseum Winterthur, Martin-Gropius-Bau, Berlin, the DESTE Foundation for Contemporary Art, Athens, the Daelim Museum, Seoul, and Dallas Contemporary, Texas. Teller's work has been acquired by numerous international collections including the Centre Pompidou and the Fondation Cartier pour l'art contemporain, both Paris, the International Center for Photography, New York, and the National Portrait Gallery, London.

Mario Testino (*1954)
Mario Testino grew up in a traditional Catholic family in Peru, remote from the world of fashion. In 1976, he moved to London, where he made his first attempts as a photographer. During the early 1990s, Testino looked to his experiences of growing up in Peru and to his long teenage summers in Brazil for inspiration, and created a unique and personal visual language. His photographs have been published in magazines such as *Vogue*, *V Magazine* and *Vanity Fair*. He has contributed to the success of leading fashion and beauty houses such as Gucci, Versace, Chanel, Dolce & Gabbana and Estée Lauder. His work has been exhibited at museums globally, including the Museum of Fine Arts, Boston, the Shanghai Art Museum, the Museo Thyssen-Bornemisza, Madrid, and the Tokyo Photographic Art Museum.

Ellen von Unwerth (*1954)
Ellen von Unwerth gained wide attention with her sensual Guess campaign in the early 1990s, which was followed by campaigns for Chanel, Dior, Miu Miu, Guerlain, Revlon and many more. Born in Frankfurt am Main, the photographer is a regular contributor to numerous publications all over the world, such as *Egoïste*, *ELLE*, *i-D*, *Interview*, *Playboy*, *The Face*, *The New York Times*, *Vanity Fair* and *Vogue*. She has also directed short films for clients such as Azzedine Alaïa, Dior, Guess and Katharine Hamnett, along with a range of commercials and music videos. Her nine major book projects are also important milestones in her career. Her works have been exhibited worldwide, and have become part of numerous collections.

Bruce Weber (*1946)
Photographer and filmmaker Bruce Weber first rose to international prominence in the early 1980s due to the success of images that combined classical styling with more visceral underpinnings of desire, mood and sexuality. His ability to switch seamlessly between romance and drama allowed him to significantly shape the public images of fashion houses such as Ralph Lauren, Calvin Klein, Versace, and Abercrombie & Fitch, as well as earning him an enduring presence as a contributor to magazines at the highest levels in the industry. Throughout his career, Weber has continued to work in various forms. He has directed ten short and feature-length films, has published more than fifty books, and has held more than sixty exhibitions worldwide. In this way his lifelong exploration of the nature of human relationships continues.

Front Cover
Richard Avedon, models: Nadja Auermann, Christy Turlington, Claudia Schiffer, Cindy Crawford, Stephanie Seymour, 1994 for Versace

Introduction
p. 1: Arthur Elgort, model: Stella Tennant, 1995 for *Vogue* US; p. 3: Ellen von Unwerth, model: Claudia Schiffer, 1990 for GUESS; p. 4: Angelica Blechschmidt, Valentino Garavani with models after his show in October 1995; p. 6: Peter Lindbergh, Seeing Spots, model: Naomi Campbell, Los Angeles 1990 for *Vogue* US; p. 9: Gilles Bensimon, model: Beverly Peele, 1991 for *ELLE* US

IMPRINT

This catalogue is published in conjunction with the exhibition

CAPTIVATE!
Fashion Photography from the '90s
Curated by Claudia Schiffer
Kunstpalast, Düsseldorf
15 September 2021 – 9 January 2022

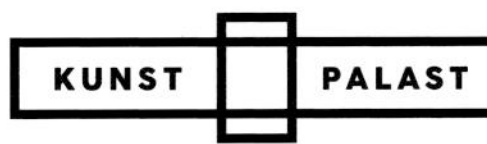

The exhibition has been made possible with the support of

Sotheby's EST. 1744

Süddeutsche Zeitung

VOGUE

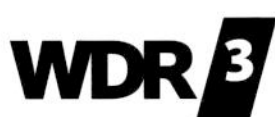

Düsseldorf
Live close Feel free

Exhibition Kunstpalast
Head of the Department of Photography: Linda Conze
Project Management: Svenja Schütte
Project Assistance: Vera Knippschild, Sonja Wittig
Registrar: Yasmin Limbach

Curator: Claudia Schiffer
Creative and content: Erin Graham, Oscar Humphries, Lucie McCullin
Project Assistance: Oliver Hastings
Press: Anna Ogundehin

Catalogue
Editor: Claudia Schiffer
Editing: Linda Conze, Erin Graham, Oscar Humphries, Lucie McCullin
Assistance: Vera Knippschild
Catalogue Management: Svenja Schütte
Project Management Prestel: Anja Besserer
Copyediting and Proofreading: Sarah Quigley
Translation German to English: Allison Moseley
Translation French to English: José Enrique Macián
Design and Typesetting: Mathias Beyer, Cologne
Production: Cilly Klotz
Repro: Helio Repro GmbH, Munich
Printing and Binding: Printer Trento, Trento
Typefaces: Akzidenz Grotesk, LL Brown, ITC Clearface
Paper: 170 g/sm GardaArt Gloss

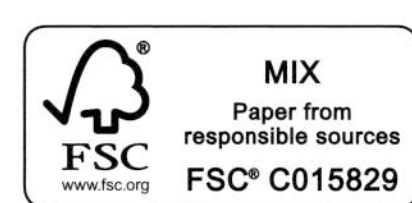

Penguin Random House Verlagsgruppe
FSC® N001967

Printed in Italy

2nd edition 2022

A member of Penguin Random House Verlagsgruppe GmbH
Neumarkter Straße 28 · 81673 München

A CIP catalogue record for this book is available from the British Library.
Library of Congress Control Number: 2021939678

www.prestel.com

ISBN 978-3-7913-7849-7
(English trade edition)
ISBN 978-3-7913-8941-7
(German trade edition)
ISBN 978-3-7913-9055-0
(English museum edition)
ISBN 978-3-7913-9054-3
(German museum edition)